AF352657

INDEPENDENT
AFRICA

INDEPENDENT AFRICA

THE FIRST GENERATION OF NATION BUILDERS

Emmanuel Kwaku Akyeampong

Indiana University Press

This book is a publication of

Indiana University Press
Office of Scholarly Publishing
Herman B Wells Library 350
1320 East 10th Street
Bloomington, Indiana 47405 USA

https://iupress.org

Manufactured in the United States of America

First Printing 2023

Cataloging information is available from the Library of Congress.

ISBN 978-0-253-06664-0 (hardback)
ISBN 978-0-253- 06665-7 (paperback)
ISBN 978-0-253- 06666-4 (ebook)

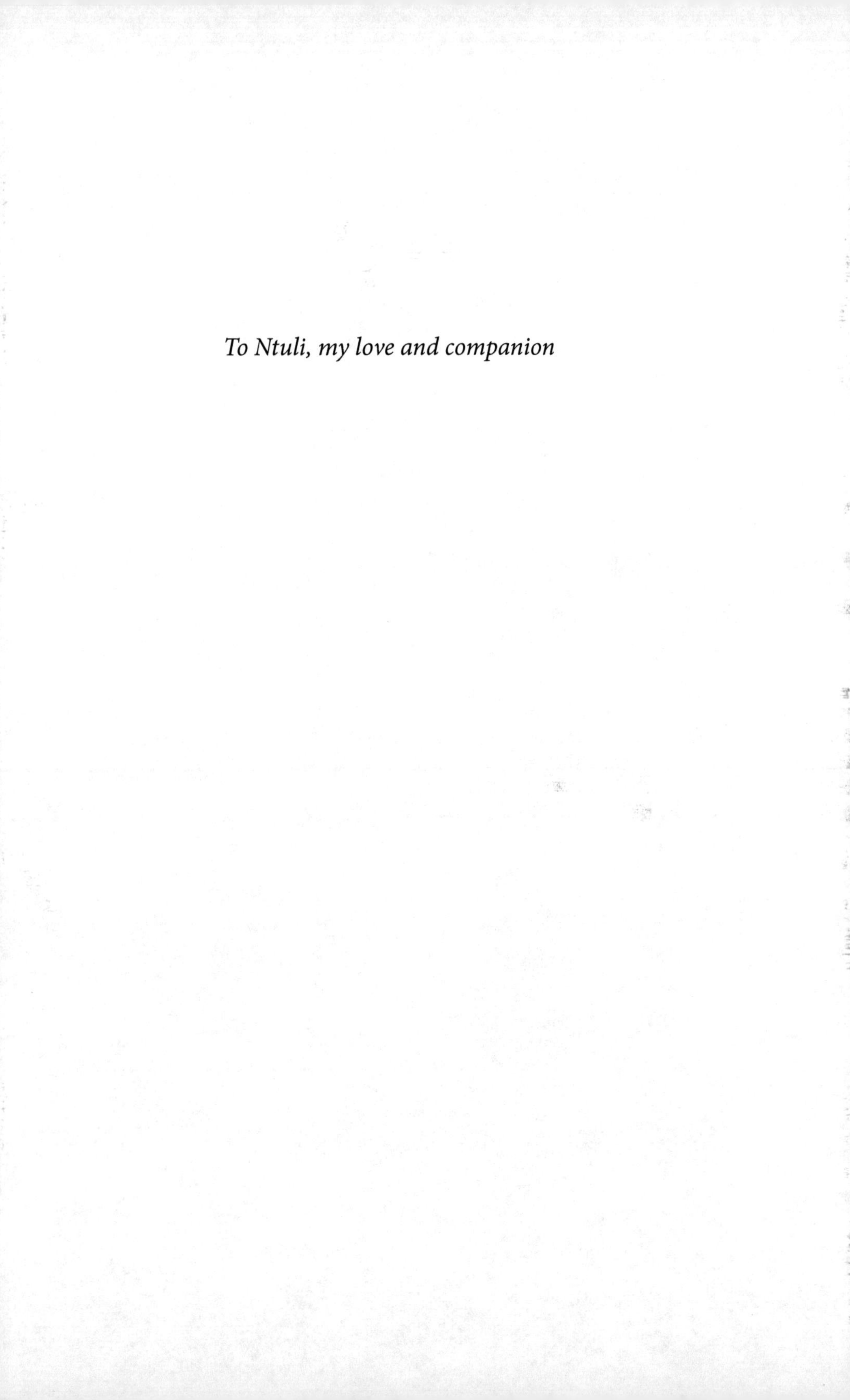

To Ntuli, my love and companion

CONTENTS

ACKNOWLEDGMENTS

An intellectual project like this one incurs many debts along the way. In the past decade, I have been fortunate to be part of networks that have deepened my interest in and knowledge of political economy and economic history. Robert Bates, Nathan Nunn, James A. Robinson, and I constituted a working group on "Understanding African Poverty over the Longue Durée," which received an Initiative Grant from the Weatherhead Center for International Affairs at Harvard University from 2009 to 2011. The initiative funded my work on business history in West Africa and a conference in Ghana that resulted in an edited volume: Emmanuel Akyeampong, Robert H. Bates, Nathan Nunn, and James A. Robinson, eds., *Africa's Development in Historical Perspective* (New York: Cambridge University Press, 2014). Nathan Nunn and I established the Workshop on African History and Economics (WAHE) at Harvard University in 2015, funded by the Center for African Studies and the Hutchins Center for African and African American Research. Its workshops extended my network of economists and economic historians to include new collaborators like Johan Fourie at Stellenbosch University. WAHE cosponsored the October 2017 conference of the African Economic History Network (AEHN), held at Stellenbosch. I presented as that year's LEAP Lecture a paper entitled "African Socialism; or the Search for an Indigenous Model of Economic Development?" (University of Stellenbosch, October 25, 2017), subsequently published in the *Economic History of Developing Regions* 33, no. 1 (2018): 69–87.

A second important network revolved around economist Yaw Nyarko at New York University (NYU). Yaw Nyarko organized and hosted two important conferences in 2009 and 2010 at NYU's Abu Dhabi Institute on "Africa and the Gulf" and "Africa and the India Ocean" respectively. Among the economists I met at these conferences was Hippolyte Fofack, then at the World Bank. Thus began a working relationship that has endured over the years, from when he was at the World Bank to his current position as chief economist and director of research at the African Export-Import Bank. I coauthored with Hippolyte Fofack two World Bank Policy Research Papers entitled "The Contribution of African Women to Economic Growth and

Development: Historical Perspectives and Policy Implications." Part I dealt with the precolonial and colonial periods (WPS 6051, April 2012) and was subsequently revised and published in the *Economic History of Developing Regions* 29, no. 1 (2014): 42–73. Part II examined the postcolonial period (WPS 6537, July 2013). Yaw Nyarko has a research interest in the production and marketing of agricultural commodities in Africa. We have conducted research together on Ghana's cocoa production and marketing and are working on a coauthored monograph on West Africa's cocoa and the chocolate industry. These networks have made me a better student of economic history and of Africa's political economy.

Earlier versions of two chapters in this book were presented at African studies seminars at American universities. At the African Studies Center at Michigan State University, I presented "Religion, Culture, and the Arts in the Making of the African Nation-State" (February 23, 2017) and benefited from comments by Jamie Monson, other colleagues, and graduate students. At the invitation of Rhiannon Stephens and Gregory Mann, I presented at Columbia University "Nkrumah, Cocoa, and the United States: The Vision of an Industrial African Nation-State" (April 20, 2017). In addition to receiving constructive comments from colleagues, I met Winifred Armstrong, a retired development economist living in New York who had served as a speech writer on Africa to John F. Kennedy when Kennedy was a senator. Winifred introduced me to the archival collection at the John F. Kennedy Library and Museum in Boston, which houses part of her private papers. I also consulted her private papers at the Schomburg Library in New York. I had the privilege of delivering the Aggrey-Fraser-Guggisberg Memorial Lectures at the University of Ghana on the theme "Nkrumah and the Making of the Ghanaian Nation-State" (March 15–16, 2018). The opportunity to share part of this manuscript with a large Ghanaian audience led to some of my distinguished attendees sharing private papers relevant to this book.

Several colleagues and friends have read and commented on individual chapters in this book. I am grateful to Kofi Adjepong-Boateng, Charles Ambler, Winifred Armstrong, Nana Dr. S. K. B. Asante, A. B. Assensoh, Abou Bamba, Robert Bates, Chambi Chachage, Mamadou Diouf, Johan Fourie, Ousmane Kane, Geoffrey Traugh, and Paul Tiyambe Zeleza. I am deeply grateful to the three anonymous readers for Indiana University Press who read the manuscript at two important junctures in 2021 and 2022 and made invaluable comments that helped tighten the arguments and structure of the book. I spent the spring semester of 2021 as a fellow at the Stellenbosch Institute of Advanced Studies in South Africa, where I benefitted considerably from discussions with colleagues as I revised this manuscript. A special thanks to my cofellow Ranka Primorac for our discussions on theory. I owe an incalculable debt to a number of research assistants, chiefly to Oluwaseyi (Shae) Omonijo. Shae was my talented research assistant from 2016 to August 2020, and we have worked on numerous projects including this monograph. She has read the chapters in this book in different draft versions, assisted with library and archival research, and supervised other research assistants we brought on from time to time. I am pleased that she now has the opportunity to pursue her own scholarly career as a doctoral student. Serges Saidi and Hans Fofack assisted in research on secondary literature, especially with French materials. Samuel Ntewusu at the Institute of African Studies at the University of Ghana assisted with archival research in Ghana. Francis Daudi Mlacha at the University of Basel assisted with archival research in Tanzania. Ashante Thomas and Anna Francis at Indiana University Press expertly guided me through the review and submission process. The Department of History at Harvard University provided a publication subsidy that covered the preparation of the index to this book.

Finally, my deepest appreciation to my family. My wife, Ntuli, who has forgiven the long hours I have spent downstairs in my study working on this book, and Emmanuel and Naledi, my kids, who together have made my life full. They have heard many promises from me on how I will spend more time with them once this book is done. May it be so.

ACRONYMS AND ABBREVIATIONS

AA African Association
AAPC All-African People's
Conference
AAPSO Afro-Asian People's
Solidarity Organization
ANC African National Congress
AU African Union
BAA Bureau of African Affairs
CCM Chama Cha Mapinduzi
CFA Colonies Françaises
d'Afrique (Franc)
CIA Central Intelligence Agency
CIAS Conference of Independent
African States
COVID-19 Coronavirus disease
2019
CPP Convention People's Party
EAMWS East African Muslim
Welfare Society
ECLA Economic Commission
for Latin America
FDI Foreign direct investment
FESMAN 66 First World Festival
of Black Arts
FESTAC 77 Second World Black
and African Festival of Arts
and Culture
FIDES Investment Fund
for Economic and Social
Development
FRELIMO Frente de Libertação
de Moçambique

GDP Gross domestic product
HIPC Heavily indebted poor
countries
IAFE International African
Friends of Ethiopia
IASB International African Ser-
vice Bureau
IBRD International Bank for
Reconstruction and Develop-
ment (World Bank)
IMF International Monetary
Fund
ISI Import-substitution
industrialization
ITUCNW International Trade
Union Committee of Negro
Workers
JRDA Jeunesse du Rassemble-
ment Démocratique Africain
KAR King's African Rifles
MIT Massachusetts Institute of
Technology
MK Umkhonto we Sizwe
MPLA Movimento Popular de
Libertação de Angola
MSAD Manufacture Sénégalaise
des Arts Décoratifs
NAB National Archives of
Britain
NAM Non-Aligned Movement
NATO North Atlantic Treaty
Organization

NDC National Democratic Congress

NGO Nongovernmental organization

NIEO New International Economic Order

NLC National Liberation Council

NLM National Liberation Movement

OAU Organization of African Unity

OECD Organization for Economic Co-operation and Development

ONCAD National Office of Agricultural Marketing and Development

OPEC Organization of Petroleum Exporting Countries

ORSTOM Office de la Recherche Scientifique et Technique Outre-Mer

PAC Pan-Africanist Congress

PAF Pan-African Federation

PAFMECA Pan-African Freedom Movement for East and Central Africa

PAFMECSA Pan-African Freedom Movement for East, Central and South Africa

PAIGC African Party for the Independence of Guinea and Cape Verde

PAMSCAD Program to Mitigate the Social Cost of Structural Adjustment

PDG Parti Démocratique de Guinée

PNDC Provisional National Defense Council

PRAAD Public Records and Archives Administration Department

RDA Rassemblement Démocratique Africain

SAP Structural adjustment program

SWAPO South West African People's Organization

TAA Tanganyika African Association

TANU Tanganyika African National Union

TVA Tennessee Valley Authority

TWAP Teachers in West Africa Program

UAC United Africa Company

UDSM University of Dar es Salaam

UGCC United Gold Coast Convention

UGFCC United Gold Coast Farmers' Cooperative Council

UN United Nations

UNCTAD United Nations Conference on Trade and Development

UNECA United Nations Economic Commission for Africa

UNESCO United Nations Educational, Scientific and Cultural Organization

UPC Union des Populations du
Cameroun
USAID United States Agency for
International Development
USARF University Students
African Revolutionary
Front
USSR Union of Soviet Socialist
Republics
VALCO Volta Aluminum
Company
VRA Volta River Authority

WACRI West African Cocoa
Research Institute
WAFF West African Frontier
Force
WANS West African National
Secretariat
WASU West African Students
Union
ZANU Zimbabwe African National Union
ZAPU Zimbabwe African
People's Union

INDEPENDENT AFRICA

INTRODUCTION

Sɛ woankɔ bi a wose yɛankɔ.
If you were not present, it is easy to say
we didn't fight. (Twi proverb)

Intellectual Framing and Arguments

Independent Africa: The First Generation of Nation Builders is a historian's interrogation of Africa's political economy in its first two full decades of independence (ca. 1957 to 1980) through the joint projects of nation-building, economic development, and international relations ("worldmaking").[1] For centuries, human societies have wrestled with two fundamental questions: how to best organize society and how to grow an economy and produce prosperity (surplus) that benefits the majority. For Scottish Enlightenment thinkers like Adam Smith, considered the founder of modern economics, civic humanism and natural jurisprudence lay at the core of both questions.[2] From his mid-eighteenth-century perspective and his observations as a moral philosopher and empiricist of how nations created wealth, Smith concluded that wealth was best created in a well-governed commercial society. For Smith, morality, politics, and economics constituted an important nexus, an integral whole that had to be examined and pursued in tandem. Jerry Evensky writes of Smith's key works: "This concept of a 'well-governed society' is the thread that stitches Smith's *Wealth of Nations*, his *Theory of Moral Sentiments*, and his *Lectures on Jurisprudence* together into a holistic moral philosophical vision of humankind's past, present, and prospect."[3] By the 1950s, when African colonies began to achieve independence, economic prosperity was associated with industrialization (or capital-concentrated manufacturing). Capitalism and socialism were the two primary paths to industrialization and economic growth, and the nation-state had become the unit of international relations.

This book makes three interrelated arguments concerning Africa's attempts at nation-building, economic development, and worldmaking in the 1960s and 1970s. First, Africa's new leaders considered it imperative for each nation to unite, suppressing "ethnic patriotisms" or ethnic and regional nationalisms in the service of development. Charles Tilly underscores the important difference between national states and nation-states, noting that with the exception of perhaps Ireland and Sweden, "very few European national states have ever qualified as nation-states," defined as "a state whose people share a strong linguistic, religious, and symbolic identity."[4] Few, if any, of Africa's artificial colonies could claim to be the nucleus of a nation-state. Yet the primacy given to the nation-state in literature on nationalism created an urgent need for Africa's new leaders to forge nation-states as a precursor to development. John Lonsdale points out that "nationalists saw their vocation as modernization, one word summarizing the fight against poverty, ignorance, and disease."[5] The early decades of independence witnessed an enormous investment of cultural creativity and energy in imagining new nations. States led the endeavor to create their nation, a social construct that paralleled an earlier trajectory in Europe. John Lonsdale and Bruce Berman note that "African nationalism was indeed, as in Europe, primarily an attempt to gain state power and control its collaborative networks and patronage services so as to domesticate modernity in the name of an imagined new community."[6] Paradoxically, the nation could not be created out of nothing; states found themselves in tension with the ethnic patriotisms they sought to subdue all while appropriating aspects of regional and ethnic material cultures and histories in the fabrication of a national culture (see chap. 2).

Second, to achieve the level of economic growth necessary to make the state an effective "distributor of hope,"[7] each state had to become developmental, prioritizing rapid economic development and redefining the economy's relations with the larger global economy (see chaps. 3 and 4).[8] On the imperative of development as a *raison d'être* of the state, Claude Ake observes of early independent Africa: "The informal and formal pronouncements of African leaders give the impression of an unshakeable commitment to the idea that they must try to achieve development, perceived as the primary condition for their own welfare, the legitimation of their leadership and the well-being of their countries."[9] African publics were prepared to make enormous sacrifices in the pursuit of development. The late-colonial developmental state after World War II had demonstrated to Africans with its intrusiveness in communities and households that development was a difficult process. Joseph Ki-Zerbo, the Burkinabe historian, reflects on the acquiescence to authoritarianism in the early decades of independence, commenting that it was as if a sign had been hung: "Silence, development in progress!"[10] Industrialization was central to the vision of economic development itself, not just in the quest to diversify economies from the colonial focus on primary commodities and fund the provision of social rights. Industrialization also had the potential to reorder the economic geography of new nations away from the vested interests of ethnic regionalisms, which could make separatist claims like that of the National Liberation Movement (NLM) in Asante in the 1950s over cocoa or the secessionist attempt of Katanga in the early 1960s over mineral wealth. Berman and Lonsdale observe that "agricultural and mineral extraction widened the regional differentiation typical of the recent colonial past; unlike industry, they did not encourage the integration of new national economies."[11]

Third, this book sees worldmaking at the national, regional, continental, and international levels as integral to strategies of nation-building and economic development for Africa's new nation-states (see chap. 4).[12] In spite of the guarantee of the right to self-determination and the sovereignty of nation-states in the charter of the United Nations, Africa's new states worried about the parity of nations, aware of their small populations and weak economies. Adom Getachew has examined how the leaders of new nations in Africa and the Caribbean sought to make the United Nations General Assembly (UNGA) the locus of transformative power and the site of executive action in contest with the Security Council, which maintained the precedence of the great powers.[13] As Third World countries came to dominate the United Nations in numbers, they transformed the politics of the United Nations, something that had not been possible with the League of Nations. Likewise, Third World nations sought to transform the politics of former colonial powers through institutions like the British Commonwealth, where the numbers of the former nonsettler colonies came to outweigh the earlier influence of the dominion states—Canada, Australia, New Zealand, and South Africa.[14]

In addition, Africa's leaders promoted South-based organizations in the "spirit of Bandung," creating solidarities among new nation-states in Africa, Asia, and the Middle East.[15] At the international, continental, and regional levels, three important organizations preceded the 1963 formation of the Organization of African Unity and inspired African worldmaking: the Afro-Asian People's Solidarity Organization (AAPSO), formed in Cairo in December 1957; the All-African People's Conference (AAPC), established in Accra in December 1958; and the Pan-African Freedom Movement for East and Central Africa (PAFMECA), created in Mwanza (Tanzania) in September 1958, then expanded in 1962 to include Southern Africa (PAF-MECSA). The penetration of African activities at these different levels expanded the parameters of international relations in novel ways (see chap. 4). Nelson Goodman, one of the first scholars to use the concept of worldmaking, notes that "worldmaking as we know it always starts from worlds already on hand; the making is a remaking."[16] Paradoxically, anticolonial worldmaking was made possible by the globalization empire created, yet it sought to subtend the strictures of empire by imagining alternative worlds not structured by empire. Pheng Cheah notes how this process of temporalization subverts imperialist cartography, disrupting European attempts to temporarily reduce the world to a spatial object.[17] A good illustration is the inaugural AAPC held in Accra, which by inviting liberation movements from colonies extended the boundaries of worldmaking beyond sovereign states.

This book has been inspired by two sets of conversations around the golden anniversary celebrations of African independence between 2007 (Ghana) and 2010 (the seventeen African countries that became independent in 1960, including most of French-speaking sub-Saharan Africa). The first raised the question of whether there was anything to celebrate, considering the failure of development efforts. In the case of Ghana, 2007 was a period of power cuts, and many asked in newspaper articles, internet blogs, and online chat groups whether the monies allocated to the golden anniversary could not have been more usefully directed toward much-needed infrastructure development. Carola Lentz and David Lowe in *Remembering Independence* remark on this particular moment in Ghana:

> Most importantly, a number of newspaper articles and radio features as well as many internet blogs debated whether the money for the Jubilee should not have been invested in infrastructure and poverty reduction

rather than the costly public festivities. Of the 20 million US dollars that Parliament had budgeted for the celebrations, 5.9 million was spent on importing new vehicles (allegedly for transporting foreign dignitaries, etc.); 4.9 million was invested in the renovation of Black Star Square (where the central ceremony was to take place), Independence Arch, and other squares and buildings in and around Accra; and 7.8 million went to the ten regions where they were to be spent on infrastructural development, particularly the rehabilitation of parade grounds, monuments, and other Jubilee-related locations.[18]

Lentz and Lowe observe rightly that remembering independence "may also become a trope for lost hopes, buried plans and frustrated futures."[19] Chat groups on online forums like Ghana Web sustained these conversations, even querying the importance of independence.

The second set of conversations consisted of rather invidious comparisons between Ghana (standing in for other African countries) and the Asian tigers like Malaysia and South Korea. I cannot count the number of times I have been reminded that Ghana and Malaysia both obtained independence in 1957 with comparable a gross domestic product (GDP) and that Malaysia came to Ghana to borrow palm oil seedlings to plant in Malaysia. In the early 1960s, Malaysia set up an exchange program with West African economies, producing palm oil in a bid to diversify its dependence on rubber and tin. Palm oil is native to West Africa and was the basis of a vibrant export trade in the nineteenth century.[20] Through scientific research, Malaysia pushed its cultivation and use of palm oil to another level; today Indonesia and Malaysia are the two leading producers of palm oil in the world in that order, an industry estimated at $60 billion in February 2020.[21] The international development community had regarded South Korea in the 1960s "as hopelessly corrupt and singularly unpromising."[22] We all know where South Korea is today—one of the most industrialized economies in the world with global brands like Samsung, LG, and Hyundai. Indeed, in 2017 South Korea's contribution to global trade at 2.93 percent was greater than that of the entire African continent (2.34 percent).[23]

But Africa's political independence was not a meaningless, token gesture of retreating colonial powers in the transition from formal colonialism to neocolonialism, the phenomenon of independent Africa's continued economic dependence on the West. Ake, in a materialist approach to Africa's political economy, notes that "the nationalist petite bourgeoisie which fought for independence had insisted that political independence was the essential preliminary to a fundamental restructuring of the colonial economy, and many students of Africa seemed to agree that the political hegemony of the colonizers was a critical factor in the underdevelopment of African social formations."[24] This was not necessarily faulty logic, as loss of sovereignty in the colonial period had been accompanied by the imposition of exactions, establishing the link between loss of political sovereignty and economic domination.[25] By 1980, attempts to decolonize Africa's economies had proved futile, but to dismiss the vision and mission of creating economically viable, politically vibrant nation-states in those early decades of independence is to sideline perhaps the most fascinating era in postindependent Africa's political economy. At the start of independence, Africa's leaders realized they had political control but no economic power or base. They believed, however, that they could use their political power to create an economic base, a vision nurtured by the fertile context of institution building in the post–World War II era. As new nation-states were born, the United Nations forged a global community of sovereign nation-states. Young institutions like the World Bank and the International Monetary Fund (IMF) found their footing, and federal experiments were pursued in Europe, Asia, and Africa. A supportive knowledge base in the social sciences, marked by the flourishing of development economics and modernization theory, affirmed the positive outlook of Africa's new leaders. The quest for economic development and the creation of a welfare society represented a powerful unifying force for African states and publics, and through the mid-1970s the state in different countries was perceived as having a genuine capacity to distribute hope. Africa's new leaders united in declaring war on poverty, illiteracy, and disease. New governments and their publics agreed on the primacy of economic development to provide access for all to education, health, jobs, and decent housing. This vision required a big push toward economic growth without neglecting social equity.

This book adopts a comparative approach to African political economy in the early decades of independence, with Ghana under Kwame Nkrumah (1951–66), Guinea under Ahmed Sékou Touré (1958–84), Senegal under Léopold Sédar Senghor (1960–80), and Tanzania under Julius Kambarage Nyerere (1961–85) as case studies. Though Ghana forms the spine of the book, it became clear in the course of my research and writing that Ghana's example is particularly instructive in comparative perspective. Nkrumah's political tenure was interwoven with those of the first generation of African leaders, and the three arguments outlined above played out in Guinea, Senegal, and Tanzania. These countries arrived at political independence through different trajectories. Decolonization in Ghana, considered a model British colony, was relatively peaceful. Guinea was the only sub-Saharan African country to vote "No" in the 1958 French referendum to create a French Community under the Fifth Republic and acceded to immediate independence without French support. Senegal obtained its independence with the rest of the French African colonies in 1960, and Senghor pursued a close political and economic relationship with France after the demise of the proposed federation of France and its former colonies. Tanganyika was a Trusteeship Territory, first under the League of Nations and subsequently under the United Nations. Its path to independence went through the United Nations. In 1964 Tanganyika and Zanzibar would unite to form the United Republic of Tanzania.

By the end of the 1970s, the economies of these four countries were in distress and had performed poorly irrespective of the ideological positioning of their leaders, who all professed some form of African socialism. The same could be said of economies like the Ivory Coast, which was explicitly capitalist in its model of development and saw remarkable growth from the 1950s through the 1970s (see chap. 3). The "Ivorian miracle" unraveled in the early 1980s, as Samir Amin had predicted in the 1960s.[26] It was my interest in understanding the failure of economic performance in the early decades of independence eventually that turned me toward political economy. I had previously considered the approach of collective biography or prosopography, especially because of the voluminous writings of Nkrumah, Sékou Touré, Senghor, and Nyerere and how their careers intersected in fascinating ways in their pursuit of nation-building, anticolonialism, regional integration, and worldmaking.[27] It is clear that context—national, regional, continental, and international—is critical. This context includes the struggle between ethnic patriotisms, nationalisms, and the purveyors of contending nationalist visions in a country like Ghana; the competing visions of regional integration and continental unity that saw early independent states in Africa divided between the radical Casablanca and the conservative Monrovia groups by 1961; the reality of how the Cold War shaped Africa's developmental agenda; and the importance of the United States and the Soviet Union as models of economic development and sources of capital and technology. By the late 1970s, the window of opportunity to build an

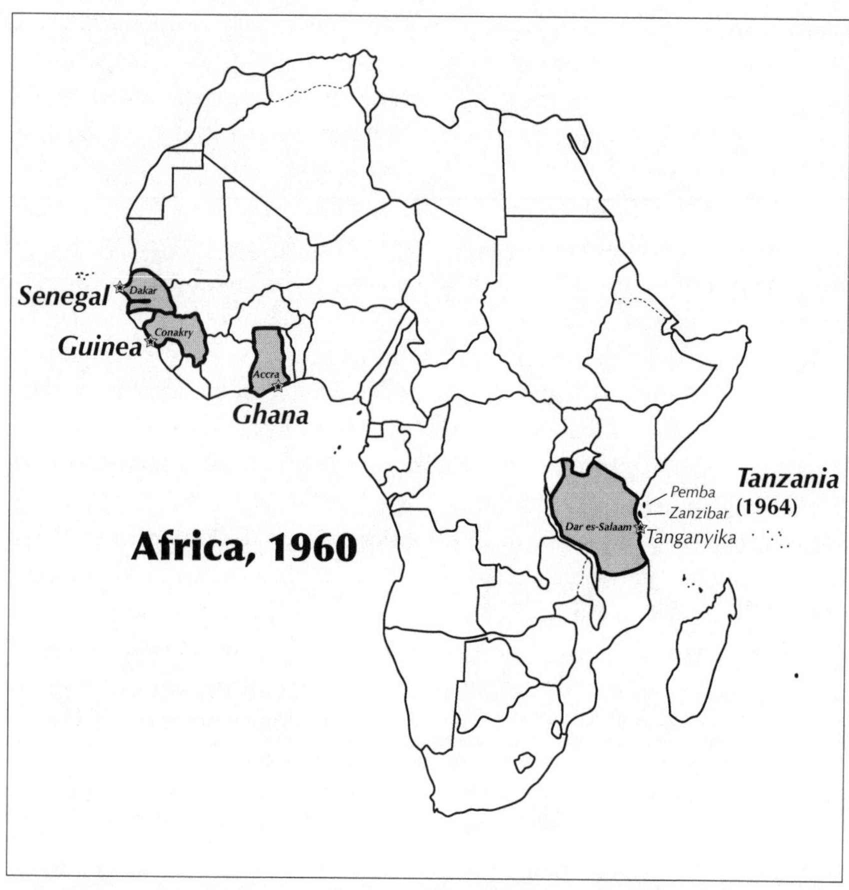

Map. 0.1 Map of Africa in 1960 showing Ghana, Guinea, Senegal, and Tanganyika. Credit: Mark Duerksen.

economically independent and united Africa had closed. Both development economics and modernization theory had been discredited. Even their replacement, the dependency theory proffered by Latin Americanists, failed to explain Africa's dismal economic performance, as authoritarian and patrimonial regimes and corruption made economic collapse more than a function of Africa's relations with the West. African states joined the rest of the Third World in the futile call for a New International Economic Order. The discipline of economics saw the rise of the monetarists, led by Milton Friedman, and the increasing assertion of market-oriented policies. We enter the era of Thatcherism and Reaganism, advocating a small state, free markets, privatization, and the control of labor. This book ends in the late 1970s. From the 1980s, Africa entered into a new era.

In the early 1960s, no one could have predicted Africa's slip into the "lost decade of the 1980s," with collapsed economies and a continent going into financial receivership under the tutelage of the World Bank and the IMF. Before the late 1970s, the only sub-Saharan African country to have received an IMF stabilization program was Ghana after the overthrow of Nkrumah.[28] Indeed, neither the World Bank nor the IMF (nor the Soviet Union, for that matter) knew much about how to promote African economic growth on Africa's independence. Samir Amin, who had taken an appointment between 1960 and 1963 with the economics and planning ministry in Mali under the independent government of Modibo Keita, reflected in his memoirs on the challenge of national economic planning with scarce economic statistics coming out of colonial rule and how he had had to develop methods from scratch:

> In Bamako I received visits from a number of "experts" in the Soviet World, the World Bank and the United Nations but I must say, without false modesty, that I learned nothing at all from any of them. The Soviets kept churning out the same "principles": it's good when the state intervenes, bad when this is not planned—never anything more precise. . . . But the World Bank people were, and are, of exactly the same type, and also speak a totally ideological language, even if their basic principle ("it's good whenever the private sector takes charge") is the diametrical opposite.[29]

The group who had begun to think about African economies—to be precise, tropical colonial economies—were economists like William Arthur Lewis in the fledgling field of development economics. It is thus not surprising that Nkrumah's young government turned to Lewis to be its economic consultant in 1952 and the economic adviser to Nkrumah on independence in 1957 (see chap. 3). It is noteworthy of the optimism of the decolonization process in Africa that Lewis in 1955 turned down an invitation from the government of Singapore to become the country's economic adviser for two years.[30] Nkrumah's Ghana became a case study in development economics.[31]

Development economics did not have all the answers, but its thinkers, many of whom were born in non-Western countries, acknowledged the need for methods of economic analysis beyond the toolkit of neoclassical economics where independent African countries were concerned. Chapter 3 outlines the key tenets of development economics, using the writings of two leading thinkers in the field: William Arthur Lewis and Peter Tamas Bauer. Development economics in Africa was blindsided by the exigencies of African politics. Lewis left Ghana in frustration in December 1958, just a year into his two-year contract. His eagerness to prove that economic men and women also lived in Africa made him unable to grasp the reality that political decisions frame economic choices and outcomes (see chap. 3). He would later reflect on the intersection of politics and economics from his experience in West Africa.[32] Bauer, once he turned his attention to the economics of independent African countries, also seemed to set aside the lessons he had gleaned in his 1954 magisterial study of West African trade on the ingenuity and entrepreneurship of Levantine and African mercantile firms and traders.[33] Both were yet to grasp Janet Roitman's later astute observation that economy must be "apprehended as political terrain."[34] It is attention to this interconnection that made the works of Claude Ake and Robert Bates in the early 1980s pathbreaking in their examination of the political economy of the early decades of African independence.[35]

The hegemonic influence of the World Bank and the IMF in Africa has given them a kind of oracular power. But this is primarily a post-1980s development, as the analysis above makes clear. The imposition of structural adjustment programs in Africa by the Bretton Woods institutions were a major turning point. These programs were introduced in a decade of economic collapse, decline of African universities, and impoverished governments—African critics of structural adjustment were easily brushed aside until the landmark study by Thandika Mkandawire and Charles Soludo.[36] Neoliberal economic suppositions were presented as scientific facts, and African governments were encouraged on a politically and economically disastrous journey. Bruce Berman notes how "the painfully won gains of national development of the 1960s and 1970s were dismissed as constraints on market-driven growth."[37] Social gains in health and education, a fledgling manufacturing base, and key infrastructure in agriculture (such as extension services) were quickly dismantled under structural adjustment as African governments retrenched and removed subsidies from social services. The neoliberal policies of currency devaluation, privatization of state-owned enterprises, and elevation of the market have not worked because they do not get at the root causes of capitalist transformation, as Hernando de Soto has argued in his influential book, *The Mystery of Capital*.

De Soto argues that the breakthrough of capitalism in the West, the ability to produce capital, occurred with the incorporation of various types of property regimes—formal and informal—into a single legal property regime. The result was a representational process that injected life into assets and made them leverageable as capital. This legal process was facilitated by the state. But the process unfolded slowly over long periods in different Western countries, so its catalytic effect has not been grasped even in the West, which purveys to the non-West ineffective economic policies.[38] Under structural adjustment, the state in Africa was seen as an obstacle to rational economic development and was instructed to oversee its own diminution. African states learned to reposition themselves to take advantage of structural adjustment, redefining dependency as a resource and not a constraint.[39] The state in Africa became a caricature of itself.

This is the point of insertion of Achille Mbembe's *On the Postcolony*.[40] Published at the turn of the century, after two decades of structural adjustment, its analysis of the deterioration of the African state and the deformation of power into something grotesque is lucid, insightful, and depressing. My point of insertion is different, focusing on the 1960s and 1970s and economic performance in early independent Africa. *On the Postcolony* is brilliant political philosophy, as Mbembe draws on social theory to give "as intelligible an account as possible of some aspects of political imagination and political, social, and cultural reality in Africa today."[41] We are both interested in political economy: Mbembe in how the economic and material informs the cultural and symbolic and the relationship between structures and representations, myself in how politics shaped economic performance before 1980. One will not find a reference in *On the Postcolony* to economists and political economists vested in understanding African economies in the early decades of independence, such as Samir Amin, Claude Ake, and Thandika Mkandawire. But the structures of our books are not dissimilar in our engagement of sites and moments.[42] Our approach is through interpretative, thematic essays, not straightforward narrative history. Thus, this book is very different from my earlier books, which mined deeply a set of related archives in Britain and Ghana and related strongly narrative histories.[43]

The African state's capacity to distribute hope endured in some countries into the mid-1970s. In others, such as Guinea, it evaporated early, despite the auspicious start that had witnessed the mobilization of a country by a dynamic grassroots party to reject de Gaulle's proposal of a French Community in 1958. The state quickly turned authoritarian under Sékou Touré, who eliminated even his close associates in government (see chaps. 2 and 4). In Tanzania, hope in the state persisted into the 1970s, dented by the state's forcible relocation of villagers into Ujamaa villages by 1976 (see chap. 4). But the Arusha Declaration of 1967, which launched Ujamaa, spoke to a broader vision of ethical politics and social equity. Its components, like the "Leadership Code," simultaneously unnerved party faithful, who had begun to accumulate wealth, and excited ordinary Tanzanians, speaking to the incipient class divide Nyerere sought so hard to ignore and to dismiss. The authors of the recent, authoritative three-volume biography of Nyerere point to how the Arusha Declaration rekindled the nationalist spirit:

> Only a few days after the public launching of the Declaration, hundreds of people from all corners of the country marched to the State House in Dar es Salaam to meet the President and pledge their support for the Arusha Declaration. To give a few examples, Mzee Sanuni Hassani, aged 75, walked 38 days from Tabora to the State House. An extant picture shows him in his tattered *kanzu* [an ankle- or floor-length robe] shaking hands with Nyerere. Eight young boys from their secondary school in Tanga walked to greet Nyerere, as did many others. Sethi Benjamin from Arusha died on his way to the State House and became an instant martyr.[44]

In Ghana, the state's capacity to distribute hope survived the overthrow of Nkrumah and lasted through changes in government into the mid-1970s. Internal developments, the OPEC oil crisis on the international stage, and deepening debt brought an end to this era of optimism.

The social background of leaders of Nkrumah's Convention People's Party (CPP) and the opposing United Gold Coast Convention (UGCC, founded in 1947)—with its successor parties the National Liberation Movement (NLM, formed in 1954), the United Party (formed in 1957), and the Progress Party (formed in 1969)—were identical with sons of chiefs and professionals playing prominent roles in both parties. Just as the Committee on Youth Organization broke away from the UGCC in 1949 to found the CPP, Asante CPP members broke away from the CPP in 1954 to establish the NLM in opposition to the CPP's policy on cocoa, of which Asante was the leading producer in the 1950s. The young men sought the endorsement of Asante chiefs, who instead divested the young men of the leadership of the NLM.[45] The military coup that overthrew Nkrumah left intact people's perception of the state's capacity to distribute hope. Lonsdale observes that "East Africa's armies entered politics as armed trade unionists. Nigeria's fell murderously apart along ethnic fault-lines widened by uneven access to colonial education. Only Ghana's soldiers lived up to expectations, marching back to barracks after reintroducing multi-party politics to a country tired of autocratic people's democracy. But they had unusually seasoned allies. An older generation of professionals and chiefs, roughly treated by Nkrumah, was there to revive an earlier, less plebian, power."[46] The National Liberation Council (NLC), an allied group from the police and armed forces that overthrew Nkrumah in February 1966, saw itself as strictly custodial and transitional. The Progress Party government that won elections in 1969 and ushered in a new civilian government traced its political ancestry to the UGCC. In Ghana, there were viable contending nationalist visions. I remember a conversation in the late 1990s with Mr. Yaw Albert Osebre, Ghana's ambassador to Algeria in 1969 and 1970 under the Progress Party. He recalled with amusement how he used to return his unspent entertainment funds to Accra at the end of each fiscal year in the spirit of patriotism that marked those years. "Can you imagine me doing that today?" he asked me. The Ghanaian public was puzzled when the National Redemption Council (NRC) under Colonel I. K. Acheampong overthrew K. A. Busia's Progress Party government in January 1972. The coup appeared unjustified: the Busia government was barely two years old, and there was no compelling reason to remove it. But, still indicative of the period's political optimism, the NRC government was able to rally the country behind it in a nationalist agenda that invoked the spirit of the developmental state. It repudiated international debts that it considered spurious under the galvanizing cry of *Yen tua* (Twi: "we will not pay"). In the pursuit of economic self-reliance, it announced two national programs, Operation Feed Yourself and Operation Feed Your Industries, which until the mid-1970s were very successful. Moved by the call to patriotism, Ghanaians created backyard farms even in suburbia, city dwellers secured land in the villages to farm, and commercial agriculture received a spurt.[47] My family still has the orange trees we grew in our backyard, and I took up the rearing of rabbits as my contribution to the economy. By 1975, the government had lost its sense of direction, and public enthusiasm waned in the face of nepotism and corruption. Africa's leaders had lost sight of Adam Smith's key insight—that for a society to be prosperous, it has to be well governed—and one could not parse morality, politics, and economics.

The Ghanaian experiment in nation-building and economic development is instructive in several ways, as I have chronicled above. But Ghana's path paralleled that of other new nation-states in Africa, hence the value of Ghana in comparative perspective. There was a rather unique cultural unity in Ghana due to a history of prominent precolonial Akan kingdoms and the fact that the geopolitical map of colonial—and hence postcolonial—Ghana was almost identical in size to that of precolonial greater Asante. The optimism of the early decades of African independence was not naive. Post–World War II economic prosperity based on the boom in commodity production and world prices extended into the late 1950s; the beginnings of import-substitution industrialization as the late-colonial state became developmental stirred African manufacturing ambitions; and the omnibus nature of anticolonial nationalism, which sought to be all inclusive and portrayed the political rejection of foreign rule as the panacea to all socioeconomic ills, generated hope in how Africans related to the future. To build on Ghassan Hage's insight on this kind of hope, "here 'the future' is not so much a 'science fiction' construction as a future that one can already detect in the unfolding of the present."[48] Ghana's attempt to decolonize its economy under Nkrumah was pathbreaking. Roger Genoud points out that what Ghana undertook and partly achieved in the economic field under Nkrumah was immense (see chaps. 4 and 5). In Ghana, Africanization proceeded in substance and Ghanaians with very few exceptions were in key positions and made key decisions. Genoud notes that "one might say that what made Ghana stand out among other tropical African countries was not so much that Ghana was doing better (this was not always true) but that Ghana, for better or for worse, was really in charge of her own affairs; if she were to commit mistakes, they were committed by herself, under her own responsibility! This was in striking contrast with the situation of most neighboring countries and this is the only true school of development."[49] This was the vision of the African developmental state. The making and unmaking of Nkrumah's vision of Ghana as an economically autonomous, industrialized nation-state thus serves as an appropriate penultimate chapter to this book (chap. 5). It represents a common struggle at independence to diversify economies from the one or two commodities that brought foreign exchange (cocoa for Ghana, bauxite and iron ore for Guinea, groundnuts for Senegal, sisal for Tanganyika) and build a manufacturing base. The book's conclusion speaks to the significance of this study to contemporary

Africa, with the current renewed enthusiasm for import-substitution industrialization, the implementation of the African Continental Free Trade Agreement, and the expectation that our post–COVID-19 world will see a return to prioritization of national economic and domestic concerns globally. The conclusion thus complements chapter 1, which provides an overview of African history from the interwar period to the beginning of the twenty-first century and extends the implications of the insights of this book to the present.

HISTORIOGRAPHICAL CONTEXTS

Nation-Building in Independent Africa

This book joins and builds on a recent body of literature that has revisited the early decades of African independence, examining the processes of decolonization and nation-building. With few exceptions, these processes have been framed as national histories. Ghana has seen a rich collection of studies in the past decade, examining Nkrumah's political thought and career and the construction of the Ghanaian nation-state. These works include books by Ama Biney, *The Political and Social Thought of Kwame Nkrumah*; Harcourt Fuller, *Building the Ghanaian Nation-State: Kwame Nkrumah's Symbolic Nationalism*; Jeffrey Ahlman, *Living with Nkrumahism: Nation, State, and Pan-Africanism in Ghana*; and Justin Williams, *Pan-Africanism in Ghana: African Socialism, Neoliberalism, and Globalization*.[50] These are useful works, and I have benefited especially from Biney's study and how it maps Nkrumah's political thought—through his writings and speeches— onto his policies as head of state. It is a particularly illuminating approach to her interrogation of Nkrumah's cultural, economic, and foreign policies. Ahlman's work and its discussion of the work of the Bureau of African Affairs, responsible for Nkrumah's Pan-African policies and his support for liberation movements, provide important context for understanding the execution of Nkrumah's anticolonial and anti-imperial campaigns. Insightful in this regard is Meredith Terretta's *Nation of Outlaws, State of Violence: Nationalism, Grassfields Tradition, and State Building in Cameroon*.[51] Terretta examines the history of the outlawed Cameroonian nationalist party, the Union des Populations du Cameroun (UPC), whose leaders received support from Nkrumah. In chapter 4, I examine Nkrumah's anticolonialism and push for continental unity, drawing on the records of the Bureau of African

Affairs. I also examine the support Nyerere and Sékou Touré provided to liberation movements, using the Tanzania National Archives, those of the ruling party Chama Cha Mapinduzi (CCM, Swahili: "Party of the Revolution"), and the archives of African National Congress (ANC), which received strong support from the early independent African governments.[52] With the partial exception of Biney's work (part of chap. 7), none of these books has a focus on economic performance, though Williams's does examine the impact of neoliberalism and globalization on Ghana's Pan-Africanism. Even Fuller's chapter on "Economic Nationalism" is more about the creation of Ghanaian currency as a symbolic expression of economic nationalism than about economic performance.[53]

Abou Bamba's deeply insightful book on the Ivorian miracle, the Ivory Coast's remarkable economic performance from 1950 to the late 1970s, *African Miracle, African Mirage: Transnational Politics and the Paradox of Modernization in Ivory Coast*, comes closest to my interest in interrogating African political economy and economic performance in the early decades of independence.[54] Indeed, I found his book so exciting that I was compelled to revisit older works by Jon Woronoff (*West African Wager: Houphouët versus Nkrumah*) and Samir Amin (*Le développement du capitalisme en Côte d'Ivoire*) and make the Ivory Coast a comparative case study in chapter 3, where I juxtapose Nkrumah's push for economic growth under the influence of development economics with Houphouët-Boigny's parallel push under the influence of modernization theory.[55] Some recent works have revisited African socialism in Ghana and Tanzania, which received quite a bit of attention in the 1960s and 1970s. Some of the older literature is reviewed in chapter 4, and more recent works include Priya Lal's *African Socialism in Post-colonial Tanzania: Between the Village and the World*.[56] In an earlier published article, I explored whether African socialism was a search for an indigenous model of economic development.[57] In chapter 4, I argue that what was pursued economically under the label of "African socialism" can be better explained through the framework of economic nationalism than through any comparison with socialism.

There is also a body of works examining the cultural politics of the early decades of independence. These are cited in chapter 2, which explores culture and the arts in the making of the African nation-state. On Guinea, I have found the contributions of James D. Straker (*Youth, Nationalism, and the Guinean Revolution*) and Mike McGovern (*Unmasking the State: Making*

Guinea Modern) highly instructive, as well as Kelly Askew's *Performing the Nation: Swahili Music and Cultural Politics in Tanzania*.[58] They all speak to the conviction of the first generation of African leaders that a new person or personality, a "new African," was necessary for the successful pursuit of a culturally authentic yet modern Africa. The perception of nationalism as a secular enterprise meant that though religion was an important component in the personal lives of Nkrumah, Sékou Touré, Senghor, and Nyerere, none sought to leverage religion as a nationalist force (even though nationalism does not have to be secular).[59] Nkrumah, Senghor, and Nyerere even contemplated priestly vocations in the Catholic Church at different points in their lives. In January 2006, the Catholic Church began the process of investigating the life of Nyerere for possible beatification.[60]

Religion could not be ignored in independent Africa because of its historical importance stretching back to the precolonial period.[61] Indeed, chieftaincy, religious cults, and power associations (also called secret societies) were common systems of government in precolonial Africa, and the first independent governments had to contend with them for legitimacy.[62] General elections and universal adult suffrage were novel mechanisms in the 1950s, and the ordinary Africans elected to political power in the 1950s and 1960s needed to assert their political legitimacy against older conceptions and forms of power (see chap. 2). It is not surprising that Nkrumah, Sékou Touré, and Nyerere all moved to prohibit or limit chieftaincy after coming to political power. Nkrumah's relations with Christian churches in Ghana, primarily mainline churches led by expatriate clergy, was complex, as he resented their presumption of speaking on behalf of the Ghanaian populace.[63] He declared himself "a non-denominational Christian and a Marxist socialist" in his desire to reject the spiritual oversight of any church.[64] Nkrumah and Nyerere led countries that were not predominantly Christian.[65] Senghor, though deeply Catholic, led a predominantly Muslim country.[66] Sékou Touré, a Muslim who claimed descent from and the legacy of Almamy Samory Touré, was reluctant to leverage Islam as a political force in Guinea, considering its close association with the precolonial Muslim state of Futa Jallon, the political opposition during his tenure.[67] But as part of its Demystification Program, the new Guinean state required traditional religionists in the Forest Region to convert to either Christianity or Islam in the endeavor to make Guinea modern.[68]

My book also engages a body of work that examines decolonization and nation-building at a transnational or federal level. Three of these works have been particularly influential in how I think about regional integration, federation, and worldmaking in francophone and anglophone Africa: Gary Wilder's *Freedom Time: Negritude, Decolonization, and the Future of the World*; Frederick Cooper's *Citizenship between Empire and Nation: Remaking France and French Africa, 1945–1960*; and Adom Getachew's *Worldmaking after Empire*.[69] Wilder examines the political thought and careers of Aimé Césaire and Léopold Senghor and how both sought a postcolonial political dispensation that included federation with France, transforming metropolitan France itself in a reimagination of ethnicity and polity. Cooper interrogates how French African politicians like Senghor and Mamadou Dia of Senegal worked assiduously with French metropolitan politicians under the Fourth and Fifth Republics to create a postcolonial federation that transcended the sum of its parts, one in which metropole and colony were truly integrated in an egalitarian way. On the other hand, African politicians like Houphouët-Boigny opted for the nation-state and national sovereignty, eager to rid the Ivory Coast of regional affiliations he believed had an economic cost. Cooper's work reveals how French metropolitan politicians bent backward to accommodate some idea of federation with the former African colonies. The historiography has often viewed the balkanization of French Africa with the 1959 abolition of the West African and Equatorial African federations as a Machiavellian and disingenuous move on the part of the French. Both works end with African independence, though Wilder in what is effectively an epilogue offers reflections on postnational democracy after independence.[70]

Getachew's *Worldmaking after Empire* has been so important to my thinking that it deserves separate consideration. Getachew is a political philosopher interested in the intersection of ideas and worldmaking—building a world after empire—among the first generation of African and Caribbean leaders. Our works intersect in our interest in Nkrumah, Sékou Touré, Nyerere, and the West Indian development economist William Arthur Lewis. We also share an interest in the flourishing of Black internationalisms in the interwar period: the subscription of this generation of leaders to Pan-Africanism, regional integration, a Third World movement, and from the 1960s the push for a New International Economic Order (NIEO). But there are important differences between our works. I am very invested in understanding the unfolding of economic development in ways that transcend ideologies to the actual performance of economies. It is my desire to understand economic performance in the early decades of independence that led to critical examination of the African developmental state in the 1960s and 1970s and the pursuit of import-substitution industrialization (ISI) as a strategy of growth. I argue that much of what passed as African socialism was in fact a nationalistic approach to economic growth and development. In a polarized world dominated by the contrasting political economies of the United States and the Soviet Union, African socialism sought a third path. In their pursuit of ISI, African states took a page from Latin America and the thinking of Argentinian economist Rául Prebisch, who was at the helm of the UN Economic Commission for Latin America (ECLA) from 1950 to 1963. Prebisch's thinking on structural dependency and framing of the global economy in terms of center and periphery, articulation of industrialization and ISI as the way to break out of structural dependency, advocacy of coupling ISI with regional integration, and shift to demanding a New International Economic Order by 1963 with the failure of ISI were key developments mirrored in Africa but separated by a timespan of one to two decades.[71] So while Latin America by the end of the 1950s had conceded that ISI was not working, Black Africa was only just becoming independent, and its frustration with ISI would occur in the 1970s. African leaders pushed ISI agendas into the 1970s, and for Nkrumah and Nyerere, regional integration—indeed, a United States of Africa, as Nkrumah argued—was integral to successful economic development. This need became particularly evident as new industries in Africa produced under capacity in the face of limited markets and declining foreign exchange reserves to import raw materials, proving unable to export as neighboring countries pursued their own ISI agendas and duplicated industries (see chap. 4).

This grounding in economic performance and sensitivity to the time gap between economic experiments in Latin America and Africa is not something Getachew pursues. Importantly, when it comes to ISI, the intellectual reflection and preparation that happened in Latin America did not happen in Africa.[72] While Getachew assumes the intellectual influence of the expatriate leftist scholars that gathered at the University of Dar es Salaam (UDSM) in the 1960s and 1970s—Walter Rodney, Giovanni Arrighi, John Saul, and others— on Nyerere's agenda, this was not the case.[73] Nyerere's animosity toward Marxists is documented extensively in the recent three-volume biography by Shivji, Saidya-Othman, and Kamata.[74] In the 1970s, leftist scholars and student movements at UDSM were purged, socialist student organizations like University Students African Revolutionary Front (USARF) and their magazine *Cheche* banned, and even Tanzanian Marxist academics redeployed from the university.

Aside from my attention to economic performance, my approach to worldmaking differs from Getachew's in my incorporation of culture and the arts (chap. 2). Goodman comments on the relevance of the arts to worldmaking and how images or "pictures make and present facts and participate in worldmaking in much the same way as do terms."[75] Goodman's insight on the arts has been elaborated in a volume on cultural ways of worldmaking.[76] Culture featured prominently in worldmaking at the national and international levels for the first generation of African nation builders. A long tradition of cultural nationalism in African political thought stretches back to Edward Wilmot Blyden (1832–1912) and his coining of the concept of "African personality." Cultural nationalism flourished in the interwar period, and for cultural nationalists such as the Sierra Leonean Orishatukeh Faduma (1857–1946, born to liberated Yoruba slaves) and Kobina Sekyi (1892–1956) of the Gold Coast, colonialism was above all the imposition of a new culture, an alien culture. Frantz Fanon writes forcefully about the psychological impact of this alien cultural imposition.[77] Toyin Falola observes that "cultural nationalists had no choice but to respond to the European-derived culture. Thus, they were both culture bearers and culture creators, who also had to invent a future for Africa."[78] The writings of cultural nationalists who dropped their European names, jettisoned European clothing, revived African cultural practices, promoted the use of African languages, studied African history and cultures, asserted their belief in racial equality, and advocated for an African personality would inspire the cultural policies of independence leaders like Nkrumah and Sékou Touré.[79]

Thinking with Nationalism

Nationalism, nation-building, and the nation-state are key conceptual lenses through which this study is framed. The nation-state, with its complex character and baggage, is at the center of this book. Erez Manela points out that one of the most important legacies of the League of Nations after World War I was its positioning of the nation-state as the framework for self-determination and international relations. The Wilsonian moment and its promise of a new international order was seized with enthusiasm in 1919 by anticolonial movements in China, India, Korea, and Egypt. "They aimed to bring into existence a vision of international relations in which hitherto dependent nations would obtain recognition of their equality and sovereignty and join a League of Nations where they would enjoy equal status regardless of size or power."[80] This aspiration was reinforced by the United Nations, which also made the nation-state the denominator of international relations. Indeed, for John Kelly and Martha Kaplan, "the era of nation-states begins in 1945, an era of formal horizontal symmetries and nations imagined as communities, dominated in fact by American power and its exigencies of 'self-determination,' 'open doors' and multilateral trade."[81] As newly independent nations took their place in the United Nations, they sought to use this international body to open the door wider for the liberation of the colonial world and to actively participate in the making of a new world.

Basil Davidson has described the nation-state as the curse of Africa.[82] Writing in 1992, just after Africa's lost economic decade of the 1980s and when the patrimonial, corrupt state in Africa had become discredited, Davidson's disillusionment with the nation-state is understandable (see chap. 1). Perceived as the product of hundreds of years of European history—involving regicide, civil wars, and revolution that put dictatorship and authoritarian rule in check and engendered a vibrant civil society— Young observes that for independent Africa, the vision of the nation-state superimposed on the former colonial territory, "reinstated a superstructure of domination severed from civil society."[83] The absence of a vibrant civil society in newly independent Africa undermined political accountability and transparency and allowed an easy slide into authoritarianism. For both Davidson and Young, the adoption of the nation-state in independent Africa preempted the possibility of Africa exploring its past history of political development for institutions with indigenous resonance and legitimacy. As Young succinctly puts it, "in fully committing itself to the nation-state model of modernity, nationalism unwittingly repudiated its ancestral heritage."[84]

But Africa's ancestral heritage had become complicated by the political and social engineering of colonial rule. Mahmood Mamdani writes of the "decentralized despotism" that characterized colonial rule in Africa, with African chiefs becoming instruments of colonial oppression rather than representatives of their peoples.[85] Martin Chanock has discussed the social invention that accompanied the codification of customary law, as African elders and chiefs with the support of colonial rule took patriarchy to new heights.[86] In short, there were no pristine political institutions Africa could revert to on independence. As historian J. F. Ade Ajayi reminds us, "more than anything else, African political institutions and the institutions of chieftaincies in particular were subjected to great pressures. States were crushed, suppressed, divided or amalgamated at will. Some chiefs were strengthened others weakened; the mighty were often made low and the lowly raised high."[87] Ajayi continues, sagely, that "change is the essence of human history; under colonialism, just as in the several ages before, some institutions changed while others continued."[88] Pivotal in the African context was loss of sovereignty, which removed African autonomy to mediate change. More important is how people adapted to changes and to what uses they put new or transformed institutions.

Africa's new leaders embraced the nation-state not out of ignorance or opportunism. They were deeply aware of the multiple worldmaking enterprises after World War II—the United Nations, the British Commonwealth, the French Union, the Dutch Indonesian Union, the Bandung Conference that spawned the Afro-Asian People's Solidarity Organization (AAPSO) and the Non-Aligned Movement, interterritorial unions that preceded the Organization of African Unity (OAU)—and believed that they could couple the nation-state, the denominator of international politics, to worldmaking and in the process transform the former colonies (see chaps. 2 and 4).[89] Lentz and Lowe note that "we need to recall that an envisaged transfer of power did not automatically entail the creation of a nation-state," and that the formation of single nation-states was not assumed by imperial or African politicians.[90] Frederick Cooper has captured in rich detail the fertile period of political imagination by French and African political leaders who explored federation and confederation in the making—and the unmaking—of the French Community under the Fifth Republic. He also examines the very brief history of the Mali Federation by Sudan and Senegal in 1960.[91] Indeed, the 1940s and 1950s witnessed the flourishing of several experiments at federalism and have been described as a "federal moment."[92] Africa's leaders believed that with the restoration of sovereignty, they were well placed to remake their worlds in an era of internationalisms and institution building. It was the desire of Africa's leaders to acquire the international agency that accompanied national sovereignty that wrecked the French Community.

For anglophone Africa, Julius Nyerere was one of the leading exponents of federation, and he worked tirelessly from 1958 for the federation of Tanganyika, Uganda, Kenya, and Zanzibar through the Pan-African Freedom Movement for East and Central Africa (PAFMECA, see chap. 4). Nyerere was keen for the four territories to agree to federation before independence, wary that to put independence before federation might create an attachment to national sovereignties and an unwillingness to cede sovereignty to a federation. Nyerere argued that "once the four nations each have their own representative at the United Nations, have their own national flag and foreign representatives, we shall have established centers of vested interests again. . . . Furthermore, Federation after complete independence means the surrender of sovereignty and all the prestige and symbols of such sovereignty."[93] While Tanganyika was further along the road to independence in June 1960, Nyerere was willing to delay Tanganyika's independence if all the territories could accede to independence together in 1961 or shortly thereafter. For Nyerere, independence and federalism were conjoined, as were the fights against colonialism and neocolonialism.

Susan Geiger has pointed to the disappointment of scholars of anticolonialism in Africa with nationalism and the nation-state in the 1960s and 1970s, a disappointment that encouraged the devaluation of the nationalist movement in the historiography. Geiger observes that "like Walter Rostow's stages of economic development, African nationalism was supposed to be, according to the anticolonial scholars of the 1960s and '70s, a story of progress told in ever more triumphant political stages. Tanzanian women participants in TANU complicate this story, and suggest the importance of refusing the characterization of nationalist movement as 'success' or 'failure.'"[94] Geiger encourages us to shift our attention from what anticolonial scholars expected and to examine how African nationalism and nation-building unfolded on the ground. I lived through much of Africa's lost decade (the 1980s) as an undergraduate and graduate student at the University of Ghana. The quality of life and education declined steadily as we became dependent on the notes of our lecturers, which we wrote down as faithfully as possible, lacking access to most of the textbooks referenced in their lectures. We lost an entire academic year when the university was closed down by the military regime of the Provisional National Defense Council (PNDC), and we were compelled to evacuate cocoa from villages to the port to aid national economic recovery. University closures continued into my graduate program. We lived through five military governments with coups in 1966, 1972, 1977, 1979, and 1981; my generation felt let down by our nation-state. As an Asante, born and raised in Kumasi, I grew up with the impression that our nationalist project and the resultant nation-state was flawed to begin with. As children in Kumasi, we would pose to each other the question of what one would do if summoned simultaneously by the president of Ghana and king of Asante. The right answer was to respond to both summons but attend to the king of Asante first. I am certain we were not the first to pose these riddles in the late 1960s and early 1970s. It was with great reluctance that I relocated to the United States in 1987 to continue graduate school, as the exodus of faculty together with poor resources undermined the viability of graduate training in Ghana.[95] Later, at the University of Virginia with its top Africanist faculty and first-rate library, I found the opportunity as a doctoral student to begin my interrogation of African nationalism and the African nation-state. I have remained a student of these processes.

Benedict Anderson's *Imagined Communities* (1983) came out in its second edition in 1991, and it was a must-read among graduate students at the University of Virginia. Its argument that nationalism and nation-ness are constructed artifacts that can be borrowed lends nationalists an exciting agency. Anderson defines "nation" as "an imagined political community— and imagined as both inherently limited and sovereign."[96] He credits nationalism with the capacity to invent nations in terms of imagining and creation. The book attributes an eighteenth-century European provenance to nationalism, grounding it in Enlightenment and rationalist secularism; tracks its manifestation in the Americas between the 1750s and 1820s, with the independence of English and Spanish colonies and the invention of the citizen republic; follows its pirating in Europe after the 1820s by peoples under imperial dynastic rule utilizing the banner of popular linguistic nationalism; and examines the assumption of official nationalisms from the mid-nineteenth century by imperial dynasties as a response to the threat of being excluded from popular imagined communities. Anderson asserts that "in effect, by the second decade of the nineteenth century, if not earlier, a 'model' of the independent national state was available for pirating."[97] This trajectory generated models of nationalism that bilingual colonial subjects could access through their Western education. The paradox of the official nationalisms of Britain and France is that these imperial powers taught their national histories to colonized subjects in Africa, making available the constructs of nationalism and the nation-state. Anderson credits two important developments as key to the imagining of the nation: print capitalism and newspapers. And central to this entire process was the development of national languages.

Colonial rule in Africa imposed European languages on colonies that comprised diverse ethnolinguistic groups brought together within artificial colonial boundaries drawn at the Conference of Berlin in 1884–85. The colonial enterprise required an army of clerks within the colonial administration. Colonial missionaries required teachers and catechists in their schools and churches, and mission schools and government schools worked together to educate Africans to meet these needs. In colonial schools, Africans from different ethnic groups learned the same colonial language, studied the same textbooks, and sat for the same standardized exams. They were being molded into a community. It was these educated Africans, mostly men under the colonial dispensation, who gained access to models of nationalism and the nation-state. As the ranks of the literate expanded across colonies, an audience was created for nationalist newspapers. Newspapers played a special role in the imagining of the nation: as dated news, they must be read on the day they come out, facilitating the simultaneous consumption of news and the imagining of a shared community.[98] While language is not emblematic of nation-ness, Anderson cautions, it has the "capacity for generating imagined communities, building in effect *particular solidarities.*"[99]

There is much in the historical record of late colonial rule to substantiate the central role of African-owned newspapers in the imagining of new nations. The 1930s witnessed the expansion of newspaper readership in British West Africa with the widening base of colonial education (galvanized by economic depression), the outcry against the Italian occupation of Ethiopia, and the protest against proposed colonial laws to restrict press freedom, curtail the import of radical literature, and impose direct taxation.[100] Newspapers were at the forefront of this protest. The Nigerian Nnamdi Azikiwe and the Sierra Leonean I. T. A. Wallace-Johnson have been credited with ushering in a new age of journalism in West Africa in the late 1930s, bold in its nationalist demands.[101] Indeed, Fred Omu has credited the newspaper press in West Africa in the 1940s for reorienting nationalism from its West African or African focus to one privileging the national enterprise and the achievement of political independence.[102] In the Gold Coast and Nigeria, the leading nationalists from the late 1940s—Kwame Nkrumah, J. B. Danquah, Nnamdi Azikiwe, and Obafemi Awolowo—were also newspapermen.[103] Stephanie Newell comments on how in West Africa in the 1940s and 1950s, "many newspapermen used the press to launch anticolonial movements and themselves as political leaders."[104] While newspapers in Nigeria were key to the imagining of the nation, they were also sucked into the regional politics that divided western, eastern, and northern Nigeria. Awolowo, leader of the western Nigerian party Action Group, opined that "Nigeria is not a nation. It is a mere geographical expression."[105] But Nigerians aspired to be a nation that transcended regional political loyalties or ethno-nationalisms, and Wale Adebanwi points to the role of the press in imagining the nation as a grand narrative in ways that reconciled or expunged regional and ethnic tensions.[106] Clearly, Anderson's argument about the role of newspapers in the imagining of the nation is supported in Africa.

But Anderson leaves several questions unanswered for the African colonial context. Other sources provide the answers. To begin with, Anderson gives too much credit to literacy, or in the African context, men, and newspapers in the imagining of the nation. This would have lent nationalism an urban bias in Africa. In colonial Africa, where vernacular newspapers were few and the vast majority of Africans did not speak or read the colonial language, there must have been other media expressing the nationalist sentiment. Ernest Gellner points out that "nationalist *sentiment* is the feeling of anger aroused by the violation of the principle, or the feeling of satisfaction aroused by its fulfillment."[107] Sentiment does not require literacy. In the Gold Coast, the nationalist spark came from rural areas with cocoa farmers at the forefront, organized in farmers' cooperatives and angered by colonial response to swollen shoot disease. Educated politicians literally climbed on this nationalist bandwagon and took the political prize (see chap. 5). Similarly, Steven Feierman describes how in Tanganyika, "peasants were forced to make alliances in order to end colonial rule, and their allies won control of the new state."[108] Nor does Anderson capture the prominent place of women, especially market women and traders.[109] The nationalist record in the Gold Coast also spoke to the important role of popular culture, of music, theater, dance, and other ways of building particular solidarities.[110] The elements of popular culture were equally important in the Tanganyikan nationalist movement.[111] Why give all the credit to newspapers? How do we explain the place of ethnic nationalisms, like that of Asante? And lastly, how did race inform colonial nationalism?[112]

The most incisive scholar in terms of ethnic nationalism has been Anthony Smith.[113] Smith's work has also addressed the "relation of nationalism to economic development and social and cultural modernization," underscoring the intimate relationship between nationalism and nation-building and the desired end of nation-building—modernization.[114] Smith, however, argues that the two processes, the rise of nationalism and the growth of the nation, can be separated.[115] This is instructive in the case of Senegal, where, as Irving Markovitz points out, there was no mass involvement in nationalism, which he considers a psychological prerequisite for development.[116] Thus, while nationalism and nation-building can be separated, it is clear that the energy of a mass nationalist movement feeds into nation-building. In *Ethnic Origins of Nations*, Smith pushes the origins of modern nation-states back past the eighteenth-century Enlightenment provenance assigned by scholars like Anderson. For Smith, the modern nation has a long ancestry in the *ethnie*, and ethnicity lies at the core of the nation. He explains that "the approach adopted here defines *ethnie* as clusters of populations with similar perceptions and sentiments generated by, and encoded in, specific beliefs, values and practices. Here the demographic element is important, but secondary to the cultural. For *ethnie* are viewed as consisting in: (1) symbolic, cognitive and normative elements common to a unit of population; (2) practices and mores that bind them together over generations; and (3) sentiments and attitudes that are held in common and which differentiate them from other populations."[117] For Smith, though the nation, defined as "a named community of history and culture, possessing a common territory, economy, mass education system and common legal rights," is a product of the modern age, its origins can be located in premodern ethnic communities.[118] Smith argues that "national sentiment is no construct, it has a real, tangible, mass base."[119] Smith and Anderson represent two schools of thought on nationalism and nations: the primordialists and the constructivists. Nationalism for Smith represents an "ideological movement for attaining and maintaining the autonomy, unity and identity of an existing or potential 'nation.'"[120] Lonsdale has discussed the local ethnic patriotisms and the ethnic moral economies that shaped territorial nationalisms. These had as important an impact on African nationalism as the imported constructs from European education did. Indeed, Lonsdale notes that local patriotisms were potential nationalisms.[121]

Between Anderson and Smith, I could make sense of Nkrumah and the CPP's imagining of a new nation without discrediting as illegitimate the claims of Asante to represent a nation that predated colonial rule and to seek recognition of status as a nation as colonial rule ended. Of our four leaders, it was the erudite Senghor whose intellectual and political vision made room for both the *ethnie* and the nation-state. Senghor differentiated between the "fatherland" and the "nation," noting that a sense of consciousness distinguished them: "Tribes really were nations but without the sense of self-identification as members of a nation that characterized Westerners. While in this first formulation, Senghor argued that the nation preceded the fatherland, what is really significant is that both were apparently conceived of as being territorially coterminous."[122] With the approach of independence and the definition of nation-building as the key task, the crucial problem became how to create a unified nation out of disparate ethnic groups. Fatherland came to represent a lesser area than nation for Senghor, who now equated the ethnic groups and areas to the fatherlands that needed to be combined into a nation. The state was assigned the instrumental role of forming the nation-state.[123] Nkrumah considered Asante's claims to nation-ness illegitimate and early in the political tenure of the CPP moved to curtail chieftaincy and its claims, as did Sékou Touré and Nyerere (see chap. 2). But the new nation could not be created out of nothing, and nationalist intellectuals needed to "reconstruct" the nation "out of pre-existing social networks and cultural elements," an endeavor examined in chapter 2.[124] Indeed, the modern nation emerged, Smith highlights, with "the conjunction, and interpenetration, of these cultural or 'ethnic' elements with the political, territorial, educational and economic ones, that we may term 'civic,' that produce a modern nation."[125]

Despite their opposing views on how nation is imagined or evolves, Anderson and Smith are not far apart in their ideological mooring, for both see the Enlightenment and the Industrial Revolution as having birthed the nation-state. Europe remains the inspiration for the phenomenon of the nation-state and, by implication, the yardstick for measuring the success of that endeavor. Smith writes:

> Historically, the formation of modern nations owes a profound legacy to the development of England, France, and Spain. This is usually attributed

to their possession of military and economic power at the relevant period, the period of burgeoning nationalism and nations. As the great powers of the period, they inevitably became models of the nation, the apparently successful format of population unit, for everyone else. Yet in the case of England and France, and to a lesser extent Spain, this was not accidental. It was the result of the early development of a particular kind of "rational" bureaucratic administration, aided by the development of merchant capital, wealthy urban centers and professional military forces and technology.[126]

The final layer of a civic society to crown the modern nation emerged during the Industrial Revolution.[127] On colonial nationalisms, Anderson concludes that "the 'last wave' of nationalisms, most of them in the colonial territories of Asia and Africa, was in its origins a response to the new-style global imperialism made possible by the achievements of industrial capitalism."[128] The paradox of nationalism and nations as constructed and exportable—yet framed by the discourse and the expectations of the West that made the nation-state the denominator of international relations—made nationalism in Africa something that imprisoned rather than liberated. But African nationalisms, as Lonsdale highlights, "have been shaped as much by African history as by imported ideas."[129]

Partha Chatterjee speaks to the irony of this predicament in his study *Nationalist Thought and the Colonial World* (1993): "Why is it that the non-European colonial countries have no historical alternative but to try to approximate the given attributes of modernity when that very process of approximation means their continued subjection under a world order which only sets their own tasks for them and over which they have no control?"[130] African colonies, having won independence through Western constructs of nationalism, were measured by their success in implementing a civic society and growing their economies. Young speaks of how European colonialism in Africa occurred at a time when civic societies had emerged and were recognized in Europe, with the common legal rights and access to a mass system of education that Smith identifies as core to the modern nation, but these features of the modern nation were denied to Africans. "Africans about to enter the sphere of sovereignty of European states encountered a status of distancing as subjects—in civil standing and racial categorization—far removed from that of the crown subjects of earlier centuries."[131] European states justified the suspension of civic rights in colonial Africa and ruled with impunity in disregard of law (see chap. 1).[132]

Yet on the eve of independence, as the colonial state retreated, it imposed on its successor "a theory and doctrine of state derived from the metropole," a new independent state that reflected the "maximal incorporation rather than repudiation of its [colonial] residues."[133]

The yardstick of the modern European nation was then used to evaluate new African nation-states in the 1960s and 1970s. In 1971, Smith reported that "even the initial wave of support for the anticolonial nationalism of the new states of Africa and Asia has ebbed. The former democratic regimes of these states have been overturned and replaced by military and presidential dictatorships, and the initial sympathy with the efforts of the underprivileged colored peoples to throw off colonial domination has cooled."[134] In short, African states had failed to establish civic societies. The economic record was no better, as failed African economies undercut the capacity to meet the welfare expectations that had framed development and become a responsibility of the modern nation. In the same year as Smith's comment above, Peter T. Bauer in *Dissent on Development* (1971) argued, in effect, that Africa and Asia could borrow the concepts of nationalism and the nation-state, but the success of the nation required deep cultural and historical roots. "Economic development is a process which requires much more than provision of money from abroad. And in this area, as in many other areas of life, experience, time and other qualifications and requirements of achievement cannot be bought. Social processes cannot be telescoped forcibly without effecting their nature as well as the outcome of the processes."[135] As Chatterjee observes, though the non-West could overthrow Western colonial rule, "it is the epistemic privilege which has become the last bastion of global supremacy for the cultural values of Western industrial societies."[136] But it is shallow history, Lonsdale points out, that "continues to dismiss African nationalism as a modernization project that failed." He notes that "patriotic potential has not failed."[137] I will return to this in the conclusion.

A Note on Sources

A Generational Cohort

What began as a book on Nkrumah transformed in the process and became a book about the first generation of independent Africa's leaders with a focus on four presidents: Nkrumah, Sékou Touré, Senghor, and Nyerere. The expanded remit of the book made it a richer study, deepening my knowledge and insights of Nkrumah as his life connected to the other protagonists in this book. My exploration of the lives and careers of Sékou Touré, Senghor, and Nyerere underscored commonalities in their lives as African colonized subjects and their shared project as nation builders and world makers. To give a few examples of the connected lives of several of the individuals mentioned in this book, let us first refer to the autobiography of Joseph Appiah and his days in London as a law student. This excerpt describes the network that developed around Trinidadian George Padmore in London in the mid-1940s:

> It was in his neat little flat in Cranleigh House, near Mornington Crescent, London, that I was to spend many evenings, lasting into the early hours of the morning, in the company of such fighters as Jomo Kenyatta, Richard Wright, Ras Makonnen, Peter Koinange, Peter Abraham, C. L. R. James, Dudley Thompson, Yacoub Osman, Burnham, and latterly Kwame Nkrumah. So close was I to George that we spent almost every free evening together for years. Dr. [Hastings] Banda and good old Kankam Boadu were always with me on these visits. Dr. Banda was another close associate in those days and bore the tedium of my company on my free afternoons on the eternal question of colonial freedom. It was here that I learned more about the doomed Central Africa Federation of the Rhodesias and Nyasaland, now Zambia, Malawi and Zimbabwe.[138]

It is remarkable how one network that met regularly in a small flat in London accounted for several of independent Africa's first leaders. And when Ghana became independent, Padmore, Makonnen, Koinange, Banda, and others relocated to Ghana.

When Nkrumah arrived in London in 1945, he was picked up at the train station by Appiah and Padmore. They were his constant companions during the two years Nkrumah was in London and key supporters when he moved to the Gold Coast as general secretary of the colony's first political party, the UGCC, and when he later founded the CPP. Appiah introduced Nkrumah to the West African Students Union (WASU), and Padmore drafted Nkrumah into the Pan-African Federation, which organized the Fifth Pan-African Congress in Manchester in 1945. Nkrumah hit the ground in London running; these were exciting political times. The Manchester Congress led to the formation of the West African National Secretariat (WANS) in 1946 to pursue the vision of an independent, united West Africa. Nkrumah, as general secretary for WANS, was dispatched to Paris in May 1946 to meet African political leaders from the French colonies. He wrote in his *Autobiography*: "I went to meet the African members of the

French National Assembly—Sourous Apithy, Léopold Senghor, Lamine Gu-eye, Houphouët-Boigny and others. We had long discussions and planned, among other things, a movement for the Union of West African Social-ist Republics. As a result of my visit, Apithy and Senghor came to London to represent French West Africans at the West African Conference."[139] In Tanganyika, the African Association, precursor of the Tanganyika African Association (TAA), heard about the Pan-African Federation and the 1945 Manchester Congress and in February 1946 wrote to the Pan-African Fed-eration for information on the federation and the Manchester Congress.[140] Worldmaking, a corollary of nation-building, began even before Black Africa's independence. It was a shared imaginary that motivated the first generation of independent Africa's leaders. Awareness of the shared politi-cal imaginary and interconnected networks that bound the first genera-tion of Africa's leaders even before independence expanded my interest in Nkrumah to include other African leaders of that generation.

Despite rivalries and disagreements, those in this generation that shared a political imaginary remained loyal to each other. Nyerere and Nkrumah had their disagreements, sometimes openly, over the approach to continen-tal unity (see chap. 4). But Nyerere long admired Nkrumah and his CPP. When Nyerere was elected president of the Tanganyika African Association, the predecessor of TANU, on April 17, 1953, he set about reorganizing the association with inspiration from Nkrumah's CPP.[141] Sékou Touré, in turn, was a loyal friend to Nkrumah and Nyerere. As African leaders distanced themselves from Nkrumah's politics by 1965, Touré remained a supporter of Nkrumah's anticolonialism and anti-imperialism. When Nkrumah proposed in November 1965 that the United Nations authorize a mission with African troops to intervene in Rhodesia and end Ian Smith's unilat-eral declaration of independence, only Guinea of the African states voted in favor.[142] On Nkrumah's overthrow, Touré declared him copresident of Guinea.[143] When Nkrumah found himself in exile in Conakry, Nyerere sent him funds.[144] Touré's friendship with Nyerere endured over the years. In 1979, Tanzania under Nyerere declared war against Idi Amin's Uganda after several provocative acts by Amin, the tipping point being Amin's annexa-tion of the Kagera Salient in October 1978. At the OAU Summit in Monrovia in July 1979, Nyerere's peers took Nyerere to task for violating the territo-rial sanctity of a neighboring country, a right he had eloquently argued for in the founding years of the OAU. Olusegun Obasanjo of Nigeria led the charge, and the matter was only diffused in a closed session through Sékou Touré's eloquent intervention.[145] And when Touré's family was imprisoned in Conakry on his death in 1984, Nyerere intervened with the new military government to secure the release of Touré's family.[146]

Sources

Reflecting the international nature of nation-building and worldmaking in the early decades of independent Africa, and the prominent role the United States came to play in the economic development agendas of Africa's new nation-states, are the number of libraries and archives consulted in the United States for this book. The usual Africanist haunts for the history of colonial and early independent Africa have been national and metropolitan archives. Documents from the Public Records and Archives Administration Department (PRAAD) in Ghana and the National Archives of Britain (NAB) in London have been consulted. Also relevant to this study are the records of the Bureau of African Affairs (BAA), located at the George Padmore Research Library in Accra. I draw on the records of the Tanzanian National Archives in Dar es Salaam and the library of the ruling party in Dodoma, the Chama Cha Mapinduzi (CCM, Swahili "Party of the Revolution"), the successor of the Tanganyika African National Union. Archival holdings in Ghana and Tanzania point to the important support Nkrumah and Nyerere provided to African liberation movements. Indeed, the Organization of African Unity (OAU) on its founding in 1963 designated Dar es Salaam as headquarters for the African Liberation Committee. I explore Nkrumah's and Nyerere's relationship with African liberation movements through the lens of South Africa's African National Congress (ANC) and its records at the University of Fort Hare in the Eastern Cape Province of South Africa.

As American universities, foundations, and national agencies have become invested in independent Africa, repositories of relevant records have proliferated. An exhaustive list is provided in the bibliography, but an illustrative few include international organizations like the World Bank Group Archives Holding (Washington, DC); national bodies like the United States Central Intelligence Agency Archives; the John F. Kennedy Presidential Library and Museum in Boston; foundation records like the Ford Foundation Records held in the Rockefeller Archive Center in Sleepy Hollow (New

York); the Hershey Community Archives with the records of the Hershey Chocolate Corporation; and university archival collections including those at Harvard University, the Massachusetts Institute of Technology (MIT), Princeton University, the University of Chicago, Lincoln University, and Howard University.[147] Photography from this period constitutes an important source, documenting the cultural imagination that informed nation-building, the relations between the leaders examined in the book, and their relations with world leaders. A guided tour of a large hall in Sékou Touré's home, Villa Sily, with wall photos of Touré meeting world leaders in Conakry or on diplomatic trips, shows how he met every notable world leader in the first two decades of Guinea's independence. It is difficult to imagine today that Conakry constituted an important stop in the itineraries of world leaders. As the nation came to be exhibited and performed, the visual and aural became important media in worldmaking.

The leaders used as cases in this book wrote extensively, and their writings are available in autobiography, subject books, pamphlets, and compiled speeches. These have constituted invaluable primary material.[148] They have been the subject of numerous biographies, which are cited in the relevant chapters of this book. A select number of interviews have been invaluable in giving me a sense of these leaders in their private lives. Their public lives, which they lived on full display, were exhaustively documented. Their biographies provide useful entries into their lives, but what was a normal day in their lives like? Interviews with family members, work associates, and others in their close circles proved invaluable. These involved travel not just in Ghana, but to Conakry, Dakar, Dar es Salaam, and Butiama, Nyerere's village (now a town). Interviewing Professor Francis Nkrumah, Nkrumah's eldest child, about his father, Mrs. Andrée Sékou Touré about her deceased husband, or Madaraka Godfrey Nyerere about his late father provided perspectives no book could have. Being in Nyerere's library in his final home in Butiama, or Senghor's in his home (now museum) in Dakar, underscored the importance of scholarship and knowledge to these individuals. It brought me close to their worlds. Though Nkrumah was a prolific writer and collector of books, the soldiers and police who overthrew him in February 1966 destroyed his library and papers. His large library in Conakry was kept after his death but was not claimed by his family or the government of Ghana. The books disappeared after Sékou Touré's death, though a valuable collection of Nkrumah's papers has been preserved through June Milne, who Nkrumah appointed as his literary executrix.[149] Several senior colleagues and friends with a closer understanding of or relationship to these leaders shared their experiences and perspectives. Outstanding in this line were interviews with the late Professor J. H. Kwabena Nketia of Ghana on Nkrumah's use of Akan culture and arts; the late K. B. Asante, pioneer diplomat in Nkrumah's Ghana; Professor George P. Hagan on Nkrumah's persona and politics; Nfaly Sangare on Touré's simple, frugal lifestyle; and an evening in Dakar in August 2018, when I was treated to an extraordinary discussion on Senghor and Senegal's politics by Mamadou Diouf, Manthia Diawara, and Ibrahima Thioub. In South Africa between January and June 2021, I conducted several interviews with South Africans—including Pallo Jordan, Albie Sachs, Paula Ensor, Nathaniel Masemola, Zine and Yagan Leeuw, and others—who had lived in exile in independent African countries like Tanzania, Zambia, Botswana, and Mozambique in the early years of independence.

one

AFRICA IN THE TWENTIETH CENTURY

INTRODUCTION

This chapter provides a narrative account of twentieth-century Africa as context for the following chapters. It tells a familiar story, inflected by the nuances and insights of three decades of research and teaching about Africa. Going beyond the time period of the subsequent chapters, it encompasses the entire century and deposits us at the beginning of the twenty-first century. The promise of new political and economic possibilities, suggested in the "Africa Rising" narrative, characterized the first decade or so of the twenty-first century, as did the African Continental Free Trade Agreement (ACFTA), which by bringing together some fifty-five countries purports to be the largest common market in the world. Indeed, it is the promise of Africa at the dawn of the twenty-first century that requires a return to those early decades of independence, as the developmental challenges of Africa at the attainment of independence remain. We cannot ignore the lessons of those early years.

The political landscape of Africa in 1900, as the twentieth century began, was very different from the landscape just a quarter century earlier. While European colonies existed—some established as early as the sixteenth century in the case of Portuguese Cape Verde, Angola, and Mozambique and the Dutch settler presence at the Cape of Good Hope from the 1650s—one could not have predicted in the 1870s that all of Africa (with the exception of Ethiopia and Liberia) would be European colonies by the close of the nineteenth century. In the era of European colonial rule, the very independence of Ethiopia and Liberia appeared anomalous. Ethiopia successfully presented itself as an old empire during the late nineteenth-century scramble and partition of Africa, embarking on imperial conquest and securing European recognition for the annexation of neighboring lands that belonged to Somali pastoralists.[1] Both Ethiopia and Liberia were treated as semidependent territories and condescendingly subjected to a subordinate status within the League of Nations (of which Liberia was a founding member) not much different from the mandated territories taken from Germany and the Ottoman Empire. Their internal affairs were open to the scrutiny of European member states, an indictment of the viability of Black sovereignty.[2] As the twentieth century opened, pacification of colonized subjects continued. The process extended into the 1910s in the arid areas of the western Sahara and the Somali desert, where nomads had evaded colonial rule. World War I completed the imposition of colonial rule, as the introduction of airpower enabled the subduing of the Tuareg nomads of the Sahara and the forces of Mohammad Abdullah Hassan of Somalia. The introduction of colonial taxes, demonetization of former currencies, resettling of colonized populations, intensification of cash crop cultivation, and institution of migrant labor to sites of European plantations, commerce, and mining underscored structural shifts in African economies. These changes signaled the subjugation of Africa and, equally important, its incorporation into a global economy. Perhaps nothing indicated Africa's absorption into the global economy at the turn of the twentieth century better than the third bubonic plague pandemic, which affected all regions of Africa by virtue of colonial port towns.[3]

John Hargreaves argues that European annexation, in the case of West Africa, was not as sudden as it might appear. In a sense, after centuries of trans-Atlantic trade, what would become colonies already existed by the early to mid-nineteenth century as spheres of European influence along the West African seaboard.[4] This could be said of French presence on the Senegambian coast or British presence on the coast of Sierra Leone, the Gold Coast (Ghana), and Nigeria. The British colony of Sierra Leone existed by 1807; an irregular protectorate had emerged in the southern Gold Coast by the 1830s, and Lagos was annexed in 1861. The scramble and partition of West Africa in the closing decades of the nineteenth century was more about European extension into the interior and carving out of geographically viable colonies. German colonies appeared suddenly, for though German missionaries from Bremen and German traders had been active in the Gold Coast, Togo, and the Cameroons, there had been no indication of German state interest. German annexation extended to South West Africa (present-day Namibia) and German East Africa (present-day Tanzania, Burundi, and Rwanda). The factors in the scramble and partition of Africa have received considerable attention. While the nationalist rivalries of France and Britain have attracted scholarly focus as precipitating factors, the second half of the nineteenth century represents a very unique moment in the relations of Europe and Africa. Scientific discoveries, such as the proper use of quinine as a prophylaxis, increasingly opened up West Africa, the "white man's grave," to European explorers, traders, missionaries, and soldiers. Technological advances led to the advent of steamship service to Africa from the 1850s and the increasingly sophisticated nature of European warfare in Africa. The British invasion of Asante in 1874 involved as many significant contributions from the army engineering corps—building bridges for the passage of troops and equipment, installing telegraph posts to facilitate communication—as from the infantry use of Martini-Henry rifles and cannons that led the Asante to name the conflict the *Toto War* after the rapid sound of fire.[5] In the 1860s, after a couple of decades of land telegraphy, underwater telegraphy came of age with the laying of cables under the sea. The discovery of minerals in South Africa, first diamonds in the 1860s and then gold in the 1880s, encouraged Europe to assume direct control over the economic exploitation of Africa. These developments in the second half of the nineteenth century underpinned European assertiveness. Daniel Headrick has commented that "the new imperialism was not the result of mere superiority, but of the unleashing of overwhelming force at minimal costs. Technological changes affected the timing and location of European conquests."[6]

European colonial rule in most parts of Africa lasted roughly from the 1880s to the 1960s. Within the context of the history of empires, this is a relatively short period. This fact has generated debate on the impact of colonial rule on African political economies. The University of Ibadan was the site of one such debate between historian Jacob Ade Ajayi and political scientist Peter Ekeh. For Ajayi, colonialism was an episode, and the ability of Europeans to chart entirely new directions in African history was limited. Ajayi acknowledged the impact of the loss of African political sovereignty under colonialism and permanent legacies such as Africa's colonial boundaries: "Far-reaching as these changes might have been, their impact on Africa was very uneven. While the lives of some communities were profoundly affected, others had hardly become aware of the Europeans' presence before they had begun to leave. What is more, colonial regimes were far from being uniformly radical. Just as the boundaries of colonial territories tended to put a brake on historical change, so the colonial regimes themselves tended to ally with the most conservative elements in society and to arrest the normal processes of social and political change."[7] While the lives of many may have been relatively untouched by colonial rule, its impact was felt not just in colonial policies or how the colonial moment affected African lives but also in decolonization. This was the position of Ekeh, who opined that "our post-colonial present has been fashioned by our colonial past. It is that colonial past that has defined for us the spheres of morality that have come to dominate our politics."[8] For Ekeh, colonialism was a defining epoch. Reflecting on the ease with which postcolonial African governments slid into authoritarian and despotic rule, Crawford Young notes that "although we commonly described the independent polities as 'new states,' in reality they were successors to the colonial regime, inheriting its structures, its quotidian routines and practices, and its more hidden normative theories of governance."[9] Unable to hold the gates closed on the rising civic society in Africa after World War II and the nationalism it engendered, colonialism implanted the "fragile graftings of a constitutional polity onto the robust trunk of colonial autocracy" as a terminal act.[10] To contemporary observers like Basil Davidson, the nation-state in Africa was a poisoned chalice (see introduction and chap. 2).

Colonial Rule and Colonial Economies

The declaration of World War I is considered as marking the transition from pacification to colonial rule proper. By 1914, 84 percent of the world's land area was dominated by Europeans, compared to 35 percent in 1800. This reality would make World War I and World War II global enterprises, as European colonial powers galvanized production in their new African colonies to support the war effort. Many Africans, unaware of the momentous developments at the Berlin Conference of 1884–85—and who may even have escaped the ravages of colonial pacification required by the Berlin Conference to confirm one's claim to a territory—now felt the weight of the new colonial dispensation through taxes, demands for labor for porterage and public works, and emphasis on cash crop cultivation. Africans in West and East Africa had for centuries been part of global transoceanic trading systems. They were keen on economic opportunities. By the mid-1840s, Zanzibar and Pemba had emerged as the world's leading producers of cloves, a crop introduced to the islands only a few decades before. West Africa dominated the global supply of palm oil and palm kernel by the mid-nineteenth century. The Gold Coast would register its first official export of cocoa, an amount of eighty pounds, in 1891, and by 1911 it had become the world's leading exporter of cocoa with 40,356 tons of cocoa that year (see chap. 5). In areas already embedded in exchange economies, like the Gold Coast and Nigeria, peasant agriculture was allowed to flourish. Across the continent colonial governments put in place infrastructure to facilitate economic extraction, as colonies were expected to be financially self-sufficient. In 1913, just before the outbreak of World War I, tropical Africa accounted for less than 1 percent of France's trade and less than 2 percent of Britain's. In a sense, the scramble and partition of Africa had been more speculative of future rewards than defensive of present economic gains. The control of African labor was at the center of colonial extractive strategies, whether in the form of concessionary companies and their brutal exploitation of labor in the Belgian Congo or in the settler colonies that emerged in Kenya, the Rhodesias, and South Africa.

Irrespective of the different ideological policies adopted by the colonial powers—assimilation by the French, indirect rule by the British, lusotropicalism by the Portuguese—naked force was always at the center of colonial rule. For the hegemonic presence of the colonial state in Africa, Young uses a description that first emerged in the Belgian Congo: *bula matari*, "crusher of rocks," the capacity of the colonial state through its superior control of technology and coercive force to command and deploy humans and machinery in ways that defied the imagination of the Congolese.[11] One key paradox of the African colonial state was that it was forged on both political and racial difference. European colonial rule in Africa coalesced at a time when civil society in Europe had become established, with ordinary Europeans as citizens enjoying a range of rights ensured by law. Electorates had become wider, and European governments had to justify colonial conquest to a wider home audience. In Africa, on the other hand, civil standing was not recognized, and racial difference allowed science and politics to construct the African as "other."[12] While law and the regulation of colonial subjects were important in the forging of colonial rule (hence the term "law imperialism"), the rule of law was absent, allowing practices, such as the *indigénat* in French colonial Africa, that could never have been contemplated in Europe. Introduced to Algeria in 1881, extended to Senegal in 1887, and later spread to the rest of French colonial Africa, *indigénat* was a regime of administrative sanctions that dealt with "offenses" and not "crimes," with "non-law" as distinct from law.[13] It enabled even the look on a colonial subject's face to be interpreted by a French colonial officer as insubordination and rewarded with a short term in prison or corporal punishment. The role of violence in everyday colonial life cannot be understated. It permitted practices such as *corvée* labor in British colonial Africa, with British indirect rule elevating racial and cultural difference as the basis of rule. Mahmood Mamdani provides a succinct summation of indirect rule as applied to the native: "Colonized, the native is pinned down, localized, thrown out of civilization as an outcast, confined to custom, and then defined as its product."[14] Colonial rule became a zone of impunity except, perhaps, in the four communes in Senegal (Saint Louis, Dakar, Rufisque, and Gorée) where residents were French citizens and constituted a civil society.

There was a uniformity to colonial economy irrespective of colonial ideology. Colonial economy revolved around commerce, mining, and agriculture. Mining was extractive, raw material exported with little processing. All large-scale mining was under expatriate control, though artisanal mining was permitted in some colonies.[15] In agriculture, colonial governments encouraged monocrop economies. These reflected the needs of the metropole and not the colonies. Emphasis was placed on cash crops, and as farmers moved away from subsistence, they became increasingly dependent on the market to meet their food needs. Commerce at the macro level was controlled by expatriate firms, though Syrians and Lebanese operated as middlemen in West Africa and Indian presence in East African commerce predated colonial rule.[16] The African mercantile class in West Africa, the "merchant princes," had become an endangered species by the early twentieth century.[17] African traders operated at the retail end or as brokers in the marketing of cash crops (see chap. 5). Albert Sarraut (1872–1962), colonial minister for France from 1920–24 and 1932–33, summed up the essence of a colonial economy in 1923:

> Economically, a colonial possession means to the home country simply a privileged market whence it will draw the raw materials it needs, dumping its own manufactures in return. Economic policy is reduced to rudimentary procedures of gathering crops and bartering them.
>
> Moreover, by strictly imposing on its colonial "dependency" the exclusive consumption of its manufactured products, the metropolis prevents any efforts to use or manufacture local raw materials on the spot, and any contact with the rest of the world. The colony is forbidden to establish any industry, to improve itself by economic progress, to rise above the stage of producing raw materials, or to do business with the neighboring territories for its own enrichment across the customs barriers erected by the metropolitan power.[18]

Infrastructure aimed at the extraction of resources, and rail and roads connected ports to areas rich in mineral resources or agricultural production. Colonial infrastructure was not intended to integrate colonial economies or provide a foundation for economic growth based on internal logic.

The BBC's The Story of Africa notes that as early as the 1920s, most of the main railway lines in colonial Africa had been completed. The motivation for constructing these lines was twofold: effective military and political control of colonies and transportation of minerals from mines to ports. "A large number of lines were built simply to transport minerals from mines to ports, with little benefit to communities on the way. In the Belgian Congo, copper from Katanga was taken to the port of Lobito in Angola on the Benguela railway. In Liberia a railway was built from the iron producing region of Nimba country to the port of Buchanan."[19] These examples can be multiplied. In Sierra Leone, the railway was limited to the capital of Freetown, built to transport European colonial officials and expatriates from segregated Hill Station to their places of work. The total mileage of railway lines in Sierra Leone is therefore only eighty-four miles and was motivated by the desire to protect Europeans from malaria-infected Africans.[20] A recent World Bank–sponsored report describes the fragmented railway systems inherited at independence:

> Although grand master plans for integrated rail systems have been proposed, none has been fully implemented and, for the most part, the African rail system remains fragmented, with lines connecting cities within a single country or linking a port and its immediate regional hinterland.

The only significant international networks are those centered in South Africa and stretching north to Malawi, the Democratic Republic of Congo (DRC), and Tanzania; the North African network in the Maghreb; and the East African network linking Kenya, Uganda, and Tanzania. A few railways cross borders to link landlocked countries to ports, and others provide inland railheads from which goods can be on-forwarded by road. But there has historically been little trade between most African countries outside southern Africa, and the financial and economic case for more integrated links is unlikely to be strong.[21]

According to this study, West Africa has some of the lowest statistics of route kilometer railways operated, as well as passenger kilometer usage of railways. It is not irrelevant that peasant economies dominated in West Africa, with small numbers of European settlers in French colonies like Senegal and the Ivory Coast. The railway map of sub-Saharan Africa today visually highlights this deficiency. Road networks, though more extensive, are also uneven in distribution and quality.[22] Deficiencies abound in other public service areas. To take the example of electricity supply, it is estimated that only a third of the population in sub-Saharan Africa has access to electricity today.[23] The colonial period left Africa with an infrastructural deficit the continent is still trying to bridge (see chaps. 3, 4, and 5).

The 1930s: Economic Depression and
the Stirring of African Nationalism

Anthony Hopkins has commented on the significance of depressions and economic recessions in Africa's colonization and decolonization. He points to how one economic recession, from 1873 to 1896, framed the context of colonial imposition, altering the terms of trade for European merchants to the point that the merchants became advocates for direct European control of African colonies. The economic depression of the 1930s encouraged the African critique of European colonial rule that became foundational for nationalist movements (see chap. 5).[24] The Great Depression of the 1930s undermined the legitimacy of colonial rule in Africa. The Depression began after the stock market crash of October 1929, which sent Wall Street into a panic. The United States' economy imploded with catastrophic global effect between 1929 and 1933, and deflation spread like contagion to Europe and through the European colonial powers to Africa. International trade declined by more than 50 percent, and commodity prices collapsed across Africa. Colonial governments responded by increasing customs duties and

Primary Roads, Rails, and Ports in Africa

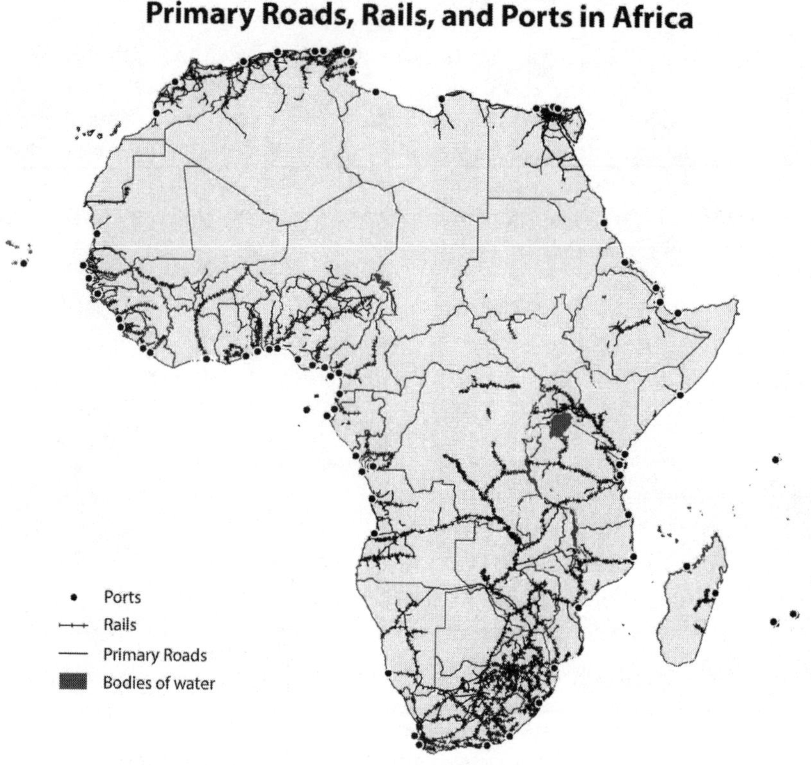

Map. 1.1 Africa's major road and railway network. Credit: Mark Duerksen.

introducing direct taxation; pursuing retrenchment by laying off workers and cutting back on expenditures on public works; and seeking to increase the production of cash crops and control its marketing. Colonial responses discredited the colonial enterprise. Hopkins comments that "after 1930 there was some pretense, but little reality about developing the estates of the Empire."[25]

In West Africa, where producers of groundnuts, palm oil, and cocoa suffered adverse terms of trade during what Susan Martin calls the "long depression" between 1914 and 1939, peasants stepped up production to maintain their standard of living.[26] In Kenya, the depression revealed the frailty of settler production—it was "the African agricultural producer and taxpayer who carried the colonial state in Kenya through the crisis of the

1930s."[27] In northern Nigeria, the colonial government laid off tin miners and railway workers, two key employments in the region. Moses Ochonu describes the rise of "self-help criminality" in northern Nigeria during the depression: retrenched tin miners resorted to theft, and laid-off railway workers stole track components and sabotaged the lines. The colonial government withdrew silver coins from the Nigerian economy for repatriation to Britain, which needed silver and gold as instruments of financial stability. Britain introduced cheap alloyed coins, which encouraged counterfeiting.[28] Colonial policies during the depression intensified gender struggles over resources; in colonial Asante, chiefs and male elders moved against young women who sought to control their own productive and reproductive labor. In the late 1920s and 1930s, several Asante women chose to invest their labor in trade and farming rather than marry and work for their husbands. Chiefs ordered the rounding up of spinsters, detained them, and mandated that they choose a man to marry or pay a heavy fine.[29] Peasant holdups of cash crops like cocoa and boycotts of European imports marked the 1930s (see chap. 5). In rural and urban Africa, protest movements agitated against colonial rule.

It is in this context that Italy invaded Ethiopia in 1935, leading to its annexation of Ethiopia for five years. Africans in Africa and the diaspora responded in outrage. That the League of Nations, of which Ethiopia was a member, did nothing to reverse this travesty for Africans revealed the duplicitous nature of this international organization that encompassed sovereign states (see chap. 4). Organizations across Africa emerged to raise funds for the free Ethiopia movement. The response was particularly sharp in West Africa, with its established tradition of African-owned and run newspapers. In the Gold Coast, I. T. A. Wallace-Johnson founded the Ethiopia Defense Committee. Nnamdi Azikiwe and Nigeria-based Pan-Africanist Duse Mohamed Ali organized protests.[30] Some fifty thousand African Americans volunteered to enlist and fight for Ethiopia—lack of funding and American laws prevented them from doing so.[31] In London the International African Friends of Ethiopia (IAFE), funded by African and Caribbean activists and trade unionists, led the campaign against the Italian invasion. It brought Caribbean and African activists like the Trinidadians George Padmore and C. L. R. James, the Sierra Leonean Wallace-Johnson, and the Kenyan Jomo Kenyatta together (see chap. 4). African responses to the Depression of the 1930s and the Italian annexation of Ethiopia saw the

1930s act as a fertile seedbed of African nationalism "and not merely as a 'background' to the more publicized events of the years which followed the end of the Second World War."[32]

WORLD WAR II AND A NEW POLITICAL AND ECONOMIC AGENDA FOR AFRICA

Unlike World War I, which consolidated colonial rule in Africa, World War II left a sense that there was no way colonialism could continue unimpaired. Whereas some of the conditions in World War II were mirrored in World War I—international pronouncements by the United States in favor of self-determination and the expressed desire for a postwar international organization to protect the rights of peoples against the predation of powerful states—Africans, except perhaps in Egypt, were newly conquered into European empires and lacked the capacity to assess the opportunities the war presented for self-determination in 1918 (see chap. 4).[33] Rather, through increased taxes for the war effort, prioritized cash crop production and mining, and encouraged "war donations" from African communities, Africans were effectively incorporated into empire during World War I. France made extensive use of African troops in the European theater of war; it was singular in its decision as a colonial power to train Africans in the modern art of warfare.[34] French Africa sent some 450,000 troops to Europe and provided 135,000 wartime workers for French factories. About 65,000 African troops from North and West Africa died in Europe fighting for France.[35] The British used African troops for military engagements on the African continent against German colonies such as Togo, Cameroon, and German East Africa. Not only did Gold Coast troops fight to take over German Togo, the cost of the entire campaign, about £60,000, was paid by Gold Coasters. The West African Frontier Force (WAFF) and the King's African Rifles (KAR) in East Africa were used by the British in military engagements on the continent.[36] The apparent consolidation of European colonial rule in Africa in 1920 was deceptive. Both France and Britain were in economic decline: France lost two-thirds of its foreign investments during World War I and suffered huge mortality and great physical damage at home; the weakening of Britain's industrial hegemony became evident, the volume of British exports between 1919 and 1939 never exceeding more than two-thirds that of 1913. Yet both Britain and France went on to acquire additional territories as they took on colonies from defeated Germany and the

Ottoman Empire.[37] The influenza pandemic of 1918–19 had a major impact in Europe, Africa, and Asia, disproportionately affecting young adults. In a sense, European empires in 1920 were already in decline, though not easily discernibly so. The cracks became more apparent in the depression of the 1930s, and World War II made imperative a new political direction.

The unraveling of European colonial rule was more evident after World War II. Allied war propaganda that presented World War II as a war against racial discrimination and rule by might positioned this global conflict very differently from World War I. This shift was captured in the Atlantic Charter, a joint declaration by British prime minister Winston Churchill and American president Franklin D. Roosevelt on August 14, 1941, broadly outlining United States and British war aims. It stated, inter alia, that after the war all peoples would have the right to determine the kind of government under which they lived. This declaration was celebrated by colonized subjects in Africa and Asia. Though Churchill would later declare it did not apply to British colonies in Africa, Labour Party leaders like Clement Attlee, then in opposition, assured African organizations like the West African Students Union in London that this declaration did apply to Africa (see chap. 4).[38]

Again, Africans made huge sacrifices in World War II. Some eighty thousand African troops fought in the French Army in France—among those taken captive and placed in a prisoner-of-war camp when Germany invaded and occupied France in 1940 was Léopold Senghor, future president of Senegal. The Free French Government under Charles de Gaulle was based in Congo-Brazzaville, and the Free French Army was an African army after the fall of France. British West Africa provided 167,000 troops to fight against Germany and Italy in North Africa and then against Japan in Burma. Britain's eastern and central African colonies supplied 280,000 servicemen. Japanese conquests of Southeast Asian colonies, beginning with French Indochina in July 1940 and continuing with the British colonies of Malaya, Singapore, Burma, and Hong Kong after 1942, severed Asian markets and producers from the metropoles. The result was a rise in demand for African commodities such as sisal, rubber, and palm oil, seen as essential to the war effort. The African percentage of British and French trade peaked.[39] African political mobilization in the 1930s and the experience of African servicemen in North Africa, Europe, and Asia during World War II deepened African understandings of empire. A parody of Psalm 23 sent by a serviceman from the battlefront to a Gold Coast newspaper, the *African Morning Post*, reveals a nuanced understanding and penetrating critique of the political economy of empire:

> The European merchant is my shepherd
> And I am in want;
> He maketh me to lie down in cocoa farms;
> He leadeth me beside the waters of great need;
> The general managers and profiteers frighten me.
> Thou preparedst a reduction in my salary
> In the presence of my creditors.
> Thou annointest my income with taxes;
> My expense runs over my income
> And I will dwell in a rented house for ever![40]

Like the cocoa farmers radicalized by the holdups of the 1930s, ex-servicemen played a leading role in nationalist struggles. Their protest march in the Gold Coast in February 1948 sparked the riots that precipitated decolonization in the Gold Coast (see chap. 5).

The international context had changed considerably when the war ended in 1945. First, there were two new superpowers: the United States and the Soviet Union. Much of the postwar economic reconstruction in Europe was financed by the American Marshall Plan; the days of empire were numbered. Funding European reconstruction, the United States demanded access to markets in Africa (see chap. 3). The Soviet Union was vehemently anti-imperialist and anticolonialist. It was the advent of the Cold War that tempered America's position on decolonization, as Britain, France, and Portugal, North Atlantic Treaty Organization (NATO) allies, presented their colonies as crucial to metropolitan reconstruction and to the fight against communism. Second, the United Nations (UN) was created in 1945, and its charter advocated self-determination. Third, as Asian countries became independent and took their place in the UN, first India and Pakistan in 1947 and then Ceylon (Sri Lanka) in 1947 and Burma (Myanmar) in 1948, they became exemplars for African colonies and advocates for self-determination in the UN. Last, in October 1945, Caribbean Blacks and Africans in Britain, spearheaded by George Padmore, Ras Makonnen, Kwame Nkrumah, Joseph Appiah, Jomo Kenyatta, and others, convened the Fifth Pan-African Congress in Manchester to deliberate on the future of Africa. This was the first Pan-African Congress to have major participation by Africans (see chap. 4).

Participants at the Manchester Congress committed themselves to the total liberation of Africa and adopted Pan-African socialism as the agenda for independent Africa.[41] Not only was the international climate auspicious for self-determination after World War II, but Africans were also ready to claim political independence.

The colonial state became a developmental state in the aftermath of World War II. Development plans included infrastructure like hydroelectric dams to facilitate industrialization (see chaps. 3 and 5). Major interventions were pursued by the British and French to increase the productivity of African agriculture. All were colossal failures. The Office du Niger in Mali was a project commenced after World War I in the Niger River Basin to produce cotton. By 1945, when the Colonial Ministry privately conceded the project's failure, some thirty thousand Africans had been forcibly resettled as part of the scheme.[42] The Richard Toll rice-growing scheme from 1949 in Senegal also failed, as did the groundnut scheme in the British trusteeship territory of Tanganyika. British attempts to modify African agricultural practices, like the building of ridges to combat hillside soil erosion in Shambaa in Tanganyika in the 1950s, equally failed.[43] In manufacturing, large expatriate companies established the first import-substitution industries in the latter years of the war, as wartime shipping shortages undercut imports for African markets. Breweries, textile factories, and other types of light industry emerged to replace imports. With a new emphasis on development, mechanized agriculture, industry, and socioeconomic reform, colonial rule became more intrusive at a time Africans expected economic and political rewards for their contribution to the war effort. This phase of colonial rule has been termed the "second colonial occupation." To promote new development projects, Britain passed the Colonial Development and Welfare Act in 1940, renewed in 1945, 1950, 1955 and 1959. France created the Funds for Investment for Economic and Social Development (FIDES) in 1946. Marketing boards were institutionalized in British West Africa to continue the colonial state's wartime control of the marketing of cash crops like cocoa, palm produce, and cotton (see chap. 5). France created in December 1945 a new monetary unit, the CFA (colonies francaises d'Afrique) franc, to be used in France's West African and Equatorial African federations convertibly with the differently valued metropolitan franc. Not only were the expected rewards for Africa's contributions to the war effort not forthcoming, but wartime shortages of imported commodities also continued. Prices remained high, sparking the boycott of European goods in the Gold Coast at the beginning of 1948.

John Gallagher makes an intriguing argument about the fall of the British Empire. He argues that the best way to maintain an empire is through neglect. Then, subjects do not feel the weight of imperial domination. One of the surest ways of losing an empire is to deepen imperial intervention. Britain saw this with its North American colonies in the eighteenth century and with African colonies after World War II.[44] It was perhaps in anticipation of the need for political concessions in Africa, with the attainment of independence by a number of Asian countries in the immediate aftermath of World War II and the launch of the second colonial occupation in Africa, that the Colonial Office in London commissioned an internal report in 1947: the Cohen Report. With Andrew Cohen as its main architect, the report served as a blueprint for decolonization in the advent of nationalism in Africa. But even Andrew Cohen in 1947 saw independence in British Africa as several decades away, with the Gold Coast perhaps achieving independence in a generation. The Gold Coast became independent exactly a decade after the Cohen Report, its process of decolonization precipitated (some believe prematurely) by the 1948 Riots and the subsequent recommendations of the Watson Commission. Based on extensive interviews, the Watson Commission concluded that nationalism had arrived in the Gold Coast and recommended constitutional reforms that eventually led to the first general elections in February 1951 and the first African government in Black Africa (see chap. 5).

With decolonization in progress in the Gold Coast, a domino effect was created; other British colonies, and even French colonies, looked on covetously as the Gold Coast made its way toward independence. France had convened the Brazzaville Conference in 1944 to present a new deal for its African colonies in the light of the herculean sacrifices of World War II. Decolonization was definitely not an option, for French colonial policy had long viewed the overseas colonies as an integral part of France. The conference was quite emphatic that "the purposes of the civilizing work which France has accomplished in her colonies exclude any idea of autonomy, any possibility of evolution outside the French imperial bloc; the eventual establishment—at however remote a date—of 'self-governments' in the colonies must be ruled out."[45] There was to be more participatory government, with African deputies to the French parliament and territorial

African assemblies. To form parties and organize elections to the metropolitan and local legislatures, the Rassemblement Démocratique Africain (African Democratic Rally or RDA) was founded in Bamako in 1946 by African politicians led by Felix Houphouët-Boigny of the Ivory Coast and Lamine Guèye of Senegal. Territorial branches of the RDA were formed to contest colony-wide elections. These included the Parti Démocratique de la Côte d'Ivoire (PDCI) and the Parti Démocratique de Guinée (PDG). As the French imperial project foundered in the 1950s, the Fourth Republic collapsing through the crisis of the Algerian war of independence, popular support swept de Gaulle back into power in June 1958. Proposing a new French Community under the Fifth Republic for overseas French territories, de Gaulle personally campaigned across Africa for a "Yes" vote in a referendum in September 1958 for African colonies. A "Yes" vote guaranteed representation in the French Parliament and French aid. A "No" vote would lead to the accession of immediate independence.

Only Guinea voted "No" and became independent in October 1958, with French support completely cut off (see chaps. 2 and 4). That Guinea was an outlier still could not prevent the march toward independence. For colonies that voted "Yes," the major attraction was French aid and the promise of an empire of French citizens. But as Black African nations gained independence and stepped onto the international stage through membership in the UN and other international organizations, national sovereignty became very attractive to the former French colonies. Their push for sovereignty and the capacity to frame their worlds led to the unraveling of the French Community. Despite the popular perception that France pushed for the balkanization of its African colonies to facilitate easier control in the postcolonial era, Cooper shows convincingly how France bent backward to accommodate a West African federation within the French Community.[46] With the floodgates open, the timing of African independence moved in advance even of receptive Britain. In 1959, Prime Minister Harold Macmillan and Secretary of State Lennox-Boyd pronounced that independence would come to British East Africa probably in the 1970s.[47] In 1960, seventeen African countries gained independence. Tanganyika followed in 1961, Uganda in 1962, and Kenya in 1963. The anticolonial march continued, with the Organization of African Union (OAU) serving as a powerful advocate of Africa's independence from 1963. The collapse of Salazar's government would lead to independence for all Portuguese colonies in 1975.

The southern African settler colonies would be among the last to attain independence: Zimbabwe in 1980, Namibia in 1990, and South Africa in 1994.

Independence and After: The Quest for Development

The newly independent African nation-states shared two major objectives: building enduring nation-states; and promoting economic growth and diversification to meet the huge expectations of their newly enfranchised citizens. Nation-building and worldmaking were two sides of the same coin, and Africa's early leaders were committed to a Pan-African vision. They were invested in a larger African political union beyond the nation-state, though leaders' opinions differed on the nature of this union and its timing. The Organization for African Unity, founded in Addis Ababa in 1963, addressed this common objective, though for some it did not go far enough when it failed to create a continental African government (see chap. 4). African nation-states assumed colonial boundaries, which had encompassed different ethnic and linguistic groups. Welding disparate peoples into one nation was an early task, and for primarily oral societies, "performing" the new nation was key. Music, dance, art, creative culture more broadly, and religious symbolism all became important materials for the fabrication of new states (see chap. 2). Tribalism was seen as the bane of the new nation-state, yet politics required ethnic and regional representation for the government to be inclusive. In Ghana, Guinea, and Tanzania, chieftaincy was weakened or abolished. Just months after independence, Nkrumah banned regional and ethnic political organizations in Ghana and declared tribalism a criminal offense. Development was a passionate goal that meant access to education (universal free primary education was pursued in many countries), good healthcare, jobs, decent housing—in short, a quality life. In 1960, less than 20 to 25 percent of Africans could read and write. Regional growth comparisons in terms of growth indicators showed that only South Asia was close to sub-Saharan Africa in adult illiteracy rates in 1970, with 55.8 percent adult illiteracy for sub-Saharan Africa and 55.5 percent for South Asia. The comparative figure for Latin America and the Caribbean was 17.4 percent. Life expectancy at birth stood at 41.1 years for sub-Saharan Africa, 45.3 years for South Asia, and 56.4 for Latin America and the Caribbean. Life expectancy at birth in industrial countries stood at 70.2 years in 1970.[48] This lends context to Nkrumah and Nyerere's emphasis that their battle at independence was against illiteracy, disease, and poverty.

On independence in 1961, Tanganyika had only two trained engineers and three medical doctors.[49]

The nexus of African nationalism, Marxism, development economics, and in the 1960s modernization theory created optimism that Africa's developmental challenges could be met. From small nation-states like Malawi, which aspired through modernized agriculture to become the Denmark of Central Africa, to Nkrumah's Ghana, which aimed for industrialization through a planned hydroelectric dam and factories established in partnership with Eastern Bloc countries, there was enthusiastic conviction that good leadership, centralized planning, foreign aid, and technical assistance could underpin economic growth in any African country (see chap. 3). That development economists queried the tenets of neoclassical economics (based on Western industrial economies) where the tropical economies of the "underdeveloped world" were concerned augured well for Africa's nation-states, which were ambivalent about capitalism and communism and sought to explore a third way through Pan-African socialism (see chap. 4). Not only was Africa's indigenous capitalist middle class weak or nonexistent, several new leaders of Africa were uneasy about the possible emergence of an African capitalist class. Douglas Rimmer notes that African governments and countries have been preoccupied with redistributive politics—sharing the small national cake instead of growing the cake, delivering welfare rather than focusing single-mindedly on economic growth.[50] The downturn in world commodity prices for many of Africa's exports from the late 1950s undermined the capacity of governments to deliver on their development promises. Most African countries had a small tax base, and government was the largest employer of labor. Development economics encouraged deficit financing to facilitate productive capacity, and the 1960s and early 1970s saw some imprudent borrowing, as interest rates were low. Africa's external debts began to mount.

Internal signs of corruption and authoritarianism were equally worrying. Ghana, the pioneer independent state in Black Africa, was already showing signs of corruption in 1953, shortly after the first general elections in 1951 and the formation of the country's first African government. For Nkrumah's African and Caribbean friends in London, who had spent an intense two years (1945–47) together thinking, planning, and working toward African independence, this was an ominous development. Joseph Appiah's brief visit to Ghana in 1953 before his eventual return from law studies in London elicited many complaints about corruption among the new African ministers. He wrote in his autobiography that "during the entire period of my stay, concerned patriots from within and without the party [the CPP] complained bitterly about the rising tide of corruption among ministers and high party officials; they made the point that at that rate of corruption in public life our future as an independent nation appeared grim and pleaded with me to draw Kwame's [Nkrumah] attention to the budding danger. George Padmore, in his report to me in London after his first-ever visit to the country in 1951, had also expressed grave concern over this unhealthy trend."[51] Appiah did confront Nkrumah privately during that visit about this growing cancer, and Nkrumah admitted that this was indeed so but resisted Appiah's advice to excise it immediately. His reasons, unacceptable to Appiah, pointed to party support from tribal networks and the connections between these tribal networks and political patronage. "Our people, he argued, had given the party their enthusiastic support on grounds other than political ideology; to a large extent, tribal and blood affinity to individual party leaders had decided their choice of C. P. P. membership; to dismiss or severely discipline any minister or high official at that time was to invite mass resignations and, consequently, the disintegration of the party."[52] Corruption undermined party solidarity and the loyalty of party rank and file and Ghanaians. The irony is that these first nationalist governments were very popular when they gained political power: Nkrumah's CPP won thirty-four of the thirty-eight popularly contested seats in 1951 and seventy-two out of one hundred four seats in the expanded legislative assembly in 1954. Touré's PDG won fifty-six of the sixty seats in Guinea's 1957 local elections. These were parties with massive internal supporters and external admirers. Nkrumah, Touré, Senghor, Nyerere, and many in their generation of leaders ended up declaring one-party states.

A series of laws trace Nkrumah's progress in this authoritarian direction. First was the Deportation Act in July 1957. Then, in November 1957, all local and ethnic organizations were outlawed and tribalism made a criminal offense. In December 1957, the Avoidance of Discrimination Act banned all religiously based parties. In July 1958, the Prevention Detention Act gave the government power to detain anyone for up to five years without trial for conduct deemed prejudicial to national security. In July 1960, Ghana became a republic, and in February 1964, Ghana became a one-party state.

With no legal recourse, the political opposition resorted to assassination attempts and coup plots, increasing Nkrumah's paranoia and isolation. This scenario played out across the continent, much to the dismay of Arthur Lewis, a strong supporter of Africa's independence.[53] Across the continent, assassination of the first leaders and military coups mounted.[54] In just 1963, assassination and coups were attempted in Senegal, Ghana, Mali, Togo, the Ivory Coast, Chad, Dahomey, and more. The Nigerian civil war from 1967 to 1970 deepened the sense of gloom. In the 1960s, the first full decade of independence in Africa, military coups overthrew governments in Algeria, Benin, Burkina Faso, Burundi, the Central African Republic, the Republic of the Congo, the Democratic Republic of the Congo, Gabon, Ghana, Libya, Mali, Nigeria, Sierra Leone, Somalia, Sudan, Togo, Uganda, and Zanzibar. Politically, the 1960s was a messy decade.

Economic performance worsened in the 1970s. Africa was not an attractive destination for foreign investment. After Africa's dismal economic and political performance, Western countries like the United States began to revise foreign aid policies toward the continent (see chap. 3). Development economics was discredited within the discipline of economics, partly due to the poor political and economic record of Africa and the developing world (see chap. 3). The Organization of the Petroleum Exporting Countries (OPEC) oil crisis in 1973 increased the debt burden of African countries, except the fortunate few like Nigeria who had discovered oil in commercial quantities. Widespread Sahelian droughts between 1967 and 1973 added to the list of woes. The first wave of emigration among Africa's professionals began from the mid-1970s, with Ghana in the forefront, and snowballed into a massive, continent-wide brain drain. The promise of independence appeared over. The 1980s would push a tottering continent into the abyss.

Failed Expectations: The 1980s as Africa's Lost Decade

The 1980s underscored how dependent Africa remained on the industrialized world and the countries in the Organization for Economic Cooperation and Development (OECD) as a market for the continent's primary commodities. The 1980s was a decade of economic recession for the OECD countries, whose markets received 85 percent of Africa's primary exports. Primary commodities still accounted for 80 percent of Africa's exports. Recession in the OECD countries resulted in a constriction of demand for Africa's commodities and a fall in world prices for Africa's primary products. Countries exporting soft commodities like coffee and cocoa experienced the sharpest declines in global prices. Economic difficulties in the developed North led to the suspension of trade agreements between the North and South that had facilitated the export of Africa's primary commodities to the consumer markets of the North.[55] Gross domestic product (GDP) in Africa declined from 5 percent in 1975–79 to 1.7 percent in 1980–85. The gains made in industrialization in the 1960s and 1970s, especially with the establishment of state-owned enterprises in Africa, suffered a reversal; Africa actually began to deindustrialize in the 1980s (see chap. 4). Then came a global stock market collapse that began in the United States in 1987 and spread to the stock markets of other countries. Japan, then the second largest economy in the world, saw its growth rates drop from over 5 percent from 1986 to 1990 to 1 percent from 1991 to 1995. Africa's share of global trade dropped from 3 percent in the 1950s to less than 2 percent in the early 1990s.

Contrasting the scene in Africa, the 1980s saw significant economic growth among countries in Asia that managed to diversify their economies away from the export of primary products and become involved in regional trade. Economic diversification and growth in South Korea, Malaysia, Taiwan, and Indonesia signaled a new trend that would strengthen in the 1990s. In the second half of the 1980s, gross domestic product (GDP) in developing Asia grew at 6.8 percent, rising further to 8.6 percent during 1991–95. Intraregional trade in Asia constituted about 27 percent of Asia's trade in 1985, and 58 percent for the European Economic Community. For Africa, intra-African trade represented a low 4.42 percent, emphasizing how extraverted Africa's economies remained. While exports declined, imports remained high in African countries, contributing to the balance of payment deficits and increasing inability to meet the servicing requirements of foreign debts. As the external debt situation in African countries worsened, international banks proved unwilling to extend loans. The result was a rise in the cost of available credit—in the 1980s, the rate of interest for intra-African trade could be as high as 40 percent.[56]

Other developments worsened the continent's political economy. HIV-AIDS reared its head on the continent from the mid-1980s, wreaking havoc in the eastern half of the continent from Ethiopia down through South Africa.[57] Economic decline adversely affected higher education, and universities that were once the pride of the continent, such as the University of Ibadan, Makerere University, and the University of Ghana, became pale shadows of their former selves. South African universities went through peculiar challenges because of apartheid and the introduction of policies such as the Bantu Education Act of 1953. From the late 1950s, key academic institutions like the University of Fort Hare—the alma mater of Nelson Mandela, Oliver Tambo, Seretse Khama, Robert Mugabe, and several other African luminaries—declined, and many Black South African teachers went to English-speaking countries, including the newly independent countries of Ghana, Nigeria, Tanzania, and Zambia. Anger over Bantu Education would explode in June 1976 with the students' uprising in Soweto, triggered by the apartheid government's decision to introduce Afrikaans alongside English as the medium of instruction. While South Africa lost some of its academic talent, it retained a strong research tradition, seen in breakthroughs like Christiaan Barnard performing the world's first human-to-human heart transplant surgery in 1967 in Cape Town. Africa's brain drain accelerated, including the medical professionals most needed to tackle the soaring AIDS epidemic.

Africa lost its voice in international academic circles, and by extension in the international development community. Whereas only Ghana had accessed an IMF stabilization program in sub-Saharan Africa before the late 1970s, thirty-three sub-Saharan African countries received adjustment loans from the IMF and the World Bank between 1980 and 1985. An early assessment of how African countries had fared under structural adjustment in its first decade was not encouraging, especially where social indicators were concerned. Infant mortality remained a high 126 per thousand; life expectancy had increased only two years from forty-six to forty-eight. For a subgroup of low-income countries, per capita outlays on education had fallen by almost half, and that of health by about a third. Undernutrition had increased in low-income countries.[58] I. G. Patel edited a volume of papers on adjustment in Africa from an IMF symposium in Botswana in 1991.[59] In a paper he wrote and published on the IMF's website in December 1992, Patel argued from the evidence of seventeen African countries that underwent adjustment in the 1980s that while eight showed significant improvements in prestructural adjustment performances, the remaining nine showed appreciable deterioration in poststructural adjustment performances. As the IMF looked to the decade of the 1990s, Patel recommended that "a new approach . . . suggests the need to design credible adjustment programs in the 1990s that are truly growth-oriented, and also take account of the needs for health, education, and other services, while being conscious of the fact that major changes in the structures and production fabric of the African economy will take time to yield results and require substantial investment."[60] These insights echoed recommendations made in the 1980s by Africa's leaders. As a fallen continent, Africa had lost its voice, and the recommendations of its leaders could conveniently be ignored. It is in the 1980s that the Bretton Woods institutions gained hegemonic influence in Africa, a development reinforced by the collapse of the Soviet Union in 1989.

Africa's leaders and economic institutions sought solutions for the catastrophic decade of the 1980s. In a keynote address in Nairobi in 2002, Adebayo Adedeji, who had been executive secretary at the United Nations Economic Commission for Africa (UNECA) from June 1975 to July 1991, referenced three strategic economic plans the continent had proposed.[61] He cited the Lagos Plan of Action for the Economic Development of Africa, 1980–2000 (1980), which the Economic Commission for Africa had worked on for four years; the African Alternative Framework to Structural Adjustment for Socio-Economic Recovery and Transformation (1989); and the African Charter for Popular Participation for Development (1990).[62] The Lagos Plan of Acton had been accepted by the OAU and the UN. The Economic Commission for Africa in 1976 had proposed four key principles that lay at the heart of strategic plans proposed by the continent in the 1980s: self-reliance, self-sustainment, democratization of the development process, and a just distribution of the rewards of development. "Unfortunately," Adedeji notes, "all of these were opposed, undermined and jettisoned by the Bretton Woods institutions and Africans were thus impeded from exercising the basic and fundamental right to make their decisions about their future."[63] By the end of the 1980s, development had ceased to be the product of international partnerships and had become something the West did *for* Africa, not *with* Africa.[64] As Adedeji correctly points out, "development should not be undertaken on behalf of a people; rather that it should be the organic outcome of a society's value system, its perceptions, its concerns and its endeavors."[65]

The Period of "Receivership": Africa under International Management

As the 1980s drew to a close, most African countries had entered into stabilization programs with the IMF and the World Bank. The fall of the Berlin

Wall in 1989 and the subsequent collapse of the Soviet Union transformed the world from bipolar to unipolar. Capitalism stood victorious, and the World Bank and the IMF confidently proposed a new agenda in the transformed landscape. Since the World Bank and the IMF represented the main source of multilateral loans, they pushed to harmonize lending policies. In 1989, the World Bank published a report on how to move Africa from crisis to sustainable growth, followed in 1994 by its report *Adjustment in Africa*.[66] Political conditionalities were introduced into the World Bank's reforms in Africa, and democratization was seen as an accompaniment to economic reform. The World Bank and IMF had come to see the state as the major obstacle to economic growth in Africa. Structural adjustment programs requested a downsizing of the state through retrenchment of the civil service; reduction in state subsidies on education, health, and other social services; liberalization of the economy; devaluation of overvalued currencies; and privatization of state-owned enterprises. The World Bank stressed the importance of returning to Africa's "comparative advantage," that is, to primary commodities, reinforcing the structures of the colonial economy African countries had struggled to break out of in the first decades of independence. Other Western institutions inserted conditionalities in their trade and lending agreements. The Lome IV Convention between the European Economic Community and African, Caribbean, and Pacific countries insisted on human rights and structural adjustment, and conditionality replaced the principle of equal partnership.[67] With only one game in town—structural adjustment with the World Bank as key lender—African politics became transformed. Party ideologies no longer contested economic policies; if anything, opposition parties argued that they would be better executors of structural adjustment if voted into power.[68] The state as culprit and impediment to development in Africa received many studies in the 1990s: the predator state, the weak state, the patrimonial state, the corrupt state.[69]

Insistence on democratization opened the political space in Africa. On the urging of the World Bank, media was liberalized, and privately owned newspapers proliferated across the continent from the early 1990s. Private radio stations also emerged—a radical departure in most African countries, where newspapers, radio, and television had been under the firm ownership and control of governments since the beginning of independence. The privatization of television stations was a slower process, as it required more capital. Civil society organizations had cohered in the 1980s, pressed into advocacy by the dire straits of Africa's political economy, and in francophone Africa a state–civil society dichotomy developed.[70] Civil society was particularly well organized in urban areas, comprising skilled and self-conscious professionals such as lawyers, doctors, nurses, teachers, and civil servants, but also students, youth, and street children. In the 1980s and 1990s, civil society strategies included strikes by trade unions, doctors, nurses, teachers, and students. Even street children organized themselves, as seen in the Mali insurrection of 1991. The fall of the Berlin Wall and the protests in Tiananmen Square in 1989 sparked an international movement against dictatorial rule. As the Soviet Union broke apart and Eastern Bloc countries became independent in 1989, the World Bank encouraged African military regimes and one-party states toward political reform.

In Benin, in what became known as the Velvet Revolution, civil society took the lead in 1989–90. Mathieu Kérékou had come to power in Benin in 1972 through a military coup d'état. In 1974, he declared Marxism-Leninism the official national ideology as part of the second wave of African socialism (see chap. 4), and in 1975 he changed the name of the country from Dahomey to the Republic of Benin. Kérékou declared his People's Revolutionary Party the sole party in Benin and had himself elected president of the country by the Revolutionary National Assembly in 1980. Benin was not exempt from the economic travails of the 1980s, and by 1989 the state was unable to pay its civil servants and public teachers. Strikes broke out, and a general strike was proposed for December 1989. Seeking to avert the general strike, the governing party a few days before the strike announced the payment of three months' backpay to government employees, abolished Marxism-Leninism as the state's ideology, and proposed a national conference to deliberate the way forward. France provided the resources for the payment of two months' backpay. France, the United States, and opposition groups were consulted concerning the national conference held in February 1990. A remarkable thing happened during the conference: the conference declared itself sovereign and persuaded Kérékou to agree to its election of an interim prime minister and a High Council, which would preside over the drafting of a new constitution and a new general election for the formation of a civilian government. Nicéphore Soglo, a World Bank economist, won the subsequent elections and became Benin's new president. This peaceful transition became a model, and civil societies pushed ruling governments along this path in Niger, Mali, Togo, Chad, the Democratic Republic of the Congo (then Zaire), and Madagascar. Enthusiasm for peaceful political transitions led observers to describe this phenomenon as the second wave of African independence.[71]

A second script developed in the Ivory Coast, where President Houphouët-Boigny chose not to go down the unpredictable path of the national conference and instead called for general elections. Houphouët-Boigny declared his support for multiparty elections. The government organized elections for the presidency, legislature, and local governments, and unsurprisingly, the ruling party won. Houphouët-Boigny managed to give the transition some legitimacy through his selection of Alassane Ouattara, the opposition leader, as prime minister. General elections without a national conference become the second option for peaceful political transition, and Cameroon, Burkina Faso, Guinea, Senegal, and Mauritania followed the Ivorian model. By 1994, not a single, legal one-party state existed in West Africa.[72]

International donor agencies encouraged the entry of nongovernmental organizations (NGOs), seeking to circumvent corrupt states and channel development funds directly to beneficiary communities. In the 1990s and early 2000s, 4x4 vehicles with emblazoned NGO logos littered town and countryside in Africa. NGO operations ranged from the health sector to the digging of boreholes for villages. Development lingo and acronyms permeated everyday language in Africa. I found to my amusement that in academic circles in Ghana in the 1990s, to "dash" or give a gift of money to your Ghanaian colleague was referred to as PAMSCAD (Program to Mitigate the Social Cost of Structural Adjustment). PAMSCAD was the program the World Bank had introduced in Ghana to soften the rigors of structural adjustment after popular outcry about the harshness of adjustment policies. It was not until the early 2000s that African academics began to publish important works presenting African perspectives on structural adjustment.[73] They argued for the importance of the state and for the state not to be marginalized in Africa's developmental agenda, irrespective of the problems associated with the African state. In the 2000s, the African state was restored to international development partnerships. For the period from 1965 to 2000, the average annual rate of growth per capita GDP for sub-Saharan Africa was negative. Adedeji in 2002 remarked on the irony that "in retrospect, the period 1960 to 1975 has, tragically, turned out to be Africa's golden era."[74]

The Turn of the Twenty-First Century: The Promise of Africa

The twenty-first century opened new horizons for Africa with auspicious changes in the global trade and growth in intra-African trade. Thus, while the golden anniversary celebrations of African independence in 2007 were tinged with ambivalence about what had been achieved since independence, there were also signs of promise. The shift in the perception of the fortune of Africa is perhaps best captured in the cover stories from the *Economist* on May 3, 2000, and December 3, 2011. The first story, from 2000, called Africa "the hopeless continent," the cover showing a map of Africa inset with a rebel wielding a machine gun. Africa had been marred by violent conflict in the years leading to the *Economist*'s story: genocide in Rwanda in 1994 left eight hundred thousand people dead in one hundred days; brutal civil wars in Liberia (1989–97) and Sierra Leone (1991–2001) led to international concerns about blood diamonds and traumatized a global audience with images of the amputated limbs of civilian casualties. There seemed little to celebrate about Africa. So what changed for the *Economist* to create a cover of "Africa Rising" on December 3, 2011? This cover showed an African boy flying a kite in the shape of a rainbow-colored Africa. In the time between the two stories, sub-Saharan Africa had posted record economic growth, compared to negative average annual growth rate per capita GDP for 1965 to 2000. Between 2002 and 2013, six of the ten fastest growing economies in the world were in Africa: Angola, Nigeria, Ethiopia, Chad, Mozambique, and Rwanda.

A significant shift in Africa's trade patterns has resulted from the rise of China and India and their relative importance to African economies. Both countries have had a long presence in Africa. China was active in Africa in the 1960s and 1970s, assisting newly independent countries with agricultural experts, barefoot doctors, and the funding and building of infrastructural projects unattractive to the West. The first hydroelectric dam China built outside of China was in Sékou Touré's Guinea between 1964 and 1966.[75] China would undertake its most expensive foreign investment outside of China in the 1970s in Africa: the building of the Tanzania-Zambia (TanZam) railway between 1970 and 1975.[76] There followed a hiatus during which China was relatively absent from Africa until the late 1990s. The

China that reengaged Africa was resurgent and economically prosperous. China-Africa trade, which stood at $1 billion in 2000, rose to $55 billion in 2008. India's trade with Africa rose significantly as well, increasing from $965 million in 1991 to $35 billion in 2008. The years 2007 and 2008 were instructive for Africa. The world found itself in another economic recession, triggered by a stock market crash in the United States resulting from the collapse of the real estate market. Global recessions undercut Africa's primary exports with the flexible demand for primary exports. In the decade leading to the 2007–08 recession, remittances from Africans abroad to sub-Saharan Africa had crept up in significance from $1.9 billion in 1990 to $4.8 billion in 2000 and were estimated to gross $10.8 billion in 2007.[77] The implications of a global recession for remittances were worrisome. Sub-Saharan Africa came through the recession of 2007–08 strongly and with a number of key lessons. First, foreign direct investment (FDI) increased, underscoring how Africa had become a preferred investment destination for China and India. Foreign direct investment rose from $36 billion in 2006 to $53 billion in 2007 and $88 billion in 2008.[78] Second, African governments responded to the recession with good fiscal measures, underscoring growing competence in this domain.[79] Third, the African countries that performed well during the recession were those strongly involved in regional trade.[80] This last fact was a strong argument in favor of intra-African trade.

China and India's importance to African economies has continued to grow. In 2009, China surpassed the World Bank as Africa's largest lender and became Africa's leading trade partner.[81] China's trade with Africa stood at $182.5 billion in 2018. In 2013, India rose to become Africa's second largest trading partner, overtaking the United States. Asia's growing significance for Africa needs to be situated within the larger context of growing South-South trade. In 2019, the South accounted for 57 percent of global trade and 50 percent of Africa's. This is a major departure from the 1980s, when OECD countries accounted for 85 percent of Africa's exports. In 2018, China and India accounted for 23.8 percent of Africa's trade.

The strong demand of China and India for Africa's primary products lay behind the "Africa Rising" story, a prosperity fueled by a commodity boom rather than structural transformation and economic diversification. The boom in commodities, combined with expanded fiscal space as a result of significant reduction in debt services enabled by the World Bank's Heavily Indebted Poor Countries (HIPC) facility, drove the rise of Africa.[82]

The decline in global prices for Africa's raw materials in 2014 quickly put a check to Africa's rising, and major oil-producing countries like Angola and Nigeria revised their budgets accordingly. But economic growth did not plummet like in past commodity slumps, revealing a new resilience to Africa's economies.[83] Africa in the last two decades has experienced infrastructural growth unknown since the early years of independence, capitalizing on China's resource-backed infrastructural loans. The rehabilitation of old railways and building of new ones, construction of highways that integrate regions, and proliferation of new hydroelectric dams and irrigation systems all have breathed new life into Africa's economic possibilities. The specter of a new phase of African indebtedness to China has engaged international attention. Austin Strange, based on extensive data analysis of Chinese loans to Africa over the past seven decades, affirms that compared to loans from the West or OECD countries, "twenty-first century Chinese development finance does not appear 'rogue' in rhetoric or practice."[84] He cautions circumspection in Africa's dealings with China, and reminds African leaders that "Chinese state financing is neither a danger nor a panacea for African countries."[85]

Two recent developments have further reinforced the prospect for stronger African economic growth. The first is the signing of the African Continental Free Trade Agreement (ACFTA) by twenty-seven countries of the African Union (AU) in Kigali in March 2018—and now by all fifty-five African countries. The African Continental Free Trade Area commenced in January 2021. Representing a closer union of African nation-states than the now defunct OAU it replaced, the AU's vision has centered on regional economic integration inspired by the principles at the heart of the Lagos Plan of Action. The AU has been working closely with the continent's Pan-African financial institutions—the African Development Bank and the African Export-Import Bank—in pursuit of an African common market. This work is evidenced in the growth of intra-African trade to 15 percent of Africa's trade in 2018 and the projected estimate of 22 percent in 2022. The second, unplanned development has been the global COVID-19 pandemic that swept the world from the beginning of 2020. COVID-19 has revealed simultaneously the weaknesses in Africa's political economy and the urgency of self-reliant, self-sustaining economic growth that benefits not only the rich, the enterprising, and the industrious, but covers everyone in a fair and just manner. As Africa's supply networks were undercut, and the continent outbid in the global demand for ventilators, test kits, and personal protective equipment, countries have stepped up their efforts at manufacturing and food production, emerging regional value chains have been affirmed in their relevance, and state and civil society have united in their acknowledgment that social services—health, education, welfare—need to be strengthened. There is much about the present that echoes the resolve and promise of independence. As Hippolyte Fofack reminds us in a recent Brookings Institute publication, not much has changed about the developmental challenges of Africa since independence.[86] In light of this reality, the following four chapters return us to those early decades of independence and to the lessons that can be learned from the first generation of independent Africa's leaders.

two

RELIGION, CULTURE, AND THE ARTS IN THE MAKING OF THE AFRICAN NATION-STATE

INTRODUCTION

On independence, Africa's first leaders faced two key tasks: delivering on economic and social development, and forging a national identity out of disparate ethnic groups brought together within shared political boundaries through colonial rule. The latter, termed "nation-building," was seen as the task of the state, which viewed nation-building as an integral foundation for economic and social development. Success at nation-building and economic development would underpin the legitimacy of the new states. It may then appear puzzling that some of the earliest measures taken by the newly independent African governments dealt with culture and the arts. On the eve of Ghana's independence, Nkrumah declared highlife Ghana's national dance music. The importance of cultural nationalism was perceptible in the early policies of Nkrumah, Touré, Senghor, and Nyerere in their call for a "new African." Culture, religion, and the arts spoke to three essential areas of nation-building and development policy in the early years of independence. First was the question of legitimacy for Africa's first independent leaders, largely commoners elected by universal adult suffrage. Culture and the arts lent themselves to the making of symbolic and substantive statements to underscore the shift in political regimes and the making of new worlds. Richard Rathbone has noted how common it was in the half century before Ghana's independence for newspapers to reference "the chiefs and people of the Gold Coast" and chiefs as "the natural representatives of the people."[1] In the Gold Coast, where chiefs had been highly visible in national politics, the nationalist government's first order of business was to establish its dominion over chiefs and other competing groups. Second was the conviction that successful economic development required a united nation and that culture and the arts lent themselves to the imagining of the new nation. Third was the importance of culture and the arts as a bridge to the African diaspora in imagining a shared community. The shortage of skilled labor and professional expertise was marked in the early decades of independence. All African countries found themselves in this predicament. Outreach to African Americans and Caribbean Africans to assist in nation-building was considered imperative, and Nkrumah and Nyerere were quite successful in attracting diasporic talent to their newly independent countries (see chaps. 4 and 5).

Chiefs as representatives of ethnic groups, both under British indirect rule and French colonial administration, were positioned as potential heirs to colonial rule, and several organized or joined political parties in the crucial process of decolonization and the transfer of power. Parties with chiefs as leaders included the National Liberation Movement in the Gold Coast (formed in 1954), the Bloc Africain de Guinée (created in 1954), and the United Tanganyika Party, established by settlers in 1956 but joined by chiefs with the support of the colonial administration. Chieftaincy had ceased to be a potent political force in Senegal, where Muslim marabouts (religious leaders) had edged out chiefs during the colonial period. The importance of chieftaincy in colonial Africa ensured the survival of political language and discourse extending to the precolonial period. Feierman, in the case of Shambaa in Tanganyika, notes the questions raised by peasant leaders or "intellectuals" about the nature of government in the transition to independent African rule: "They debated the nature of *demokrasi*. Was it rule by a council of elders? Was it a system in which only the best-educated held jobs? Would all power be given to the lineages of nonroyals? Would a peasant king sit on the throne? Should each man and woman be given a vote in formal elections? And they debated the nature of *freedom* and *slavery*. Was control by old men over young men compatible with freedom? If a chief took a woman arbitrarily and by force, was that characteristic of a regime of slavery?"[2]

As late as 1966, five years after Tanganyika achieved independence, Feierman recorded peasants in Shambaa still taking tribute cows to old chiefs reputed to be powerful rainmakers to facilitate rain and fertility of the soil ("the healing of the land").[3] General elections and universal adult suffrage in the 1950s were novelties in a colonial context where civil society had been repressed. The nationalists elected to power, often commoners who could not claim chiefly or religious legitimacy, had to establish new claims to political legitimacy. This made Africa's new leaders highly sensitive to criticism and generated an intolerance to political opposition that put them on the path to authoritarianism. The nation-state had to be built within and without, its success recognized nationally and internationally.

This chapter examines the roles religion, culture, and the arts played in the making of the African nation-state. Whereas culture and the arts constituted key building blocks for states in the construction new national identities, bolstering claims to Africa's ancient civilizations, subscription to the secular state gave religion a more subdued place in state policies. The centrality of religion in African life, however, made it an inescapable force. Nkrumah in his philosophical work *Consciencism* described religion in Africa as a "social fact," but stressed that "it is essential to emphasize in the historical condition of Africa that the state must be secular."[4] Nkrumah wrote of "Africa's triple heritage" and the reality of Africa's vibrant religious and social traditions at the time of independence: "African society has one segment which comprises our traditional way of life; it has a second segment which is filled by the presence of the Islamic tradition in Africa; it has a final segment which represents the infiltration of the Christian tradition and culture of Western Europe, using colonialism and neo-colonialism as its primary vehicles."[5] In 1949, barely a decade before Ghana's independence, those who subscribed to indigenous African religions comprised 66 percent of the population. In 1960, the year Ghana became a republic, a significant 38.2 percent still identified as followers of indigenous religions.[6] The close relationship between chieftaincy and indigenous religion, a source of chiefly legitimacy, is seen in the abovementioned rain chiefs in Tanganyika. Indeed, it can be argued that British indirect rule reinvigorated indigenous religions by privileging chieftaincy.[7] Islam's presence in North Africa, the sahel and savanna regions of West Africa, and the East African coast has a long history. Christianity has an even older presence in North Africa, displaced by Islam in the seventh century CE. While Ethiopia remained Christian from at least the fourth century CE, and Christian outposts could be identified in the precolonial period in the Senegambia region, in the Gold Coast and Kongo, the expansion of Christianity has been a post-nineteenth-century phenomenon, especially through the provision of Western education.

Even in predominantly Muslim states like Guinea and Senegal, Christian missionaries had been major providers of Western education, instrumental in the education of nationalist leaders and bureaucratic elite. It was noted in the introduction that Nkrumah, Senghor, and Nyerere were all products of Catholic missionary education, and at different points in their lives all considered the Catholic priesthood. As universal religions, Islam and Christianity have a strong associational life, with international corporate or organizational forms. And these religious faiths claim primacy in the lives of adherents, which was problematic for several of the first generation of independent African leaders—even those faithful—as they sought to build new unifying national identities. Their policies included nationalizing church schools to make education secular and open to all. Chieftaincy and ethnic and regional patriotisms were strongly associated in the minds of nationalist leaders, and to build the new nation, these had to be sidelined. The regional and ethnic factionalisms that collapsed the young Congolese state soon after its independence, promoted secessionism, and led to the assassination of the country's first prime minister, Patrice Lumumba, frightened Africa's new leaders. Nyerere, a neighbor and witness to the unraveling of the Congolese state, moved quickly to abolish chieftaincy in the 1960s, leaving peasants and bureaucrats as the only "centers of gravity" in independent Tanzania and paving the way for the ascendance of bureaucrats.[8]

But religious and chiefly symbols remained attractive to nationalist leaders seeking to establish legitimacy. As we will see later in this chapter, Nkrumah would persecute chiefs in Ghana while usurping the material culture and symbols of chieftaincy. He chose the title of "Osagyefo" (Twi: warrior), an appellation for a warrior chief, befitting of one who had led the nationalist struggle. Akan chieftaincy was associated with titles and appellations, and the king of Asante was "Otumfuo," the "holder of power." Some pointed to the religious connotations of Nkrumah's title, translating Osagyefo to "redeemer." Touré claimed descent and legacy from the late nineteenth-century Malinké state builder (later declared jihadist) Almamy Samory Touré.[9] In Ghana, where nationalist mobilization had preceded Nkrumah and where the educated elite was more expansive than in independent Tanganyika or Guinea, rival political leaders, such as the philosopher and lawyer Joseph Boakye Danquah, sought to correct Nkrumah's narrative of being the principal architect of Ghana's independence. Indeed, Danquah had been the driving force in the choice of "Ghana" as the name for an independent Gold Coast.[10]

The cultural and artistic elements the new states leveraged to build national identities were not unproblematic, as they came with histories and were not empty vessels to be deployed irrespective of the older meanings individuals and communities attached to them. We see this in the rich and complex histories of the musical forms Nyerere's TANU party and government sought to manipulate during the nationalist struggle and after independence to build a new national identity: *ngoma* (men and women's traditional competitive dance groups), *dansi* (dancehall music), and *ta-arab* (Swahili sung poetry).[11] Other examples include Nkrumah's efforts to make highlife music a national art form under state supervision[12] and Touré's elevation of militant theater and ballet in Guinea.[13] The building of national identities, this chapter argues, was a complex process rife with contradictions, incomplete even today, but not without significant impact. While these processes defy being labeled as successes or failures, as nation-building "always and necessarily . . . remains a work in progress," they mirror important lessons in the subsequent chapters as they underscore the futility of state attempts to direct—exclusively—cultural, political, and economic projects from the top.[14] Askew puts it well: "Trouble arises in the persistent refusal to recognize that the nation's cultural direction is not determined solely by intellectuals and government bureaucrats who assume that cultural development is their exclusive responsibility. Failure to take the roles and activities of citizens into account results in a defective plan of action."[15] Despite the pitfalls and missteps in the processes of nation-building, Africa has yet to witness another period like the first two decades of independence, when so much thought, creativity, and energy were devoted to imagining new nation-states.

CHRISTIANITY, ISLAM, AND AFRICAN RELIGIONS: THE TRIPLE HERITAGE IN THE NATION

Religion was hugely important in the personal lives of Africa's early political leaders, even beyond the fact that many had been products of missionary schools. In their pursuit of African socialism, Nkrumah, Touré,

Senghor, and Nyerere sought accommodation with their religious faith. Nkrumah held a bachelor's degree in sacred theology from Lincoln University in Pennsylvania and had been a licensed preacher in the Presbyterian Church while in school in Pennsylvania. Nkrumah later declared himself a nondenominational Christian and a Marxist socialist. Touré's socialism embraced Islam, and we will see below how his government's "Demystification Campaign" required citizens of Guinea's Forest Region, viewed as the stronghold of "fetishism," to convert to Islam or Christianity. Senghor was a Christian socialist, crediting the Jesuit priest Pierre Teilhard de Chardin for affirming his faith as a Catholic and steering him away from Marxism.[16] Nyerere was also a Christian socialist and devout Catholic with strong antipathy toward Marxists (see introduction). It is striking that in their study of personal rule in Black Africa, Robert Jackson and Carl Rosberg classify Nkrumah, Touré, and Nyerere as "prophets" for their revolutionary socialist visions and pursuit of a new and better world. The prophet, they opine, "is a political agent, but he is also a moral agent—a political-religious man."[17] While all four leaders were committed to a secular state, the centrality of religion in African lives necessitated that they negotiate delicate relations with religious institutions and leaders. Senghor noted that "religion, whatever it may be, more generally faith, is as necessary to the soul as bread, rice, or millet to the body . . . The problem is not to suppress it; it is to assign it to its true place and to purify it by making it one of the elements of the humanism of today."[18] Ironically, while the first generation of Africa's leaders stressed the importance of grounding the new nation-state in Africa's history and cultures, few extended this privilege to indigenous African religions.

Nyerere and Tanzania's Triple Heritage

The son of a chief from Zanaki, a small chiefdom in Tanganyika's Mara Region on the eastern shore of Lake Victoria, Nyerere came into contact with Christianity at the age of twelve, when he began formal schooling. Brought up in the traditions of the Zanaki, he waited until his father's death in 1942 before being baptized as a Catholic on December 23, 1943. He took the baptismal name of Julius.[19] Nyerere's Catholic faith became a central pillar in his life. Though he seldom spoke publicly about his faith, he attended mass daily whenever possible. The combination of Nyerere's Christian faith and missionaries' status as key providers of formal education in Tanganyika made the emerging bureaucracy in independent Tanzania very Christian, though Christians on independence were not a majority in the country. In the 1957 population census of Tanganyika, Muslims accounted for 31 percent and Christians for 25 percent of the population. Christians had numbered only 2 percent of Tanganyika's population in 1914, underscoring the impressive growth in their numbers after World War I.[20] TANU and its precursors, the Tanganyika Africa Association (TAA) and the African Association (AA), had strong Muslim input in formation and membership. Nyerere accepted Muslim patronage in his early political career, as he was dependent on Muslim finances and networks. But he would change TANU's leadership and his government to become heavily Christian. None of this transformation was explicitly set out as policy, but the result was very evident.[21] Of the founding members of TANU in 1954, with strong Muslim representation, Nyerere was the only one left in the Central Committee of TANU in 1961.[22] This shift displaced the early influence of Muslims in the political life of Tanganyika.

In 1955, Nyerere traveled for the first time to the United Nations in New York to address the Trusteeship Council on the independence of Tanganyika. The Muslim elders of Dar es Salaam helped raise money for the trip, with fundraisers including a taarab dance at Anatouglo Hall in Dar es Salaam. They took Nyerere through Islamic rituals to ensure the success of the trip. Perhaps, though bemused by the entire experience as a Catholic, Nyerere needed the support of the Muslim elders and so submitted to the rituals. In a speech recorded in 1985, Nyerere recalled being summoned to the house of Mzee Tambaza in 1955 prior to the UN trip:

> We arrived there and sat. We met the elders who had already sat down. Their sons called me to make a prayer for me. At night. . . . It was filled with elders and Jumbe's house was filled. I was prayed for—Me, a Christian! But all were Muslims! They prayed for me and burnt incense—then we finished. When we were finished, these elders said a prayer in honor of their ancestors—they didn't forget them. Then they led me out. We went out. Now, those prayers were those of the Koran, and those of many other affairs. There came the prayers for the ancestors. They had a he-goat, and they dug a hole like this. They came and told me "stand up" and I stood up. The he-goat was slaughtered. The blood flowed into the hole. When it was slaughtered thus, I was told prayers have been finished. They now told me "Cross over (the hole) with honor." OK I crossed the hole. And they told me, "It is finished, go home." Today the prayer has finished.[23]

Intriguingly, Nyerere refers to prayers "of the Koran" and "prayers for the ancestors." It is unclear whether these prayers were conducted by two different groups present at Mzee Tambaza's house, or whether one group combined these different prayers in recognition of different religious traditions. One can be certain that as Nyerere assumed control over TANU and the government, he never put himself in such a predicament again.

Another occasion on which Nyerere found himself subjected to the ministrations of others of a different faith was on his swearing in as president of Tanganyika on December 9, 1962. The actors in this instance were chiefs, closely associated with indigenous religions, who had on the whole opposed TANU in the nationalist struggle. One can read in their actions at the presidential inauguration a desperate bid for inclusion in the new political dispensation:

> When he [Nyerere] arrived at the National Stadium in Dar es Salaam, the drums of the royal house of Mwami Theresa Ntare of Buha sounded a rhythmic welcome. Chief Petro Itosi Marealle greeted the president and prayed that God would bless him. Then Chief Mazengo presented Nyerere with a robe, so that "the favour of your leadership be spread all over the country in the same way as this long robe has spread all over your body," with a spear for the protection of the citizens of Tanganyika, and with a shield for the defense of the country from enemies. The president left to the sound of the great Haya drum, after being anointed by Chief Mazengo with a mixture of flour and water.[24]

These acts signaled not only the association of chiefs with ritual power but also their past roles as defendants of their communities. But for a government that had come to power through elections in the face of opposition from chiefs, Nyerere's political vision did not make room for chieftaincy or any form of political representation that was not elective. He viewed chieftaincy and its ethnic bases as potential agents for factionalism and the ritual sources of chiefly legitimacy and power as illegitimate. On January 1963, soon after becoming president of the Republic of Tanganyika, Nyerere abolished chieftaincy.[25] The TANU government considered acknowledgments of chiefly power such as "tribute collection and rainmaking as treasonous activities, challenges to governmental authority."[26] The rainmakers themselves, perhaps as an act of self-preservation, converted to Islam and Christianity.[27]

On one of the few occasions on which Nyerere spoke about the church and its relationship to the state, a conference of Maryknoll Sisters in New

York in 1970, he was clear that both were involved in social justice and that for the poor of the world, "the church should accept that the development of the peoples means rebellion."[28] He argued for open partnership between church and state and for church involvement in the social, economic, and political development of peoples in societies in which the church was present. This was a challenge the Catholic Church in Tanzania accepted—the church's pastoral bishops in a 1968 statement endorsed Nyerere's Arusha Declaration (1967) that outlined his vision for African socialism.[29] But Nyerere all the while insisted that the state must be secular: "Nyerere's refrain which he never tired of reiterating was that the state or the ruling party did not have a religion, nor did it favor a particular religion though the right and the freedom of its people to pursue whatever religion they wished, or no religion at all, was fully guaranteed and respected."[30] Nyerere's African socialism would lead him down the path of nationalization—of businesses, commercial properties, and church schools. He decided in 1969 that all schools should be secular and nationalized mission schools, including those of the Catholic Church, much to the unhappiness of the Catholic Church.

Nyerere was clearly aware of the disparity in access to secular education between Muslims and Christians, and he worried that it would create tensions in the new state. Iliffe comments that the deprivation of Muslims in secular affairs, "and especially in education . . . had reversed their status during colonial rule."[31] As early as November 1963, Nyerere wrote to the Catholic Secretariat of the Tanganyika Episcopal Conference expressing his concerns at the growing gap between Christians and Muslims with access to secular education. He pointed to the historical reality that the colonial administration had done little to provide secular education in Tanganyika, making the church the main source of education. Suspicion of Christian proselytization had discouraged Muslims from patronizing church schools. Nyerere now explicitly asked the church to partner with the state in building secular schools with open access to all citizens in addition to existing mission schools, seeking to make primary education compulsory. Shivji, Yahya-Othman, and Kamata, in their recent multivolume biography of Nyerere, note that Nyerere underestimated the Catholic Church's deepseated hostility toward Islam and communism. The Catholic Church worried about the visible presence of Muslims in party organs of TANU, and statements by leftist leaders in the party deepened the church's concern that

Ujamaa could be a doorway to communism.[32] The church was unrespon-
sive to Nyerere's appeals to assist in the establishment of secular schools. So
Nyerere nationalized all schools, including the church's schools. For Nyerere, state and church shared a similar mandate: the uplifting of humankind
so that humans could live in freedom and dignity. The church's remit was
even larger than that of the state for Nyerere, as the Catholic Church is
universal.[33] It was unacceptable to him that the church would be partisan
when it came to development. This was not Nyerere opposing the church;
he wanted the Catholic Church in Tanzania to put on an African garb and
shed its European disposition. It is not insignificant that between 1970 and
1975, the Ministry of Education was headed by a Christian pastor.[34]

Senghor and Muslim Marabouts in Senegalese Politics

It was evident to the French colonial administration by 1919 that traditional
authorities in Senegal (for example, the Wolof kingdoms of Kajoor and Ba-
wol), enmeshed in the Atlantic slave trade and with the wanton pillage of
royal soldiers or *ceddo*, had been discredited in the eyes of their peasants.[35]
French colonialism had also taken its toll on precolonial Wolof political
institutions, which could not be reconstructed to effectively meet the need
for political communication between the state and peasants.[36] In their
place had emerged Muslim Sufi leaders or marabouts, rural religious leaders who, with their disciples, entered heavily into cultivation of peanuts or
groundnuts—the crop that became the basis of Senegal's economy from the
mid-nineteenth century through independence. Donal Cruise O'Brien examines the structures that emerged in Senegalese state and society to connect Wolof politicians, Wolof traders, Wolof marabouts, and their peasant
followers between 1850 and 1973.[37]

The Wolof constituted about a third of the population of Senegal, its
largest ethnic group, and lived adjacent to the seacoast between the Senegal and Gambia Rivers, at the very heart of French colonial presence. The
group was the dominant producer of peanuts, the colonial and postcolonial lifeline. Cruise O'Brien explores how Sufi leaders from the three major
tariqas (orders or brotherhoods)—the Qadiriyya, the Tijaniyya, and the
Mouride—emerged as key intermediaries in the state's relations to Wolof
peasant producers of peanuts. These marabouts, referred to as "saints"
by Cruise O'Brien, were seen as repositories of *baraka*, spiritual grace or

blessings, and as more legitimate representatives in the eyes of their peasant followers.[38]

Marabouts as major producers of peanuts and leaders of large populations of peasants came to play an important role in French colonial rule, once the French were able to transcend their prejudices against Muslim leaders and orders (acquired from their experience in Algeria).[39] Cruise O'Brien argues that, deficient in moral authority, state bureaucracies under colonial and postcolonial rule "to work effectively among the Wolof, have been irrevocably compelled to come to terms with Sufi saints."[40]

Relations between the devoutly Catholic Senghor, head of state of Senegal, and powerful marabouts, such as *khalifa* Falilu Mbacke, head of the Mouride order, and Cheikh Ibrahima Niasse of the Tijaniyya order, provide fascinating illustrations of the relations between religion and politics in early independent Africa. Senghor and other major state officials made it a point to attend the annual festivals of these orders—the Mouride *Magal* in Touba and Ibrahima Niasse's *Gamou* in Kaolack—which provided an occasion for the state to discuss its economic agenda, as these constituencies were the major peanut producers in Senegal. Relations between the state and Muslim marabouts were not always harmonious; one example had international ramifications. Ibrahima Niasse considered Kwame Nkrumah his friend and spiritual protégé, although Nkrumah was not a Muslim. Lucy Behrman writes that "Nkrumah's belief in the Senegalese marabu's power manifested itself in generous gifts of various kinds throughout his years in office," a relationship that may have been unknown to most Ghanaians.[41] Niasse rallied to Nkrumah's support when Nkrumah was overthrown in a military coup in February 1966, provoking a confrontation with Senghor, whose government had recognized the new National Liberation Council government in Ghana. Behrman provides details from interviews she conducted with Niasse, his disciples, and government officials in March 1966:

> When Nkrumah was removed from office, the marabu came out publicly on his side. On the occasion of a trip to Mali in March, 1966, Niass sent a telegram to the President of Guinea thanking him for supporting Nkrumah. At the time, the government of Senegal had already acknowledged the military regime in Ghana and had definitely refused to support the movement by Sekou Touré to reinstate the former Ghanaian president. Naturally the Guinean government publicized Niass' telegram on Radio Guinea and Touré's official message of thanks. In this instance the government of Senegal felt obliged to ask the marabu to be more circumspect in

his actions, but these efforts were unsatisfactory: Niass was furious, for he felt the government has no right to intervene between him and his *taalibé* [disciple]. He wrote a letter to the President in which he said that he had been humiliated by the request and that he refused "categorically" to do as he had been asked.[42]

In the end it was Senghor who backed down, extending an apology to Niasse through his presidential adviser on religious affairs, Cheikh Tahorou Doukouré. Senghor's accommodationist response to Cheikh Niasse fits the mold of "princely rule," which is how Jackson and Rosberg characterize Senghor's style of rule in Senegal. They write that the "legitimacy of the modern African Prince depends upon his respect for the *private* understandings and agreements he has made with other members of the oligarchy over whom he presides and with whom he rules."[43] In Senegal, Senghor depended on the marabouts to deliver the rural vote, maintain law and order in the countryside, and continue their invaluable contribution to Senegal's economy through agriculture. The role and the influence of Muslim brotherhoods in Senegal have been historically exceptional, a situation not paralleled in Guinea, where major marabouts have been excluded from national politics.[44] Senghor had deep respect for religion, and his own piety elicited respect from the marabouts he treated with courtesy. The indispensable role of the marabouts as intermediaries with peasant cultivators of peanuts brought together economic and religious roles for Senghor, who viewed religion as born out of the relationship between people and agriculture.[45]

Sékou Touré and the War on "Fetishism" in Guinea's Forest Region

In Guinea, Touré waged war on indigenous religious leaders in Guinea's Forest Region. The area was home to the Loma, Kpelle, Kissi, and Kono, small nonstate communities from the precolonial era whose social and cultural lives revolved around membership of power associations (also called secret societies), like Poro for men and Sande for women. The Forest Region had low conversion rates to Islam and Christianity and, in the PDG government's drive for modernity, came to encapsulate all that Guinea sought to leave behind. The forest's denseness came to represent its physical and cultural impermeability to the outside world. With male initiation rites that could last for seven years among the Loma, absenting male youth from Guinea's schools, the Forest Region and its sacred rituals became the embodiment of all the obstacles that interfered with independent Guinea's drive to develop. The war against the fetishism of the Forest Region took the form of iconoclasm: the destruction of sacred masks and ritual objects of the Forest Region, the exposure of masks of male power associations to women and youth in a process called "demystification," and the humiliation in public of elderly priests and ritual leaders. McGovern notes that monotheistic religions consider masks (graven images) as forbidden, and by authorizing the destruction of masks, Touré—in addition to claiming descent from Almamy Samory Touré—"appropriated the idiom of religious renewal as a source of political legitimacy."[46]

The height of Touré's Demystification Campaign was from 1959 to 1961, and local youth who joined the youth wing of the party (Jeunesse du Rassemblement Démocratique Africain—JRDA) were required to display their zeal in the Demystification Campaign to be promoted within the ranks of the party. Indeed, Touré turned "toward rural youth as the most promising heroes of the entire nation-imagining, nation-building, and nation-governing adventure."[47] This choice stemmed from his conviction that urban youth had been contaminated by the corruptive influences of European colonial education and Western lifestyles. Rural youth had been isolated by social and physical distance from agents and institutions of colonialism. The result of the Demystification Campaign was to turn communities against themselves, as rural youth spied and informed on their elders, shattering the trust that had guaranteed the security of these face-to-face communities for generations.[48] Whereas rainmakers in Shambaa converted to Christianity or Islam of their own volition in independent Tanganyika, in the Forest Region the Guinean state mandated that its denizens convert to Islam or Christianity.[49] For the Christian Nyerere and the Muslim Touré, the spiritual claims of Shambaa rainmakers and Forest ritual elders were false and needed to be demystified, archaic cultural practices to be eliminated rather than viable religious beliefs and practices. It is revealing that Touré's book on the cultural revolution in Guinea contains no real discussion of religion.[50] And in a bizarre turn of events resembling social imperialism, though each cycle of the Demystification Campaign was declared highly successful, it was relaunched the following year, making it a campaign that endured from 1959 until Touré's death in 1984.[51] As Guinea's economy worsened, and political space shrunk as the state became even more dictatorial, the peoples of the Forest Region became the enemy within, the site of the fumbling state's catharsis.

Yet the same state saved some masks from the Forest Region for display in museums and pushed the youth of the region to stage theater and create ballet pieces promoting the objectives of the Demystification Campaign. In militant ballet, "masks and other traditional objects once seen as magical icons were presented as profane artifacts of *previous*, more or less admirable or repugnant forms of social-artistic creativity and control."[52] District, regional, and national theater and ballet competitions were held annually, climaxing at the *Quinzaines Artistiques* in Conakry, with the intention of facilitating the imagining and bonding of the new nation. This was an ambivalent experience for Foresters, who, while enjoined by the state to shed their past, were also caught in the reenactment of that very past to the amusement and ridicule of their fellow citizens.[53] Straker observes that "it is no accident that the country's remote *région forestiere* became a primary site for uniquely aggressive stagings of state power."[54] Under the watchful eye of the state, initiation rites were shortened to accommodate school schedules and eventually abolished when a rural community in Macenta became implicated in what was believed to be a ritual murder to consecrate a new mask for Poro initiation.[55] The attack on fetishists intensified. But belief cannot be legislated, though ritual practices can be abolished. The forest in Guinea's southeast region borders with Liberia, and the Loma crossed into Liberia's Lofa county to be initiated with their ethnic colleagues across the boundary. This was considered a crime, and culprits were punished on their return. With the death of Touré and the new government's declaration that it would not continue Touré's "socialist cultural revolution," Foresters quickly resumed their initiation and other ritual practices, and masks appeared or were made for these sacred rites.[56] Indeed, the outbreak of civil war in Liberia and Sierra Leone put a premium on the ritual powers of Foresters; combatants came to Guinea's Forest Region for amulets said to provide fortification for military engagement.[57]

Nkrumah and the Church in Ghana

In Ghana, with its fast-changing twentieth-century religious landscape, Nkrumah publicly exploited the symbols of Christianity and cultivated the aura of a mystic.[58] The twentieth century witnessed the phenomenal growth of Christianity in Ghana from a fringe religion at the beginning of the century to the majority religion by the end of the century. Even in the first half of the twentieth century, those who self-identified as Christian rose in number from 30,000 in 1900 to 641,427 in 1948. In 1949, when the population of the Gold Coast and the British mandated territory of Togoland stood at 4,501,218, adherents of Christianity represented 30 percent of the population, Islam 4 percent, and African traditional religions 66 percent. In 1960, the year Ghana was declared a republic, the share of the Christian population had increased to 42.8 percent, Islam 12 percent, and African traditional religions 38.2 percent. Though Christianity had the largest proportion of religious adherents in 1960, Pobee points out that Ghana was in no way a Christian country and underscores the penetration of traditional religion into other faiths. He also highlights the goodwill Christianity enjoyed from the provision of education and welfare services such as health, ensuring that Christian influence extended beyond professing Christians.[59] In this section, I examine Nkrumah's relationship with the church.

Christian language and symbolism permeated the nationalist and political struggle of the post–World War II era. Nkrumah did not introduce Christian language and symbolism into Ghanaian politics. He discerned the enormous influence of Christianity on Ghanaian life and sought to exploit this in forging his political kingdom. The song that became the CPP's favorite rally song, John Henry Newman's hymn "Lead, Kindly Night," had been the rallying song of the Cape Coast Dwarfs football team in the 1930s, and Kwesi Dickson recalls often hearing the team sing this hymn the night before their football engagements.[60] Perhaps Nkrumah's favorite biblical verse, "Seek ye first the kingdom of God and his righteousness; and all these things shall be added unto you" from Matthew 6:33, was reproduced in 1958 (the year after independence) on the pedestal of Nkrumah's statue in front of Parliament House as "Seek ye first the political kingdom and all other things shall be added unto you."[61]

The church in Ghana viewed itself as a supranational body above partisan politics but claimed to speak on behalf of Ghanaians. It was the largest organized body in the country. Naturally, it protested Nkrumah's use of Christian symbolism and language. While the party machine may have been creative in its deployment of Christian language, as Nkrumah was increasingly likened to the messiah, it is important to remember that Nkrumah was a theologian, keenly aware of the place of religion in the forging of polity and society. At the same time, it cannot be assumed with certainty whether the use of religious discourse and motifs had Nkrumah's express endorsement or whether such use was the creativity of the party faithful. In 1949, the Christian Council in the Gold Coast issued a statement on the Christian and politics. It expressed its position as above party politics, yet in favor of all parties that had Christian principles. Following the Gold Coast riots of February 1948 and the formation of the CPP in July 1949, the church, as if in anticipation of impending political conflict, sought to define its neutrality without ceding its platform as representative of Gold Coasters. In the subsequent years, it clashed with the CPP and Nkrumah over the use of Christian language and symbols. These included the wording on the pedestal of Nkrumah's statue mentioned above, the formation of the Young Pioneers Movement (which the Christian Council considered incipiently atheistic), and what the church viewed as the divinization of Nkrumah through titles or honorifics. Nkrumah and the CPP were not willing to countenance any institution—church or chieftaincy—interposing itself between the state and citizens.

The deportation of the Anglican bishop of Accra, Rt. Rev. Reginald Richard Roseveare, a prominent member of the Christian Council, on August 13, 1962, drew a line in the sand. Nkrumah set up the Ghana Young Pioneer Movement in June 1960 as a voluntary organization for children between eight and twelve years old.[62] It later became compulsory, and Dr. Elizabeth Amoah recalls how even in the elite female mission school of Wesley Girls, a Young Pioneer branch was established during her student days. She remembers the excitement of those days; the girls seemed more interested in Young Pioneer activities than ideological education.[63] Bishop Roseveare's Synod Charge of 1962 concerning the Young Pioneers drew the ire of the press and the CPP. He opined that "not only myself, but all heads of Churches in Ghana, are shocked by the godlessness of this movement and by some of its phrases and songs for the children to repeat or to sing. We made our views known to the Minister of Education last April (1962), saying that we found it impossible to give our support and co-operation in the development of the movement as at present constituted."[64] He went further, stating that "moreover, it seems that the movement confuses the work and example of a great man with divine acts which are unique in history. The incipient atheism is quite foreign to the traditional concept of the African Personality."[65] The press backlash was impressive, and the bishop was soundly castigated as an interfering neocolonialist and saboteur of the ongoing national revolution. He was deported in August 1962—his deportation order stated that his "presence in Ghana was not conducive to the public good." Roseveare and the Christian Council petitioned Nkrumah for his return, a request granted in October 1962. Roseveare returned to the country on November 13, 1962. The intimidated church was effectively silenced, and no criticism from the Christian Council came for the remainder of Nkrumah's rule.[66]

Nkrumah and the CPP rode roughshod over Bishop Roseveare because Roseveare was an expatriate, and it irritated Ghanaian nationalists that an expatriate head of a Christian denomination would propose to lecture the nationalist government on its revolution. It did not matter that many heads of churches and clergymen shared this position. A clash in 1963 between Nkrumah and Archbishop John Kodwo Amissah, the head of the Roman Catholic Church in Ghana, had a very different outcome, emphasizing the importance of having Ghanaian or African heads of the historic churches—only they could claim to speak on behalf of Ghanaians. Rev. Father Damoah, a priest at the Roman Catholic Church in Saltpond, was invited to the Saltpond police station for a message and detained on arrival without explanation. That same evening, Archbishop Amissah called at Saltpond and was informed that Father Damoah had been detained. Amissah marched to the police station and refused to leave without his priest unless the priest was formally charged. Pobee recounts how the news spread like wildfire in the community, and Catholics gathered in support outside the police station. A vigil was kept all night, ending in the celebration of communion the following morning.[67] Instructions came from Accra that Father Damoah be transferred to Elmina police station. An old center of Catholicism, at Elmina the crowds got even larger. Attempts by Catholic cabinet ministers like Kofi Baako to get the archbishop to back down were unsuccessful. The archbishop got his wish: Father Damoah was released. A key figure in this controversy was J. E. Hagan, minister for the Central Region, who Pobee describes as a "Roman Catholic and a great bully."[68] Hagan happened to be the uncle of Professor George Hagan, who educated me on what transpired behind the scenes to get Father Damoah released. The point of contention seems to have been some critical articles Father Damoah had written about Nkrumah:

> Nkrumah couldn't handle Amissah the way he handled Roseveare. This was not a foreigner. He could not deport him. This was a Ghanaian and a very highly intelligent Ghanaian at that, who had risen to the high position

of a leader of the Catholic faith. And everybody knows if you touch the Catholic Church, you are in trouble. It is a worldwide organization, and nothing would work. You could not deal with [President] Kennedy [who was Catholic]; even the Protestant heads would not talk to you. In fact, my uncle was ordered by Nkrumah to release Damoah immediately. . . . What Nkrumah said was *"Amissah ono o ye ruffian nti yi Damoah na y'asom mdwo yen"* [that Amissah is a ruffian, so release Damoah and let us have peace of mind].[69]

An African voice and face representing the church made a big difference. Ironically, Damoah was sent to the United States to study and returned as a Marxist, perhaps more radical than even Nkrumah.

While Ghana, Guinea, Senegal, and Tanzania all declared themselves secular states on independence, religion was too intimately woven into the fabric of African lives to be ignored in the nationalist march to independence or the building of new national identities. Through moments and episodes, this section has reflected on Africa's triple heritage in the new nations. As political rule became authoritarian and corruption eroded the integrity of the African state, calls increasingly came by the end of the century for the faithful to step into the political arena and take over the running of states. A 2010 Pew Forum on Religion and Public Life report of a survey on religion in sub-Saharan Africa entitled *Tolerance and Tension: Islam and Christianity in Sub-Saharan Africa* established that the majority of Africans seek to make their faith central to the organization of state and society while also committing to democratic pluralism. The percentages of Muslim populations who favored the introduction of Sharia as the official law for their countries ranged from 82 percent in Djibouti, 71 percent in Nigeria, 64 percent in Kenya, and 63 percent in Mali, to 58 percent in the predominantly Christian country of Ghana and 55 percent in the predominantly Muslim state of Senegal.[70] The lines between secular and sacred, difficult to keep apart in the early years of independence, have become even more blurred.

FORGING A POLITICAL CULTURE:
A ROLE FOR CHIEFTAINCY IN THE NATION-STATE?

The Demise of Chieftaincy in Senegal, Guinea, and Tanzania

French colonial rule downgraded chieftaincy, and chiefs did not play the unifying role in French local governments that they did under British colonialism. We have seen in the case of Senegal that Muslim marabouts had already edged out chiefs as spokespersons for the people in the early colonial period. Not only were chiefs under French colonial rule appointed by the colonial regime, but they were appointed without regard to whether a candidate came from a ruling family or was even native to the area. The French paid no regard to precolonial polities in the structuring of colonial rule.[71] Once Senegal attained independence in 1960, the office of *canton chef* (district chief) was abolished, and only at the village level have traditional positions persisted into the present. The decline of chieftaincy and the rise of marabouts as the fulcrum of religious, social, and economic life in the countryside have had major implications for state-society relations and economic development in Senegal. Drawing on Max Weber's concept of charisma and its routinization, Leonardo Villalón observes how the maraboutic or Sufi organization has been routinized as an institution or system in Senegal, constituting "what might be described as a religiously based 'civil society' in Senegal."[72] Over the course of the twentieth century, the charisma of three prominent Sufi leaders in Senegal—Ahmadou Bamba of the Mouridiyya, Malik Sy of the Tijaniyya, and Abdoulaye Niasse also of the Tijaniyya—has translated into an institutionalized charismatic system anchored by the towns they founded—Touba, Tivaouane, and Kaolack respectively—and their families. These families and their religious followers were prominent cultivators of peanuts, Senegal's leading export. The prominence of the maraboutic system as a type of civil society has meant that even ethnic sentiments are expressed not through chiefs or clan leaders, but through the maraboutic institution, which has become the accepted model for organizing state-civil society relations.[73]

But whereas the maraboutic system has served as a model for religiously organized civil society and helped maintain law and order in the countryside, it has not lent itself as the instrument of socioeconomic transformation in the countryside that Senghor's government hoped for. Chapter 4 documents the failure of Senghor's government to transform the rural economy through increased production and diversification of its monocrop base. Jackson and Rosberg observe that "the marabouts can be important auxiliaries of rule and order, but not of policy and change. They have been deployed for maintaining law and order, securing taxes and military service from their followers, and mobilizing votes for the PS [Parti Socialiste], but they have resisted most attempts by the government to reorganize rural life in a developmental direction."[74] Chapter 4 shows how Senghor's government gave up in the early years of independence its initial attempt to directly mobilize the peasantry and remove the intermediary role of the marabouts. Unable to transform the rural economy on which government revenue was heavily dependent, Senegal remained dependent on French funding.

One of the first decisions by Guinea's ruling PDG party when Guinea became independent on October 2, 1958, was to abolish chieftaincy. But in the case of Guinea, there was a more viable tradition of chieftaincy, especially in Futa Jallon—seat of a precolonial Islamic state forged through jihad—the traditional leaders of which had become important partners in French colonialism in Guinea. The colonial state in Guinea comprised of four regions: Futa Jallon; Upper-Guinea, centered on Kankan; Lower-Guinea, where the capital, Conakry, was located; and the Forest Region, abutting the territories of Liberia and Côte d'Ivoire. That chieftaincy in Futa Jallon would constitute a strong foundation for French colonial rule is not surprising, as the French to an extent practiced indirect rule to minimize cost of administration. The colonial administration delegated the mobilizing of forced labor and collection of taxes to the chiefs of Futa Jallon. In this case, what Mahmood Mamdani has described as the "decentralized despotism" of indirect rule overlaid the extensive practice of slavery in precolonial Futa Jallon, exacerbating tensions between Futanke aristocracy and their non-Fulbe peasant subjects.[75]

An additional layer of conflict was added in the contest between the leftist-oriented PDG and more conservative parties led by Futa Jallon elites with the advent of territorial politics in the French colonies from 1947. In the Forest Region, Canton chiefs had been appointed where none existed before. A number of ethnic parties emerged in opposition to the PDG, such as the Union Franco-Guinéenne, founded in 1947 and backed by the chiefs and elites in Futa Jallon. In 1954, various ethnic and regional groups with the support of the chiefs and traditional aristocracy came together as a single political party, the Bloc Africain de Guinée (BAG). With over 95 percent of Guinea's population living in rural areas, the colonial government viewed ethnic parties and their backing of chiefs as key partners in the process of decolonization, not the 5 percent of educated Africans who lived in Conakry and other urban centers.[76] The loi-cadre of 1956 that introduced a degree of internal self-government and universal adult suffrage in Guinea altered the political contest between chiefs and peasants, as peasants in the Forest Region and in Futa Jallon showed massive support for the PDG. Peasants in these regions had been resisting chiefs since the material exactions of World War II. Elizabeth Schmidt notes that in Futa Jallon, a region where a quarter of the population was of servile descent, a large proportion of the PDG's votes in 1956 came from former slave villages.[77] In short, the abolition of chieftaincy in Guinea had popular support.

Tanzania presents an intriguing anglophone example of a postcolonial state where Nyerere, the son of a chief, presided over the abolition of chieftaincy. Chiefs and native authorities were casualties of Nyerere's attempt to create a centralized state that set aside the legal and administrative structures of British indirect rule. Mamdani succinctly explains the vision: "To do away with ethnic-based distinctions in customary law, Nyerere mounted a political project that did away with native authorities. The objective was to build a centralized state structure, one that would do away with the colonial legacy of a division between customary and civil law on one hand and civil and native authorities on the other."[78] In this endeavor, Nyerere had the support of rural or village dissidents, who did not grasp the larger political imperatives that motivated Nyerere. As in Guinea, peasants who harbored grievances against chiefs rallied to support Nyerere and TANU in the opposition to chieftaincy. Andreas Eckert points to how the nationalist party used peasants in its move against the chiefs: "Perhaps most pressing was the need to replace chiefs who, as colonial native authorities, had been associated with the colonial order. In its struggle for independence, the nationalist movement owed its support, at least in part, to unsophisticated local dissidents and village rebels who could easily use independence to justify the immediate banishment of chiefs against whom they harbored long-standing grievances."[79] With the chiefs gone, the two centers of gravity left in the politics of Tanganyika were peasants and bureaucrats. Feierman has discussed insightfully how TANU, in its nationalist mobilization, borrowed from the discourse of peasant struggle against chiefly collaboration and colonial policies after World War II, drawing strength from peasant organizations. But on independence, "the peasant intellectuals of the 1950s, who were effective actors on the national stage, found themselves removed from positions of influence."[80] Senghor is unique in that his political vision made room for the coexistence of ethnic and regional divisions in the quest to create the nation-state, with the first being a building block for the second.[81] In his case, there was not much of the institution of chieftaincy to work with by the 1960s. In place was the maraboutic system, and Villalón has observed that "state power and maraboutic power in Senegal coexist and interact."[82] It is the state's use of the political and material culture of chieftaincy that makes Nkrumah's Ghana such an instructive example.

Nkrumah and Chieftaincy in Ghana

The British policy of indirect rule set up chiefs as legitimate rulers of the people. Until World War II, the place of chieftaincy in the colonial dispensation was unquestioned: chiefs were partners in colonial rule. European reconstruction after World War II placed priority on accelerating economic development in African colonies to better assist European reconstruction. Colonial governments turned to educated African nationalists as partners in this new phase of colonial rule and development. This left in question the role of chiefs in soon-to-become independent Ghana. In the years before 1957, chiefs used the pages of the *Daily Graphic*, founded in 1950 by the Daily Mirror Group of Britain, to make their claim to political engagement. It is clear that the *Daily Graphic* imagined a place or role for chiefs in the Gold Coast political process. As was discussed in the introduction, the support of chiefs in the colony and Ashanti for the National Liberation Movement (NLM) in 1954 brought chiefs into direct confrontation with the ruling CPP party.[83] The emergence of the NLM after the 1954 general election, which the CPP won, led to the colonial government's request for a final general election in 1956 before the grant of independence. The CPP won the 1956 election, making clear its preeminence, as it won all three elections in the years leading to independence—1951, 1954, and 1956.

Richard Rathbone highlights how Nkrumah and the CPP viewed chieftaincy as an anachronism. Indeed, African nationalists and scholars enamored by the nationalist struggle and the march to independence in Africa assumed that "chieftaincy would die just as religion was supposed to fade as material progress and scientific endeavor made for its social and emotional redundancy."[84] Controlling the countryside was central to the CPP's plan for political control of Ghana, and this required overcoming chiefs and their institutions.[85] The assault on chiefly power began in the last decade of colonial rule. Frustrated by the inability of chiefs to assist in increasing the volume and value of Gold Coast exports to assist the war effort, the colonial government in 1944 passed the Native Authorities Ordinance. This ordinance limited state councils to the realm of tradition and ritual.[86] The CPP would push forward these reforms after its first electoral victory in 1951, passing a new Local Government Ordinance. Local government was now to be the realm of democratically elected councils, limiting the purview of chiefs to "customary functions." Rathbone sums up the import of this ordinance:

> Under the ordinance, chiefs of the Colony (the South) and in the Ashanti Region effectively lost control of what were traditionally called stool lands, even if the general ownership of those lands remained vested in the stools and hence the communities which owed allegiance to these stools. The revenue from these lands, derived from local taxes on farmers, land and concession sales as well as from royalties on timber forests, auriferous and diamondiferous tracts, was the ancient basis of chiefly patrimony; from now on that revenue was to be collected by the newly created democratic local councils as one element of revenue. Chiefs were no longer at liberty to alienate stool lands without the assent of local councils.[87]

Chiefly agitation from this major shift in fortunes was expressed in the *Daily Graphic* and took organized form in the NLM. In his exasperation with the chiefs, Nkrumah threatened that if they were not careful, they would run away and leave their traditional sandals. A barefooted chief is a destooled or dethroned chief; the warning was clear.

A clear signal on the locus of political power in the newly independent Ghana was sent just months after independence in March 1957. Indeed, though the CPP had convincingly won the 1956 elections, the paramount chiefs of Akyem Abuakwa and Asante, the Okyenhene and the Asantehene, remained defiant, articulating competing sovereignties for their kingdoms with the Asante demanding federation or threatening secession.[88] On October 16, 1957, the CPP government withdrew its official recognition of the Okyenhene, Ofori Atta II. Rattled by this unprecedented move, paramount chiefs in the Joint Provincial Council quickly began to declare their support for the government in power. In 1958, the government commenced two high-profile commissions, or stool probes, into the affairs of Akyem Abuakwa and Asante, whose kings had been at the forefront of the NLM. On receiving the report of the Jackson commission of enquiry into the affairs of Akyem Abuakwa in May 1958, the CPP government confirmed the permanent removal of the Okyenhene. The Asante stool probe was a public display of CPP power. Of grand proportions, the probe lasted several months. It held twenty-nine public sessions, took two hundred statements, and examined five thousand files and documents. Though not explicitly, what was under investigation were the pro-NLM activities of the Asanteman Council and the Kumasi State Council and their punitive actions against CPP supporters in Ashanti. The government's findings in September 1958 harshly condemned the Asanteman Council, the Kumasi State Council, and the Asantehene. The government introduced the Ashanti Stool Lands Bill to take control of Ashanti stool lands, arguing this was necessary for the preservation of chieftaincy. Now the government would not need the Asantehene's consent to lease, sell, or otherwise use Ashanti lands. The impact of the government's move against chieftaincy in the immediate years after independence was profound, as noted by Rathbone: "The entire basis of chiefly legitimacy and illegitimacy, however robustly contested they were, had been destroyed."[89] Not only had chiefs lost control of the revenue of stool lands, but the government now also claimed the right to recognize or not recognize the appointment of new chiefs. With chiefs subdued, the government confidently went on to declare Ghana a republic in July 1960. In 1962, parliament passed a law authorizing the government to acquire land for public purposes and placed all stool lands under the authority of the state.

In a country where an estimated 70–80 percent of national territory fell under chiefly jurisdiction, this law had enormous implications for development.[90] While Nkrumah's desire to modernize agriculture in the South was obstructed by the existence of small, family-owned farms in densely populated areas (see chap. 5), northern Ghana with its open lands and sparse populations lent itself to large-scale, mechanized commercial farming based on irrigation. With control over land vested in the state, the North became the site for commercial rice farming under both state and private initiative, a pattern which continued under successor governments to the CPP.[91] It is perhaps not surprising that though post-Nkrumah governments from 1966 reversed some adverse policies regarding chieftaincy, it was not until 1979 that recognition of the control of traditional authorities over land was extended to the northern regions.[92]

Ironically, Nkrumah's appreciation of the loyalty to and the embedded nature of chieftaincy also grew in the years after independence. The prominence of chiefs' sons and nephews in the leading ranks of the CPP and opposition parties was conspicuous. Even "commoners," or what were called in Asante parlance "nkwankwaa," were loyal to their chiefs. In the tussle between the CPP and the NLM, it is reported that Nkrumah at one point contemplated arresting the Asantehene. He mentioned this to his close confidantes, including Krobo Edusei, a minister in Nkrumah's cabinet. Krobo Edusei that night drove to Kumasi to warn the Asantehene. Krobo Edusei, on being appointed minister for the interior on August 30, 1957, was noted for his hard stance against the Okyenhene and Asantehene.[93] But he could not contemplate the arrest of the Asantehene. Preempted, Nkrumah decided against making any physical move on the Asantehene.[94] Nkrumah had to come to terms with chieftaincy. Professor George Hagan insightfully describes Nkrumah's conundrum: "Chieftaincy was a bother to him [Nkrumah] because chieftaincy represented the people. I have always claimed that chieftaincy in Ghana has its roots deeply planted in the soil because of one or two things. Almost every family in Ghana claims to be connected to a chiefly family. It is not like England, for example, that you have a class of royals. Everybody in Ghana is a royal. Look at funeral announcements. Everybody who dies has connections to a chiefly family."[95] It does not matter if the connection is to a minor stool or chief; royalty is royalty. Nkrumah found it extremely difficult to manipulate chieftaincy. Major Akan kingdoms had flourished in the Gold Coast since the seventeenth century: Bono Manso, Denkyira, Akwamu, Akyem Abuakwa, and Asante. Their footprint in the history of the Gold Coast could not be easily erased. In addition to the popularity of chieftaincy in Ghana, chiefs also controlled land. As we have seen above, a major weapon Nkrumah used against chiefs was deprivation of control and revenues from land. In the end, Nkrumah co-opted the institution and its material culture in his endeavor to forge the aura of an African nation-state.

Akan chieftaincy has long depended on the visual and aural in the presentation of power to oral societies. Orality has remained important in Ghanaian and other African societies despite the advance of literacy.[96] Oral societies understand power as "lived moments of action," more narratively than analytically.[97] In the Asantehene's court, the royal past and present are conveyed through oral genres such as praise poems (*apaee*) and poetry (*ayan*), recited by *asafo* or courtiers and played on state drums (*atumpan*) during state occasions. Praise poems by the *abrafuo* (warriors) retell the military exploits of Asante. Professor J. H. Kwabena Nketia has documented the praise poems and poetry of the king of Asante.[98] In the realm of material culture, symbols of royal power—staffs, horns, drums, swords, palanquins, umbrellas—were indispensable in conveying royal majesty and authority in a preliterate setting.[99] Kwame Amoah Labi has observed that "chieftaincy regalia comprise some of the most significant art works in Ghana."[100] Agya Ko Nimo, an Asante royal court musician, drew my attention to another function of the royal display of regalia during state ceremonies. Each incoming king of Asante or chief of an Akan polity is given an inventory of royal regalia. Any industrious chief or king is expected to add to this regalia, commissioning new artifacts. Royal processions during state ceremonies provide occasion for the display of regalia, serving as a "mobile museum" and allowing the community to assess what a chief has added to the regalia since his enstoolment.[101]

Nkrumah turned to the oral and material culture of Akan chieftaincy to represent and elaborate the Ghanaian nation-state, especially when Ghana assumed republican status on July 1, 1960. The declaration of Ghana as a republic in 1960, removing the British Crown as the symbolic head of the Ghanaian nation-state, provided the occasion to commission works underscoring the Ghanaian-ness of the new republic. For the Republic day celebration, Nkrumah turned to two artist/scholars for creative input: J. H. Kwabena Nketia, with his work on Akan traditional poetry and royal verbal arts; and Kofi Antubam, an artist/sculptor who had been drawn into symbolism by teacher H. V. Meyerowitz at Achimota College.[102] Center stage at Nkrumah's presidential inauguration in 1960 was the state stool or throne (Twi: *ohene akongua*), state sword (Twi: *afena*), and state mace (Twi: *okyeame poma*) designed by Antubam. Chief Justice Sir Kobina Arku Korsah swore Nkrumah into office, Nkrumah standing on the foot stool, which was part of the state stool, and holding the state sword.[103] To the right of a dais stood the state's okyeame, or linguist, with the state mace or the equivalent of the traditional linguist staff in hand. With their elaborately carved finial tops depicting proverbs and other metaphorical associations, linguist staffs are above all political art forms.[104] Nkrumah was dressed in traditional kente cloth, the cloth of royalty, worn toga-style.[105] The scene was deeply symbolic and reminiscent of the enstoolment of an Akan paramount chief (*omanhene*) or king. Doran Ross notes that the most important political function of the sword is in the enstoolment of an Asante chief.[106] The king of Asante is sworn into kingship holding the state sword, the *Mponponsuo*.

It is not surprising that the Asante objected to what they considered state appropriation of Asante symbols.[107]

The evening concert for the celebration of Ghana's Republic Day equally elevated the place of Ghanaian music and reflected Nkrumah's commitment to the arts as a way of building the new nation, affirming Pan-African solidarity, and showcasing African genius and cultural creativity. Nketia captures the evening for us:

> It was because of his ardent commitment to Pan-Africanism that he [Nkrumah] suggested that an evening concert be included in the official programme of the celebration of the First Republic, and that Philippa Schuyler, the African American composer-performer whom he had known during his student days in America, be invited as special guest for this auspicious state occasion. The first half of the programme consisted of choral works by Ephraim Amu, Isaac Riverson and myself, while the second half consisted of my Republic Suite (in seven movements) for flute and piano played by Charles Simmons (flute) and myself, and the piano works of the guest artiste, Philippa Schuyler, played by herself.[108]

The evening blended national and international artists, a symphony of Africa and its diaspora. Ephraim Amu was a product of Presbyterian missionary training and a distinguished Ghanaian composer who had introduced traditional instruments like the bamboo flute (*atenteben*) into church music. His patriotic song "Yen Ara Asase Ni" ("This is our Homeland") is often performed at national functions. Isaac Riverson had compiled Akan songs and authored some of the textbooks used in the instruction of music in Ghanaian primary schools on independence.[109]

The imperative to create African art to express the spirit of political independence and exhibit African creative culture was explained very eloquently by Antubam: the West points to its cultural and artistic heritage as evidence of its civilization—"great art galleries, sculpture-illumined parks . . . museums and theatres that their countries have built through the years and still maintain. . . . But poor Africans, they say, what have they to show in concrete to substantiate their great desire for telling the twentieth century world that they, too, own a great past which grants them the right to their claim to have a lesson to teach that will help to better the future of the world?"[110]

Under Nkrumah, the creative and performance arts flourished. Nketia composed state poetry with accompaniment on drums, horns, and flutes, drawing on his work on the courts of the Asantehene, Kokofuhene, and Mamponghene. Antubam not only carved the state stool, sword, and mace,

Fig 2.1 Nkrumah at the podium on Republic Day, Ghana, July 1, 1960. Source: Shirley Graham Du Bois Papers, Schlesinger Library, Harvard University.

but later even made the Ghanaian cultural artifacts that Nkrumah gave as state gifts.[111] This is when the title of *Oman Panyin* (Twi: head of state) was innovated, as well as the phrase that became the call of address: Ghana *Muntie*! (Twi: Attention Ghana!)

A state linguist, Okyeame Kwasi Akuffo, was appointed, and traditional libation became a part of state ceremonies. The state eclectically and creatively drew on the indigenous political traditions of various ethnic groups of Ghana. Hagan captures well the irony of the situation: "The presidential stool was of gold and designed in traditional motif. Kente became his costume on formal occasions, though he appeared at times uncomfortable in it. (It is reliably learnt that at least initially his kente was held in place with safety pins). A state umbrella appeared over him; and traditional drummers and horn-blowers became part of formal ceremonies. Nkrumah had a linguist to pour libation and praise him with traditional praise from all the major chiefdoms of Ghana. Had he destroyed chiefship, in what way could he have projected this cultural personality?"[112] Himself from the chiefly lines in Wassaw Fiase and Aowin, and assuming a chiefly position later in life, Nkrumah as Hagan rightly points out "loved chieftaincy as the embodiment of Ghanaian culture; but he disliked it as a force of reaction which had to be reduced."[113] As the independent Ghanaian state cracked down on ethnic, regional, and religious dissent through the Avoidance of Discrimination Act (1958), physically reduced Asante through the creation of the Brong Ahafo Region, and left an obviously chastened Asantehene in place, chiefs aligned themselves with the CPP's political agenda.

As Ghana became a republic in 1960 with a new constitution, Nkrumah extended an olive branch towards the chiefs, assuring them of the central place of chieftaincy in Ghanaian life and its continued existence. In an address to the Asantehene and his chiefs in a colorful durbar in Kumasi on December 10, 1960, Nkrumah encouraged the forgetting of the recent unpleasant conflict between the CPP and the NLM and affirmed his commitment to chieftaincy:

> As the frontiers of our social and economic development widen, the institutions of chieftaincy cannot afford to remain static. We are a modern nation with modern and progressive ideas, and we will always wish our chiefs to move abreast of us in our forward march. To ensure the existence of a cordial relationship between the Government and the Chiefs, the first prerequisite is cooperation between the Government, the Chiefs and the People.
>
> The question of the maintenance of traditional authorities is actively engaging my attention and that of Government. I assure you Nananom, that the matter will be objectively pursued, and the result will no doubt rebound to your prestige and dignity. All I expect from you is Trust, Loyalty and Honesty.[114]

This was an important overture, considering that the symbols of the Ghanaian nation-state Nkrumah had constructed were distinctly Akan. Perhaps nothing better expresses this change in Nkrumah's relations with chiefs than the photo of him and his Egyptian-born wife, Fathia, dancing to highlife music on the grounds of Flagstaff House in January 1963 flanked by paramount chiefs.

CELEBRATING CULTURE AND THE ARTS IN THE NEW NATION

For Senghor, everything was culture. He valued how the cultural policy of the state could forge and express a national identity, exploiting history and culture as resources, but created and maintained by public authorities as

Fig 2.2 Kwame Nkrumah, wife, and chieftains dance to highlife, January 20, 1963. Photo by Bettmann. Reproduced with permission from Getty Images.

an enterprise.[115] Senegal under Senghor was extraordinary for the resources devoted to the state's cultural agenda: "Twenty-five percent of the state's budget was allocated to the Ministry of Culture to build museums, art schools, presses, theaters, archives, and workshops for the emerging generation of young artists."[116] This was an appropriate investment for Senghor, for whom the priority of development did not have to overshadow the primacy of culture as a contribution to the universal civilization, an integral humanism.[117]

Sékou Touré equally stressed the urgency of a cultural revolution to reverse the inimical effects of European colonial rule on Africa: "All imperialism is always accompanied by cultural aggression, an acculturation enterprise, an action of cultural alienation for the purposes of a complete conditioning, necessary for political and economic subjugation. And this is why for peoples emerging from colonial enslavement, the task of cultural dis-alienation for the return to national culture is imperative for the consolidation of national independence and concrete sovereignty, meaning the full exercise of popular will in all fields."[118] Though Touré was a strong critic of Senghor's négritude—what he believed was Senghor's indiscriminate endorsement of European (French) culture and his cession of logic and abstract thinking as what characterizes the European versus emotion in the African—Senghor was not uncritical of the impact of European colonial rule on Africa. Senghor was aware that European colonial rule had denigrated and undermined African culture and confidence, and that this attitude or mentality could not be carried into the proposed French Community. In an article in *Le Monde* in September 1957, he stressed the need to decolonize the mind on both the part of the colonizer and the colonized:

> *j'entends l'abolition de tout préjugé, de tout complexe de supériorité dans l'esprit du colonisateur, et aussi de tout complexe d'infériorité dans l'esprit du colonisé.*[119]

> I mean the abolition of any prejudice, of any superiority complex in the mind of the colonizer, and also of any inferiority complex in the mind of the colonized.

Africa's leaders shared an ambivalence about the cultural impact of European colonial rule while appreciating the benefits of secular education and its contributions in areas such as science and technology (see introduction). For Touré, the fact that secular education had come largely through the medium of Christian missions, focused on religious and cultural proselytization, and that European expatriates modeled lifestyles and shaped the expectations of educated Africans made urban educated African youths and their social expectations a challenge to the Guinean revolution. He pronounced educated Africans as alienated from true African culture, which "flourishes away from them in the villages amongst the common people, whose mentalities and social behavior are the authentic foundation of African humanism."[120] He elevated rural youths as the ideal agents of the Guinean revolution, advocated for reforms in education to equip them for their designated roles, and assigned teachers the task of fashioning them into revolutionary agents.[121]

Africa's new leaders were keenly appreciative of the role of the arts in forging symbols of nationalism and nation-building in their primarily oral societies. Objects portraying the new nation-state that could be seen, heard, or touched were effective media for symbolic nationalism. Harcourt Fuller's observation on the instrumentality of symbolic nationalism is instructive: "But why are visual symbols of nationhood such as national flags and anthems, and in particular postage stamps, banknotes, and coins such effective means of spreading political propaganda to the populace of a country and internationally? They are issued and controlled solely by the central government . . . they are cheap to produce, they can be graphically imprinted with considerable detail, despite their small size; they circulate among millions of people both within and outside of the country's borders; they do not require a high degree of literacy (or none at all) to understand the messages."[122]

Nothing better signaled the end of colonial rule than these visual symbols of nationhood. Literature, theater, poetry, music, dance, and the visual arts flourished under the first generation of independent African leaders. These media were avenues to shape a "new African," rid of the superstitions of the past, confident of her or his African identity, and equipped and positioned to lead Africa in the modern era.[123] For Frantz Fanon, the psychologist of the African national liberation, the struggle for liberation was itself a cultural phenomenon. The disappearance of colonialism went hand in hand with the disappearance of the colonized subject. A new humanity was birthed, requiring a new humanism with culture at its center.[124] The nation-state was exhibited and performed. National museums proliferated in capital cities.

The role of language was keenly debated. Touré stressed the importance of education in indigenous languages; the plays and ballets the state requested party branches at village, district, and regional levels to create were to be performed in indigenous languages. "Africa cannot, and should not, underestimate in her development the need of her people to use their own languages and to enrich them so that they are able to express succinctly all the shades of their thoughts, both in the written and spoken form."[125] This was a sentiment Nyerere shared. Nyerere promoted Kiswahili as a national language and an official language in Tanzania in addition to English. To underscore the suppleness and capacity of the language, and hence its suitability for conducting government business, Nyerere translated Shakespeare's *Julius Caesar* and *The Merchant of Venice* into Kiswahili.[126]

Whether through participation in international exhibitions in the arts, the export of highlife music from Ghana through cultural ambassadors E. T. Mensah and the Tempos Band, the celebration of Guinean ballet by Fodéba Keita's Ballets Africains, or world-class events like the First World

Festival of Black Arts hosted in Dakar in 1966, the first two decades of African independence witnessed a period of innovation and state patronage of culture and the arts more fertile than any other period in the postcolonial era. Africa stepped out onto the world stage, and the world took notice of the new African nation-states. The international showcasing of African arts and culture was built on the state's production of culture. National competitions in the arts proliferated across the continent. The artistic festivals in Guinea, the *Quinzaines Artistiques*, have been referenced. On the rise of militant theater, especially with the launch of the Guinean socialist cultural revolution in 1968, Straker notes that "by the end of the first decade of independence, each of Guinea's two thousand *comités*—the country's smallest administrative unit consisting of a village or urban neighborhood—was required to present at least one new play, one ballet, and one choral work at local competitions every year."[127] Tanzania had its National Arts and Language Competitions, where government-sponsored and private local cultural troupes competed. In 1965, the TANU government requested that Cultural Committees be established at the village, district, regional, and national levels and that competitions be held at each of the four levels to promote the arts.[128]

Nkrumah, Touré, Senghor, and Nyerere all viewed the arts as an important avenue to forge a national identity. On the eve of independence in 1957, Nkrumah declared highlife Ghana's national dance music.[129] On Independence Day, March 6, 1957, celebratory dances took place across all regions in Ghana, with thousands of men and women dancing to highlife music. Nate Plageman points out that on July 1, 1960, when Ghana became a republic, the government made two major pronouncements concerning highlife music: the first claimed highlife as Ghana's national dance music; the second advocated pruning highlife of foreign influences and making it more Ghanaian.[130] Plageman comments on the CPP's use of highlife in nation-building: "Eager to carry out its own plans for development and modernization, it used dance band highlife to translate official rhetoric about abstract ideas—the nation, citizenship, and the African Personality—into clear domains of individual practice and communal identification."[131] Perhaps no image gave highlife international standing and signaled new worlds in the making like the photograph of Queen Elizabeth II and President Nkrumah dancing to a highlife tune at a farewell ball in Accra in 1961.[132] Highlife music did for Ghana what militant theater did in Guinea. The CPP set up the Arts Council in 1955, making it a permanent body by legislation in December 1958. It was tasked with controlling quality, training highlife bands, and ensuring bands fit the government's expectations to merit government patronage. From this period, highlife ceased to be simply recreational and became a tool of education. State patronage could be inimical, and "in the early 1960s, the [Arts] Council provided the Government Passport office with firm instructions about which bands should be allowed to perform outside the nation's boundaries."[133]

The arts were an important sphere for Nkrumah in his construction of the Ghanaian—and African—nation-state. In his opening address for the Institute of African Studies at the University of Ghana on October 25, 1963, Nkrumah gave the study of the arts of Africa special mention, "for the study of these can enhance our understanding of African institutions and values, and the cultural bonds that unite us."[134] He tasked the institute with developing "new forms of dance and drama, of music and creative writing that are at the same time closely related to our Ghanaian traditions and express the ideas and aspirations of our people at this critical stage in our history."[135] On January 24, 1965, Nkrumah inaugurated the Osagyefo Players, a drama group, at Flagstaff House. Nkrumah's comments on this occasion revealed his intellectual architecture for the arts in his building of the nation. He had "initiated the establishment of the Institute of Art and Culture, the Institute of African Studies, and the School of Music and Drama at Legon [the University of Ghana]. We also hope to launch a film and television school for training producers and artistes. We already have a Ghana Symphony Orchestra which are showing great promise. All these institutions and this drama group which we are initiating today mark a step forward in the development of the Arts in Ghana."[136] The overthrow of Nkrumah in 1966 ended a vibrant period of artistic and cultural production and the intellectual interrogation of African studies in Ghana.

Similarly, in Tanzania the TANU government that had exploited popular culture in its nationalist mobilization on independence sought to use it in nation-building. With Tanzania's long history of competitive dance societies, music and dance lent themselves as important instruments in imagining of the new nation.[137] The colonial government's ban on civil servants joining political organizations deterred the small group of educated Africans in government employ from joining TANU in 1954. It was women in Dar es Salaam, mostly illiterate and semiliterate Muslim women, who carried the new political party. Women in Dar es Salaam were already organized in dance associations, or *ngoma* groups. Bibi Titi Mohamed, who was co-opted to head the TANU Women's Section, was a singer in a *ngoma* group. She described to Geiger how these groups framed women's social worlds:

> There were many *ngoma* groups at that time [from the late 1940s]. "Good Luck," eehe? "Safina" [ship, or Noah's Ark], "Submarine," "Snow White," "Ratusudan" [Pleasure of the Blacks], "Ratulail" [Pleasure of the Night], "British Empire." These were *lelemama* groups. They were organized. On Saturdays, they dressed in *sare* [uniforms made of similar cloth, usually matching *kanga*]. They had their own dances and they sang and had their own arrangements and order of singing. The leader would sing and the rest would dance. Do you understand? It was like this: groups competed with each other. I found myself coming into the world.[138]

Bibi Titi was an expert in composing songs and led the singing at *ngomas*. Men were paralyzed by the fear of losing their jobs; in Muslim communities in Dar es Salaam, where men could not easily circulate among women who were not close relatives, women had to become ambassadors of TANU in the early years.

Bibi Titi described the process of contacting women's dance groups and informing them of TANU and its message: "To mobilize the women, I went to the *ngoma* groups. First of all, I went to their leaders. The leaders got together in a meeting, and after I spoke to them, they told me that on a certain day at a certain time they would call all their people so that I could come and talk to them about TANU—what it does, what it wants, where it is going."[139] Not only did the women join TANU in their numbers, but they also composed songs for the nationalist party. One by Hiari ya Moyo from 1954, the year TANU was founded, was entitled "Amka Msilale" ("Wake up, don't sleep").

Amka Msilale	Wake up, don't sleep
Msiwe wajinga mu Tanganyika	Don't be stupid, you are in Tanganyika [territory]
Tanganyika ni mali tetu	Tanganyika is our property
Tukidai tutapewa	If we demand it, we'll be given[140]

Penina Mlama notes that the arts' invaluable role in mobilizing the masses in Tanganyika's independence movement is what led Nyerere on independence to create a full Ministry of Culture in the first cabinet.[141]

Announcing the formation of the Ministry of National Culture and Youth in Parliament on December 10, 1962, Nyerere reflected that "of all the crimes of colonialism there is none worse than the attempt to make us believe that we had no indigenous culture of our own; or that what we did have was worthless—something of which we should be ashamed, instead of a source of pride. . . . So I have set up this new Ministry to help us regain our pride in our own culture. I want it to seek out the best of the traditions and customs of all the tribes and make them part of our national culture."[142] Unfortunately, the state's commitment to the production of culture was more rhetorical than substantial, and the Ministry of National Culture came to represent one of the most underfunded and unstable ministries. Askew described it as a "Migrant Ministry" in regard to how it was constantly shunted around, merged with other ministries and even demoted to a department within a ministry.[143]

Culture and the arts played key roles in the international relations of new African nations. As TANU formed its policies as a government, one of its priorities was the liberation of Africa (see chap. 4). Designated as the headquarters of the Organization of African Unity's Liberation Committee, Dar es Salaam became the base of several liberation movements from white-ruled settler colonies in southern Africa. Liberations songs were composed and taught in Tanzania's schools. One such popular song went like this:

Vijani twendeni	Rise up young people
Vijana twendeni	Rise up young people
TANU inaita Msumbiji	TANU is calling us to go to Mozambique
Tukawaokoe ndugu zetu	To liberate our brothers and sisters[144]

In the first decade of Tanzania's independence, the government formed the National Ngoma Troupe in 1963, the National Acrobatic Group in 1969, and the National Drama Group in 1972.[145] Exchange visits and foreign tours of cultural troupes became such an important part of international relations that liberation movements like the South African ANC created a cultural ensemble in exile as part of its efforts at worldmaking (see chap. 4).[146] In 1980, the ANC in exile formed the Amandla Cultural Ensemble, led by renowned trombonist Jonas Gwangwa, which served as the ANC's official artistic group and toured the world building support for the movement. Its music was regularly played on Radio Freedom, the ANC's radio station broadcasted from Zambia.[147]

Touré also saw theater and ballet as cultural ambassadors of the Guinean state and its revolution. A key player in this development was Guinean choreographer Fodéba Keita, who had founded Les Ballets Africains in Paris in 1952. The group enjoyed the support of several heads of state and performed around the world.[148] On Guinea's independence in 1958, Touré requested that the group relocate to Guinea-Conakry and serve as the country's cultural ambassadors. Lansine Kaba notes that even before Guinea's independence, two nationals, Fodéba Keita and Laye Camara, "had achieved wide recognition within France and her sub-Saharan dependencies, respectively as a producer of African dances and folklore, and as a novelist who specialized in the portrayal of indigenous culture in contact with the European value system."[149] A product of École Normale William Ponty, Fodéba Keita was from a griot background and had mastered the art of performance and musical composition even before going to Paris for further studies. In Paris he formed in 1947 the Ensemble Fodéba-Facelli-Mouangué, a result of his exposure to other musicians from West Africa who lived in the Latin Quarter, later renamed Les Ballets Africains.[150] The group's repertoire was extensive, and while based in Paris it earned the label of "Ambassador of African Culture" in its tours of Europe.[151]

By 1955, Kaba points out that Fodéba had become the most popular writer and artist in French West Africa.[152] Sékou Touré met Fodéba in Paris when Touré was elected to the French National Assembly as the deputy for Guinea in 1956. Fodéba returned to Guinea as a representative of his district in Guinea and became minister for internal affairs in 1957. He remained an active artist on his return to Guinea and inspired the national ballet, an instrumental ensemble, and cultural festivals that annually brought leading regional troupes to the capital, Conakry, to compete.[153] For the first decade after Guinea's independence, under the direction of the Ministry of Arts and Culture and Fodéba, there was a veritable cultural renaissance.[154] Plays and ballets became media for national education with arts companies organized at village, district, regional, and national levels. The youth division of the PDG, the JRDA, was entrusted with oversight of the national arts system.[155] African Americans who had been introduced to Guinean and French West African music and dance during the 1959 American tour of Les Ballets Africains and inspired by Guinea's "No" vote traveled to Guinea. Visitors included Julian Bond, Fanny Lou Hamer, Miriam Makeba, and Harry Belafonte. Makeba and Belafonte were collaborators, and Belafonte

Fig 2.3 Les Ballets Africains on stage in Paris, March 1953. Photo by Walter Carone. Reproduced with permission by Getty Images.

visited Guinea after Makeba took up residence there at the invitation of Touré. Indeed, Touré would offer Belafonte the artistic directorship of the Ballet Djoliba, a new national company established in 1964.[156]

This artistic fluorescence came under critical review when Sékou Touré launched his "cultural revolution" in August 1968, seeing the artistic and cultural works that had flourished in the decade after independence as elitist. Touré in his pursuit of socialism decided that culture must reflect the lived reality of the masses as defined by the leadership of the PDG. New educational reforms sought to make rural schools the norm.[157] Touré was uncomfortable that Europe remained a reference point for much artistic creativity in Guinea. He shared this discomfort with Nkrumah, who sought to prune highlife music of foreign influences, and Nyerere, who pushed back against *dansi* for its European influences and *taarab* for its Arab and Indian influences. Fodéba and other notable Guinean artists fell from grace. Fodéba was arrested as a conspirator in a plot against Touré in 1969 and condemned without trial to death in 1971; intellectuals including historian Djibril Tamsire Niane either went into exile or were imprisoned.[158] Many Guineans relocated to Senegal, where Touré's vehement denunciation of négritude had more political than philosophical basis.

Senegal under Senghor also sought to define how artists should practice nationalism through art. Laura Cochrane examines how state patronage was applied to the weaving craft. She discusses how Papa Ibra Tall, an artist from the independence era, helped set up a state-sponsored tapestry factory, the Manufacture Sénégalaise des Arts Décoratifs (MSAD) at Thiés. A distinct artistic style emerged under the watchful eye of the state, and a select group of weavers at MSAD worked under supervision to create tapestries for official functions and presentation to visiting dignitaries as state gifts.[159] For Senghor, art was the supreme medium for the expression of négritude. But the privileging of a tapestry style as "national" was detrimental to regional styles, as Senghor like other African leaders pursued his statist vision of national unity. Tall also ran the Workshop for Research in Black Visual Arts in the 1960s and, like Fodéba, had been encouraged to return from art studies in Paris to direct these initiatives. But there was resistance to the state's imposition of national styles even among prominent artists, as the career of Ibrahima Mané in Senegal illustrates. For Mané, artistic diversity, "specifically that of ethnic heritages [was necessary] for artistic nationalism to thrive."[160]

Senghor's social engineering with the arts went beyond weaving and tapestry, and he used public spaces throughout his twenty-year presidency to mold public opinion in accordance with négritude and African socialism. Senghor set up the Department of Arts and Letters in 1964, under his direct responsibility, with the mandate of encouraging Senegalese participation in international art exhibitions. This would become the Ministry of Cultural Affairs in the early 1970s. A Dakar School emerged between 1960 and 1980, as artists such as Papa Ibra Tall, André Seck (head of sculpture and ceramics), Chérif Tham, Amadou Ba, and others dominated artistic life at home and abroad. Artists who challenged translating

Senghor's philosophical vision into the arts were marginalized, and it was not until after 1980, a period of economic decline, that the autonomy of Senegalese artists grew. But even in the 1970s, several artists trained at the National Institute of the Arts in Senegal began to meet at the Terrace Café, close to the Theater National Daniel Sorano, to explore ways in which to "unblock" artists and to promote freedom of expression, practice, and interpretation.[161]

Perhaps the event that best put Senghor's Senegal on the world map in terms of the arts was his hosting of the First World Festival of Black [Negro] Arts in Dakar in April 1966 (FESMAN 66). Planning for the 1966 First World Festival of Black Arts, however, goes back to the 1950s and transcends the efforts of Senegal. Pan-Africanism from the 1930s flowed in two streams: an English-speaking world, with Britain and the United States as one axis; and a French-speaking world, with its hub in Paris that drew in colonial subjects from the Caribbean and Africa. Paris witnessed the flourishing of négritude in the 1930s with Césaire and Senghor as key exponents, and Senegalese writer Alioune Diop established the Pan-African journal *Présence Africaine* in Paris in 1947. The desire to create a cultural movement brought the francophone and anglophone worlds together at the First Congress of Black [Negro] Writers and Artists in Paris in 1956. Convened by *Présence Africaine*, this congress was inspired by the Bandung Conference of 1955, which sparked the desire for a cultural Bandung. In attendance were sixty-three delegates from twenty-four countries, including distinguished Black writers like Césaire, Senghor, Fanon, and Richard Wright. The 1956 Congress gave birth to the Society of African Culture, which organized a Second Congress in 1959 in Rome. The need to restore cultural authority and initiative to African artists and their publics preoccupied delegates at both congresses, and the Arts Commission formed at the Second Congress proposed—and resolved—to invite African governments to create a "Festival of Black [Negro] Arts" to take place periodically and simultaneously with the Congress of Black Writers and Artists and illustrate a chosen theme. This fascinating journey resulted in the Dakar Festival of 1966, a colloquium on the theme "The Significance of Art in the Life of the People and for the People." The chosen theme for the second festival was "Black Civilization and Education."[162] More than a decade elapsed after the Festival in Dakar before the sequel, the Second World Black and African Festival of Arts and Culture (FESTAC 77), was held in Lagos in 1977.

The Dakar Festival, occurring the year after the 1965 US Voting Rights Act and just two months after the military overthrow—with American Central Intelligence Agency assistance—of Nkrumah in February 1966, brought into sharp focus the ongoing fight against colonialism and neocolonialism in Africa and the unfinished struggle of the US civil rights movement. Sponsored by the government of Senegal, UNESCO, the American Society of African Culture, the US State Department, and the US Agency for International Development, the Dakar Festival was notable both for its impressive list of attendees and for those who boycotted it in political protest. African American participants included jazz composer and bandleader Duke Ellington, choreographer Alvin Ailey, gospel singer Marion Williams, writer Langston Hughes, filmmaker William Greaves, and anthropologist, choreographer, and dancer Katherine Dunham. Those who boycotted the festival included Harry Belafonte, James Baldwin, Ralph Ellison, Ossie Davis, and Sidney Poitier. In all, twenty-five hundred artists and twenty-five thousand guests attended the 1966 Dakar Festival.[163] With art exhibitions featuring works from across the continent; a book exhibition displaying the works of African and African American writers; musical concerts and traditional dance performances by newly independent nation-states, older independent African states like Ethiopia, and groups from the Americas; and an academic colloquium, the festival through this large-scale display of African and diasporic artistry and talent brought international attention to the need to cultivate spaces for Black artists to thrive on the continent. The festival made Dakar a cultural landmark in the world.

The focus of the Dakar Festival on culture and the complete absence of political discussion or mention of African liberation was striking. Alioune Diop, president of the 1966 Festival Association, decided to limit participation to nation-states. African liberation movements were not represented at the Dakar Festival, and African American delegations had to be approved by the US State Department. Senghor ensured that négritude dominated the theoretical discussion at the colloquium, unlike the open discussion that had characterized the international Black writers and artists congresses in 1956 and 1959. Both had witnessed critical reviews of négritude by writers such as Fanon and Wright.[164] Proceedings at Dakar in 1966 set the stage for the 1969 Pan-African Cultural Festival in Algiers.

In contradistinction to the Dakar Festival of 1966, the organizers at Algiers in 1969 allowed the participation of African liberation movements and gave official recognition to groups such as the Black Panther Party from the United States.[165] Even American Eldridge Cleaver, then living in exile in Cuba, was given festival "citizenship" and sanctuary in Algiers.[166] Several African leaders criticized négritude as a philosophy of elite Blacks in Paris seeking inclusion in French society, not a philosophy equipped to liberate Africans from colonial oppression. Nkrumah used the occasion of the inauguration of the Institute of African Studies at the University of Ghana in 1963 to take a swipe at négritude: "When I speak of the African genius, I mean something different from Négritude, something not apologetic, but dynamic. Négritude consists in a mere literary affection and style which piles up word upon word and image upon image with occasional reference to Africa and things African. I do not mean a vague brotherhood based on a criterion of color, or on the idea that Africans have no reasoning, but only a sensitivity."[167] Nkrumah and Senghor's political differences also played out in their approach to decolonization, with Nkrumah favoring armed struggle and a militant push and Senghor preferring a gradualist approach (see chap. 4). Senegal would be one of the early states to recognize the military government that overthrew Nkrumah. It is perhaps not surprising that Senghor made no reference to the Ghana coup in the 1966 Dakar Festival. Touré was another vehement critic of négritude, as we have seen above. Participants at the 1969 Algiers Pan-African Cultural Festival uniformly denounced négritude. Andrew Apter notes that the discursive deck was stacked against the négritudistes, who were reduced to observers and not full-fledged participants. Touré, though absent from the Algiers Festival, set the stage with a forty-minute recorded message dismissing négritude.[168] Other African leaders followed. The effect, in short, was a complete discrediting of Senghor's philosophy.

Bad blood from the Algiers Festival carried over to FESTAC 77, when Senghor as copatron invoked the cultural boundaries of Blackness to strongly demand that North African nations ("Arabs") be only given observer status at the Lagos Festival. This was clearly an outcome of the Algiers Festival and out of character with Senghor's own scholarly writing, including the lecture he gave at the University of Cairo on his receipt of an honorary doctorate in 1967.[169] The Nigerian government pushed back, insisting on the full participation of all members of the Organization of African Unity (OAU), liberation movements recognized by the OAU, and Black governments and communities outside of Africa. Importantly for our purpose of imagining the nation, Apter argues that what emerged within and between these cultural festivals from 1966 through 1977 was a "transnational form of black cultural citizenship."[170] Africa's new political leaders believed that they could forge distinctly African nation-states. Considering the strength of Pan-African networks in the 1930s, Africa's new nation-states could not be devoid of a Pan-African imaginary. Imagining the African nation-state thus proceeded at two levels: the level of the nation-state, creating a national identity out of disparate ethnic groups; and the level of the Pan-African state, uniting Africa and its diaspora. We see this endeavor most clearly at FESTAC 77, when Nigeria, flush with oil wealth, was able to sponsor FESTAC on a scale unimaginable in Dakar in 1966 and at the extraordinary cost of over US\$3 billion. Seventeen thousand artists from fifty-seven countries participated, with the United States sending a five hundred-member contingent. Nigeria held itself as beacon for the Africa-descended world.[171]

It was mentioned above that the inspiration for the 1956 Congress of Black Writers and Artists in Paris was the Bandung Conference of 1955. In an era of Cold War where the Soviet Union had outlined its "Two-Camp" slogan and the United States under Eisenhower had assumed an equally intransigent position (either with us or against us), Bandung suggested an alternative conception of political community.[172] For Samir Amin, Bandung was a critical moment that initiated a different pattern of globalization, one he termed "negotiated globalization," which had the potential to delink Africa and Asia from years of entanglement in a capitalist world forged through Western imperialism.[173] It was out of the 1956 and 1959 Congresses of Black Writers and Artists that the idea to create a Festival of Black Arts was birthed. These congresses were Pan-African gatherings, and it is not surprising that the arts festivals they generated were Pan-African in their conception. Christopher Lee's comments on the "spirit of Bandung" dovetail instructively with Apter's observation that emerging at the festivals of Black arts was a conception of Black cultural citizenship. Lee underscores the relevance of *communitas* in the political imagining that Bandung spawned. Distinct from *community*, which is rooted in geography, a physical reality that defines the boundaries of the nation-state, *communitas* is defined by "social relatedness," a "community of feeling." Equally important, "*communitas* is in movement, an interval of creative possibility and innovation, and therefore an active rite of passage thought to be necessary, yet equally perceived as destabilizing."[174]

Watching the William Greaves' documentary of the Dakar Festival in 1966 or reading articles by African Americans on the Dakar and Lagos festivals underlines the "community of feeling" that festivals engendered and the *communitas* that mobility or travel had made possible. Romi Crawford shows how African American participants of FESTAC 77 from Chicago connected the articulation of Black consciousness in Lagos with the local articulation of Black consciousness from Chicago's South Side.[175] The colloquium at FESTAC 77 involved papers by some seven hundred scholars. For Arthur Monroe, the most impressive paper was that delivered by the African American Ron Karenga, "who stressed the need for Africans to redefine the parameters of who and what is an African; and that any redefinition would have to include 'black communities outside of Africa' for they could not be ignored."[176] Dependent on external funding, including that of the United States and French governments, the Dakar Festival was unable to assume an independent position capable of forging a community of feeling—a Black cultural citizenship—that transcended the strictures of imperialism and capitalism. Algiers in 1969 and Lagos in 1977 made bolder steps in imagining Black cultural citizenship. But this enterprise of forging a Pan-African or Black cultural citizenship was vitiated by the economic—and therefore political—weakness of the African nation-states (Nigeria in 1977 was exceptional) and by the nature and politics of decolonization. These factors destabilized the rite of passage that could have birthed a meaningful and enduring Black cultural citizenship. Economic collapse in Africa in the 1980s torpedoed Pan-African dreams.

Conclusion

This chapter has examined how the first generation of independent African leaders deployed religion, culture, and the arts in the making of the African nation-state and in worldmaking broadly. The chapter has demonstrated that the process of nation-building and forging national identities was a contradictory one, and the state assumed the lead in cultural production. After years of state cultural production in Tanzania, Askew opines that what came to symbolize national identity comprised Kiswahili as the national language, the national flag, the national anthem, national holidays, national monuments, and a national dance troupe. And these symbols displayed their own contradictions: the national anthem was that of South Africa's ANC with the lyrics changed to Kiswahili, and the national dance troupe had received training in China and performed Chinese acrobatics.[177] We have seen how Foresters in Guinea reverted to their banned initiations and other rituals once Touré died and the succeeding government pronounced the socialist cultural revolution over.

What was the impact of these experiments at nation-building? Should we consider them failures? Nation-building is a never-ending process, not a completed process with clear identifiable effects. But even unfinished, the process has not been without impact. Askew points to how cultural production under Ujamaa did create a sense of Tanzanian identity that distinguished Tanzania from neighboring countries, which succumbed to civil wars and armed conflicts at one time or another—the Democratic Republic of the Congo, Rwanda, Burundi, Uganda, Kenya, and Mozambique.[178] Guinea escaped the civil wars that marred the lives of its neighbors in Liberia, Sierra Leone, and the Ivory Coast, and even Guinean Foresters cite their sense of national identity as what sets them apart from their ethnic counterparts in Liberia.[179] Senegal is one of the few African countries that has not experienced a military coup, and the elevation of culture and the arts under Senghor has made Senegal, and Dakar in particular, a cultural oasis in Africa to the present day. Ghana has exercised an influence in Africa out of proportion to its geographical size and population. That this is associated with Nkrumah's leadership in Africa's first independent Black African nation cannot be contested. It is not insignificant that his statue with an outstretched hand stands outside the headquarters of the African Union in Addis Ababa, as if signaling the way Africa should go. But the examples of Ghana, Guinea, Senegal, and Tanzania also underscore that all national projects—cultural, political, economic—implemented from above by the state as if the state exists in isolation are deeply flawed. I have discussed the exploration of a Black cultural citizenship embracing the African diaspora through the festivals of Black arts and culture in the 1960s and 1970s. This endeavor's failure was not disconnected from the failure of political and economic integration in Africa (chaps. 3 and 4).[180] The next chapter will examine how the first generation of independent leaders engaged development economics and modernization theory to build modern economies.

three

ECONOMIC IMAGINARIES
African Leaders and Development Economics

INTRODUCTION

The rise of development economics from colonial economics in the post–World War II period intersected with decolonization and the birth of new nation-states in Asia and Africa.[1] Holding itself as a new economics appropriate for economic growth in the Third World, for which orthodox economics from Western economies lacked tools, development economics stirred the economic imaginaries of African nationalists. Development economists and African nationalists shared the same dream of rapid economic development. The field's diagnosis of what ailed economies of the Third World and its prescription of foreign aid, industrialization, and state-centralized planning externalized the causes of Africa's poverty and meshed with nationalist understandings of underdevelopment. For African nationalists like Nkrumah, who sought to decolonize Ghana's economy, development economics promised a solution in its very critique of Western-grown classical economics. The Keynesian influence on development economics was apparent, based on John Maynard Keynes's appreciation of the necessity of state intervention and the market's inability to manage uncertainty during the Great Depression years of 1929 to 1932.[2]

Modernization theory shared intellectual space with development economics, though it arose in very different circumstances. It emerged in the 1950s and 1960s in the context of the Cold War, as America offered a path

113

to economic prosperity to Third World countries as an antidote to the allure of communism. The works of Walt Whitman Rostow best captured this American optimism: *The Process of Economic Growth* (1953) and *The Stages of Economic Growth: A Non-communist Manifesto* (1960).[3] Rostow assured the Third World that economic growth was within the capacity of every country with the right fundamentals in place and with American (Western) financial and technical support. This was not a critique of classical economics, like development economics, but an endorsement of classical economics' capacity to bring prosperity through capitalism to the Third World. Reflecting its impact on the developing world, Rostow's *Stages of Economic Growth* went through three printings in 1960, another three printings in 1961, and popularized the concept of "take-off into self-sustained growth." Industrialization rooted in highly productive commercialized agriculture was the objective, as in development economics, and modernization theory assumed that the prosperity of high mass-consumption society, made possible by Western science and technology, would spell the death of Marxism and communism.[4]

A product of American social sciences—economics, political science, sociology, and anthropology—modernization theory's primary task was to modernize traditional agricultural societies and position them on the path to sustained economic growth. The process, it was believed, would involve new social values in meritocratic societies, changes in productive structures and relations, and an effective centralized national state. Frederick Cooper observes that postwar critics in Europe wrestled with how to develop large-scale agricultural production in Africa but failed to theorize or conceptualize how to get there from the existing, dominant small family farms.[5] It is here that the American social sciences proved instrumental, conceptualizing in a dualistic approach how to move societies "from primitive, subsistence economies to technology-intensive, industrial economies; from subject to participant political cultures; from closed, ascriptive status systems to open, achievement-oriented systems; from extended to nuclear kinship units; from religious to secular ideologies; and so on."[6] American social scientists at the forefront of modernization theory included Marion Levy, Daniel Lerner, S. N. Eisenstadt, David Apter, and Samuel Huntington, several of whom had conducted studies on the Third World.

These competing understandings and prescriptions of development economics and modernization theory informed an exchange between Félix Houphouët-Boigny of the Ivory Coast and Nkrumah, during a visit of the latter to Abidjan in April 1957, that became enshrined as "the West African wager." The differences in their politics had already created a cooling of relations, and Houphouët-Boigny did not attend Ghana's independence celebrations on March 6, 1957. The following month, Nkrumah passed through Abidjan on April 5 on his way to Conakry to see Sékou Touré. Houphouët-Boigny gave Nkrumah a tour of Abidjan, a city that had undergone significant physical transformation since World War II through funds provided by the French government's Investment Fund for Economic and Social Development (FIDES). Through FIDES, roads, bridges, railways, canals, an airport, and Abidjan harbor had been constructed, mostly through grants made possible by the American Marshall Plan to rebuild Europe.[7] Houphouët-Boigny took Nkrumah to see the new Abidjan port, and they drove along the canal connecting the port to the sea. Perhaps Houphouët-Boigny had listened to and found irritating the independence speeches of Nkrumah the previous month. He asked Nkrumah, after showing Abidjan, how Africa could develop without the generous support of the metropole. Somehow the two made a wager there and then to see whose country would have the most social and economic development in ten years' time. The following day, the bet became public when their disagreement showed up in their speeches before the Ivorian Assembly.[8]

Ghana under Nkrumah and the Ivory Coast under Houphouët-Boigny have often been compared through the analytical lenses of socialism and capitalism. This comparison reveals as much as it conceals. In comparing public and private sector enterprises in the economy, Ralph Austen points out that the state was central in the economies of both irrespective of ideological discourse, the public sector accounting for 56 percent of enterprises in Ghana in 1966 and 50 percent in the Ivory Coast in 1973.[9] This chapter argues that the two regimes also differed in two important ways: their proposed relationship with the former colonial power; and their relationship to the two camps that had emerged in the context of the Cold War—the United States and the Soviet Union. The Ivory Coast valued a close relationship with the former colonial power and was explicit in its commitment to the United States. In contrast, Nkrumah privileged the decolonization of the Ghanaian economy and viewed the Ivory Coast's continued relations with France as neocolonialism. Nkrumah and other radical independence leaders like Touré and Nyerere insisted on their right to have amicable relations with both the United States and the Soviet Union. Not being forced into one camp expanded economic opportunities to deal with countries in the Eastern and Western Blocs, a practice they termed "positive neutralism." For Houphouët-Boigny, this was double-dipping, and he urged America to penalize such countries in its financial aid. Touré pointed out in exasperation, not incorrectly, that the United States maintained cultural relations with the Soviet Union, the United Kingdom continued its economic relations with the People's Republic of China, and France retained cultural and scientific relations with the Soviet Union. So "why do they want to deny newly independent countries the right to establish relations freely, in keeping with their interests and with their people's needs?"[10] Nkrumah saw in development economics the opportunity to decolonize Ghana's economy and redefine its relationship with the larger global economy. Indeed, Tony Killick views Ghana under Nkrumah as a case study of development economics in action.[11] Houphouët-Boigny turned to modernization theory and its affirmation of capitalism, his country becoming, for the United States, a showcase for the success of capitalism. These knowledge systems were underpinned by contrasting ideologies, and this chapter shows the power academic ideas exercised among the public (including politicians) and policy makers in the early decades of Africa's independence. Both development economics and modernization theory failed in Africa, as both were top-down approaches that privileged the vision and the agency of the state.[12]

The next section of the chapter examines the tenets of development economics. I compare the ideas of two leading economists in the early decades of independence on how to grow Africa's economies: development economist Lewis and economist of developing economies Thomas Peter Bauer.[13] Lewis served the Nkrumah government in a consulting capacity from 1952 and in 1957 became chief economic adviser to Nkrumah. Bauer was a critic of the policy prescriptions of development economics, though an ardent advocate of African development. The subsequent section offers Ghana as a case study of development economics in action. I then look at modernization theory and the Ivorian economic miracle. The concluding sections reflect on the failure of development economics, what role Africa played in its demise, and the afterlives of the field.

TENETS OF DEVELOPMENT ECONOMICS

The key objectives of independent African governments—with Ghana leading the way—were to reduce economic dependence on the West, industrialize, and increase the role of the state. Killick notes that these objectives interfaced with three policies advocated by economists engaged with the problems of underdeveloped countries (or the Third World): a "big push" to catalyze economic growth through major investment; the privileging of industrialization with emphasis on import-substitution industries as the driver of growth; and structural change in a not wholly open economy achieved through the instrumentality of the state.[14] The consensus about what constituted development economics present at the beginning of the 1960s no longer exists. Classical development economics was also referred to as high development theory. Let us briefly outline what its key tenets were.

Why Poverty?

Killick writes that "the poverty of nations is the special concern of development economics."[15] How did the rich countries get rich? Why does poverty persist in Africa and other parts of the underdeveloped world? How can poor countries become rich? Attempts to answer these questions in the 1950s created the core literature of development economics. Contributions came from several economists, notably Estonian international economist Ragnar Nurkse (1907–59), Ukrainian Jewish economist Harvey Leibenstein (1922–94), Swedish economist Gunnar Myrdal (1898–1987), Argentine economist Raúl Prebisch (1901–86), and American economist and politician Walt W. Rostow (1916–2003). This was a very international field, with major contributors in the West and East. Nurkse pointed to the intersection of low per capita income, low savings, and a small market in poor countries and how this created a vicious circle of poverty.[16] Leibenstein added a Malthusian dimension, underscoring how population growth in poor countries could reinforce the vicious circle highlighted by Nurkse.[17] Thus, it was important to build not only physical capital but also human capital. In his contributions on the international economy and underdeveloped regions, Myrdal noted how market forces tended to reinforce and perpetuate global inequalities.[18] This was an aspect Prebisch and Latin American economists had highlighted from the early 1950s, pointing to how the benefits from technological progress and international trade were unequally shared between industrialized "center" and nonindustrialized "periphery." Thus, the gap between the two widened over time and required a restructuring of international trade.[19] For Rostow and others from the modernization school, traditional societies tended to face a ceiling on level of productivity and output per head because they either did not utilize or could not maximize the potentialities that flow from modern science and technology.[20]

Breaking out of the traditional mold, becoming modern, was an important step toward economic development.

How to Grow Poor Countries

Investment was critical to growth in poor countries. Development economics argued that the importance of investment transcended the private value of the individual investment and gained a social value, adding to the larger attractiveness of an economy to further investment. Thus, every act of investment would expand the market and promote capital formation by others. The major thinkers in development economics—Paul Rosenstein-Rodan, Nurkse, Leibenstein, and Albert O. Hirschman—all subscribed to this position.[21] The role of global trade as a driver for growth in poor countries was not clear to early development economists, as most poor countries exported one or two primary commodities that had inflexible demand and were subject to market volatility. Singer and others also did not see foreign private investment as the solution, as this type of investment tended to go toward the production of primary products for export, often creating enclaves that did not have an impact on the larger economy.[22] In short, development economists cast doubt on traditional avenues of growing economies in mainstream economics. In the developing world, markets were small, factor markets were highly imperfect, information flows were poor. Lewis and Nurkse also pointed to a general dearth in entrepreneurial talent. Myrdal and others, like Seers and Prebisch, criticized neoclassical economics for being grounded in Western or industrial economies; evidently, there was need for a new economics for the underdeveloped world.[23] Most development economists argued for more aid to underdeveloped countries from industrialized countries and for encouraging or promoting domestic savings. Both avenues required the state playing an instrumental role through the establishment of relevant financial institutions and tax policies.

While development economists were not unanimous in terms of how to grow poor countries, by the 1960s there was some consensus around the following necessary steps.

- That economic development requires structural transformation, which tends to be discontinuous.

- That as per capita income reaches a certain critical level, growth will become self-sustaining.

- That a "big push" is required to break out of the poverty trap.

- That the single most important component of the big push is a massive increase in the ratio of investment to national income.

- That development involves industrialization, which must first meet the home market's need for manufactures, hence import-substitution industries.[24]

- That the foregoing points presuppose a central role for the state as the only conceivable institution capable of providing the big push.

Industrialization was seen as so central to development that Tibor Scitovsky simply referred to development theory as "the theory of industrialization."[25] United Nations reports tended to support the positions of development economists in the late 1940s and 1950s. A 1949 UN report underscored that primary products on the world market tended to fluctuate in price compared to manufactures, a trend documented from the 1870s. Countries dependent on primary commodities clearly needed to diversify toward manufacturing. A 1951 UN Report indicated the need for investment rates of at least 10 percent of national income in most underdeveloped countries to get on the path to growth.[26] That development economists like the Argentine Prebisch came to head the United Nations Economic Commission for Latin America (1950–63) provided a powerful platform for high development theory. Prebisch and the economists at the ECLA advocated import-substitution industries as the path to economic diversification and growth in the 1950s, to be pursued simultaneously with the expansion of primary production. These insights from Latin America were adopted by the African developmental state in the late 1950s and 1960s, which embarked on import-substitution industrialization (see chap. 4). Whereas neoclassical economics privileged the market, mainstream development economics was very interventionist.

GROWING NEWLY INDEPENDENT AFRICA—INSIGHTS FROM LEWIS AND BAUER

Through a body of works, Lewis outlined proposals for the economic development of former tropical colonies (or the underdeveloped world). While Bauer did not propose a vision for the development of the underdeveloped world, he was a consistent and eloquent critic of several ideas of development economists. And while Bauer was an outlier at the height of development economics, by the mid-1970s, as Killick puts it, he found "himself coming into fashion."[27] Juxtaposing Lewis and Bauer's ideas gives an instructive sense of the competing ideas for the development of Africa in the early years of independence. Both were connected to the London School of Economics (LSE), an influential institution in development economics. The Saint Lucian-born British citizen Lewis obtained a BSc in economics from LSE in 1937 and a PhD from the same institution in 1940. He taught on the faculty of LSE until 1948, when he joined the Economics Department at the University of Manchester. On Ghana's independence in 1957, Lewis was invited by Nkrumah to serve as his economic adviser. From Ghana, Lewis went on to serve as vice chancellor of the University of the West Indies and in 1963 was appointed professor of economics at Princeton University, where he stayed until his retirement in 1983. While at Princeton, Lewis left for a three-year period to serve as the first president of the Caribbean Development Bank. The Hungarian-born British citizen Bauer studied law in Budapest, then moved to Britain in 1934 to study economics at the University of Cambridge, graduating in 1937. Bauer spent most of his career on the faculty of LSE. Bauer brought together a collection of his essays published over the 1960s in a 1971 volume entitled *Dissent on Development: Studies and Debates in Development Economics*, and a revised edition appeared in 1976. Bauer's arguments and insights from these works were reinforced in his 1984 book *Reality and Rhetoric: Studies in the Economics of Development*. With two to three decades of Asian and African independence behind them, Bauer's criticisms of development economics gained more force in the 1980s.

Lewis and the Development of Tropical Countries

One of Lewis's early interventions in economic development was a small book called *The Principles of Economic Planning*, a study prepared on behalf of the Fabian Society and published in 1949.[28] Originally supposed to be a thirty-page pamphlet, it ballooned into a 120- page manuscript and was published as a book. The focus was Britain, its economic challenges in the summer of 1948, and ways in which government could encourage or persuade private enterprise to align itself with the government's economic agenda. Lewis's position on government planning was nuanced, and he saw himself as "both planner and anti-planner, according to the circumstances of the problem, and the major purpose of the book is to analyze the circumstances in which one means is preferable to the other."[29] Lewis affirmed that all societies plan, distinguishing between visible controls (the state) and invisible controls (the market). The point at issue is the right balance of visible and invisible controls. The purpose of planning is to make resources mobile. For Lewis, the state "can plan as much as it wants, but it should plan not by direction, but by the manipulation of the market."[30]

In appendix II of the book, Lewis shared his thoughts on planning in "backward countries." Several of the ideas explored in the appendix informed his later works and almost sketched a blueprint for development in newly independent African countries. He noted that planning required a competent, strong, and incorrupt administration: "Now a strong, competent and incorrupt administration is just what no backward country possesses, and in the absence of such an administration it is often much better that governments should be laisser-faire than that they should pretend to plan."[31] In contrast to the prevailing wisdom in development economics that industrialization was the path to growth for poor countries, Lewis assigned priority to agriculture, observing that an "agricultural revolution and industrial revolution always go together, the first releasing the labor which the second draws off the land."[32] Lewis worried about the small sizes of farms in underdeveloped countries and the importance of large-scale farming. In the historic past, the push to aggregate land for large-scale farming had always been accompanied by violence, and Lewis wondered in the current spirit of democracy how nonviolent ways of aggregating land could be pursued. He placed emphasis on food farming in particular: "In most backward countries, output is low partly because people are undernourished or malnourished. Investments which increase the output of food, such as irrigation, or reclaiming lands, or increasing manuring or livestock, are of greatest urgency."[33] With a solid agricultural base and a well-nourished population, productivity would increase and the local market expand. Then a country could think about industry, depending on the availability of industrial resources and a source of energy or power. Since industry depends on the size of market, and it would be absurd for every economically backward country to embark on industrialization, Lewis recommended "political and economic federation, which, by widening the market, increases specialization, and makes it possible to develop economically."[34]

Not only was Lewis a Fabian socialist, several of the first generation of independent African leaders were also Fabian socialists, including

Fig 3.1 William Arthur Lewis. Source: W. Arthur Lewis Papers, Seely G. Mudd Manuscript Library, Princeton University.

Nkrumah, Nyerere, Kenneth Kaunda, Senghor, and Jomo Kenyatta.[35] Indeed, Nkrumah first met Lewis at a 1946 conference in London organized by the Fabian Colonial Bureau.[36] In Lewis's appendix are several of the building blocks that informed Nkrumah's policy to develop the economy of Ghana: large-scale agriculture, the drive toward industrialization, the fixation with the Volta River Project and the Akosombo Hydroelectric Dam, and the passion for continental African government. And Nyerere's inspiration for villagization, which he pursued before the more concerted move to African socialism or Ujamaa, could have come from this same appendix, where Lewis observed that underpopulated backward countries might need to concentrate peoples in areas and begin development there because of limited resources.[37] In concluding the appendix, Lewis raised the rhetorical question of why backward countries embark on planning, considering the challenges involved and the tasks it imposes on government. He answered his own question: "Because their need is also so obviously greater. And it is also this that makes them carry it through in spite of error and incompetence."[38] Lewis was not cavalier about planning, as Bauer would make most development economists out to be.

In his 1949 article "Colonial Development," perhaps a fuller development of his thoughts from the appendix to *Principles of Economics Planning*, Lewis more centrally engaged the issues that would come to define development economics in the 1950s and 1960s. Why are colonies poor and their production so low? For Lewis, the answer was easy: "The colonies are so poor because they apply so little knowledge to production, use so little capital, and operate on so small a scale."[39] Scale was key. "The small scale on which everything is done is the third cause of backwardness. This applies universally. The political units are too small, and overburdened with trying to maintain a full service at a low level of efficiency. The peasant farms are too small. The factories, such as they are, are too small. The units in which the peasants' output is processed—the rice mills, sugar factories, cotton ginneries—are too small, and so on."[40] Lewis viewed private foreign investment and international lending as important avenues to scaling up. He noted that while private foreign investment was unpopular in the colonies, it was instrumental to early capital formation and the transfer of skills to indigenous people, both necessary to scaling up development. For Lewis, the training of entrepreneurship was one of the most important requirements in development. Lewis observed that the colonial government and foreign private investment had been remiss in these areas, especially in mining, where concessions had been granted on terms that did not reflect the spirit of trusteeship. "This is true, for example, of gold mining in the Gold Coast, of copper in Northern Rhodesia, of oil in Trinidad, and of diamonds in Sierra Leone. The principal examples are in mining, where responsibility towards the colonial interest has been least adequately safeguarded."[41] But this did not detract from the value of private foreign investment if properly directed. In the case of postwar Britain, which was itself cash-strapped, Lewis suggested that international lending could be an avenue for the colonies, especially from the International Bank for Reconstruction and Development (the World Bank).

Lewis returned to the primacy of agriculture. "The truth is that governments must prepare to invest capital in a big way in native agriculture," he opined. A prosperous agriculture, he continued, "cannot be based on a 3-acre unit with shifting cultivation."[42] He stressed the need for governments to find methods of demonstration and persuasion to pursue the aggregation of land in Africa, considering how peasants are attached to their lands. In the examples of enclosure in England and collectivization in Russia, converting small-scale agriculture into large-scale agriculture had not been peaceful. For Lewis, colonials overrated the importance of industrial development, assuming the developed state of advanced countries was due to industry. Lewis identified the real causes or drivers of development—knowledge, capital, and organization—and believed that these could be applied to agriculture to make countries prosperous, as seen in Australia and New Zealand. Lewis argued that industrialization is needed in two clear cases: where power and raw materials are found together and where labor is superabundant.[43] He made an impression on Africans studying or living in Britain even before the Convention People's Party (CPP) won the 1951 election in the Gold Coast and entered into a power-sharing arrangement with the British colonial government. Lewis was a natural choice when the young CPP government in late 1952 decided to recruit a leading economist to advise the Gold Coast on a plan to industrialize.

The CPP government through its minister of commerce and industry, Komla A. Gbedemah, invited Lewis in 1952, then a professor at the University of Manchester, to visit Ghana and advise on the development of secondary industries. Lewis visited Ghana in December 1952 and January 1953 and submitted his *Report on Industrialization and the Gold Coast* to the minister of commerce and industry in June 1953.[44] On the very first page of his report, Lewis set out the conditions for industrialization: "Industrialization starts usually in one of three ways: (1) with the processing for export of primary products (agricultural or mineral) which was previously exported in crude state; or (2) with manufacturing for an expanded home market; or (3) with the manufacture for export of light manufactures, often based in raw materials."[45] For Nkrumah, determined to make Ghana a showcase for industrialization in Africa, Lewis's rather strong recommendation to focus on agriculture, and on food farming in particular, must have been a disappointment. Lewis directed that "the most certain way to promote industrialization in the Gold Coast is to lay the foundation it requires by taking vigorous measures to raise food production per person engaged in agriculture. This is the surest way of producing the large and ever increasing demand for manufactures without which there can be little industrialization."[46] Lewis did not foreclose industrialization in the Gold Coast; he felt it was premature. It was first important to raise the standard of living, which could not be done in "an economy in which half the people are scratching the ground for food with a hoe."[47] Lewis advised Nkrumah's government to focus on expanding agricultural and public services. The latter would lower the cost of manufacturing and make the Gold Coast attractive to new industries. Lewis concluded on a very definitive note: "Very many years will have elapsed before it becomes economical for the government to transfer any large part of its resources toward industrialization and away from the more urgent priorities of agricultural productivity and public services."[48]

In his article "Colonial Development" (1949), Lewis stipulated the two conditions for industrialization in the underdeveloped world: labor must be superabundant, and power and raw materials must be found together. In the article that would establish his reputation as a leading thinker on the science of economics, Lewis turned to the issue of economic development in countries with unlimited supplies of labor, like Egypt and India.[49] In the underdeveloped world, Lewis observed, there tends to be low productivity in sectors such as agriculture, retail trade, and domestic service. A retail firm may have several messengers where just a couple would do. An affluent couple may have three domestic servants because of social expectations or obligations to kin. A family farm may have more hands than required for the small size of the farm. The price of labor in these economies is a subsistence wage. Economic growth can therefore be fueled by the low cost of abundant labor, as "shortage of labor is no limit to the creation of new sources of employment."[50] It is the rise of productivity in peasant agriculture that raises wages against the capitalist. Lewis emphasized that his comments applied to unskilled labor only. But for an industrial revolution to occur requires significant increases in saving among productive capitalist classes, who finance capital formation out of profits and credit. This is where backward countries are challenged, for their dominant classes—landlords, traders, moneylenders, soldiers, priests—do not think this way, making it necessary, sometimes, for the state to become capitalist. But once investment in manufacturing takes off, the existence of surplus labor gives manufacturing a head start in the form of low wages. By the mid-1950s, Lewis had a body of work that spoke directly to the challenges and opportunities of growing underdeveloped countries.

Bauer: A Voice of Dissent

In his 1971 collection of essays *Dissent on Development*, revised and republished in 1976, Bauer took issue with several of the key tenets of development economics. Bauer disagreed with the hypothesis that a vicious circle of poverty prevailed in underdeveloped countries; that their terms of trade tended to decline persistently because they were exporters of primary commodities; and that central planning and foreign aid were indispensable for their growth. He took issue with the allegation that rich countries had caused the poverty or underdevelopment of the less developed world, as Walter Rodney would famously put it in 1972, an ideological position that would not have endeared him to that first generation of African nationalists.[51] For Bauer, too much had been made of the importance of monetary investment to economic development.[52]

Bauer's arguments were not without merit, and time has lent empirical substance to several of his positions. Bauer critiqued the Malthusian dimension of the circle of poverty hypothesis, arguing that there was no proof that population growth was a major independent cause of poverty and ruling as invalid the positioning of birth control as indispensable to economic growth and prosperity.[53] For Bauer, the very premise that the vicious circle of poverty required major sacrifices domestically and large-scale foreign aid was erroneous. He pointed to the economic growth of several poor countries since the late nineteenth century, citing the example of cocoa in the Gold Coast and rubber from Malaya. By 1911, the Gold Coast had become the world's leading exporter of cocoa, a veritable peasant revolution with enormous implications for peasant accumulation and quality of life. Yet the Gold Coast had exported no cocoa in 1890, and Malaya no rubber in 1900. By the early 1960s, the Gold Coast exported four hundred thousand tons of cocoa per year and Malaya eight hundred thousand tons of rubber in 1963. Bauer argued that "the level of income in underdeveloped countries is by definition low, but this is still compatible with advance, indeed even rapid advance, if that advance has begun only comparatively recently and has started from a very low level. This is the position in many underdeveloped countries."[54] Bauer opined that the attractiveness of the vicious circle of poverty hypothesis for both its advocates and the governments of underdeveloped countries lay in its rationalization of centralized planning and large inflows of foreign aid. All developed countries started off poor; poverty did not disqualify a country from embarking on economic development.

Foreign aid politicizes economic life and does not represent a simple inflow of funds or resources. Bauer argued that foreign aid "is plainly not indispensable to economic progress, and is indeed likely to obstruct it."[55] He continued that foreign aid is a "system of gifts" not targeted at or designed for development. For the recipient of foreign aid, "if the mainsprings of development are present, material progress will occur even without foreign aid. If they are absent, it will not even occur with aid."[56] Moreover, foreign aid distorts priorities. In underdeveloped nations, the receipt of aid has led to the neglect of agriculture, as governments assume external assistance will come "to their rescue in the event of a serious food shortage, and consequently feel freer to direct their resources to industrial and to prestige projects."[57]

In regards to centralized or comprehensive planning, which had been twined with foreign aid, Bauer was insistent that planning is "much more likely to obstruct economic progress than to advance it."[58] Planning only enhances the authoritarian tendencies of underdeveloped governments; Bauer was caustic in his observation that the new governments of these countries "seem anxious to plan and unable to govern."[59] And for those who viewed foreign aid and planning as essential to government capacity to create physical infrastructure in new nation-states, and infrastructure as a prerequisite to economic development, Bauer was keen to point out, citing historical examples, that "infrastructure develops in the course of economic progress, not ahead of it."[60]

As noted above, Bauer's arguments gained even more force in *Reality and Rhetoric*, published in 1984. He noted how centralized planning and the entry of the state into economic activity conferred greater power on political rulers, especially from the 1950s. This made politics a zero-sum game and the state the most important actor in the economy. The state became the prize to capture and "thereby diverted people's energies and resources from economic activity to the political arena."[61] With hindsight, Bauer commented on how foreign aid had brought into existence the Third

World, also called the South, creating a North-South divide in the global political economy. "The one common characteristic of the Third World is not poverty, stagnation, brotherhood or skin color. It is the receipt of foreign aid. The concept of the Third World and the policy of official aid are inseparable."[62] On key issues in development, such as emphasis on peasant agriculture, ambivalence about state planning, and value placed on entrepreneurship and management skills learned through apprenticeship in foreign direct investment, Lewis and Bauer cannot be seen as diametrically opposed. Lewis would not have disagreed with Bauer's position that "economic achievement and progress depend largely on human aptitudes and attitudes, on social and political institutions and arrangements which derive from these, on historical experience, and to a lesser extent on external contacts, market opportunities and on natural resources."[63] This conviction made Bauer reluctant to advance a general theory of economic development. In this, he was thinking like a historian.[64] But there were notable differences even where both endorsed the importance of peasant agriculture. Bauer, based on the entrepreneurship and economic astuteness of West African peasants like the cocoa farmers of colonial Ghana and Nigeria, believed that laissez-faire policies would propel economic growth with actors such as peasant cocoa farmers in the forefront.[65] Lewis, as senior economic adviser to Nkrumah, would endorse the government's appropriation of a significant part of the earnings of Ghana's cocoa farmers through the marketing board to fund the government's development projects.[66]

It is in political sentiment and ideological positioning that Lewis and Bauer were poles apart. A product of the colonies and Americas shaped by slavery and its legacy, Lewis did not view the West as a hero in his understanding of the global political economy. In this, Lewis was ideologically close to the African nationalists of his generation. For Bauer, Western influence was instrumental to positive economic change in the underdeveloped world, making the position that developed countries had contributed to the underdevelopment of poor countries untenable. Indeed, Bauer was an apologist for colonialism in Africa. "And whatever its objectionable features, nineteenth- and twentieth-century colonialism, which is what is meant by colonialism in this context, was of great benefit to the peoples of these countries. For instance, Ethiopia and Liberia, which were not colonies, are among the most backward countries in Africa."[67] Bauer even rose to the defense of the West concerning the Atlantic slave trade. "What about the Atlantic slave trade? Most Western countries were not involved in it at all. Asian countries, the largest foreign aid recipients, were unaffected. And horrible and destructive as this trade was, it was not a cause of African backwardness. The region most affected, namely West Africa, had by 1914 become the most advanced part of Black Africa."[68] Bauer's understanding of the West's relations with Africa was very problematic, and he was historically inaccurate in his assertion that Asian countries were unaffected by the European slave trade.[69]

Statements like the above and the following in reference to the habitus of Africans and Asians would not have endeared Bauer to African nationalists like Nkrumah or to other development economists: "Examples of significant attitudes, beliefs and modes of conduct unfavorable to material progress include lack of interest in material advance, combined with resignation in the face of poverty; lack of initiative, self-reliance and a sense of personal responsibility for the economic fortune of oneself and one's family; high leisure preference, together with a lassitude often found in tropical climate; relatively high prestige of passive or contemplative life compared to active life; the prestige of mysticism and of renunciation of the world compared to acquisition and achievement."[70] While Bauer saw these traits as more pronounced in Asians, he believed that Africans also held strong beliefs and attitudes not conducive to material progress. With views like these, it is not surprising that Bauer was on the margins of the discipline during the heydays of development economics. Neither is it surprising that he was not among the list of development economists in demand by the new African nationalist leaders.

Ghana as a Case Study for Development Economics in Action

The title of this section of the chapter derives from Tony Killick's book *Development Economics in Action: A Study of Development Economic Policies in Ghana* (1978). In the preface to the book, Killick makes an important assertion: "Many of the things which Nkrumah and his successors tried to do were rather accurate reflections of policies which economics had been urging upon the third world for some time. The Ghanaian experience thus represents a case study in applied development economics and the general conclusion which has been reached will add to the literature on economic development."[71] He observes that the influence of development economics and the changing concerns of the field continued under successive governments to Nkrumah's, as key civil servants, such as J. H. Mensah and E. N. Omaboe, trained in development economics or familiar with the field and its readings, served as advisers.[72] For the National Liberation Council (NLC) that overthrew the Nkrumah government in February 1966, Omaboe, Nkrumah's government statistician, became the major shaper of economic policies.[73] With the return to civilian rule and the Progress Party government in 1969 under K. A. Busia, Mensah, who had served as executive secretary to the National Planning Commission under Nkrumah, emerged as the government's chief economic adviser, combining portfolios of finance and planning.[74] The military coup that ended the Progress Party government in 1972 also brought back into play some key individuals who had been influential in Nkrumah's government—"economic policies had come full circle."[75] Tignor, from his deep familiarity with Lewis's private papers and other memoranda and private correspondence to which Killick did not have access, makes an important correction to Killick's observation above on development economics in Ghana. Development economists such as Lewis did make policy prescriptions, but the Ghanaian government under Nkrumah had its own political priorities and often set aside the policies recommended by Lewis and other development economists.[76] The commitment to development economics was at best partial.

Before we turn to development economics in action in Ghana, a brief discussion on how the appeal of development economics lay in its intersection with nationalism, modernization theory, and socialism/Marxism is in order. This confluence of ideas reinforced the attraction of development economics. Lewis, for example, was very explicit in his anticolonialism, and Myrdal related economic backwardness to colonialism. Bauer was short-sighted in his dismissal of this position, noting that "it is emotionally comforting to be told that external factors explain the failure to achieve specified goals, including material prosperity."[77] The "big push" was particularly attractive to nationalist leaders, and the stress on import-substitution industries addressed the consumption needs of growing, vocal urban populations, who constituted a major market for these products. Across the newly independent tropical countries, development economics was in high demand, as Killick notes: "In the newly emerging nations of the third world, politics and economics marched together. The profession enjoyed unaccustomed popularity and the leading figures in development economics were in great demand as advisers to the governments of underdeveloped countries."[78] Ginelli notes how West Africa from the 1950s became an important region for the exhibition of US postcolonial planning expertise in the spirit of modernization theory. Foundations such as Rockefeller and Ford, the Marshall and Rhodes Scholars Programs, and the United States Agency for International Development (USAID) from 1961 recruited American and African researchers to work on local urban and regional planning schemes drawing on Western technology and theories.[79]

As early as 1951, the Rockefeller Foundation appeared before the United States Senate to urge the US government to consider a comprehensive development and foreign policy plan for emerging Third World nations.[80] A few months later, the Center for International Studies (CIS) at the Massachusetts Institute of Technology (MIT) was founded by Max F. Millikan, former assistant director of the Central Intelligence Agency (CIA). Evidently, the initial seed grant for the CIS came from the CIA, a fact undisclosed at the time; an additional grant of $875,000 came from the Ford Foundation.[81] In this instance, we see the beginning of a decades-long relationship between US government foreign policy interests, the spread of technical and theoretical knowledge through major research universities, and the rise of development programs directed and funded by private family foundations. By 1952, Rostow had joined Millikan in the Department of Economics at MIT and begun to lay the foundations for modernization theory, drafting papers on stages of economic growth and the purpose of foreign aid.[82]

That modernization theory held out the prospect of development irrespective of how small or underresourced a country might be was particularly appealing. Kevin Baker captures this spirit of expectation well: "Unlike other, earlier theories of economic development, modernization theory denied the relevance of racial or geographic barriers to capitalist development. In the work of Rostow and his colleagues, some countries may be 'ahead' of others in terms of economic 'progress,' but there were not intractable barriers that would prevent a nation like Nigeria from becoming an urbanized, industrial, and commercial society like the US."[83] It is with this sense of optimism that the Malawian political prisoner Dunduzu Chisiza taught himself development economics while in detention. Geoffrey Traugh writes of Chisiza's learning process: "Chisiza was a student of the American modernization theorist [sic], Walt Rostow, though not in the conventional sense. He was a self-taught economist who started his studies in earnest in a Rhodesian detention camp during the 1959 Emergency."[84]

Chisiza encountered Rostow's work in the pages of the *Economist*, which had published Rostow's Cambridge lectures based on his acclaimed book *The Stages of Economic Growth*. Traugh reflects on how Chisiza sought to extend the parameters of Rostow's conceptualization of modernization, embracing the possibility of an agrarian revolution as the driver of modernization in place of Rostow's privileging of industrialization.[85]

Chisiza was in good company; USAID from the 1950s had become interested in rural transformation through agricultural modernization and sought to demonstrate American competence in this area in the newly independent African nations. Nigeria, Africa's largest nation, was an attractive case study for USAID, as Kevin Baker has documented. "From an early stage, American officials and development experts saw Nigeria as providing the setting for a 'significant historical demonstration' of the quality of American technical assistance. Wolfgang Stolper, a Harvard PhD and former student of Joseph Schumpeter, played an important role in defining economic policy of the newly independent nation. With Ford Foundation backing, the economist was dispatched to Nigeria to head its Economic Planning Unit."[86] In 1962, Malawi, then Nyasaland, hosted the first international symposium on African Economic Development to be held on the continent.[87] The symposium brought twenty-three experts from America, western Europe, and India and over fifty African experts and observers to deliberate economic development in Africa on topics ranging from agriculture and industry to fiscal and monetary policies and planning. How the symposium ended up in Malawi is intriguing. In the closing address, the prime minister for Nyasaland, Dr. Hastings Kamuzu Banda, expressed delight at hosting the symposium and remarked that it was "Dunduzu Chisiza [who] told me that economists in America were thinking of holding a symposium somewhere in Africa, and that he wanted my consent and blessing to hold it here. . . ."[88]

Chisiza's paper, which opened the conference, was entitled "The Temper, Aspirations, and Problems of Contemporary Africa." In it he commented on the rise of "African socialism," querying what exactly African leaders meant by this term: "Are we talking about guided capitalism and the parody of communism? Or are we trying to draw inspiration from *Das Kapital* to enable us evolve an [sic] 'African Economic Ideology'?"[89] Few African intellectuals and politicians in the 1950s and 1960s overtly described themselves as capitalists—not with the knowledge of the impact of over three centuries of European export slave trade and colonial rule. It is naive to dismiss this intellectual reality. Bauer mentioned that Marxist ideas in the underdeveloped world were largely transmitted through Lenin's small book *Imperialism: The Highest Stage of Capitalism*. Marxism-Leninism held, inter alia, that the developed world's exploitation of the underdeveloped world is a major cause of the poverty of these countries.[90] Killick notes that Marxism was principally concerned with inequality, just as an important premise of development economics was the desire to create a more egalitarian world.[91] Stanford-trained Ghanaian economist J. H. Mensah, a key figure in economic planning in Ghana in the 1960s and the 1970s, reflected in a much later interview that "at that stage . . . any self-respecting anti-colonialist would be a critic of the laissez-faire economics policies taken up by the political right, and later by the World Bank and the IMF."[92] Killick observes that in the early 1960s, Nkrumah talked of socialism "as if it was simply a superior way of decolonizing and modernizing the country."[93] The confluence of African nationalism, development economics, modernization theory, and Marxism made the 1950s and 1960s an intellectually exciting and promising era.

Lewis as a key thinker in development economics had the opportunity to shape Ghana's economic policies in the 1950s and 1960s at three distinct stages. The first was in late 1952 and 1953, when he was invited by the young Nkrumah government to submit a plan for industrialization. The second was in 1957, when he was invited by Nkrumah on independence to be chief economic adviser and architect of the 1959–63 five-year development plan. The third was in 1963, after Lewis's departure from Ghana in late 1958, when he returned with a group of international economic experts to discuss Ghana's Seven-Year Development Plan (1964–70), meant to transform the economy into a socialist one. Lewis was also an important consultant in the CPP government's Volta River Project.[94] In terms of Lewis's *Report on Industrialization and the Gold Coast* (1953), we have noted how Lewis was emphatic that Ghana focus on agriculture, in particular on food farming, and on provision of public services rather than industrialization—it would be several years before changed conditions would warrant the transfer of resources to industrialization. In Nkrumah's drive for an industrialized Ghana, Lewis recommended only a small range of industries, such as processed timber, and a few import-substitution industries in areas such as cement and breweries. Douglas Rimmer notes how Nkrumah's CPP government ignored

Lewis's advice and set up an Industrial Development Corporation in the 1950s to lead the drive for industrialization—with disastrous results.[95]

By the time Lewis assumed his formal position as economic adviser to Nkrumah in 1957, the cocoa boom that had underpinned the Gold Coast's prosperity from the early 1950s had begun to wane, with major implications for proposals to use cocoa surpluses to diversify the Gold Coast's economy. Colonial officials became pessimistic about the financial capacity of the Gold Coast to continue its economic development projects, particularly the Volta River Project, which was supposed to produce the electricity needed for Nkrumah's industrialization vision. Lewis was aware of the changing financial circumstances of the Gold Coast but was eager to assist the first independent sub-Saharan country in its developmental agenda. The Gold Coast had come to the end of a ten-year development plan (1947–56) the British colonial government had introduced in 1947. Lewis was tasked with designing the Gold Coast's first independent economic development plan.[96] In a spirit of caution that would prove strategically wise, Lewis took a two-year leave of absence from his academic position at the University of Manchester and proposed that Nkrumah request his services for a two-year period through the United Nations.[97] Lewis declined Nkrumah's offer of a chair in economics position at the University of Ghana.[98] The expectations of Lewis were high: for Nkrumah and the CPP, he would help build an economy independent of the former colonial power; for the British, the Americans, and institutions like the World Bank and the International Monetary Fund (IMF), Lewis was expected to exercise "a moderating influence [on Nkrumah], pro-capitalist and pro-Western."[99]

A key point of contention was the relative importance Nkrumah and Lewis attached to electricity as a driver of industrialization and hence the Volta River Project. For Nkrumah, it was the centerpiece of his developmental vision, what Stephan Miescher describes as "Nkrumah's baby."[100] For Lewis, the Volta River Project was "of only marginal significance" and was not to derail more important projects that would position the country for economic growth based on its reserves of some £200 million sterling.[101] An exchange between Lewis and Nkrumah in late October and early November 1958 indicated clearly that Nkrumah had drawn a line in the sand where the Volta River Project was concerned. Lewis wrote to Nkrumah on October 31, 1958, following a conversation with Eric Taylor that gave Lewis the impression Taylor had been sent by Nkrumah to "persuade me that cheap power is the secret of industrialization."[102] Lewis was not convinced and wrote to Nkrumah to explain why. Nkrumah returned Lewis's note, his reply handwritten at the bottom and dated November 1, 1958. "I did not ask Taylor to persuade you about any cheap power. My mind is fully made up, and irrespective of anybody's advice to the contrary I am determined to see that at all cost the Dams at Bui and Ajena are built within the shortest possible time."[103] Clearly, relations between Nkrumah and his economic adviser had become frayed by late 1958.

Lewis wanted the five-year development plan from 1958 to work within the parameters of Ghana's financial resources and to prioritize economic projects that would bring immediate revenue and improve the government's financial position. He estimated that the cost of the plan should not exceed £70–£80 million over the five-year period. But the politicians had a mind of their own. By the time the ministers' departmental projects had been incorporated into the plan, the price tag had ballooned to £185 million. More problematic for Lewis was Nkrumah's unwillingness to back him against the impositions of the ministers. In addition, the ministers' requisitions targeted projects that brought them political capital but were not economically productive. For Lewis, it was always important to put the horse of economic growth before the cart of welfare. Rimmer has accurately observed that Ghana, like several other African countries, has been preoccupied with equity issues, with dividing the small national cake equitably instead of just growing the cake—or keeping a single-minded focus on economic growth.[104] Of the total budget for the five-year development plan, only 12 percent was allocated for manufacturing and 8 percent for agriculture, with public and social services taking the lion's share.

Correspondence between Nkrumah and Lewis in December 1958 documents that tensions reached a crisis that month, precipitating Lewis's resignation. The exchange pitted the primacy of politics against economics and signaled to Lewis the wisdom in a dignified retreat. From Lewis's analysis of the second five-year development plan in his private papers, there were five priorities: agriculture and industry, electric power, secondary education, rural water supplies, and public health. Electricity could be supplied by generation plants and not necessarily by tapping a Volta Dam grid. In his final analysis, "agriculture and industry have priority beyond all others because economic development is needed to support everything else. From this point of view the First Development Plan must be written off as a failure. We spent £93 million on development between 1950 and 1957, but in this period the product of manufacturing, agriculture and mining taken together increased only by 13 per cent."[105] Lewis continued: "It would obviously be an error merely to repeat the pattern of the First Development Plan. The major objective of the next five years must be a substantial increase in agricultural and industrial output."[106] Unwilling to be mere window dressing for Nkrumah's political agenda, Lewis wrote to Nkrumah on December 18, 1958, to inform the prime minister that he had been offered a position at the United Nations to assist with the creation of a development fund. He would only consider staying in Ghana as Nkrumah's economic adviser under specific conditions. He would attend cabinet meetings whenever economics issues were to be deliberated; the CPP government was not to invest more than £25 million of the government's money in the Volta River Project; and the first phase of the five-year plan was not to exceed £120 million. Lewis's statements like the following on the prestige projects inserted in the budget by the government were bound to irritate Nkrumah: "In the first place I find it immoral to tax the poor people all over the country and use the proceeds mainly to beautify Accra, when 80 per cent of our people still live in towns and villages with no water, or other elementary amenities. And secondly, wasteful expenditure on prestige objects seems to me the worst form of inferiority complex."[107] Nkrumah's response on December 19, 1958, was polite but firm. Nkrumah understood that Lewis had an international reputation, that Lewis had staked his reputation by coming to Ghana as economic adviser, and that his political decisions could undermine Lewis's international stature:

> I appreciate that I cannot expect you to risk this reputation by political decisions which I consider I must make. The advice you have given me, sound though it may be, is essentially from the economic point of view and I have told you on many occasions that I cannot always follow this advice as I am a politician and must gamble on the future. . . . I feel that [it] would be best for you to accept this appointment so that we may part at this stage in a friendly manner and not run the risk of parting on an issue which might be embarrassing to either or both of us.[108]

Lewis resigned his position at the end of 1958, fourteen months into his two-year contract.

Matters got worse. By the time the CPP finished the budget for the five-year plan, which was published in early 1959, the total price was £343 million.

Of this total, £103 million was assigned to the Volta River Project, aside from other prestige projects. Clearly, the government had decided to ignore the advice of its expert economist. This was not a failure of economic policy; it was a failure arising from lack of appreciation of how politics would shape economic policy in the developing world.

Lewis returned to Ghana in 1963 as one of a number of economic experts invited by the Nkrumah government to review its seven-year development plan set to commence in 1964. Ghana had begun to move toward a state-led economy in 1960, the year the country became a republic, vesting more power on the president. The seven-year plan was to effectively move the country toward socialism. In the foreword to the published plan in 1964, Nkrumah outlined the vision: "It is our hope that by the end of the plan in December, 1970—which would coincide with the tenth anniversary of the Republic—firm foundations will have been laid for the complete transformation of Ghana into a strong, industrialized, socialist economy and society."[109] Lewis's five-year plan had been suspended in January 1962. In charge of the planning process was a National Planning Commission established in 1962 with J. H. Mensah as executive secretary. Given a leading role in crafting the seven-year development plan was the Hungarian economist József Bognár. Eastern European countries in the Soviet Bloc like Hungary sought to decrease their dependence on the Soviet Union by developing trade relations with African and Asian postcolonies and earning hard currencies, as these postcolonies used the currencies of their former colonial masters. A professor at the Karl Marx Economic University from 1956, Bognár served as mayor of Budapest from 1947 to 1949 and then as minister of domestic and foreign trade in the communist government in Hungary from 1949 to 1956. He was also the author of a small book entitled *Planned Economy in Hungary* (1959). Nkrumah was sufficiently impressed by Hungary's economic achievements and Bognár's credentials during his visit to Budapest in July 1961 to invite Bognár to come to Ghana and serve as chief adviser to Ghana's seven-year plan.[110] Ginelli describes Ghana's seven-year plan as a transnational product with input from Eastern and Western development economists. For advice on tax matters, Nkrumah turned to Hungarian-born British economist Nicholas Kaldor. The seven-year plan received input from Polish economist Czeslaw Bobrowski of the Planning Commission of Poland and other Polish development economists.[111] Tignor notes that Bognár was edged out after drafting the preliminary statement;

the seven-year plan became the product of one individual, Mensah, with direction from Nkrumah and the newly appointed governor of the Bank of Ghana, the socialist Kwasi Amoako Atta.[112] The World Bank took a keen interest in the plan, and its representatives in Accra followed its development closely. Again, the plan exceeded the level of government expenditure recommended by the World Bank.

In March 1963, an international conference to review the seven-year plan took place in Accra, attended by what Tignor describes as a "who's who of development economics":

"Nkrumah delivered the opening remarks, which were followed by a critique of the plan design, undertaken by N. C. Bos, Czeslow Bobrowski, and Osvaldo Sunkel. Lewis, Hirschman, and Weekes reviewed the economic policy on which the plan was based while Kaldor and [Leon] Baranksi [World Bank representative in Accra] reported on the financing of the plan. K. N. Raj and P. Vuscovic submitted a document on planning in general, and Dudley Seers, Sunkel, Carney, and P. H. Ady considered whether the plan would help to expand inter-African trading. Not a single aspect of the plan escaped critical review."[113] Killick, who was present at the conference, opines that "in short, constructive professional advice was offered but very little by way of fundamental criticism of the strategy. Nkrumah's planners could reasonably go away from that meeting in the belief that the principal ideas of the plan had found general acceptance."[114] Tignor disagrees with the assessment that the international development economists present generally approved of the plan, having access to the correspondence and unpublished memoranda of participants like Lewis and Baranski.[115] The plan with its budget of £840 million received serious criticism from the international experts assembled, and the conference ended with the expectation that Ghanaian technocrats such as Mensah and Omaboe would respond to criticisms and revise the investment figure. Considering Nkrumah's prickliness about Ghana's sovereign status, it is unlikely that any external criticism was harsh. When the final version came out, Mensah had revised the investment figure upward to £1 billion.[116]

Perhaps all this was moot anyway. Though published in 1963, the plan was never implemented because of lack of resources resulting from the continued decline in world prices for cocoa, Ghana's cash cow, and the unwillingness of governments and foreign banks to lend to Ghana with its socialist rhetoric. All the government's development plans from the 1950s had been funded by cocoa, and the stabilization fund created by the Cocoa Marketing Board to cushion cocoa farmers from fluctuations in world prices had been increasingly directed to the government's development projects.[117] Nkrumah was overthrown in a military coup in February 1966. The biggest shortcoming in development economics was not the soundness of its prescriptions, but the assumption that economics could be separated from politics or that politics could ride shotgun to economics, "that politicians, properly instructed by economic advisers, could become benevolent promoters of economic progress."[118] It is fair to end this section of development economics in Nkrumah's Ghana with Killick's own nuanced assessment:

> This suggests what indeed is the chief contention of this study, that what Nkrumah was trying to do in the sixties was in consonance with the ideas of most development economists. The view of the economists themselves had some influence on Nkrumah's decisions but what was decisive was the congruence that existed at the beginning of the sixties between the ideas of mainstream development economists, Marxists and nationalists. The mutual reinforcement of economics, socialism and nationalism gave this set of ideas an intense attraction to statesmen such as Nkrumah. The claim, then, is not that Nkrumah adopted his strategy primarily because it was being advocated in the development literature, but rather that the prescriptions of the literature coincided in most essentials with the natural predilections of a leader of Nkrumah's background and persuasions.[119]

But the negative outcome of Nkrumah's big push is not in doubt, as we see in the failed attempt at industrialization "socialist-style" (see chap. 4) and the declining fortunes of the cocoa sector (see chap. 5). Rimmer concludes that Nkrumah's economic policies "saddled the country with liabilities in the form of debts and inappropriate productive capacity . . . that were to drag down [Ghana's] economic performance for the next twenty years."[120]

Modernization Theory and the Ivorian Miracle

Reflections on what has been described as the Ivorian economic miracle in the Ivory Coast—almost three decades of sustained economic growth between the early 1950s and the late 1970s—are instructive in the discussion on development economics, modernization theory, and African nationalism. The Ivory Coast's economy built on policies from late colonial rule that shaped its early decades of independence and its economic prosperity. In the 1950s, before independence, French policies privileged agriculture, ensured a cheap agricultural labor force, and facilitated labor migration from the poorer countries of Mali and Burkina Faso. Unlike Ghana or Guinea, where new nationalist leaders envisaged an independent country radically different from the colonial one, Félix Houphouët-Boigny believed in continuing a strong relation with France in the postcolonial period, viewed agriculture—and agriculture dominated by African planters and peasants—as the driver of economic change, and privileged nation-building over Pan-African aspirations. Gross national product (GNP) in the Ivory Coast between 1960 and 1975, the first fifteen years of independence, grew by 7.4 percent per annum. Peter Marden observes that "the major dynamic behind this growth has been the substantial exports of agricultural products. Between 1960 and 1975, total exports grew almost on a parallel with GNP at 7.2 per cent per annum."[121]

French influence in early independent Ivory Coast remained so heavy that visitors commented on how little had changed, including street names. But the Ivory Coast was itself undergoing important change under the influence of American modernization theory. The French desperately sought to act as a buffer and retain hegemony in what had become their most prosperous West African possession by the early 1950s, while Félix Houphouët-Boigny actively courted American technical assistance.[122] Here was Chisiza's model of agriculture-led modernization envisioned for Malawi rather than the usual privileging of industry in modernization theory and development economics; here was a demonstration of Bauer's arguments about how agriculture had produced prosperous economies in the West and could do so in a newly independent Africa, his assertion that colonialism and Western influence was a positive economic good. But the Ivorian miracle did unravel. It became a mirage, in Abou Bamba's words, and its modernization path failed. The timing of its demise is intriguing: it overlapped with the decline in development economics and modernization theory, the latter a casualty of the Vietnam war. But it was also clear that when it came to Africa, the United States lacked the accumulated knowledge of a former colonial power like France, and the absence of epistemic depth caused major lapses in project implementation, to the discredit of American companies. Woronoff, writing in 1972, prematurely concluded that Houphouët-Boigny had won his wager with Nkrumah.[123] But Amin already in the mid-1960s predicted that the Ivorian miracle would unravel, unsustainable because it showed all the characteristics of structural underdevelopment: dependence on primary production and exports, agriculture of an evolved colonial type, heavy dependence on foreign resources, an extroverted economy, and the absence of real industrialization.[124]

Houphouët-Boigny believed in capitalism. In the era of the Cold War, he was explicit in his support of America, contrasting with African leaders who flirted with socialism and communism.[125] Houphouët-Boigny was also appreciative of how French technical knowledge and investment had transformed his country, once considered the "Cinderella of French West Africa," into the economic powerhouse of French Africa.[126] The Ivory Coast's economic rise dates from infrastructural developments that opened the country up from about 1951: the construction of the port of Abidjan, the Vridi Canal, and road and rail networks. This development was accompanied with the leveraging of what Bamba describes as the French "colonial library" and "epistemic memories." France deployed researchers in earth, crop, and social sciences through new research institutions created after World War II to conduct pioneering research and regional studies, which underpinned the agricultural revolution that was the Ivorian miracle.[127] The most prominent of these new research institutions was the Office de la Recherche Scientifique et Technique Outre-Mer (ORSTOM). But Houphouët-Boigny and his key cabinet ministers were aware that the funding that had enabled these French investments in infrastructure and knowledge through FIDES had originated in the American Marshall Plan fund. An admirer of American modernization, particularly as encapsulated in the Tennessee Valley Authority (TVA) and its transformation of rural America under the New Deal, Houphouët-Boigny believed it made sense to approach the Americans directly for technical assistance and funding, thereby minimizing the Ivory Coast's overwhelming dependence on the French.

Bamba notes that within twelve days of the Ivory Coast's independence in August 1960, Houphouët-Boigny wrote to the American ambassador in Abidjan requesting technical aid to modernize his country.[128] He made several visits to the United States beginning in 1959. In his in-depth and nuanced study of the Ivorian miracle, Bamba traces the evolving relationship between the Ivory Coast and the United States—and the resultant tensions between America and France, described by Bamba as a "hot peace" in contradistinction to the Cold War. France sought to protect its preeminence in its prosperous former African colony, countering American funding with French funding and American research teams with its own deep, epistemic knowledge through specialized research institutions that had mushroomed after World War II. Admired for economic success from the early 1950s through the mid-1960s, the Ivory Coast had no difficulty borrowing. It went on a spending spree to promote regional development and a diversified economy, intending to extend the benefits of the Ivorian economic miracle, incubated in the center and southeast of the country, to the forested region in the southwest and the savannah north. Hydroelectric dams were constructed at Kossou on the Bandama River together with integrated development of the river valley in the spirit of TVA; the San Pedro project in the southwest revolved around a new deep-water port at San Pedro and opening of the Forest Region through roads, rail, the extension of cocoa and coffee cultivation and new cash crops, and the exploitation of timber; and the creation of a new Ivorian sugar industry was positioned to breathe new economic life into the northern savannah.[129] In the spirit of modernization theory, these were huge, top-down projects, pursued with little consultation with the ordinary people envisaged as their beneficiaries and with indifference to the advice against indiscriminate borrowing that came from the French and the IMF.[130]

As these state-led projects suffered internal setbacks with labor, ordinary people refusing to align themselves with the state's plans, and internal criticism of the direction of the economy's growth, a global recession set in from the late 1970s with an oil crisis and sharp drops in prices of commodities including sugar. The Ivorian miracle unraveled, as predicted by Amin. Amin described the Ivory Coast as a classic case of "growth without development."[131] Whereas technocrats in the Ivory Coast had predicted the country would reach the "takeoff" stage by 1970, the level of savings reaching a point sufficient to assure an internally generated, self-sufficient growth, Amin opined that the "type of growth that the Ivory Coast has experienced since 1950 . . . does not automatically result in an economic 'take-off,' but in an increased external dependency and the blocking of growth."[132] France shouldered a significant part of the cost of the Ivorian miracle.[133] The Ivory Coast's external debts had ballooned to almost US$4 billion by 1980 from an estimated $400–$450 million in the early 1970s, with France and the World Bank as major creditors. But American financial institutions like the Exim Bank and Citibank were also major lenders, with Citibank being responsible for about 10 percent of the total Ivorian debt. In 1981, the Ivory Coast became a ward of the World Bank and the IMF's structural adjustment program (SAP).[134]

Ideologically, Houphouët-Boigny and Nkrumah were very different. The former was an ardent supporter of capitalism and modernization theory; Nkrumah was ambivalent about capitalism, viewing socialism and development economics as a more secure path toward economic decolonization and the building of a welfare economy. But they also shared important commonalities: authoritarianism, commitment to state-led development, and a desire to make their countries an economic showcase, including through prestige projects. Both fleeced smallholder farmers in their countries through marketing boards to fund development projects—cocoa and coffee in the case of the Ivory Coast and cocoa in the case of Ghana.[135] Whereas Nkrumah turned earlier to the Eastern Bloc to counterbalance the role of the West in Ghana's economy, Houphouët-Boigny sought that balance in the Ivorian economy by counterposing two Western allies, France and the United States, turning them into competitors. Both Houphouët-Boigny and Nkrumah valued economic growth and its potential for improving the lives of citizens, but both clearly subordinated economic decisions to political imperatives. Neither was a good student of economics, as both viewed economics as the handmaiden of politics. Ghana crashed early, undermined by the West, which wanted the Ghanaian socialist experiment to fail. The Ivory Coast, the idol of the West, crashed a little over a decade later, ironically toppled by debt from the same West, which then took the country into receivership through its financial institutions. Neocolonialism was a specter that haunted both countries in different ways. The Ivory Coast could not shake its image as a neocolonial possession of France, leading the United States to extend commercial loans instead of grants to the newly independent nation; Ghana in its determination to avert neocolonialism drove Western investment away through its radical politics. As much of Africa came under the sway of structural adjustment programs from the 1980s, it seemed not to matter whether a country had pursued socialism or capitalism. The failed experiments at economic development were not because independence was an empty political shell with no potential for real economic change. The examples of Ghana and the Ivory Coast point to the contrary. The convergence of development economics, modernization theory, socialism, and nationalism convinced the leaders of both countries that development could be a top-down process, pursued as a state enterprise without national consultation or consensus. With that parochial focus, both the West and East became simultaneously assets and liabilities.

By the 1970s, it had become clear that modernization theory could neither bridge nor explain the persistent gap between wealthier and poorer nations. The American exuberance of the 1960s, when the John F. Kennedy administration (with the urging of Walt Rostow) declared the 1960s the "development decade" and modernization theory in the spirit of the TVA promised the transformation of rural economies across Africa, faltered. Out of disillusionment in the Third World, dependency theory emerged from the late 1960s to explain the hegemonic relationships between wealthier and poorer nations. Andre Gunder Frank, the leading dependency theorist, argued that underdevelopment was due to the exploitative nature of capitalism that purposely maintains or increases the wealth of the First World at the expense of the Third World.[136] A shift in United States foreign policy acknowledged the demise of modernization theory. Whereas the "development decade" had touted economic cooperation between the United States and African countries, by the early 1970s the United States had begun to cut back on aid, believing that aid had not been effective.[137] From the mid-1970s, American foreign policy changed under Jimmy Carter to focus on giving aid to low-income countries and poor people.[138] Gone was the vision of development through economic cooperation.

Did Development Economics Fail Africa? Did Africa Fail Development Economics?

Killick notes the collapse of the consensus in development economics by the mid-1960s. Rostow's theory on the stages of growth was one of the first casualties, the victim of a major critique by Kuznets.[139] Rostow in a reflexive paper entitled "The Historian and the Analysis of Economic Growth" conceded that "we have discovered in many areas, and we have discovered the hard way that economic factors do not enjoy an automatic priority in the process of economic growth."[140] By this period, almost a decade of African independence had elapsed for the gathering of internal evidence on the responsiveness of African economies to the policy recommendations of development economics. Some of the findings bore out the dissenting voice of Bauer, underscoring the importance of knowledge and technical progress. Killick observes that the chief areas of disappointment, however, related to the performance of import-substitution industries (ISIs) and the effectiveness of state planning.[141] The section above about the ideas of Lewis and Bauer noted that Lewis was ambivalent about planning, conceding the necessity of planning on the part of the new governments in Africa but preferring that governments allocate resources—the major goal of planning—through market incentives. Bauer argued for an agriculture-led economic revolution in the tropical economies, and we have seen that Lewis's report on industrialization in Ghana suggested focus on industrialization be postponed for a couple of decades. Whereas Bauer applauded the agency and economic savviness of West Africa's farmers, Lewis worried about scale, recommending large-scale, mechanized farming. Ghana and the Ivory Coast both experimented with state-led agriculture through parastatals. The results were devastating.[142] Disillusionment on the African end in the first decade of independence was witnessed in three military coups in West Africa: in 1963 in Togo and Dahomey (now the Republic of Benin) and in Ghana in 1966.

In his essay "The Rise and Decline of Development Economics," Hirschman opined that development economists had underestimated the problems facing Third World economies. "Had the toughness of the development problem and the difficulties in the North-South relationship been correctly sized up from the outset, the considerable intellectual and political mobilization for the enterprise would not have occurred."[143] This may have been a fair assessment for the Americans, who lacked the colonial library and deep epistemic knowledge that almost a century of colonial rule had given European powers like France and Britain. The years Lewis spent at the British Colonial Office during World War II and its immediate aftermath and his exposure to economic conditions in the British colonies through reports and memoranda at the Colonial Office shaped the core precepts of his development economics. The British Colonial Office, as it looked forward to the reconstruction of postwar Britain, assisted by the colonies, had by 1943 envisaged a leading role for the colonial state and in the need for economic planning. A 1943 memorandum by Sydney Caine, a graduate of LSE and appointed chief financial officer of the Colonial Office, laid the basis of colonial economics, the predecessor of development economics. "In August 1943, he wrote what was regarded as the new manifesto of colonial economics, a three-thousand-word memorandum that called for economic planning in the colonies, stressed the large role that colonial states would need to play in promoting economic growth, and even cited Russian five-year plans and the TVA project in the United States as models for the kind of centralized state intervention in the economy that

Britain's colonies needed."[144] This idea resonated with Lewis, even though Caine pushed back as Lewis followed the logical implications of the 1943 memorandum. Lewis knew that the British colonies, and consequently the newly independent countries, were ill-equipped to plan. National statistics were patchy, and as economic adviser to the government of Ghana Lewis mentioned to the executive chairman of the United Nations Technical Assistance Board the challenge of finding trained staff to assist in economic planning.[145] And Ghana's education system was way ahead of other British colonies in tropical Africa. Rimmer, who had the opportunity to work with the newly independent African governments (including Ghana's), commented on the poor state of statistics and how this impaired planning.[146]

Working with poor statistics led to disappointment in the African experience with development economics. American officials saw in newly independent Nigeria an opportunity to showcase the effectiveness of American technical assistance. It was mentioned above how on Nigeria's independence, the United States (with Ford Foundation backing) dispatched Wolfgang Stolper in 1961 to head the Nigerian Economic Planning Unit. Stolper was tasked with drafting Nigeria's Development Plan for 1962–68. In addition to frustration with corrupt Nigerian officials, Stolper ran into the problem of poor statistics. Baker writes of Stolper's Nigerian experience: "Furthermore, he lamented the 'lack of facts' available from the colonial period while drafting the national development plan, arguing that the lack of statistical and social scientific knowledge about the country made planning exceedingly difficult."[147] This challenge led Stolper to write a book, *Planning without Facts*, in which he argued for decentralized decision-making in the reality of poor numbers.[148]

Poor statistics and faith in state-led development projects, which implied a dismissal of the wisdom, input, and agency of ordinary farmers in newly independent countries, were major factors in the abysmal performance of development economics. Bauer had long argued for the economic intelligence of West Africa's farmers, whose industriousness underpinned the emergence of Ghana and then the Ivory Coast as the world's leading producers of cocoa, a crop grown solely for export. In the mid-1980s, with development economics in disarray, the seasoned economic anthropologist Polly Hill urged the field to rally, as its work had intrinsic value. She cited how development economists had been misled by bad official statistics: "Owing to the acceptance of bad official statistics, relating particularly to the value of crop production over wide areas, development economists must be regarded as mainly responsible for the contemporary mood of demoralization over third-world prospects, which has overwhelmed the public in the Western world—a public which so often feels that 'it is too late for anything to be done.'"[149] She highlighted several gaps in development economics from the perspective of economic anthropology, which from the 1960s was conducting pioneering work on rural Africa. An important lapse in development economics was the invisibility of African women. Hill pointed to the example of West Africa, where women were conceivably responsible for a larger proportion of the gross domestic product than men.[150] Western disillusionment deepened with the drought and famine in Ethiopia and Sudan in the 1970s. Hill affirmed "the viability of tropical economies," and insisted that "much third-world 'doom-mongering' has no sound intellectual basis."[151]

Hirschman in his essay "The Rise and Decline of Development Economics" also pointed to the deflating impact on the field of disastrous political developments in the Third World from the 1960s:

> But there was a more weighty reason for the failure of development economics to recover decisively from the attacks it had been subjected to by its critics. It lies in the series of political disasters that struck a number of Third World countries from the sixties on, disasters that were clearly *somehow* connected with the stresses and strains accompanying development and "modernization." These development disasters ranging from civil wars to the establishment of murderous authoritarian regimes, could not but give pause to a group of social scientists, who, after all, had taken up the cultivation of development economics in the wake of World War II not as narrow specialists, but impelled by the vision of a better world.[152]

Political developments in the Third World hit hard at the hopes of development economists. For Lewis, who had retreated from Ghana in disillusionment after having gone to assist in the economic development of the first Black African country to become independent, painful lessons had been learned on the interface of economics and politics. His bruising experience with Nkrumah left deep emotional scars that made the occasion of his Whidden Lectures in 1965 on "Politics in West Africa" at McMaster University cathartic. He shared with his audience that "I have wanted to write this monograph for the past eight years for emotional reasons. The invitation to give the Whidden lectures at McMaster University forced me to control the emotion, to do extensive research which academic standards require, and to meet the deadlines without which the material might never have been completed."[153] The result was a deeply thoughtful set of connected essays on the development of the single-party system in many West African states barely a decade from independence, the worrying absence of democratic tolerance, and the winner-takes-all mentality in West African politics. Focusing on West Africa, the region with which he was most familiar, Lewis argued for a fundamental change in the political philosophy of those in power in West Africa's plural societies. He advocated governance through coalitions in which the voices of all could be heard, distinct from the governing party–opposition party alternative that made politics a zero-sum game. He affirmed his faith in West Africa's future: "Democracy was set back in West Africa partly because of the heat of the moment [referring to the nationalist struggle for independence], but mainly because the ideas and institutions of democracy inherited from Europe were inappropriate, and confused and weakened its supporters. As the emotions of independence recede, and the problems of the area are better understood, the existing regimes will be displaced, and democracy will again have its chance."[154] Not until 1989 would the fall of the Berlin Wall and the wave of democratic protests across Africa led by civil society bodies usher in regime changes in what has been described as Africa's "second wave of independence." The results of this post-1989 movement lie beyond the purview of this book.

The Decline of Development Economics: Africa's Lost Decade

The 1980s ushered in Africa's worst economic decade in its postindependence history, referred to as "Africa's lost decade" (see chap. 1). The early 1970s through the mid-1980s had seen weak global economic growth and contraction in the economies of countries belonging to the Organization for Economic Cooperation and Development (OECD). In this period, OECD countries received over 85 percent of Africa's exports, so contraction in OECD economies had major implications for African economies.[155] The preceding decade, the 1970s, had witnessed a series of reverses that undermined African economies: the oil crisis of 1974, and for the Sahelian and savannah countries severe drought from 1967 to 1974 and from 1979 through 1985. By 1985, Senegal had lost so much arable land to desertification that the production and export of peanuts, its main industry, declined dramatically (see chap. 4).[156] Belief in the utility of deficit financing to jumpstart economic growth in the 1960s and 1970s coincided with a period from the

1960s through the early 1970s when interest rates on international loans were as a low as 3 percent. Interest rates jumped in the mid-1970s to as high as 20 percent, and African countries accumulated huge debts. Unable to meet their schedules of debt repayment, several African countries became wards of the IMF.[157] Poor economic performance in the 1960s and 1970s was worsened by a sharp drop in world prices for Africa's primary exports in the 1980s. For countries that had built an industrial and manufacturing base in the quest for industrialization in the 1960s and 1970s, when manufacturing in Africa grew about 7 percent a year, the 1980s saw a reverse—growth went into negative figures and Africa actually deindustrialized (see chap. 4). Economic decline loosened trade ties between many African countries and their former colonial powers, and the United States emerged in this period as the leading trading partner for several African countries. Africa's share of world trade declined from 3 percent in the 1950s to less than 2 percent in the early 1990s. In the 1980s, intra-African trade constituted less than 5 percent of Africa's total trade.[158]

Development seemed to have eluded Africa. In the first two decades of independence, development was pursued as an international collaboration between African states, the developed world, and international development institutions. Now, a disillusioned West redefined its relations to Africa, seeing its role as one of poverty reduction instead of wealth production. Development economics had made wealth production a feasible aspiration for Africa. But with the field in disarray and with Africa's dismal economic performance in its early decades of independence, even stalwart development economists like Hirschman by 1979 wondered whether it had been a pipe dream. With the state in Africa discredited by political predation, development as a process negotiated between sovereign states no longer appeared tenable.

These developments mirrored shifts in the discipline of economics. The late 1970s saw the rise of the monetarists, led by Milton Friedman. Changes in the theoretical area of economics generated skepticism about the effects of planning and control and witnessed an increasing assertion of the efficacy of market-oriented policies.[159] These shifts elevated mathematical formalization in economics (mathematical economics or econometrics), and models came to the forefront. Amin complained that "Marx and Keynes have been erased from social thought and the 'theoreticians' of 'pure economics' have replaced analysis of the real world with that of an imaginary capitalism."[160] By the early 1980s, 54 percent of the papers in the *American*

Economic Review contained "models without data."[161] Marion Fourcade reflects on how in the 1970s and 1980s the economics department at the University of California at Berkeley was divided into two camps. Originally housed in Barrows Hall with other social sciences such as sociology and political science, the department split in the 1970s when a group of economists moved to Evans Hall, home to the departments of mathematics and statistics. This group of seven or eight economists were inclined to mathematical economics. Those who stayed in Barrows Hall were "not anti-technical," they just used statistics in more descriptive ways and were heavily involved in "practical work" with governments, foundations, and other institutions; in short, they were more into applied economics.[162] The Department was reunited in Evans Hall in 1989. This interesting anecdote by Fourcade speaks to Paul Krugman's argument in his 2012 article "The Fall and Rise of Development Economics." Krugman argues that the crisis in development economics was methodological in the refusal of its advocates to model. Paradoxically, it was not because theorists of development economics like Hirschman could not model, Krugman observes. They refused to, in ways that were dramatized in the split at Berkeley. "The irony is that we can now see that high development theory made perfectly good sense after all. But in order to see that, we need to adopt exactly the intellectual attitude Hirschman rejected: a willingness to do violence to the richness and complexity of the real world in order to produce controlled, silly models that illustrate key concepts."[163] In conversations with governments, international bodies like the United Nations, and politicians in newly independent countries, development economists were not writing just for those in the discipline of economics and wanted their work to be broadly accessible. In pursuit of this larger objective, they refused to model. Krugman delivers the verdict within economics: "Like it or not, however, the influence of ideas that have not been embalmed in models soon decays. And this was the fate of high development theory."[164] By the 1970s, when Krugman was an economics student, he observed that development economics "had come to seem not so much wrong as meaningless."[165] With the apostles of development economics in the wilderness, "development" had disappeared from the vocabulary of international experts by the end of the 1980s.

THE AFTERLIVES OF DEVELOPMENT ECONOMICS

But there was light at the end of the tunnel for development economics. The concerns of development economics were too important and pressing for the field to be discarded. Hirschman's essay "The Rise and Decline of Development Economics" was written in 1979 on the occasion of the awarding of the Nobel Prize in Economic Sciences to Lewis. Commenting on the resilience of the material conditions that birthed development economics, Hirschman wrote that "the problem of world poverty is far from solved, but encouraging inroads on the problem have been made and are being made. It is therefore something of a puzzle why development economics flourished so briefly."[166] Lewis went from the Nobel Prize in Economic Sciences to become president of the American Economic Association, a pattern followed by subsequent economists. Instructively, Krugman notes that Lewis was one of the development economists who did model, pointing to his influential model of his concept of surplus labor.[167] Thus, Lewis straddled the transition in economics and signaled the revival of development economics. Fellow development economists were excited by Lewis's recognition with the Nobel Prize. Moses Abramowitz, professor of economics at Stanford and president of the American Economic Association (1979–80), wrote to Lewis on October 17, 1979, that Tibor Scitovsky, also a professor of economics at Stanford and a pioneering development economist, had just left his office overjoyed by Lewis's Nobel Prize.[168] Marking the shift in the field was the award of the Nobel Prize in Economic Sciences to Gérard Debreu in 1983. Debreu was part of the group of mathematical economists at Berkeley who moved to Evans Hall in the 1970s. Like Lewis, Debreu went on to become president of the American Economic Association.[169]

Fourcade in her book *Economists and Societies* comments that even with mathematical economics coming to the forefront of the field in the United States from the 1970s and American economists dominating the international scene, "*pure* mathematical formalism never dominated the U.S. field."[170] Her book charts the development of three distinct but not disconnected economics traditions that emerged in Britain, France, and the United States over the course of the twentieth century. Economists in the United States and France, perhaps the two most important players in the field of economics, occupied polar opposites in their approach to markets and the state. Fourcade notes that "Americans always displayed a much higher level of general consensus on a number of standard economic propositions and were significantly more favorable to economic ideas based on free trade and market competition. The French, on the other hand, stood out for their distrust of the price system and their support for political control of economic institutions, such as the central bank or the exchange rate."[171] British economists were in the middle of these two poles. One could characterize economists in the US as "scientific and commercial," the British as "public-minded elitism," and the French as marked by "statist divisions."[172] These positions were the products of these countries' distinct political cultures. In Britain, political culture has situated economics in a tradition of public service. Fourcade writes of this tradition that "this has produced a scientific field that is organized around the authority of elite institutions and personalities, but where the ability to communicate economic ideas in plain and eloquent language (through personal networks and contributions oriented toward the general public, for instance) is also highly valued."[173] It is not surprising that development economics was inspired by British colonial economics. French economics gained its statist form post–World War II, when the country was faced with reconstructing and modernizing its economy after the devastation of the Great Depression and a disastrous war. The state's response was to develop a specially trained elite corps of public economic managers and technicians.[174] A proliferation of state institutions charted this course in France and French colonies, as the state explicitly harnessed the scientific production of knowledge.

The different economics traditions in Britain and France (which informed welfare economics and state-led development respectively), the fact that these two European powers held most of the colonies in the world, and the training in economics of citizens from former colonies in British and French universities meant that development economics saw a rebirth. The internationalization of economics meant that these currents fertilized economics globally. After a decade in the 1990s of dismissing the state in Africa as the obstacle to development and good governance, the World Bank returned at the beginning of the twenty-first century to a position that saw relevance in the state and its role. This view was very much in line with Killick's position in the mid-1980s, when he wrote *A Reaction Too Far*, that the important question in Africa is not the size of the state, but what kind of state and how state performance can be improved.[175] That two Nobel Prize laureates in Economic Sciences in 2019 worked in the economics of development bears evidence to the rehabilitation of development economics: Esther Duflo's title at MIT is Professor of Poverty Alleviation and Development Economics; and Michael Kremer at Harvard University was Gates Professor of Developing Societies. Global poverty remains undefeated, and as Killick reminds us, the "poverty of nations is the special concern of development economics."[176]

four

PAN-AFRICAN SOCIALISM

The African Developmental State, Regional Integration, and Worldmaking

INTRODUCTION

In various publications and statements, Nkrumah, Touré, Senghor, and Nyerere sought to explain their socialism, often qualifying their subscription to Marxism. Nkrumah was unequivocal in describing himself as a "Marxist socialist."[1] Senghor insisted that "we are not 'Marxists' in the sense given the word today, in so far as Marxism is presented as atheistic metaphysics, a total and totalitarian view of the world."[2] Answering students' questions at the University of Dar es Salaam in February 1976, Nyerere declared, "I'm not a Marxist . . . but you would be amazed if you knew how much of Marx I do accept."[3] An exasperated Touré, desperate for financial aid after the abrupt withdrawal of the French from Guinea in 1958 and irritated with Western attempts to brand him a socialist/communist and deny him assistance, had a most revealing conversation with the US ambassador to Guinea, William Attwood, in 1961. Attwood reported on this conversation in a telegram to the Department of State: "He [Touré] insisted no [Soviet] bloc technicians in any operating or executive positions but here only to make studies and advise. He said whether technician Communist Socialist Liberal or Capitalist unimportant to Guinea so long as things get done. He said Guinea so poor cannot be concerned ideology only action."[4] Historiography agrees that what these leaders sought to implement was not traditional socialism. Regarding Nkrumah, perhaps the most ideological of our four leaders, Roger Genoud, after a detailed study of Ghana's political economy under Nkrumah (1951–66), concluded that "the experience of Kwame Nkrumah's Ghana was basically that of nationalism in modern Africa and had little to do with socialism, despite the claims of a clamorous and highly ideological press."[5] Touré until 1967 even resisted the socialist label.[6] Senegal's socialist experiment limped along after the ouster of Prime Minister Mamadou Dia in December 1962.[7] Mamadou Diouf notes of Senegal that by 1980, the "gap between the socialist discourse of the regime and its liberal economic practice illustrates, in a derisory and comical manner, the end of the enterprise of development."[8] The Egyptian Marxist Samir Amin was even more dismissive of Nyerere's claims to socialism, describing him as a populist "pastor"—a not inaccurate swipe at the Catholic influence on Nyerere's political thought.[9] Frantz Fanon in the early 1960s expressed dismay at this lack of ideological coherence: "For my part, the deeper I enter into the cultures and the political circles the surer I am that the great danger that threatens Africa is the absence of ideology."[10] The historiographical description of two waves of socialism in Africa, African socialism from the 1960s through the mid-1970s and Marxism-Leninism from the mid-1970s, creates the impression—perhaps unintended—of a purer ideological variant taking over from failed African socialism.[11]

In an earlier paper, I interrogated whether "African socialism" was actually a search for an indigenous model of economic development.[12] In this chapter, I would like to shift the focus away from a comparison of African socialism with Marxism or Marxism-Leninism, clearly not the intended purpose of our historical actors. They did not miss the mark because they were ignorant of Marxist theory. I also want to move away from an assessment of whether African socialism failed or succeeded. I pursue two objectives in this chapter. First, I trace the historical developments that led to the declaration of Pan-African socialism as the vision statement for an independent Africa at the Manchester Congress of 1945. That history sheds light on the intentions of our nationalist actors and how they sought to position themselves differently from the Soviet (communist) and capitalist camps. It is clear that what was presented as African socialism in the early decades of independence was often just a nationalistic program of development. I particularly like the label "Pan-African socialism" from the 1945 Manchester Congress because it underscores that this vision of nationalistic development was pursued within the larger framework of Pan-Africanism. Second,

I examine the substance of what emerged in the countries under the four leaders in the 1960s and 1970s as they sought to implement Pan-African socialism. All four leaders were active on three levels: first, the aggressive pursuit of economic development at the national level (the state assuming the form of a "developmental state"); second, the pursuit of regional integration, seen as indispensable to economic development and premised on the total liberation of Africa; and third, the importance of agency at the continental and international or world stages (worldmaking)—membership of sovereign states in international institutions and the creation of new institutions in the South to bolster the sovereign autonomy of Africa's new states. These levels were intimately linked; success in national economic development bolstered credentials for regional leadership and gave international visibility.[13] Senghor was exceptional among the four in his insistence that France be a partner at all three levels.

It was an appreciation of these connections that encouraged Americans to put together a development package for Guinea to woo Touré from the Soviet to the American side. The Americans astutely discerned that aid from the Eastern Bloc had not strengthened Guinea's claims to regional leadership after Guinea's sensational achievement of independence in 1958. "Hard look at economy implies realization Bloc aid showy but not rational. Radio station, luxury hotel, printing plant, municipal loud-speakers and sports stadium, though welcomed by GoG [government of Guinea] contribute little to building sound economic base. Result is Guinea being bypassed economically by other West African states and therefore becoming increasingly irrelevant politically."[14] Touré, similar to Nkrumah, desired a dam on the Konkouré River and a smelter for Guinea's vast bauxite reserves. These criteria informed jockeying for regional and continental leadership, as Nkrumah, Touré, and Nyerere adopted strong anticolonial positions and offered their countries as bases for liberation movements. While they forged developmental states, assuming the agenda of the late colonial state, their intent was to flip developmentalism on its head. Cooper has pointed to how the colonial government retreated on independence, convinced that the new African governments—which had assumed the colonial government's development agenda and state apparatus—would continue on the path of the late colonial state.[15] Though Nkrumah, Touré, and Nyerere may have appropriated the colonial developmental agenda, they sought to decolonize the economy, to sever expatriate control and end structural dependence.[16]

This position was a key factor in Nkrumah's and Touré's antagonism toward Senghor and Houphouët-Boigny, perceived as too close to France.[17] I turn next to the contending internationalisms between the two world wars and the evolution of Black internationalism that shaped the agenda of the Manchester Congress of 1945 and its vision of Pan-African socialism. I then examine the three aspects that came to define the agenda of Pan-African socialism: the African developmental state, regional integration and continental unity, and anticolonialism and worldmaking. The endeavor here is not to hang an ideological tag on the programs of these early leaders, but to discuss what they did and what their objectives were.

Contending Internationalisms: Background to the 1945 Manchester Congress

The intellectual antecedents that shaped the Cold War after World War II date back to the contending visions proffered by liberalism and Bolshevism for a new international order that emerged in the closing years of World War I (or the Great War). The United States did not enter WWI until April 1917. But increasingly from 1916, President Woodrow Wilson began to articulate a vision of a new international order that would eliminate "rule by might" in the operation of empire that he saw as having caused the Great War. In statements widely distributed by the American propaganda campaign that stressed the importance of principles like government by consent, equality of nations, and the need for new institutions and norms to regulate international relations, Wilson captured the hearts and minds of the colonized world in what has been described as the "Wilsonian moment."[18]

In a series of policy statements that began with his "Peace without Victory" speech to the United States Senate on January 22, 1917, and continued through his address to Congress on the "Fourteen Points" on January 8, 1918, Wilson laid out his agenda for the armistice and the postwar world. The Fourteen Points outlined in comprehensive fashion the United States' war aims and Wilson's vision for world order after the war. The plan has been seen by some as a response to the Bolshevik declaration of a peace plan by Vladimir Lenin and Leon Trotsky. The Fourteen Points included Wilson's first reference to the rights of colonized peoples, indicating a dissatisfaction with the existing imperial order. In an address before Congress the following month on February 11, 1918, Wilson for the first time explicitly used the term "self-determination" in the discussion of his peace plans. This was clearly a move to appropriate the language and appeal of the Bolsheviks, though Wilson's version of self-determination was very much in line with his earlier principle of consent of the governed.[19] Erez Manela has examined Wilson's and Lenin's use of self-determination: "However, these distinctions between the Wilsonian and Leninist versions of self-determination, compelling as they may appear in retrospect, were hardly so clear-cut at the time. To many around the world, and especially in the colonial world, Wilson and Lenin appeared to be more similar than different. Both advocated a new, open diplomacy, both were sharply critical of imperialism, both called for a radical transformation of international relations, and both advocated a peace based on the principle of self-determination."[20] Between Wilson and Lenin, Wilson was the more internationally recognized statesman in 1918. The acceptance of the Fourteen Points as the basis of the armistice on November 11, 1918, together with Wilson's decision to attend the peace conference in Paris—making him the first sitting American president to travel to Europe—turned the Wilsonian moment into a crucible of global hopes for a transformed international order. Whereas the president saw himself as an advocate for weaker nations in Europe, the impact of his pronouncements on the colonized peoples of the world in Asia, the Middle East, and Africa was equally profound, even if he was unaware of how colonized peoples had latched onto his words of hope about a new world order that privileged self-determination.[21] Popular legitimacy and not the self-centered interests of great states, Wilson opined, would shape the new world order.

The Bolsheviks, Lenin and Trotsky, were in April 1917 the first to put forward a peace settlement based on self-determination. In March 1917, the Bolsheviks had overthrown Czar Nikolai II of Russia in a revolution and brought an end to Romanov rule. On April 4, 1917, Lenin delivered his April Theses in Petrograd. He drew on his recently published book, *Imperialism, The Highest Stage of Capitalism* (1917), to denounce the Great War as an imperialist war fomented by capitalist interests.[22] Lenin advocated a peace that did not entail annexations, akin to Wilson's "Peace without Victory," and called for the establishment of a new, revolutionary International to pursue the demise of imperialism and capitalism. The new government announced its war aims on April 9, 1917, declaring that it would seek a permanent peace based on the self-determination of peoples.[23] When Lenin spoke of self-determination, he like Wilson was not thinking beyond Europe. But his use of the term applied to ethnically defined nations, and he envisaged the term to express the right of immediate secession from imperial rule.[24] The Bolsheviks, having entered a separate peace agreement with the Central powers in 1918 and embroiled in civil war in Russia, were not party to the Paris Peace Conference, which began on January 18, 1919. Wilson was the focus of international attention, his policy statements having inspired expectant responses among colonial and dominated peoples. Delegations and petitions from Europe, the Middle East, North Africa, and Asia poured in as the Paris Peace Conference commenced. From eastern Europe, Croatians, Albanians, Ukrainians, and Estonians claimed self-determination; in western Europe the Catalans sought independence from Spain, and Sinn Fein demanded an independent Ireland; Syrians, Lebanese, and Armenians submitted petitions in favor of self-rule; the Vietnamese wanted independence from French colonial rule, as did Tunisian nationalists. African Americans from the United States attended, despite the efforts of the State Department to restrain them, to remind the world that they were a disenfranchised people. The African American scholar and activist W. E. B. Du Bois, together with representatives from the Caribbean and Africa, organized the Second Pan-African Congress in Paris in February 1919 to coincide with the peace conference, highlight colonial conditions in Africa, and advocate for good governance. Instructively, as Manela notes, "all praised President Wilson's vision for a new world, noted the support his principles gave to their claims, and often quoted at length from his speeches."[25]

The outcome of the peace conference was disillusioning for the many who saw Wilson as a champion of self-determination. Wilson came to the peace conference equipped with a draft covenant for the League of Nations that he had written personally. This draft included "a provision that explicitly established the principle of self-determination as a central instrument for adjudicating disputes that come before the league."[26] As head of the commission that drafted the covenant of the league, Wilson spent weeks trying to ensure the provision on self-determination would remain despite the opposition of his own advisers and allies. Bowing to pressure, Wilson on February 3 deleted the clause that made self-determination central to claims for territorial readjustment. When Wilson faced the expectant world press on February 14 to present the text of the League of Nations covenant, the term "self-determination" had been excised. The league would be controlled by the imperialist powers. The mandate system, another of the principles advocated by Wilson, survived in the league's covenant. The mandate system was intended to provide effective oversight over colonial territories, but, reflecting the continued influence of the imperialist powers, mandated territories would be governed in ways that did not differ from actual colonies. The mandate system would not transform the nature of colonial rule. By March 1919, Wilson's international stature had declined sharply. Britain and France sought to benefit from the peace conference, casting aside Wilson's call for "peace without victory" and seeking territorial acquisitions and reparations from the defeated Central powers. Wilson's Republican opponents had wrested Congress from Democratic control, and the Senate voted to reject the covenant of the League of Nations in its current form. Wilson found himself on the retreat at home and abroad, and the League of Nations developed under the firm imprint of the imperial powers, including the United States.[27] The United States Senate on March 19, 1920, rejected the Treaty of Versailles and with it the League of Nations covenant; the United States never joined the League of Nations, Wilson's brainchild.

This was a disappointing but perhaps not surprising outcome. Manela points to Wilson's poor record on domestic race matters and his thoughts on American colonial rule in the Philippines to underscore that he could not be labeled progressive in either race or colonial relations.[28] The two principal architects of the League of Nations covenant were Wilson and his ideological ally, Jan Smuts of South Africa. Believers in segregation, Wilson and Jan Smuts "excised the revolutionary implications of the Bolshevik right to self-determination and repurposed the principle to preserve racial hierarchy in the new international organization," Getachew has argued.[29] The Wilsonian moment, which promised to be revolutionary, became counterrevolutionary in its preservation of the status quo. With the collapse of the Wilsonian moment and Russia's return to stability, Lenin's reputation eclipsed Wilson's in the colonized world.[30] For African American radicals disappointed with Wilson and the gravitation of the white American working class to the nationalist and imperialist cause, Robin Kelley points to how "Lenin turned out to be something of a friend."[31]

While Lenin's earlier pronouncements on self-determination had also focused on Europe, he had in a sense begun in the early twentieth century to expand the works of Karl Marx and Friedrich Engels, originally focused on industrialized Europe, to the colonized world. Marx and Engels were preoccupied with the industrialized world of western and central Europe, its imbrication with capitalism, and how this system produced an alienated proletariat that would overthrow the capitalist order through a socialist revolution. Lenin's works extended the heuristic value of Marxism to create Marxism-Leninism, or scientific socialism. Russia at the beginning of the twentieth century was an agricultural economy with peasantry as its main workforce. With a fledgling industrial base, there was no established urban proletariat to comprise the revolutionary force envisaged by Marx and Engels. Lenin's first innovation in his book *Two Tactics of Social Democracy in the Democratic Revolution* (1905) was to elevate the peasantry into a legitimate revolutionary force in countries that were not industrialized.[32] The import of this extension was profound for the agrarian economies of Asia and Africa, as noted by Fritz Schatten. "By politically rehabilitating the peasantry and allowing them into an alliance with the proletariat, Lenin introduced a new basic factor into communist revolutionary movements in countries which were not sufficiently developed, economically and structurally, to comply with the original Marxist conditions for a socialist upheaval."[33] Lenin's innovation would inspire Mao Zedong of China, where the peasantry took on even more political significance. In *Imperialism, The Highest Stage of Capitalism* (1917), Lenin added another plank to the foundation of colonial understanding of empire and capitalism. Highlighting the value of colonial territories to capitalist accumulation (raw materials and markets), Lenin pointed to the implication of decolonization and the overthrow of empire as a blow to the capitalist system. In pursuit of overthrowing colonialism, the Third International would draw from a third important work by Lenin, *Left-Wing Communism: An Infantile Disorder* (1920). Drawing on the experience of the Bolsheviks in Russia, Lenin encouraged communists in western Europe to ally with noncommunist trade unions and participate in parliamentary elections and politics as strategies to win over the masses and seize political power.[34] By extension, communists could collaborate with noncommunist nationalist forces in the colonies, even with bourgeois-democratic liberation movements, to advance the cause of weakening imperialism and capitalism. These ideas gained greater import through the revolutionary Communist International (Comintern) or the Third International, established in 1919. The Third International, juxtaposed with the League of Nations, became another reference point for peoples from the colonized world in the increasingly internationalized world after World War I.

The Wilsonian moment—and the League of Nations—and the Bolshevik Revolution set the stage for a new international order after the Great

War. Both positioned the sovereign, self-determining nation-state as the only legitimate political form in international relations.[35] The Third International's strategic and theoretical accommodation of nationalist forces in the colonized world, even those not socialist or communist, was an astute recognition of the nature of the educated elites in the colonies. The educated elite in African colonies in the interwar period were products of Western education, much of their early education having been acquired through Christian missionary schools. Though anticolonial, their ambitions were to remake their societies along Western liberal democratic lines. The Communist International could partner with African educated elites in the overthrow of imperialism without necessarily foregrounding the need for a world communist revolution, which, however, remained the ultimate objective.

The interwar period witnessed the proliferation of internationalist bodies. In the 1920s and 1930s, youth leagues and movements multiplied across West Africa, including the Gold Coast Youth Conference (founded in 1929), the Nigerian Youth Movement (1934), and the West African Youth League (1935). Emmanuel Asiedu-Acquah points to how the World Youth Peace Conference in the Netherlands in 1928 was a galvanizing moment. The peace conference brought some five hundred youth delegates from around the world to express unanimous opposition to imperialism and racial inequalities. This conference and its liberal-international language of self-determination informed the formation of the Gold Coast Youth League under the leadership of J. C. Degraft-Johnson and Dr. J. B. Danquah.[36] The West African Youth League, set up by the Sierra Leonean I. T. A. Wallace-Johnson in the Gold Coast in 1935, also owed its origins to different internationalist influences inspired by the Third International. Wallace-Johnson had traveled in communist networks since the late 1920s and lived at different times in Moscow, Hamburg, Paris, and London. A journalist and labor organizer, he sharpened his journalistic skills by working for the *Negro Worker*, the newspaper of the International Trade Union Committee of Negro Workers (ITUCNW), which was part of the Third International.[37] Black internationalism flourished during the interwar period.

The interwar period, which witnessed intense participation and mobility within internationalist networks by Africans and diasporic Africans, also saw increasingly critical attitudes of Blacks toward the international bodies they had viewed as emancipatory. C. L. R. James offered a sharp critique of the League of Nations and its racial hierarchies, which were embedded by the cofounders of the league, Wilson and Jan Smuts.[38] The Italian invasion of Ethiopia in 1935 and its subsequent annexation laid bare the racial hypocrisy behind the League of Nations.[39] Both Italy and Ethiopia were members of the league. But the two independent African states, Ethiopia and Liberia, were incorporated into the league in ambivalent ways that subordinated them to supervision by the white nation-states in the league. Liberia was a founding member of the league in 1919, and Ethiopia joined in 1923. Condescendingly, both states were subjected to investigations about the persistence of slavery within their territories, enabling the league to raise questions about the viability of Black sovereignty.[40] The Western countries conveniently forgot their leading roles in centuries of slave trade and slavery and the colonial use of forced labor that would persist into World War II.[41] Other member states of the league made no strong effort to deter Italy's plans to invade Ethiopia, which had been brought before the league by Ethiopia in January 1935. Impugning Ethiopia's level of civilization, its capacity to self-govern, and by extension its worthiness of membership of the league, Italy circulated a sixty-page memorandum in September 1935, a month before its invasion of Ethiopia, indicting Ethiopia for its inability to abolish slave trade and regulate arms trade, two conditions incumbent on all league members. The memorandum concluded that Ethiopia "does not possess the necessary qualifications . . . to raise herself by voluntary efforts to the level of other civilized nations."[42] In short, Ethiopia needed to be brought under white tutelage. Italy invaded Ethiopia in October 1935 and in 1937 claimed conquest of the country. Other Western powers accepted Italy's claim in 1938. Italy's occupation of Ethiopia would prove short lived, coming to an end in 1943 when Italy was defeated as one of the Axis powers in World War II.[43]

Ethiopia's annexation was a transformative moment in Black internationalism and nationalism. It hugely discredited the League of Nations in the eyes of Black internationalists. But Soviet Russia equally lost face when it was discovered to have kept a vibrant trade in 1935 and 1936 with Mussolini's Italy, including supplies of oil crucial to the Italian war effort.[44] The league had imposed sanctions on Italy effective November 18, 1935, on enumerated commodities considered war materiel. Petroleum was on this list, and Italy acquired over half of its oil supplies from Soviet Russia and Romania. Soviet Russia did not want to lose this oil market and pointed to the persistence of other powers like the United States in supplying oil to Italy to continue its oil trade. While Soviet Russia immediately ceased exports to Italy of other enumerated commodities, such as phosphate, manganese, and chromium, it compensated by increasing exports to Italy of other un-enumerated commodities like oats and wood.[45] These developments could not be concealed, and J. Calvitt Clarke III notes that "this duplicity redounded against Soviet influence in Africa for many years."[46] That Stalin in 1943 dissolved the Third International so as not to alienate Russia's wartime allies, the United States and Britain, underscored Soviet Russia's accommodationist politics. The People's Republic of China would step up from the 1940s to challenge Soviet Russia's claim to leadership in the communist world. Chinese communists presented their revolution in agrarian China as a model for colonial and semicolonized worlds and a better product of Marxist-Leninist theory. Turning away from the political compromises of Soviet Russia, the People's Republic of China argued in its propaganda in Africa and Asia that "all political power goes back to the barrel of a gun," and that liberation movements must arm themselves to take power rather than strike alliances with nonrevolutionary groups.[47]

It is in this context of disillusionment with the Soviet Union and the Comintern that West Indian and African radicals began to explore opportunities to create an autonomous Black international movement independent of the Comintern and great powers. Brent Edwards has examined how the West Indian George Padmore and the francophone West African Tiemoko Kouyaté, both expelled from the Communist Party in 1933, were at the helm of this turn. They planned to establish a Negro World Unity Congress (Congrès Mondial Nègre) in July 1935. Padmore and Kouyaté forged plans for this Congress between 1933 and early 1935, when both resided in Paris and shared an apartment. Though the Congress did not take place as planned in July 1935, the Italian invasion of Ethiopia later that year galvanized Black internationalism. C. L. R. James formed the International African Friends of Ethiopia (IAFE) in London, which Padmore joined on relocating to London from Paris in early 1935. Padmore and James were childhood friends from Trinidad. In Paris, Kouyaté formed the Comité de Défense d'Ethiopie (Ethiopian Defense Committee). Paulette Nardal, who served as secretary to the Ethiopian Defense Committee, was its liaison to IAFE because of her fluency in English. Out of IAFE emerged the International African Service Bureau (IASB) in 1937, an anti-imperialist organization headed by Padmore. The IASB was at the center of a number of small groups that came together in 1943 to form the Pan-African Federation (PAF), which planned the 1945 Manchester Pan-African Congress. The congress was initially planned for Paris to coincide with the World Trade Union Conference in September 1945, but complications led to its relocation to Manchester in October 1945.[48]

Padmore would exercise enormous influence in West Indian and African nationalist circles in London from 1935, forging a particularly close relationship with Nkrumah from 1945 until Padmore's death in September 1959. Padmore had worked actively in communist networks since his college days in the United States in the late 1920s. A gifted writer and organizer, he was invited by the Communist Party in the Soviet Union to stay on in Moscow after a conference in 1929 at which he delivered a report on the formation of the Trade Union Unity League before the Communist International.[49] He lived and worked for the Communist International in Moscow, Hamburg, and Vienna and was instrumental in the founding of the International Trade Union Committee for Negro Workers (ITUCNW), editing its monthly magazine, the *Negro Worker*. A committed activist for the liberation of Africa, Padmore became disillusioned as the Kremlin moved into closer diplomatic ties with imperial powers Britain, France, and Italy as it sought to counter the rise of the Nazi Party in Germany.[50] Padmore cut ties with the Communist International in late summer of 1933 and was formally expelled by the Communist Party in February 1934. While Padmore remained a socialist, he became disinterested in the politics of the Soviet Union.[51] For writers such as Basil Davidson, Italy's invasion of Ethiopia lent coherence to African nationalism. Protests spread across Africa in response to the Italian invasion. In the Gold Coast, Wallace Johnson started an Ethiopian Defense Committee. Expelled by the Gold Coast government in 1937 for sedition, he moved to London and joined Padmore and James in organizing the International African Service Bureau, an anti-imperialist organization. The Nigerian Youth Movement passed its charter in response to the annexation of Ethiopia, demanding independence from Britain.[52] Nkrumah, who in 1935 was passing through England en route to the United States and college, would write later in his autobiography how he felt on receiving news of Italy's invasion of Ethiopia: "At that moment it was almost as if the whole of London had suddenly declared war on me personally."[53]

It is important to note, then, that by the end of World War II and the inception of the Cold War, African nationalists and Black internationalists had become wary of both the United States and the Soviet Union. In 1945, as Western powers gathered in San Francisco to found the United Nations, Padmore and the International African Service Bureau organized a parallel conference in Manchester, Britain, named the Fifth Pan-African Congress. Nkrumah had met James in the United States and been introduced by James to Padmore as he traveled to Britain in 1945. Padmore roped Nkrumah and Jomo Kenyatta, two future heads of African states, in the organization of the Manchester Congress in October 1945. Du Bois, who had been instrumental to Pan-African conferences between 1900 and 1927, was invited as honorary international president of the conference.[54] The Manchester Congress was inspired by the need to put forward an agenda for the independence of Africa in the wake of World War II.[55] African students and Black activists in Britain had jubilated in 1941 at the joint declaration of the Atlantic Charter by US President Roosevelt and British Prime Minister Winston Churchill, which promised that after the Allies won the war all peoples would have the right to choose the government under which they would live. At a meeting in August 1941 with the West African Students Union (WASU) in London, Labour Party leader Clement Attlee assured the West Africans present that the Atlantic Charter applied "to all peoples of the world."[56] Churchill would later deny that the Atlantic Charter applied to colonies within the British Empire. For observers like Du Bois, who had followed the process of the peace conference and the formation of the league in 1919 with expectation, 1945 seemed like déjà vu, as personalities like Jan Smuts and the imperial powers played a leading role in the formation of the United Nations.[57]

The Manchester Congress adopted Pan-African socialism as the ideology and agenda for liberating Africa and developing postcolonial Africa.[58] The ideology and vision of Pan-African socialism remained tentative at this stage, understandable in a fledgling and evolving Black internationalist movement. But by 1945, the tenets of Pan-African socialism were emerging and discernible. The Provisional Committee for the 1945 Pan-African Congress, under the initiative of Padmore, drafted a "Manifesto to the United Nations." Three of its six demands would become pillars in Pan-African socialism as practiced in independent Africa: the rapid economic and social development of African peoples; the opportunity for Africans to participate in the United Nations at all levels of administration; and the advancement of Africans to "full self-government within a definite time limit."[59] On independence, Pan-African socialism gave birth to anticolonialism and the push for the total liberation of Africa; the African developmental state and its agenda of aggressive economic development; regional integration and continental unity acknowledging that the many small states of Africa could not stand alone; and worldmaking and the desire of African states to be active participants in international organizations. The new African states considered worldmaking as the path to enforce the principle of the parity of sovereign nations irrespective of size. But ambivalence toward international organizations like the United Nations, sponsored by the great powers, remained, as we see in the criticisms of the United Nations by James, Du Bois, and Fanon and the hostility of Touré and Nyerere to the IMF (see below). So, an important dimension to worldmaking was the creation of new international institutions or organizations based in the developing South, inspired by the Bandung moment. The spirit of Bandung became concrete when the vision of nonalignment, outlined by Jawaharlal Nehru at the 1955 conference, received institutional form in September 1961 in Belgrade with President Josip Tito's convening of the Non-Aligned Movement (NAM). The spirit of Afro-Asian solidarity also assumed concrete form when in December 1957, the Afro-Asian People's Solidarity Organization (AAPSO) was established in Cairo. This moment culminated in the bid for a New International Economic Order in the late 1970s.

The Challenges at Independence

Expectations of African independence were huge. There were the expectations of scholars of nationalism and the nation-state, who saw political independence as the precursor to economic independence and the development of a welfare state after the models of the West (see introduction). There were the expectations of development economists and social scientists who believed in modernization theory and looked forward to growing Africa's economies under democratic rule (see chap. 3). Then there were the African populations, who had come to see political independence as the panacea for all that was wrong with colonial society. Cyril Daddieh has described African nationalism as an omnibus; nationalist politicians promised everything to everyone once the colonial rulers were expelled.[60] Popular expectations of development included jobs, decent housing, schools, hospitals—in short, a better life. Once in power, the political and economic landscape looked very different for Africa's new rulers. The state was underresourced materially and in human capacity, and the evaluation of deficiencies underscored the demerits of colonial rule. Chapter 1 referenced the handful of African medical doctors in Tanzania on independence. On the eve of independence, Nyerere, anticipating the repatriation of British civil servants from Tanganyika, asked the ANC to assist with the recruitment of nurses to uphold Tanganyika's health system. The ANC arranged for twenty-one highly qualified and experienced South African nurses to move to Tanganyika.[61] Advocate Nathaniel Mashilo Masemola of South Africa narrated how, newly qualified as a lawyer after his education at the London School of Economics and Political Science and the Inns of Court (Gray's Inn) School of Law, he had applied to the government of Zambia on the eve of independence looking for a job. Not having heard from the government, he traveled to Zambia in October 1964 and was present for Zambia's Independence Day on October 24, 1964. An overwhelmed government had not responded to his mail. But on his arrival, discovering that he was a qualified lawyer, the government quickly made him its first Registrar of Lands and Deeds.[62] In terms of statistics, Guinea, all its records having been destroyed by a retreating France in 1958, did not even have a baseline from which to plan economically. As late as 1994–95, 85 percent of the employed workforce in Guinea had no formal education, 7.3 percent had received primary education, 4.5 percent had passed through secondary education, and just over 1 percent had received professional training or higher education. In 2001, only 10 percent of Guinea's roads were surfaced, and only 0.8 percent of Guinea's rural population had access to electricity.[63]

Senegal and Ghana, in contrast, seemed better positioned. As the federal capital of French West Africa, Dakar was the site of institutions, infrastructure, and industries that served all of French West Africa. Colonial subjects from French West Africa went to Dakar to be educated at the secondary level at institutions like École normale supérieure William Ponty, established in 1903 to educate the sons of the traditional elite into a new educated elite. Its alumni included future heads of state like Mamadou Dia of Senegal, Houphouët-Boigny of the Ivory Coast, Modibo Keita of Mali, Hamani Diori of Niger, and Maurice Yaméogo of Upper Volta (Burkina Faso). The Pasteur Institute of Dakar, established in Saint Louis in 1896 and relocated to Dakar in 1913 after it became the capital of the federation of West Africa, and the Dakar-Fann University Hospital Center, established in 1956, trained medical personnel from all over French West Africa. Senegal was also heir to an extensive infrastructure of industry and commerce. Federation had provided economies of scale for Senegal's industries based on groundnut oil, fish products, other food industries, and textiles. In April 1959, a year ahead of the blanket granting of independence to France's African colonies, France formally dissolved the federation of French West Africa. With the breakup of the federation, a primary concern for Senghor was securing markets for Senegal's industries, as the component states of the former federation now pursued their own industrialization.[64] Senegal's population comprised about 80 percent peasants, with groundnuts as the major export. Senegal needed to strengthen rural economies and diversify its dependence on groundnuts. Compared to Tanzania, Guinea, and Zambia cited above, Ghana in 1960 had 410 university professors and lecturers, 220 jurists, and 350 physicians, surgeons, and dentists.[65] In addition to a relatively competent civil service, Ghana on independence had a sterling reserve of £200 million, accumulated just before independence from the soaring world prices for cocoa, Ghana's principal export.[66] But the appearance of Ghana as an economically prosperous country was deceptive, an impression encouraged only by comparing Ghana to poorer African countries. While its income per head in 1950 was £45, about three times greater than Nigeria or Uganda, it was insignificant compared to Britain's—£265 in 1950.[67] As Roger Genoud notes, "the country was more prosperous, but this was a colonial type of prosperity."[68] Ghana exported primary commodities—cocoa, timber, gold, diamonds, manganese—and imported manufactured items in return. And with the rural prosperity caused by cocoa, Ghana was not self-sufficient in food production and imported foodstuffs.

The period from the late 1950s witnessed a decline in world prices for Africa's primary exports. The timing, though coincidental with the advent of African independence, was not necessarily a response to African independence. Coulson points to how the global economic ascendance of the United States after World War II changed Africa's trade dynamics. Europe under reconstruction after the destruction of World War II was more in need of capital goods from the United States than raw materials from Africa. With its huge landmass and different soil and climate conditions, the United States was nearly self-sufficient in raw materials and did not depend on colonies or tropical exports. The production of chemical substitutes for sisal, rubber, and other agricultural exports further undercut African exports. The Korean War in the early 1950s occasioned the last global boom in demand and prices for traditional raw materials.[69] These shifts had major implications for African economies. To give one concrete example, Tanzania's first five-year plan was launched in 1964. The plan's projections hinged on the export price of sisal, the country's major export, and on assistance from foreign aid. The world price for sisal dropped from £100 per ton in 1964 to £60 per ton in 1967. In February 1965, West Germany, one of the three largest sources of aid to Tanzania, withdrew its aid. Zanzibar had imploded in a socialist revolution in 1964; Nyerere moved quickly to bring the new government into a union with Tanganyika to create the United Republic of Tanzania (see introduction), preventing the island from becoming a site for Cold War battles. Socialist East Germany had a diplomatic presence in Zanzibar and, by extension, Tanzania, now that the two countries were united. West Germany operated a rigid foreign policy of declining aid to any country that recognized East Germany. Southern Rhodesia's unilateral declaration of independence (UDI) in 1965 led to another financial setback for Tanzania, which severed diplomatic ties with Britain for its passive response to Ian Smith's UDI. Britain halted its £7.5 million loan that had been approved for Tanzania but not yet signed into effect. The financial assumptions of Tanzania's first five-year plan fell apart.[70] This experience would encourage Nyerere to actively court investment from the West and the East to prevent a vulnerable dependence on any one camp. China would become a major investor in Tanzania, financing and building the most expensive Chinese investment outside China in the 1970s, the Tanzania-Zambian Railway.

Africa's newly independent states faced certain political economic imperatives. Of topmost concern was diversifying primary dependence on the export of raw materials. In the context of declining world prices for raw materials and declining demand for these products, adding value to raw materials through processing was urgent. Governments needed to expand sources of revenue, and industrialization promised to be the solution. In the immediate aftermath of World War II, Latin American economies, under the aegis of the Economic Commission for Latin America (ECLA) and the leadership of Prebisch (see chap. 3), formalized import-substitution industrialization (ISI) as a strategy of growth for developing countries.[71] Considering the limited size of the markets of developing countries, it would be counterproductive if all countries in one region embarked on the same

ISI strategy. Who would sell to whom? Regional integration represented a meaningful avenue to plan for national and regional economic development. The withdrawal of foreign aid for Tanzania in 1965, which torpedoed its first five-year development plan, underscored the fragility of national sovereignty for poor, newly independent African governments. Regional and continental integration offered protection against the manipulation of rich, developed countries.

Nkrumah, the champion of continental unity, summed up the African situation in 1962, recognizing and stressing the need to transcend the allure of national sovereignty: "It is natural that each one of us should be proud of his own state, its national flag and national anthem. We of this generation shall never forget the price that we had to pay in order to hoist the flag and to sing that national anthem in our own free and independent territory, even though the barriers between their territories are artificial and not of our own making."[72] But symbolic political independence was not enough. Nkrumah continued: "As things stood, three possibilities were open to African states: to look to each other and pool their resources, to look to one or other of the foreign powers and become dependent upon them, or to isolate themselves and regress. There could be no question in the mind of any African that an overall economic, industrial and agricultural planning on a united continental basis would increase the industrial and economic power of Africa. But that could not be achieved until African States come together in a political union to give political direction."[73] While continental political unity along Nkrumah's lines proved elusive, the ideas of aggressive economic growth and economic decolonization caught on. It was imperative that new governments grow their economies if they were to meet the expectations of independence, and for this, states had to become developmental. This became one facet of Pan-African socialism, but the rhetoric of socialism just clouded what was at heart a nationalistic agenda.

THE AFRICAN DEVELOPMENTAL STATE AND AGGRESSIVE ECONOMIC GROWTH

Mkandawire has pointed out that for a state to become developmental, it has to meet both ideological and structural requirements. The developmentalist ideology requires the state to assume rapid growth as its mission, pursuing high rates of accumulation and industrialization. Indeed, the capacity of the state to pursue high growth rates and transform the structure of the economy and its relation to the international economy becomes the *raison d'être* of the developmental state—its claim to legitimacy. Structurally, the state must have the capacity to implement economic policies effectively. This presupposes state autonomy and freedom to pursue long-term economic policies.[74] Building the state's capacity to plan ended in the growth of a large bureaucratic bourgeoisie in developmental states. The developmental state at its inception had popular mandate in Africa, as both political leaders and societies were eager to embark on development and reap its benefits. That the developmental state paved the way for authoritarianism was unfortunate. And that it failed to deliver on its economic promise does not make the state any less developmental, as Mkandawire reminds us.[75]

Chambi Chachage and Chachage Seithy Chachage provide an excellent description of the developmental state in reference to the first decade of Tanzania's independence:

> Very briefly, the Tanzanian development model in the first decade of independence stressed the need for state intervention in the economy as a means to achieve development. It was premised on the need for the concentration of powers in the executive arm of the state with the intention of bringing social services, industries and infrastructure to the people—a form of welfarism or a quasi-socialist model. The common interests of the people were made subject to government activity, from building schools, dispensaries, etc. to village communal property. In return, people were expected to accept a high degree of economic control and at the same time offer united political loyalty.[76]

Developmental states thrived on a sort of social contract that united leaders and people with the vision of a better material future.

Two important international developments facilitated the ideology and structure of the African developmental state and gave form to Pan-African socialism. The first was the turn toward import-substitution industrialization by Latin American countries in the 1940s. This turn was given formal articulation by 1950 with the creation of the ECLA in 1948 and the pioneering work of its first executive secretary, Prebisch. The ECLA gave birth to one of the most important theories of development in the 1950s and 1960s: the "structuralist model" of development.[77] Perhaps more than any other institution, the ECLA—as the most important economic institution in the Third World in the 1950s—was responsible for putting development on the international agenda in that decade, an item that had not featured prominently in the work of the World Bank and the IMF.[78] The ECLA made two key arguments. First, the global capitalist system was ordered around center and periphery. The center lay in the West, where industrialized economies produced manufactured products. The periphery lay in the developing world, assigned the production of primary materials by the capitalist system. That the terms of trade constantly declined for producers of primary products was a primary reason for the underdevelopment of the Third World. In a major study in 1950 that has been described as the manifesto of the ECLA, Prebisch provided a "ringing critique of the international division of labor and declining terms of trade for producers of primary products, [and] called for industrialization as the only path to development in the underdeveloped countries of Latin America."[79] Second, the ECLA provided theoretical justification for import-substitution industrialization (ISI) as a growth strategy, to the point that the "name ECLA became virtually synonymous with ISI and structuralist economic thought."[80] Import-substitution industrialization was presented as a strategy of growth for developing countries.

The second important international development was the Bandung Conference of 1955, its pronouncements, and the spirit it engendered. For what was to become the Third World, Bandung was as galvanizing as the 1945 Manchester Congress had been for African participants. The Bandung Conference "not only condemned imperialism and colonial rule but saw the 'right to industrialization, as a legitimate pursuit.'"[81] Diouf comments that "the philosophy that emerged following the Bandung Conference and persisted through 1975 is defined as the new developmentalism that was supported by independence, modernization, and industrialization."[82] As the spirit of Bandung promoted new international bodies in the global South, the ECLA's encouragement in the late 1950s and 1960s that Latin American countries couple regional integration with economic growth plans solidified the economic agenda for the African developmental state and the vision of internationalists like Nkrumah.[83] Genoud stresses that "Nkrumah's almost desperate plea for a united Africa, whatever the merits of Ghana's approach to this problem . . . [was significantly connected] to the experience of Ghana, i.e., a country on the threshold of real industrialization."[84] There was an important economic argument for regional integration and continental unity. Ghana's attempt at a form of economic development that reduced its dependency on the West speaks to the politics of development and how regional, continental, and international contexts framed the national agendas of the newly independent African states.

Ghana

Despite the seeming prosperity of the Ghanaian economy, Nkrumah was aware that Ghana's economy on independence was colonial and had undergone little structural change since the introduction of cocoa at the turn of the twentieth century. Central objectives for Nkrumah were to diversify the economy from its overwhelming dependence on cocoa (see chap. 5), to decolonize the Ghanaian economy and break its structural dependence on the West, and to make Ghanaians—in this case, the state—the dominant force in the economy. For Nkrumah, the absence of a capitalist middle class meant that the state would play the lead role in industrialization and in wresting control of the economy from expatriate interests. Though this approach was described as socialism and seen as a historical necessity in the absence of an indigenous capitalist class, Genoud concludes that it was nothing more than "a straightforward nationalist program of development."[85] And though the CPP may have marked the period from 1964 as a distinctively socialist phase, Genoud argues that an existing thread connects the CPP's economic policies from 1951 through to the overthrow of Nkrumah in February 1966.[86] Even the socialist program of the Seven-Year Development Plan (1964–70) did not anticipate nationalization, and throughout Nkrumah's tenure a mixed economy of state and foreign involvement was allowed with the intention that the state, through its investments, gradually become the dominant player in the economy by the end of the 1970s.

On independence, only 10 percent of the Ghanaian economy was in industry, of which 41 percent was in mining, all expatriate owned. Commerce (wholesale and retail trade) made up 30 percent of the economy, with 80 percent of wholesale and retail trade controlled by a handful of European and American firms. Only agriculture was wholly controlled by Ghanaians, and largely by small-scale peasant farmers. In the small manufacturing sector, a handful of European and American firms accounted for over 90 percent of the income.[87] Banking was in the hands of two major expatriate banks, Barclays and the Bank of West Africa. In short, Ghana's economy was very much an open economy, typical of colonial and neocolonial economies. It was economically dependent on a few Western countries, primarily Britain and the United States, and 60 percent of foreign exchange earnings came from cocoa.[88]

To move from an open to a closed economy and lessen foreign control of the Ghanaian economy, Nkrumah's development strategy was three pronged: massive investment in education, especially technical and university education; infrastructural development; and investment in manufacturing activities through import-substitution industrialization.[89] The period from 1951 to 1957 witnessed huge investment in education. The number of students enrolled in primary, middle, and secondary schools, technical institutions, and universities expanded phenomenally between 1951 and 1966. Nkrumah saw education as playing three important roles in independent Ghana: first, producing a scientifically literate population; second, tackling the environmental causes of low productivity; and third, producing knowledge to tap into Ghana's economic potential.[90] Nkrumah saw the building of infrastructure as the path to breaking the West's stranglehold and decolonizing the Ghanaian economy.[91] Between 1951 and 1961, massive investment in education, health, roads, the Tema Harbor—the largest artificial harbor in Africa—and a doubling of electricity production (even before the Akosombo Dam) were pursued with an eye to industrialization. Nkrumah's vision of an industrialized, modern, Ghanaian nation-state informed the invitation of Arthur Lewis to provide a blueprint for industrialization in 1953 (see chap. 3) and the dogged pursuit of the Volta River Project (see chap. 5). After 1960, when Ghana became a republic, the emphasis shifted to the building of industries. Hirschman notes that import-substitution industrialization has been pursued under four conditions: during balance of payment difficulties; in times of war; in response to the gradual growth of income; and as a deliberate development policy.[92] In West Africa, initial experiments with ISI occurred during World War II, when the shortage of shipping space due to wartime exigencies encouraged expatriate companies in imports and exports to establish a few factories to produce the consumer goods they previously imported.

Nkrumah's pursuit of ISI was a deliberate development strategy, ideologically not predisposed to cultivating and supporting indigenous Ghanaian businesses. The agenda for ISI was the state taking the lead through state-owned enterprises. William Steel writes that "Nkrumah specifically stressed the import-substituting role of domestic manufacturing industries, in order to reduce dependence on former colonial powers for those goods. He saw industrialization as a dynamic development force, not only for diversifying the economic structure, but for training workers, providing capital for further investment and motivating Ghanaians. IS industrialization was thus initially conceived primarily as a means of achieving economic independence and growth, rather than as a response to foreign exchange needs."[93] What followed was Nkrumah's big push to establish a wide range of industries, several with the assistance of countries in the Eastern Bloc. Nkrumah's distrust of Western imperial powers led him even to solicit Soviet assistance for new geological surveys in Ghana to gain a better sense of Ghana's natural resources. The communist countries of the Eastern Bloc and China offered interest-free or low-interest loans repaid over longer periods of time. They also offered economic and technical aid that could be repaid in African commodities. After a delegation from Ghana traveled to Moscow in August 1960, the Soviet Union gave Ghana aid to the tune of 160 million rubles, which could be used by Ghana to exploit natural resources, build hydraulic power stations, develop industrial plants, and train technicians. The Soviet Union accepted in return cocoa, coffee, rubber, and fruit.[94]

Exploring investments from both the West and the East was Nkrumah's understanding of "positive neutralism," an active but nonideological engagement with the two Cold War camps. Ghanaian newspaper the *Daily Graphic* published a gazette notice in 1962 "[that] indicated that in the sixty-three agreements signed in 1961 with foreign governments; forty-four were with East European countries on trade and payments as well as scientific, technical, and cultural co-operation; five were with China; five were with Yugoslavia; and one was with the United States, on the operation of the Peace Corps."[95] The Accra correspondent of the *Frankfurter Allgemeine Zeitung* in December 1961 astutely recognized a pattern emerging in Nkrumah's economic engagement with the United States and the Soviet Union. Commenting on the £38.1 million in credit granted to Ghana by various countries from the Soviet Bloc, the reporter noted that "as a result of these credits Ghana is to receive an iron ore plant, a steel works, boot and shoe and textile factories, several shipbuilding yards, assembly works for Soviet tractors, sugar, rubber and yarn factories, a glass works, and so on. It will all be industrial plant [*sic*] that Ghana badly needs, and some of it will consume a great deal of power. Without the Volta Project this power would simply not be available."[96] But Nkrumah was far from fully embracing the Soviet Union. He did not intend to exchange Britain's imperial hegemony for Russia's, and Nana Osei-Opare is correct in his argument that Nkrumah was circumspect in his relations with "the Soviets in large part due to . . . fear of being recolonized by another white superpower—the USSR."[97] To balance Soviet influence in Ghana, Nkrumah showed a preference for dealing with smaller countries in the Eastern Bloc like Hungary, as these Second World countries also sought to minimize dependence on the Soviet Union through trade in noncommunist, postcolonial markets.[98]

It did not take long for Ghana's ISI push to run into difficulties. The 1950s witnessed a surge in public and private consumption as cocoa wealth fueled consumer imports, and the size of government grew. With the addition of capital expenditures from 1961 for the establishment of factories, Ghana quickly depleted its foreign exchange reserves and began to run budget deficits (see chap. 3). The lack of foreign exchange warranted foreign exchange restrictions and import licenses. The government resorted to supplier credit to continue its acquisition of capital goods for industrialization, leading to the purchase of equipment often not ideal for the country and on unfavorable terms. The equipment obtained from suppliers was usually capital intensive, and the inability to import raw materials because of scarce foreign exchange resulted in the underutilization of plant capacity. Whereas only six investment projects had been started through supplier credit in 1959–60, these increased to nineteen in 1961, twenty-five in 1962, and in 1963 alone a total of fifty-five. Incredibly, of "the 210 supplier credit contracts signed by the end of 1965, 137 (65 percent) were payable within five years or less, and only 23 (11 percent) in ten years or more."[99] Poor implementation and foreign exchange difficulties undercut Ghana's ISI program. New factories were simply inefficient and could not compete against imports without high tariffs. The push toward industrialization diverted resources from agriculture (see chap. 5) and resulted in a decline in agriculture's share of the economy. Moreover, Ghana was unable to find new markets for cocoa, and while the Eastern countries were happy to export machinery to Ghana, they bought little in terms of cocoa. In 1963, only 11 percent of Ghana's imports came from the Eastern Bloc, and 13.7 percent of its exports went to the Bloc.[100] By the end of 1965, Ghana was bankrupt.

But to look at the balance sheet from only this perspective obscures the government's motivation and what it achieved. In 1960, private capital (mostly foreign) accounted for 67.6 percent of manufacturing and annual growth rates, state-owned enterprises another 19.5 percent, and joint state-private capital ventures the remaining 12.7 percent. In 1966, when the Nkrumah government was overthrown, the state's share of manufacturing had increased to 33.5 percent, and joint state-private capital investments to 50.3 percent. The sphere of private capital operating independently in manufacturing had shrunk considerably.[101] And Ghana grew at a quite impressive rate of between 5.5 and 6 percent per annum between 1955 and 1963, exceeded in West Africa by only the Ivory Coast (see chap. 3).[102] Kwesi Jonah shows the long-term control of Western capital of Ghana's economy between 1951 and 1965 and how it began to change in 1965. On independence in 1957, foreign investment in Ghana—primarily Western—totaled about £151 million. "Within the sixteen year period 1950–1965, the return of foreign investment in Ghana repatriated abroad was £127,764,000. Within the same period, Ghana lost £165,746,000 to foreign shipping and insurance companies handling its foreign trade. Remittances of foreigners working in Ghana within this period was £50,222,000. Such is the cost of foreign economic dominance in Ghana."[103] A different picture was emerging by 1965. "By 1965 the state-owned Ghana National Trading Corporation (G.N.T.C.) handled about 35% of the country's commercial imports; the State Insurance Corporation transacted about 50% of insurance business, the Ghana Commercial Bank accounted for 60% of total deposits, the Black Star Line, Ghana's state shipping line, carried about 17% of Ghana's sea-borne commerce, the Ghana National Construction Corporation handled all state-awarded contracts and fully or partially owned state factories accounted for 27% of total manufacturing output."[104]

The numerous commissions set up in 1966 and 1967 by the military government that overthrew Nkrumah to inquire into different aspects of the Ghanaian economy underscore how the state had displaced foreign private capital. A good illustration is the state's control of the purchasing of cocoa, the lifeblood of the Ghanaian economy. In May 1961, the government made the United Ghana Farmers' Cooperative Council (UGFCC) the sole buying agent for the Cocoa Marketing Board, and the UGFCC, clearly with the assistance of the government and the Bank of Ghana, made use of only the Ghana Commercial Bank in its produce financing transactions. Barclays and Bank of West Africa were certainly peeved to be pushed aside, and their heads complained about discrimination in the commission of inquiry into the local purchasing of cocoa set up after Nkrumah's overthrow, pointing to their long record of service to the country.[105] Set up in 1961, the Ghana Cargo Handling Company was given the monopoly of handling cargo at all ports in Ghana.[106]

Operating under the received wisdom of the IMF, which had placed Ghana under a stabilization program in 1966 (the first in sub-Saharan Africa), the new military government, the National Liberation Council, divested itself of state-owned enterprises. Minor ones were sold to Ghanaians, but the more substantial investments were operated as joint ventures between the state and private foreign capital or sold outright to foreign capital. The result was the restoration of foreign control of the Ghanaian economy.[107] Based on a sample of forty factories established in Ghana in the 1950s and 1960s, Steel reaches the conclusion that "there is no indication that state investment is necessarily any more efficient than investment of international corporations. On the other hand, it may be surprising to critics of Ghana's state enterprises that they do not appear to be significantly less efficient."[108] In ridding the state and country of industrial capacity built under the CPP government in the 1950s and 1960s, Ghana essentially deprived itself of industrial capacity that could have been the basis for an indigenous entrepreneurial bourgeoisie.[109] A new phase of state capitalism started in the 1970s under a different military government, the National Redemption Council, which also promoted Ghanaian businessmen. This new stock of industrial investments, including those by private Ghanaian businessmen, were seized by the military regime of John Jerry Rawlings in 1979 or on his return to military power in 1981. The industries were sold to foreign investors under Ghana's structural adjustment program from 1983. It is instructive that Africa's deindustrialization in the 1980s coincided with the imposition of structural adjustment by the IMF and World Bank.

Thus ended Nkrumah's revolutionary experiment to decolonize Ghana's economy and chart an autonomous path to sustained economic development. For Genoud, Ghana's development effort represents the only genuine endeavor to develop an economy under the true direction of Africans in that first generation of independence. He opines that "in the *economic field* what was undertaken, and partly achieved, by the Nkrumah-CPP Government is immense."[110] Africanization in Ghana proceeded in substance, and Ghanaians with very few exceptions were in key positions and made key decisions. Genoud concludes that "one might say that what made Ghana stand out among other tropical African countries was not so much that

Ghana was doing better (this was not always true) but that Ghana, for better or for worse, was really in charge of her own affairs; if she were to commit mistakes, they were committed by herself, under her own responsibility! This was in striking contrast with the situation of most neighboring countries and this is the only true school of development."[111] This was the vision of the African developmental state. That ISI failed in Nkrumah's Ghana was not because of some inherent deficit in the approach, but due to inefficient utilization of resources as the government pursued its "'big push' on all fronts."[112] Moreover, a decade of ISI is not sufficient time to rule on its viability as a path to economic growth. In the case of the failure with ISI in Latin America in the 1960s, Hirschman points to political and institutional factors that undermined the capacity of industries to export as key factors more than the cost-price structure of the new industries.[113] For Nkrumah, as we will see below, new political and institutional arrangements for Africa were integral to the success of economic development.

Tanzania

In Tanzania we again encounter the disjuncture between rhetoric (socialism) and what was in reality a nationalistic economic agenda. Tanzania, like Ghana, remained a mixed economy with a role for foreign capital. The state nationalized foreign investments, providing compensation to the expatriate owners for the loss of their businesses—something Nkrumah did not do, as he believed the state sector could out-compete foreign investors. The Tanzanian state took the path of a developmental state, outlining a developmental ideology in the Arusha Declaration of 1967 and structurally expanding the capacity of the state to plan and direct the economy.[114] In its launch of Ujamaa (familyhood) after 1967, the state embarked on what has been considered one of the most thorough attempts to bring development to rural Africa and achieve equity across the rural-urban divide and at individual (communal) and regional levels.[115] Tanzania did not make a serious effort to decolonize its economy in terms of lessening its external dependence on the West. Indeed, in the heyday of Ujamaa, the West was a major investor in Tanzania's socialist endeavor. By 1980, the cutoff point for this study, Tanzania's economy remained a neocolonial one, exporting traditional agricultural products and importing manufactured products.[116]

A number of factors help explain this rather peculiar development of a developmental, self-defined African socialist state, which also remained a ward of the West. Nyerere and TANU were uncomfortable with the reality on independence that much large-scale agriculture was either expatriate-controlled plantations or settler farms. There was very little manufacturing in Tanzania aside from first-stage processing for exports of agricultural products like sisal, cotton, and tea. In East Africa, Kenya had emerged as the hub for import-substitution industries and had the jump on Tanzania of thirty to forty years in manufacturing. Nyerere was particularly keen on the creation of an East African Federation, a point we will come back to later. He was actually prepared to delay Tanganyika's independence if the British would grant independence simultaneously to Tanganyika, Uganda, and Kenya so that the three countries could enter a federation right from independence. This federation would have built on the East African High Commission that had connected the three countries since colonial times, and Nyerere was deeply disappointed that the East African Federation did not materialize.[117] It became clear that Tanganyika would have to embark on its own, separate developmental path, and its first five-year plan (1964–69) was designed with this in mind. The limitations of human and financial capital quickly became apparent. The five-year plan was formulated by an expatriate team led by French planner M. J. Faudon.[118] We have mentioned above how Tanzania's first five-year plan suffered early setbacks from the drop in the world's price of sisal, Tanzania's major export, and the withdrawal of aid by West Germany and Britain over diplomatic differences with Tanzania. It is ironic that the five-year plan, dependent on Western aid, "appeared to be a determined attempt to break away from the inherited structural dependence."[119] It sought to modernize agriculture through a "transformation approach" and to industrialize through import substitution.

Tanzania remained closely connected to the World Bank after independence in 1961; the World Bank under the influence of modernization theory was an enthusiast of agricultural settlement schemes, including Tanzania's early villagization program. Tanzania launched its first three-year plan from 1961–63 with the assistance of the World Bank. Tanzanian professor of law Issa Shivji writes of this stage that "the heart of the World Bank's villagisation programme was the modernization theory which was rampant at that time. Traditional peasants had to be pulled into and integrated in the international commodity circuits. The programmme was based on the so-called transformation and improvement approach. Model farmers would be settled in villages, given modern technology and they would farm under the supervision of managers."[120] This program of villagization left untouched the structures of Tanzania's colonial economy, which exported primary materials and imported manufactured items. At this stage, villagization was more about the provision of social services than it was a model of economic development. Indeed, Nyerere's pro-poor policies would mesh with the agenda of the World Bank from 1968 under its new president, Robert McNamara, who made poverty a key platform.[121] Thus, the World Bank remained a supporter of Tanzania even with the declaration of Ujamaa.

Nyerere's ideology and practice were rife with contradictions. Of the two highly educated, English-speaking presidents from the first generation, Nkrumah and Nyerere, Shivji notes that Nyerere was not a theorist, pointing to the "virtual absence of his theorizing village development as charting out a new path of development."[122] Nyerere just wanted to see the standard of living rise for Tanzanians. He was uncomfortable with the accumulation of wealth, whether by urban workers and entrepreneurs or rural peasants. Shivji continues: "Mwalimu's thought did not capture the political economy aspect of his central emphasis on the village. I would dare suggest that this is because Mwalimu, unlike, for example, Nkrumah, did not fully understand or appreciate the political economy of imperialism. As is well known, he never accepted that building socialism was a process of class struggle. He did not therefore accept that the state he was leader of had a class character. He believed that the state could carry out the reforms he genuinely believed in so long as it had a selfless, committed leadership."[123] Nyerere naively believed that if he could prevent accumulation in rural and urban Tanzania, he could avert the formation of classes and the concomitant class struggle that had torn European society apart. There had been a burst of import-substitution industries from 1958 with Tanzania's approach to independence, as the Asian community in Tanzania invested in manufacturing at the encouragement of the Aga Khan to protect its future in the country. Multinational companies in East Africa that had supplied Tanzania from factories in Kenya or Uganda also established subsidiaries in Tanzania.[124] Tanzania's economy grew between 1961 and 1966 at a GDP rate of 4.8 percent per annum. But Nyerere considered this rate and the dependent nature of the economy unsatisfactory. Though the country enjoyed balance of payment surpluses, the huge needs of the country required a more robust growth rate.[125] Nyerere also worried that a dependent but growing African capitalist class was emerging in Tanzania.[126] Moreover, rural areas had benefited little in the economic growth up to 1966. This state of affairs was the backdrop to the Arusha Declaration in early 1967.

Being a soft theorist had its advantages in the age of Cold War, especially compared to Nkrumah's strident rhetoric, which alienated the West and neighboring countries in West Africa. Even Nyerere's 1967 Arusha Declaration, which launched Tanzania's socialist project with a focus on agriculture and self-reliance, state-led import-substitution industrialization, and expansion of manufacturing under state control, still branded itself as a third path.[127] Pointing to how the Agrarian and Industrial Revolutions in Europe had generated classes and made class struggle a driver in European history, Nyerere stressed that the foundations of African socialism instead lay in the extended family: "'Ujamaa,' then, or 'Familyhood,' describes our socialism." It opposed capitalism and doctrinaire socialism, the first based on exploitation of man by man, the second on the "inevitable conflict between man and man."[128] Within a week of the publication of the Arusha Declaration on February 5, 1967, the government announced the nationalization of all commercial banks, the major grain-milling firms, and the largest foreign-owned import-export business. It would take controlling interest in the subsidiary plants in Tanzania of multinational corporations. But this government pursuit was not done in a combative spirit; existing commitments were honored and assets acquired were duly compensated.[129] This soft theoretical or ideological position explains the anomaly of a socialist country upheld by Western aid throughout the 1970s.

The center stage of Tanzania's socialist drive post–Arusha Declaration was rural development through Ujamaa villages. We have seen attempts at villagization in the early 1960s with the support of the World Bank. The focus in these early attempts was to make social services available to concentrated rural settlements. Then came the transformation approach under the first five-year plan with assistance from the World Bank, establishing capital-intensive agricultural resettlement schemes designed to take advantage of river valleys, irrigation, mechanization, fertilizers, and improved seeds. The transformation approach failed. The Ujamaa village envisaged a small group of politically committed peasants living together as a group and working on a communal farm. In spirit, this movement was supposed to be voluntary. Seeing that the majority of the country's peasants were unwilling to relocate from family lands and homesteads, the relocation to Ujamaa villages ceased to be voluntary; the government applied force from 1973. Tanzania underwent one of the major episodes of social engineering in independent Africa's history, with the government compelling nine million peasants to relocate to Ujamaa villages within a period of four to five years under "Operation Vijiji." The government resorted to compulsion when it became evident that peasants were not interested in communal production. About 70 percent of the Tanzanian population had moved their homes by 1975.[130] By 1976, about 91 percent of the rural population lived in Ujamaa villages. Nyerere envisaged communal production in these villages, but low production and low expectations reinforced each other—peasants were not motivated to work on cooperative farms, exerting themselves instead on their private farms. By the mid-1970s, government insistence on communal farming had softened.[131]

The Arusha Declaration in 1967 announced the government's intention to nationalize industries. Coulson observes that "in less than ten years from the Arusha Declaration, the State had taken a controlling interest in virtually all productive institutions that could easily be nationalized."[132] When Nyerere took stock of the Tanzanian economy in 1977, he admitted honestly that it had done badly both in agriculture and industry. He conceded that "the truth is that the agriculture results have been very disappointing."[133] In terms of industry, Nyerere noted that "almost all our industrial plants are running well below capacity; sometimes less than 50 per cent of what could be produced with existing machinery is actually being manufactured and put to the market."[134] Import-substitution industries underperformed in Tanzania, as "many of the new factories involved only the last stage of manufacture or assembly of imported inputs, and were consequently intensive in their use of foreign exchange."[135] Like in Ghana, factories in Tanzania post-Arusha tended to be capital intensive and built on expensive supplier credit that needed to be repaid in foreign exchange.[136] This was problematic for a country whose foreign reserves had declined to almost zero by 1975. Whereas the economy had grown in the 1960s, the only sector that showed growth in the 1970s was subsistence agriculture.[137] Economists Mwase and Ndulu provide the reasons for this dismal failure: "The egalitarian undertones in government policy-making resulted in the subordination of economic incentives to political objectives. Economic policy-making during the 1970s and early 1980s was designed to support the political goal of achieving equity at the interpersonal, inter-regional, and rural-urban levels."[138] By the late 1970s, Ujamaa had been abandoned. There was no incentive for peasants to exert themselves when they did not reap the rewards of their labor. While communal farming in Ujamaa villages had failed, Ujamaa delivered in other areas, particularly in the realm of social services like health, education, and water supply systems. The provision of social services was part of the inspiration for Nyerere's early villagization project. Dean McHenry concluded in 1979, a few years before Nyerere gave up Ujamaa, that Tanzania of all countries had come closest to achieving many of its objectives under African socialism, "but there is a paradox: the more steps taken toward realizing the vision of Ujamaa village life, the less confidence there is that it can ever be *fully* achieved."[139]

Strikingly, unlike Ghana under Nkrumah, which was penalized by the Western donor community for Nkrumah's socialist policies, donor money flowed into Tanzania throughout Nyerere's period in government. Here we see the benefits of a soft ideology, as Tanzania despite its adherence to socialism managed to appeal to the liberal ideals of the West because of its pro-poor policies. In this, Tanzania offered a convenient recourse for the West to appear nonideological by offering aid to a socialist country. As Coulson puts it, "Western governments did not wish to be seen as offering all their aid to avowedly right-wing regimes: 'Socialist' Tanzania was a useful corrective."[140] Likewise, the World Bank legitimized itself by extending loans to a socialist country. Indeed, most of "McNamara's recommendations about rural development, education, and income distribution in successive annual reports of the World Bank were already official policy in Tanzania."[141] Relations with Western multilateral finance institutions continued even when Nyerere was dismissive of an IMF delegation that had visited Tanzania in 1979 to discuss retrenchment and the devaluation of the Tanzanian shilling.[142] Not until Nyerere stepped down in 1985 were his successors able to steer Tanzania toward the IMF and neoliberal policies.[143] And though the West may have disagreed with some of Nyerere's policies in his socialist drive, there was respect for the sincerity of his endeavor and his integrity. Mwase and Ndulu comment that "it is quite striking that even the 'hard control' phase of Tanzania's development received quite strong endorsement by development partners, as evidenced by the large inflows of aid and official credit to fund the country's socialist programs. Despite the enunciation of African socialism as the basis for government policy-making, aid inflows increased significantly during the period 1967–77, in both absolute terms and relative to other SSA [sub-Saharan countries] countries. The 'socialist' vision of Mwalimu Nyerere's presidency excited widespread admiration and support from academics and policy makers in the capitalist West."[144] In contrast, the American pushback against Nkrumah was extraordinary, including the CIA's (Central Intelligence Agency) complicity in his overthrow.[145]

But Nkrumah's policies were not markedly different from Nyerere's. Both led developmental states. Both resorted to import-substitution industrialization. Both declared one-party states, and their governments were both clearly authoritarian. Both were supportive of African liberation movements, as we will see in the next section. Both courted (played off) the West and the East in their pursuit of investment—their definition of "positive neutralism." Unlike Nyerere, Nkrumah refrained from nationalizing expatriate investments. But what was distinctively different under Nkrumah, drawing the antagonism of the West, was his effort to decolonize the Ghanaian economy, to sever the traditional dependence on the West. Genoud's reflections on this endeavor are instructive:

> In this sense, one may wonder whether Ghana was not, in the last analysis, the victim of its own inability to free itself from its economic dependence on the West, rather than the victim of its official choice of a "socialist path of development." A pro-Western, nonsocialist Ghana might have attracted more private foreign investments than a neutralist Ghana such as Nkrumah's Ghana, but a neutralist Ghana which would have managed with the assistance of the socialist countries to free itself from its overwhelming dependence on its traditional Western partners might have attracted even more foreign capital, perhaps with a different composition. In any case, a rather weak neutralist country, unable to balance better its economic partners, represented the worst possible bargaining position.[146]

Ghana was the pioneering Black independent African nation and an exemplar to many, and the West could not countenance that a new African nation-state successfully decolonize its economy. After flirting briefly with decolonizing Tanzania's economy, Nyerere turned in a different direction.

Guinea

The Republic of Guinea on independence struggled to follow in the mold of the developmental state. While its dramatic attainment of independence abruptly severed Guinea's ties with France—effectively decolonizing Guinea's economy—Guinea's economy was very underdeveloped, though the country was rich in natural resources. So Guinea's start as an independent country after its famous "No" vote in 1958 was rocky. France retaliated by withdrawing financial and material support, and French officials as they left stripped Guinea of records, equipment, and anything that could be moved; they destroyed what could not be moved. Even telephone lines were severed. Guinea became independent on October 2, 1958. It was Kwame Nkrumah's loan of £10 million pounds sterling in late November 1958—after the two countries had entered a vaguely defined union—that prevented Guinea's collapse.[147] The heroic, nationalist vote that birthed an independent Guinea would shape Touré's entire tenure as president. France's incessant schemes to undermine Guinea's independence, which included opposing its application for membership to the United Nations, supporting coup attempts, and lobbying its Western allies and other francophone African countries to ostracize Touré and Guinea, put the country on a path that it has "yet to recover, long after the death of de Gaulle (1970) and Touré (1984)."[148] "Indeed, from October 1958 (Guinea's independence from France) to October 1982 (Touré's only state visit to France) Guinea's sovereignty was largely framed in terms of defending the country from a French perennial plan of neo-colonial reconquest, or else from a sustained sabotage of the regime's policies and international relations."[149] In a postcolonial Africa where most francophone countries had entered into dependent relations with France, France could not afford to allow the Guinean option of complete independence to be admired and seen as a model.

Guinea's economy on independence was based on banana and other fruit plantations and the mining of gold, diamonds, bauxite, and iron. France's withdrawal and the country's isolation by the West left Guinea at the mercy of the Eastern Bloc countries. The rift between Guinea and France required Guinea, politically, to introduce its own currency. In March 1960, Guinea introduced the Guinean franc, which was not convertible with the CFA franc instituted by France as a currency for francophone Africa. This effectively ended Guinea's official trade with its francophone neighbors. Touré tried to put on a brave face, asking the francophone countries still using the CFA franc "how then can one consider oneself economically free, if the currency being used in one's country has been put into circulation in the interests of foreigners."[150] Touré advocated for an authentically African monetary zone. Mohamed Camara notes that no sooner had Guinea introduced its new currency in 1960 than the French secret service attempted to flood the Guinean market with counterfeit.[151] Guinea struck out on a nationalistic path on independence. "Immediately after independence, the PDG created import and export enterprises to reduce reliance on French companies and nationalized banks, insurance companies, transportation, and the public utilities. In March 1960, the government created its own currency . . . The national economy was designed according to some general socialist guidelines. A three-year plan of development was formulated at the Kankan Conference in April 1960 to bring about industrialization and higher agricultural productivity through modernization and collectivization."[152] But the three-year plan (1960–63) was formulated on the assumption that foreign investment and aid would come. That was an optimistic assumption. Aid and investment were not forthcoming, and many major projects would have to be abandoned or modified.[153]

Though communist countries quickly signed trade agreements, extended credit, and sent technicians, there was little follow-through on their economic agreements, and Guinea found itself in dire straits by the end of 1961. The country's three-year plan had been made with the promises of the Eastern Bloc countries in mind.[154] The Eastern Bloc did not deliver. Meanwhile, communist propaganda materials flooded Guinea with visits of delegations and instructors from Eastern Bloc countries. Economic dissatisfaction with the government climaxed with widespread political unrest by trade unionists, teachers, and students in November 1961 and a demand for the imposition of communism.[155] Announcing a "communist-inspired conspiracy," the government acted swiftly to end the disturbances, and Touré demanded that Khrushchev recall the Soviet ambassador to Guinea, Daniel Semyonovitch Solod.[156]

In January 1961, John F. Kennedy became the thirty-fifth president of United States, and his personal approach to diplomacy and courting of African nationalist leaders opened a new window of opportunity for Touré and Guinea. Kennedy's position was that Africa's leaders were mostly nationalists and not communists and that there existed a platform for collaboration if the United States was sensitive to their need for economic development.[157] Kennedy declared the 1960s the "decade of development," and more African heads of state visited the White House in the three years of Kennedy's administration than under any other president in US history.[158] Kennedy

Fig 4.1 Kwame Nkrumah visits John F. Kennedy, March 8, 1961. Credit: Abby Rowe, National Park Service, John F. Kennedy Library and Museum.

appointed William H. Attwood as American ambassador to Guinea, an astute choice. A trained journalist, Attwood in 1959 had obtained an exclusive interview with Fidel Castro and was a strong advocate in the Kennedy administration of the possibility of rapprochement with Cuba.[159] In an early consultation with Touré, who was eager to attract American aid and investment, Attwood expressed American unease at Guinea's uncritical endorsement of Soviet positions in world issues, American investors' fear of nationalization, and the difficulty in financing development in Guinea due to Touré's refusal to join the IMF and the World Bank. Attwood assured Touré that the US was open to assisting Guinea's developmental effort, so long as it was not building up a Soviet satellite.[160]

Touré responded to Attwood that on the abrupt French withdrawal from Guinea, the first country he approached for assistance was the United States through President Eisenhower, who had not even responded to his correspondence. Touré reassured Attwood that nationalization of industry

Fig 4.2 Leopold Senghor visits John F. Kennedy, November 3, 1961. Credit: Abby Rowe, National Park Service, John F. Kennedy Library and Museum.

was not the objective of the Guinean government, and the only reason water, electricity, and the diamond enterprises had been nationalized was because of their inefficient operation and the need to attract investment for their further expansion. The presence of technicians from the Eastern Bloc was more a reflection of the lack of trained Guinean technicians and administrators than a preference for Soviet assistance. Touré expressed an interest in securing American assistance to train Guineans for the public and private sectors and as teachers, warming up to Attwood's description of the Peace Corps. And though the Soviets were completing a survey for the construction of a dam on the Konkouré River, key to building light industry and electrifying cities, Touré was emphatic that no agreement had been signed with the Russians.[161] Pending a favorable survey, the Russians had offered to construct a dam and build an aluminum smelter for Guinea's vast bauxite reserves. The ground was set for subsequent discussions between the United States and Guinea, resulting in an aid package for the struggling country.

Fig 4.3 Ahmed Sékou Touré visits John F. Kennedy, October 10, 1962. Credit: Abby Rowe, National Park Service, John F. Kennedy Library and Museum.

John F. Kennedy approved an aid program for Guinea despite the protestations of French President de Gaulle, as Muehlenbeck notes. "It was agreed that Guinea would be offered the construction of a dam on the Konkouré River that was capable of providing power for light industry, staffing for an English-language teaching program, food aid, a training program for Guinean administrative and technical personnel involved in industry and government, and a Peace Corps contingent."[162] Touré gladly accepted the offer.[163] Under Attwood's encouragement, Touré overcame his reservations about the World Bank, which he viewed as under French influence, and in 1962 Guinea applied to join the World Bank and the IMF with American support.[164] Guinea also signed an agreement allowing a Western consortium to develop the Nimba iron deposits. The exploitation of Guinea's mineral resources remained in the hands of large Western companies, and Touré was willing to accommodate this arrangement because it represented a lifeline for Guinea's economy. This was especially true regarding

Fig 4.4 Julius Nyerere visits John F. Kennedy at the White House, July 16, 1963. Credit: Abby Rowe, National Park Service, John F. Kennedy Library and Museum.

the exploitation of bauxite, and the mining concerns in Boké and Fria existed in a special category. It was important to the US that Russia not build the dam on Konkouré and be in a position to command Guinea's bauxite. A Russian-funded hydroelectric dam would imperil Western investments in Boké and Fria, which the Soviets could take over. On the other hand, the US did not want to build the large dam and smelter that the developmental French colonial state had planned before independence to exploit Guinea's newly discovered bauxite. Doing so would make Guinea an economic powerhouse, which was Touré's desire. The US would provide sufficient support for Guinea to meet its immediate economic and social needs and improve the living conditions of its population—that would woo Touré from the Soviet camp. Considerations of a larger dam or smelter could be undertaken in the future by the private companies involved in Fria and Boké.[165]

Touré proved that he was not an ideologue in his position toward the Soviet Union during the Cuban Missile Crisis, when he refused Soviet planes permission to refuel in Conakry en route to Cuba.[166] During Kennedy's tenure through 1963, Guinea's economy was marked by soft government control. The state's policy later changed to one of hard control as state planning replaced the market.[167] Whether the assassination of Kennedy in 1963 influenced this turn is an interesting question. When informed of Kennedy's death, Touré lamented: "I have lost my only true friend in the outside world."[168] From 1964 through 1984, Guinea switched to a state-controlled economy, and it adopted scientific socialism as official policy in 1967. The state marketed agricultural produce, and farmers were required to deliver a part of their produce to state shops. The state also set producer prices. But while the state guarded against indigenous capitalism and the internal divisions this could cause, it allowed the foreign-controlled Fria Bauxite Complex to operate as a capitalist enclave for several years after independence, as the government depended on it for more than 60 percent of the country's foreign exchange.[169] Lansiné Kaba, writing in 1977, observed of Guinea's bauxite industry that "for instance, the French Pechiney Corporation has been operating the multi-national bauxite and aluminum complex of Fria since 1957, and its installations and assets have never been threatened by nationalization. The French *Société des Bauxites du Midi*, which substantially reduced its activities after independence, was nationalized and transformed into a joint enterprise between Guinea and Aluminum Limited of Canada. The Government has 49 per cent of the shares in the most important multi-national corporation in Guinea: the Boké industrial complex created by the California-based Harvey Aluminum Corporation."[170] But outside these select Western-run industries, Guinea's economy declined sharply. The economy demonetized as citizens disengaged from the market economy, and Touré by 1973 requested that citizens pay their taxes in cattle and food crops and stated that these were acceptable fares for the pilgrimage to Mecca.[171] In 1982, Guinea with its economy in crisis became a ward of the World Bank and the IMF and adopted a structural adjustment program.[172]

Senegal

Senghor on Senegal's independence in 1960 had two major tasks in terms of the economy: to find markets for Senegal's manufacturing sector in the wake of the dissolution of the French West African Federation, which had constituted a secure market for Senegal's industries; and to improve productivity in the groundnut industry and diversify agriculture away from overwhelming dependence on groundnuts. What distinguished Senegal's developmental efforts from those of Ghana, Guinea, and Tanzania was that they were pursued in close affinity with the former colonial power, France.[173] The first objective made Senghor an ardent champion of federalism. The second gave Senegal's economic development program on independence an agrarian orientation, even though Senghor noted that colonialism had relegated the dominated to agriculture and that "there is no development without industrialization."[174] Diouf points to the huge influence of French and Catholic thinkers on Senegalese understandings of development and the impact of Dominican priest Louis-Joseph Lebret and development theorist Francois Perroux on Senghor and his prime minister Dia.[175] The Dominicans led a movement on economics and humanism, which had at its center land use planning. The Dominicans' interest in land use reinforced the Senegalese emphasis on agrarian reform. To put in place the new policies of land use and economic planning, an extensive bureaucratic infrastructure evolved in the pattern of Ghana and Tanzania, where the endeavor to create an African developmental state resulted in a technocratic state with a huge bureaucratic bourgeoisie. Senegalese socialism revolved around two strategies, both intended to transform the countryside: functional education in rural areas, including the training of female teachers and leaders (labeled broadly as a program of "animation"); and the encouragement of cooperatives, which were seen as the nexus or crucible of rural education, liberalization of the peasantry, and development. Through cooperatives, the state hoped to equip the Senegalese peasantry with technical competence. Envisaged under Dia, these policies continued in some form even after his removal in 1962, though agency shifted from the peasant as envisaged by Dia to technocrats. The result was the paradox that while Senghor underscored the importance of industrialization to development, the Senegalese government focused its energies on peasants and the countryside. The single-party system, declared in 1966, was meant to channel these energies.[176]

Regional Development Agencies were set up across the country to be engines of rural transformation, providing agricultural extension services and agricultural inputs such as fertilizers, pesticides, seeds, farm equipment, and credit to farmers. As an umbrella for these activities, the government created the Agricultural Marketing Board (Office de Commercialisation Agricole) in 1960, renamed the National Office of Agricultural Marketing and Development (ONCAD) in 1966. ONCAD not only provided inputs for farmers; after harvest, it collected the produce of farmers, arranged for transport, and collected payment for the inputs advanced to farmers. The Regional Development Agencies acted as liaisons between farmers' cooperatives and ONCAD. Credit to farmers was not in cash but in kind, in the form of inputs.[177] As we have seen in other state-led development programs, farmers had different priorities (see chaps. 3 and 5): "The credit components of the government programs never operated as policy-makers had intended. Inputs were frequently not used by the designated beneficiaries. When farmers became short of cash or food they would obtain credit in any form available. Often they would acquire more agricultural inputs than they wanted or needed. They would sell them immediately for cash, at a discount, or post them as collateral to borrow cash or food from local merchants."[178] Cattle would be fattened and sold to butchers instead of used for plows as intended. Many farmers did not repay their debts, collapsing the entire system. That the government forgave farmers' debts in bad harvest years encouraged farmers to default on loans. With recurrent droughts in the 1970s, there were several years where groundnut productivity fell below seventy thousand tons, which had never happened in the 1960s and compelled the government to annul some or all the debts of farmers on five occasions in the 1970s. By late 1980, the amount of unpaid farmers' debt for agricultural inputs totaled 30 billion CFA franc—over $100 million by the prevailing exchange rate. It had become clear that the entire system was untenable, and the government abolished the system and canceled the debts of farmers and ONCAD.[179]

Senegal's industrial sector also struggled as the state adopted protectionist policies in the interest of manufacturing companies that had lost access to the market of federated French West Africa on independence in 1960. Assured of a captive market under colonial rule, industries in Senegal seemed unable to think beyond the parameters of the colonial economy. New import-substitution industries established during independence also benefited from protective tariffs, which sheltered them from market forces and made them uncompetitive.[180] As a resource-scarce country, Senegal's major assets were the institutions and industries it had inherited as a federal capital under French colonial rule. From the 1960s, Sahelian droughts and the extension of desiccation undermined the viability of Senegal's groundnut industry. Senegal, due to massive indebtedness, would come under an

IMF stabilization program in 1979, a year before Senghor stepped down. The following year, Senegal embarked on structural adjustment.[181] On a per capita basis, Senegal's income grew at an annual rate of 2.9 percent between 1960 and 2000, with population growing at a rate of 3 percent. Ndiaye sums up the economic policies and results under Senghor, who stepped down from the presidency on December 31, 1980: "A study of Senegal's growth record between 1960 and 1993 reveals the dramatic impact of poor policy choices—notably a 'soft' control syndrome and an episode of unsustainable spending—that resulted in heavy market control, a poor investment environment, a large and inefficient government sector, a high level of trade protection, and an unsustainable debt strategy. To make matters worse, economic performance was badly hit by adverse climatic conditions, especially droughts, and declining world prices for the country's main exports."[182] The government not only interfered in manufacturing but it also depended on rent from the agricultural sector to underwrite the huge increase in the civil service from 34,900 employees in 1965 to 61,000 in 1973.[183] True to Senghor's commitment to partnership with French capital, foreign businesses were not nationalized, and Senegal's membership of the CFA franc zone and its closeness to France guaranteed external funding and protected it from devaluations until 1994, when France devalued the CFA franc by 50 percent.[184]

One irony of the Senegalese state was how it abandoned attempts to transcend the nature and limitations of the colonial economy and become a developmental state in ideology and structure with the departure of Dia in 1962, remaining dependent on French and Western technical support and funding. Visiting Dar es Salaam in April 1967, when ten African countries had military regimes, Senghor commented in a press conference that personal ambition and impatience at the rate of economic progress were to blame for the recent spate of coups on the African continent. In a rather resigned spirit, he stated that "he believed African countries might develop into nations in around 100 years, but at present they were in too much of a hurry. The President claimed that Senegal was now actively practicing Socialism, but said the country would need foreign capital for another 100 years."[185] Senegal remained very much a neocolony under Senghor. "Senghor never diversified Senegal's groundnut economy, which depended on an unpredictable international commodities market. He counted increasingly on French development aid, technical experts, and private investments. Senghor's government passed policies favorable to French companies, became a reliable ally of the French state, and avoided displeasing powerful provincial marabouts. His failures to meet popular expectations through effective development programs eroded public support for Senghor's regime by the 1970s."[186] Gone after 1962 was Dia's vision of a developmental state that would directly mobilize the peasantry by removing the intermediary role of marabouts, nurturing a prosperous rural peasantry in a decolonized economy.

African Liberation, Regional Integration, and Continental Unity

For Nkrumah, Touré, Senghor, and Nyerere, regional integration was a necessary dimension to economic development. Both Senghor and Touré had wanted a continuation of the French West African Federation on independence. But Senghor's vision went beyond African integration and included France, the former metropole with deeper pockets. After France's decades of exploiting the material wealth of Africa, Senghor believed it would be shortsighted on the part of African nationalists to give France a pass in an era when even "'European nations . . . feel the need to associate together within a larger community,' [and] small colonies as isolated countries could never be 'truly independent.'"[187] African regional integration was premised on the total liberation of Africa, starting with support for regional liberation movements. Not only did our leaders become advocates of Africa's total liberation, but they also took each other to task on any sign of compromise on this cardinal principle or collaboration with imperialists. We have seen Senghor's endeavors to preserve the French West African Federation in some form, with Senegal entering the short-lived Mali Federation after the demise of the French West African Federation (see introduction). Ghana, Guinea, and Tanzania all included clauses in their first republic constitutions giving priority to regional integration and continental unity over national sovereignty. We have seen above the market constraints of the experiments at import-substitution industrialization, as factories operated well below capacity because of restricted markets. Yet the newly independent countries embarked on their own forms of industrialization. Even Zanzibar, after its union with Tanganyika to form Tanzania in 1964, insisted on pursuing its own import-substitution industrialization, duplicating many of the industries on the mainland.[188] Robust economic growth and anticolonialism became two important precepts of Pan-African socialism and of any claim to leadership in newly independent Africa.

Nkrumah, who insisted Ghana's independence was meaningless without the total liberation of Africa and who pursued a continental vision that transcended the nation-state, devoted considerable effort and resources to the liberation struggle and the creation of a United States of Africa. In April 1958, Nkrumah convened the Conference of Independent African States (CIAS) in Accra; in December 1958, he hosted the All-African People's Conference (AAPC) in Accra with representatives from independent African countries and independence movements from territories still under European colonial rule. Nkrumah met Patrice Lumumba of the Belgian Congo at the December 1958 conference. The liberation movements invited to take residence in Accra included the Union des Populations du Cameroun (UPC), headed by Dr. Félix-Roland Moumié, who had replaced Reuben Um Nyobé when the latter was killed in September 1958.[189] It was Moumié who encouraged Nkrumah to consider a relationship with communist China in his fight against colonialism and imperialism.[190] Ghana recognized the People's Republic of China and established full diplomatic relations on July 6, 1960, becoming the second Black African country (after Guinea) to recognize China. Leaders of independence movements who lived in Ghana under Nkrumah included Hastings Banda of Nyasaland and Robert Mugabe of Southern Rhodesia (and his Ghanaian wife Sally), and Ghana provided offices for the ANC and Pan-Africanist Congress (PAC) from South Africa and the Zimbabwe African People's Union (ZAPU) and Zimbabwe African National Union (ZANU) from Southern Rhodesia.

Nkrumah's support for African liberation movements and dissident political groups from independent countries became a sore point for Ghana's neighbors and the United States. Relations with Ghana's immediate neighbors, the Ivory Coast and Togo, were tense. For the United States CIA, there was nothing ideological or principled about Nkrumah's championing of a United States of Africa. According to a CIA report from April 17, 1963, "Ghana's vain and egocentric Kwame Nkrumah is driven by his dreams of primacy in a united Africa and of a world role as a leading figure among the non-aligned states."[191] Even though the CIA believed Nkrumah was pro–Soviet Union, the agency considered his professed socialism insincere: "However, while he has a strong affinity for socialist doctrines, as adapted to the African milieu, he is primarily concerned with advancing his own designs."[192]

What the CIA seemed unable to recognize was the emotive and political significance attached to supporting liberation movements. Indeed, supporting these movements had become part of the credentials to leadership in Africa, though it came with considerable financial cost, as liberation movements were completely dependent on the financial support of the host country. Radical states like Egypt, Ghana, Guinea, Tanzania, and Algeria put in place extensive infrastructure to support liberation movements. As one of the early independent countries in Africa, Egypt attracted liberation movements from all over the continent. Sindiso Mfenyana, posted to Cairo as the ANC representative in 1970, described the state infrastructure for liberation movements: "As part of his commitment to the total liberation of the African continent, the Egyptian President, Gamal Abdel Nasser, set up an African Association. Located in the isle suburb of Zamalek, it housed the office of national liberation movements from South Africa, Angola, Mozambique, Zimbabwe and Namibia. Each mission of the National Liberation Movement (NLM) fell directly under the Office of the Egyptian President and representatives of liberation movements received monthly allowances from the Presidency."[193] The files of the Bureau of African Affairs, established by Nkrumah in 1959 under Padmore's direction to oversee Ghana's Pan-African affairs, reveal the extensive network that emerged from 1959 to underpin Nkrumah's support of freedom movements. Airline tickets were provided for freedom fighters to travel to Ghana, exiled youth were enrolled in Ghanaian schools, country representatives of the liberation movements were given housing and offices, and fighters were placed in military camps for training.[194] Joe Matlou, sent by the ANC to Accra in August 1965 as a country representative, reported back to the ANC's headquarters in Tanzania on his endeavors to find suitable accommodation and office. "I have been given a Flat in a building occupied by freedom-fighters from several other countries. The Bureau has not been able to find office premises for me: I am therefore using one of the rooms in the flat for an office. This arrangement starts today."[195]

Many Ghanaians, including ordinary Ghanaians, considered the government's "substantial investment in African liberation" misplaced, especially from the early 1960s when the Ghanaian economy was in decline and budget deficits had become commonplace.[196] But this role was powerfully symbolic and substantive for the rest of the continent under colonial and settler rule, which looked to the premier independent, Black African nation-state for leadership. South African ANC member, lawyer, and former exile Albert (Albie) Sachs recalled how the ANC looked to Nkrumah and

Ghana for ideological direction when Ghana became independent.[197] Alfred Hutchison's *Road to Ghana*, which tells of his overland escape from apartheid South Africa to Tanganyika and then by air to Ghana in time for the All-African People's Conference in December 1958 as a representative of the ANC, underscores how hugely significant Ghana was to parts of Africa still under colonial rule or on the verge of independence.[198] The December 1958 conference in Accra, by bringing liberation movements together with the eight independent African countries to deliberate over the political situation in Africa and how independent countries could support anticolonial struggles, opened the door to worldmaking for nonsovereign political organizations. Representatives from liberation movements were appointed to the steering committee of the AAPC, including Joshua Nkomo of ZAPU and Tennyson Makiwane of the ANC.[199]

International revolutionaries considered Ghana an important stop: Fanon led the Algerian delegation to the All-African People's Conference in Accra in December 1958, returning in 1959 as Algeria's first ambassador to Ghana; Malcolm X visited Ghana in 1964; and Che Guevara came through Accra in 1965. Conakry and Dakar were not to be outdone, and Touré offered UPC's Moumié, Amilcar Cabral, and the African Party for the Independence of Guinea and Cape Verde (PAIGC) bases in Guinea. Several freedom fighters came through Dakar, including Amilcar Cabral.[200] Nkrumah, cherishing his role as Africa's most prominent Pan-Africanist, was unhappy when Tanzania emerged as a rival hub for Pan-Africanism. In jockeying for preeminence, Nkrumah and Nyerere often found themselves in contention instead of collaboration in pursuit of their shared goal of African unity. Two developments aroused Nkrumah's ire: Nyerere's pursuit of federation in East and Central Africa; and the OAU's designation of Dar es Salaam as the headquarters of the African Liberation Council.

In September 1958, just three months before the December 1958 AAPC in Accra, Nyerere convened a meeting of nationalist organizations from East and Central Africa in Mwanza, Tanganyika. The moving spirits behind this meeting were Nyerere and Tom Mboya, the Kenyan trade unionist. Kenya was then in a state of emergency because of Mau Mau, so the meeting took place in Tanganyika. The conference sought to advance the struggle against colonialism by coordinating the activities of various nationalist organizations. Thirteen nationalist organizations sent representatives to Mwanza, where the Pan-African Movement for East and Central Africa (PAFMECA) was founded.[201] A second important objective for this body was regional integration through federation. Azaria Mbughuni writes: "As the chairman of PAFMECA in 1960, and as President of Tanganyika after December 9, 1961, Nyerere pushed for the idea of East African Federation; he wanted to establish a Federation made up of Tanganyika, Uganda, Kenya, Zanzibar, and Ruanda-Urundi (Rwanda and Burundi). Nyerere's strategy was to start with regional unity and eventually establish a 'United States of Africa,' as he argued eloquently in 1963."[202]

Nkrumah, perhaps because of the unsatisfactory experience of the late 1958 Ghana-Guinea Union that Mali joined after the collapse of the Mali Federation in August 1960, had decided that regional federations were a diversion and that Africa should concentrate on continental unity. Nkrumah also did not want PAFMECA to become a competitor to the AAPC. He wanted to be the "popular symbol of African liberation in East Africa; he had aided political movements there, and cultivated leaders."[203]

Nkrumah took Nyerere to task when Nyerere shared the idea of an East African Federation at the second Conference of Independent African States in June 1960. Nkrumah wrote to Nyerere in November 1960, questioning his pursuit of an East African Federation and its implications for continental African unity. He insinuated that Nyerere was perhaps motivated by the promise of some reward from the West. Nyerere was furious. He wrote back to Nkrumah demanding an explanation for the slight: "Your question does not come out of the heat of a moment of misunderstanding, and its implications are therefore so serious that I must ask you to elucidate."[204] That the British were supportive of an East African Federation made Nkrumah even more suspicious of the endeavor.[205] In June 1963, it seemed that the East African Federation was to become a reality. Nyerere, Jomo Kenyatta of Kenya, and Milton Obote of Uganda issued a joint declaration on June 5, 1963, in favor of federation. Then, for complicated reasons, Ugandan politicians pulled back, and the four hereditary monarchs in Uganda declared against federation.[206] The British between 1900 and 1933 had entered into agreements with Buganda (1900), Toro (1900), Ankole (1904), and Bunyoro (1933), and these kingdoms came to be known as "the agreement states." It was these agreements that gave Uganda protectorate status, and the chiefs did not want to lose their privileges in a federation with Tanganyika and Kenya.[207] Indeed, in 1963 the Kabaka (king) of Uganda, Sir Edward Mutesa, was elected first president of Uganda. Kenyatta's interest became lukewarm.

By the end of August 1963, the prospect of an East African Federation was as good as dead.[208] Still, when the OAU was formed in Addis Ababa in 1963, it was the advocates of regional federation as a stepping stone to continental unity that won the day. Nkrumah's vision to immediately embrace continental unity was shelved.

January 1964 was traumatic for Nyerere and Tanganyika: first, there was a revolution in Zanzibar as anti-Arab nationalists overthrew the sultan; then, the Tanganyikan army mutinied. Armies in Kenya and Uganda also mutinied, creating a regional crisis. There could be no internal regional solution, as all the armies of the three East African countries had mutinied. Nyerere appealed to Britain to intervene and restore order in Tanganyika. Nyerere himself knew it was a problematic solution—he dispatched the British forces as soon as order was restored and requested Nigerian soldiers to be posted to Tanganyika through the intercession of the OAU. At the OAU summit in Cairo in July 1964, Nkrumah took Nyerere to task for having invited the former colonial power to intervene to quell a mutiny. Nkrumah called Nyerere's response "neocolonial" and called Tanganyika an unworthy host of the OAU's African Liberation Committee. Nyerere was stunned. He locked himself in to write his rejoinder, and delivered a devastating attack on Nkrumah on July 20, calling Nkrumah "power hungry."[209] It is sad that these two champions of African unity, who admired each other, fell out over the strategy to be adopted toward a United States of Africa. Tanzania made incredible national sacrifices to support Africa's freedom fighters and provided bases for several southern African liberation movements: the ANC and PAC from South Africa, ZANU and ZAPU from Zimbabwe, SWAPO from Namibia, MPLA from Angola, and FRELIMO from Mozambique. For Nyerere, support for these freedom movements was imperative, as he noted in a lecture at the University of Toronto in 1969, because Tanzania constituted "a border state between free Africa and colonial Africa."[210] Strong ties connected East, Central, and Southern Africa. Bantu linguistic and cultural ties aside, the dominance of South Africa's economy had drawn in migrant labor from this entire region. And the prominence of two institutions of higher learning forged links among educated elites from this region: the University of Fort Hare, whose graduates included Oliver Tambo, Nelson Mandela, Seretse Khama, and Robert Mugabe; and Makerere University, whose alumni included Nyerere, his contemporary Kabaka Edward Mutesa, Ugandan president Milton Obote, and Aboud Jumbe, who

Fig 4.5 Julius Nyerere and Oliver Tambo, Dar Es Salaam, 1960. Source: Oliver Tambo Papers, ANC Archives, National Heritage and Cultural Studies Center (NAHECS), University of Fort Hare.

became president of Zanzibar. Nkrumah could not claim such substantive ties to Guinea or Mali.

In February 1966, Nkrumah was overthrown in a military coup; Touré immediately invited him to take residence in Conakry, symbolically appointing him copresident. The Ghana-Guinea-Mali Union may have been moribund, but there was clearly genuine friendship and admiration. Nyerere called 1966, when Ben Bella of Algeria and Nkrumah were overthrown, a "year of humiliation and shame for Africa."[211] He saw it as a triumph for the imperialists. Nyerere from his own resources remitted funds to Nkrumah in Conakry.[212] It is clear from the frequency with which Nyerere referenced Nkrumah in interviews that he missed his colleague. With Nkrumah's overthrow in 1966 and his death in 1972, Africa lost its most vocal champion for continental unity. The most architecturally distinguished building for years on the campus of the University of Dar es Salaam, and its main assembly hall, has been Nkrumah Hall. It is also worth noting that of all the attempts in those early decades of independence at federations, the only one that has stood the test of time (not without its challenges) is the union of Tanganyika and Zanzibar in 1964 to form the United Republic of Tanzania.

WORLDMAKING AND THE QUEST FOR A
NEW INTERNATIONAL ECONOMIC ORDER

There were two defining moments for African worldmaking in the early decades of independence: the founding of the United Nations in 1945 and the institutions the UN has spawned; and the Bandung Conference in 1955 and the institutions established in pursuit of the spirit of Bandung. The UN represented the international community of sovereign nation-states, and admission and membership extended recognition of sovereignty to Africa's new nations. As the membership from Asia, Latin America, and Africa grew in the 1960s, the United Nations General Assembly became the forum for claims making, distinct from the Security Council that was controlled by a few powerful nations. Bandung was a turning point, not just in Afro-Asian solidarity, but in African perception of the continent's possibilities. Bandung took place without the participation of the two superpowers—the United States and the Soviet Union—giving currency to a Third World. Indeed, for the Soviet Union, which had pursued accommodationist politics with the West in the 1930s and 1940s, Bandung was an indication of the dent in its image in the non-West and the rise of China as a champion for liberation in colonized and semicolonized countries.[213] The ten principles passed at Bandung spoke to the concern for sovereign rights and parity of nations for these new nation-states. The closing communiqué addressed the issue of economic dependence on the West and industrialized nations and encouraged participants of Bandung to work to reduce this dependence and assist each other with development projects through the sharing of knowledge and technology. Regional research and training institutions were proposed as one way to share knowledge and technology.

Two organizations sprang from the spirit of Bandung: the Afro-Asian People's Solidarity Organization (AAPSO) in 1957 and the Non-Aligned Movement in 1961. Both sought to carve neutral paths in the era of the Cold War, but for the United States under the Eisenhower administration, they were thinly disguised, procommunist institutions. For the Soviet Union, the independence of Ghana and Guinea, earlier than the West anticipated, underscored its turn away from Africa, and it became urgent for the Soviets to develop an African policy and seek allies in Africa. Allies did not have to be communist proselytes. The Soviet Union sought the friendship of newly independent African and Asian countries through economic assistance. The Soviet objective of global communist domination had not changed; securing allies in the global South drew them into the Soviet camp and away from the American camp. Chinese communists were not interested in an accommodationist position: they were wedded to a revolutionary policy and revolutionary tactics.[214]

The founding meeting of the AAPSO took place in late 1957 in Cairo with the arrival of thirty-nine delegations from Africa and Asia. In attendance were the Soviet Union, North Korea, North Vietnam, the People's Republic of Mongolia, and the People's Republic of China, underscoring a heavy communist presence in what was supposed to be a nonaligned organization. The conference affirmed the principles from Bandung and condemned imperialism in all its forms and manifestations. The Afro-Asian Solidarity Conference became very involved in the African independence struggle. The venues for the first four Afro-Asian Solidarity Conferences gave a privileged role to African countries in the forefront of the fight against colonialism and imperialism. The founding conference took place in Cairo in 1957, the second in Conakry in 1960, the third in Moshi, Tanganyika, in 1963, and the fourth in Ghana in 1965.

Much as the AAPC give visibility to the liberation movements, AAPSO extended recognition to freedom movements from southern Africa, the Middle East, and Asia. It provided airline tickets for representatives from African liberation movements to AAPSO conferences, gave them a platform to present statements, and included them in its resolutions. From the 1960s, the ANC regularly attended AAPSO council sessions and conferences. The ANC delegation to the Eighth Council Session of AAPSO in February 1967 in Nicosia, Cyprus, comprised Robert Resha (leader of delegation), Alfred Nzo, Tennyson Makiwane, Johnny Makatini, and M. Piliso.[215] At the Eleventh Council Session of AAPSO in Baghdad in March 1974, AAPSO decided to create a Presidium comprised of representatives from thirteen countries and organizations. Included in the Presidium were Samora Machel (Mozambique, FRELIMO), Agostinho Neto (Angola, MPLA), Oliver Tambo (South Africa, ANC), and Sam Nujoma (Namibia, SWAPO).[216] The liberation movements also had representation at the OAU, which provided funding, albeit limited, through its African Liberation Committee.

With Africa-based and Third World organizations extending recognition to southern Africa's liberation movements, especially the OAU, other international organizations began to grant them audience. As acting president-general of the ANC of South Africa, Oliver Tambo delivered a statement to the United Nation's Special Committee on the Policies of Apartheid of the Government of the Republic of South Africa in Stockholm, Sweden, in June 1968.[217] Travel to international conferences now absorbed such considerable time for the leadership of the ANC that cadres complained their leaders were preoccupied with international travel and conferences and that members of the National Executive Committee were often away from the ANC's headquarters.[218] But after disastrous attempts at military infiltration of cadres from the armed wing of the ANC, Umkhonto we Sizwe (MK), into Southern Rhodesia and South Africa in the late 1960s, the ANC quietly conceded the superiority of apartheid South Africa's security and military system.[219] Clearly, the path to political change in South Africa would be through worldmaking and the exertion of diplomatic pressure on the government in South Africa, not through armed struggle. This was a paradoxical situation: the ANC as an armed liberation movement had become wary of military confrontation. Dependent on financial contributions from foreign governments and organizations, the ANC in exile kept up the charade of an armed struggle, Stephen Ellis argues, as it needed to "play to an international gallery to survive."[220] Appreciative of the gains of worldmaking, the ANC came to see the international isolation of the South African government as crucial to the ANC's success and ability to establish itself as "a credible government-in-waiting." The achievement of independence in the Portuguese colonies in 1975 was an important development for the remaining liberation movements, as the international community now viewed the movements as governments-in-waiting. The OAU in partnership with the UN began to provide training in several fields to equip the liberation movements with skills for governing.[221]

In 1961, a select group of leaders from Asia and Africa met in Belgrade, Yugoslavia, with President Josip Broz Tito, host for the first conference of heads of states of nonaligned governments. In addition to Tito, the moving spirits were Jawaharlal Nehru of India, Sukarno of Indonesia, Nasser of Egypt, and Nkrumah of Ghana. The Non-Aligned Movement (NAM) was formally born. During the Cold War, its membership expanded to as many as 120 countries, representing the largest international body outside of the

United Nations. Though professedly nonaligned, both the United States and the Soviet Union worked to secure allies in the Third World. When the Soviet Union awarded the Lenin Prize to Touré in 1961, it sought to make an open, international statement of Guinea's affiliation to the Soviet Union, even though Touré may not have seen it as such. Another attempt to brand nations as pro-Soviet was the extension of an invitation to the ruling parties of Guinea, Ghana, and Mali—the radical Ghana-Guinea-Mali Union—to attend the twenty-second Congress of the Communist Party of the Soviet Union in October 1961.[222] These were complications Touré had to explain as he sought American economic aid under Kennedy. Attwood, America's ambassador to Guinea, opined that Touré may not have been aware the Lenin Award was intended to make it more difficult for Touré to convince the West that he was neutral or nonaligned. Likewise, America felt the need to explain in advance to its allies in West Africa—the Ivory Coast, Nigeria, and Senegal—the reason for its extension of aid to Guinea to avoid the conclusion on the part of African leaders that "positive neutralism" (actively playing both sides) paid.[223]

With the East and the West having allies in the Non-Aligned Movement, it made sense that the most important bid by the Third World in the late 1960s and 1970s, the quest for a New International Economic Order (NIEO), would be fought out on the floor of the United Nations General Assembly. This movement garnered enormous support from Latin America, Asia, and Africa. The inspiration emerged, again, from Latin America, with Prebisch at the forefront. By the early 1960s, it had become clear that ISI had not worked in Latin America. Africa would come to that conclusion in the mid-1970s. Ironically, it seemed that the adoption of ISI had created new, lucrative opportunities for multinational or transnational companies, which remained embedded in the economies of the developing world as purveyors of capital equipment and technology. Unlike Latin America's adoption of ISI, Africa's had not been prefaced by any theoretical reflection.[224] Federation, which the ECLA had proposed as an important accompaniment to ISI in Latin America, had not worked either. In the case of Africa, with its wave of authoritarian regimes in the 1960s and 1970s, Mkandawire notes sardonically that "there has never been a federation of dictators."[225]

Prebisch resigned as executive secretary of the ECLA in 1963, having directed the institution since 1950. His next major assignment would be as the founding secretary-general of the United Nations Conference on Trade and Development (UNCTAD). Leading to the 1964 conference in Geneva, where UNCTAD would be proposed as an institution, Prebisch visited a number of developing regions to confer on trade problems and met with government officials to discuss developmental challenges. These discussions informed the agenda for the Geneva Conference from March 23 to June 15, 1964.[226] Out of the Geneva Conference came the demand for a New International Economic Order (NIEO), a term Prebisch coined in 1963. The nineteenth session of the United Nations General Assembly in December 1964 approved the creation of UNCTAD as a permanent body of the General Assembly, and on February 10, 1965, the General Assembly unanimously confirmed the appointment of Prebisch as the founding secretary-general of UNCTAD.[227] UNCTAD was thus created to engage economic relations between industrialized and nonindustrialized nations. At the crux of the NIEO were the unchanging and unequal relations of trade between these two groups. The NIEO was premised on the idea that sovereign equality, the parity of nations, required an equitable distribution of global wealth. Getachew argues that "the view that sovereign equality had material implications marked anticolonial nationalists' biggest departure from the postwar international order."[228] Advocates of the NIEO pointed to imperialism as the creator of the inequalities in the global economic system: "The claim that imperialism had produced an uneven but integrated global economy allowed proponents of the NIEO to represent the international arena as a site for demands for redistribution that extended far beyond aid and charity."[229] The NIEO sought not to redefine the international division of labor, which had clearly come to stay, but to propose that developed and developing nations work together to create egalitarian economic relations that reduced dependency. For the developing nations, the forum for such a dialogue was the United Nations General Assembly, a forum open to all sovereign nations where each nation had one vote.

African nations signed onto the NIEO from the mid-1970s, after the failure of ISI and the financial crises and indebtedness deepened by the OPEC oil crisis from 1973. But the landscape of international development had already begun to change significantly. We have seen how by the 1970s development economics was in decline, and the rise of Milton Friedman and the monetarists and the economic policies of Reagan and Thatcher from the late 1970s placed the free market at the center of the global economy (see chap. 3). The failure of African developmental states and the "big push" of the 1960s and early 1970s had increased inequality within African countries. At the World Bank, there was a new focus on poverty in thinking about international development from 1968 under the presidency of McNamara.[230] As the developing world demanded a New International Economic Order, the developed West responded with the demand for governments in the Third World to address poverty within their countries. Debates on basic needs strategies were thus introduced as the counterpoint to the NIEO.[231] Nyerere remained one of the few African leaders with international visibility and goodwill in the 1970s. But his championing of the NIEO did not meet the same positive response from the West as Ujamaa had received in the previous decade, nor did his arguing that structural inequality in the global economy undermined endeavors to achieve domestic equality.[232]

The discussion turned to reform within the developing world and away from reform of the relationship between the developed and developing worlds—to the reduction of poverty in the developing world and not the creation of wealth or its redistribution between nations. Mkandawire has pointed to the lack of interest by African governments in the West's discussion of basic needs strategies.[233] Getachew has discussed developed nations' rejection of the United Nations General Assembly as the forum for making decisions about the international economy and their insistence that the appropriate forum would be international financial institutions like the IMF and the World Bank. The failure of state planning and market intervention in the Third World strengthened the argument that markets are self-regulating and create desired equilibria and that the entire global economy should be regulated by the same rules.[234] Neoliberal ideology was not just ascendant on the global stage; Nyerere would discover that even within his own ruling party many had abandoned Ujamaa and become converts to neoliberalism. The biographers of the recent three-volume biography of Nyerere note that by the end of the 1970s, "the era of national sovereignty and the right of people to self-determination was over, imperialism was on the offensive and neoliberal ideology and globalization would make mincemeat of all notions of sovereignty, Third World solidarity, and the New International Economic Order. He [Nyerere] would have to beat a retreat on both the national and international front."[235] The stage was set for the structural adjustment programs of the 1980s and after. By 1980, African leaders had already become pessimistic about the chances of the NIEO. Mkandawire notes that at the OAU economic summit in Lagos in 1980, the "main focus was now on some kind of pan-African self-sufficiency and co-operation."[236] That desire would crystallize in the African Continental Free Trade Agreement four decades later.

CONCLUSION

African nationalists after World War II claimed the right to forge a third path to a political future; they called that path Pan-African socialism. While expressing reservations about Western capitalism and Soviet communism, they borrowed elements of both that suited the African condition without adopting entire systems. Nonalignment facilitated this flexibility. Those who actively courted both camps to secure the maximum economic benefits called this strategy positive neutralism. Africa's past had been framed by capitalism, one of expropriation and exploitation. And while Black internationalists between the two world wars had their reservations about Soviet communism, the Soviet Union's remarkable, material development in a single generation was impressive. A visit to the Soviet Union left them in admiration of its material achievement, if not its political system, and a desire for similar transformation in Africa in their lifetimes. That the state had been at the center of Soviet transformation lent support to the prospect of the developmental state in Africa as the agent of economic transformation. That all four leaders declared their countries one-party states speaks to the authoritarian nature of the state in early independent Africa. Unlike Russia, the small, poor former African colonies could not separate from the West to pursue their path of growth. Colonial rule had embedded their extraverted economies deeply within the global capitalist system. Economic development could only come through engaging the West and the East, but within the security of a liberated, integrated, and united Africa. Pan-African socialism gained coherence.

Independent Africa faced daunting odds. From European colonial metropoles like Portugal that struggled to hold onto African colonies, to defiant settler regimes in southern Africa that made Hutchison's *Road to Ghana* seem like walking a minefield to freedom (safety), the forces of empire seemed determined to stay. And the forces of capitalism seemed equally determined to keep Africa in its place as a supplier of raw materials in the global economy, from the providers of supplier credit who overcharged for capital goods not ideal for Africa's economies, to representatives of multinational companies who arranged lucrative management contracts with

African governments to establish new industries, to the United States' pressuring of countries like Ghana and Guinea to desist from bartering raw materials for capital goods from the Eastern Bloc (thereby undercutting a global economic system based on the American dollar), to the IMF and the World Bank encouraging the selling off of state-owned manufacturing plants the moment African countries came into receivership. Two chronological periods now mark independent Africa's political economy: before structural adjustment, seen through Western eyes as when economic policies were bad; and after structural adjustment, when economic policies became sound. One must return to works written in the 1960s and 1970s to encounter detailed accounts of state-led development and the first wave of import-substitution industrialization after independence. This is the story of the rise and fall of the African developmental state, of the push for continental unity that ended up with a watered-down version of the Organization of African Unity, of a compromised Africa that was easily dismissed in the 1970s when it made claims for a New International Economic Order. But this is still a story worth remembering, worth telling, as the bases seem reloaded in the twenty-first century for another push at development within the framework of a continental common market (see conclusion). The story in the next chapter of Ghana's attempt to create a modern, industrialized nation-state under Nkrumah, what Genoud has called the only true African attempt in the early years of independence to decolonize an economy, build a modern infrastructure, and establish an industrial base, is a worthy conclusion to this book. In the 1950s and 1960s, Ghana was at the center of the African imagination as *the* African path to "self-rule and postcolonial development."[237]

five

NKRUMAH, COCOA, AND THE UNITED STATES

The Vision of an Industrialized African Nation-State

Introduction: Independence and the Modernist Dream

Nkrumah on Ghana's independence inherited a relatively prosperous economy based on cocoa exports, of which Ghana was the world's leading producer. While Nkrumah appreciated the cash cow the cocoa industry was, he was ambivalent about its premodern infrastructure and the dominance of small family farms, which he considered an inadequate driving force for his industrialization schemes. Cocoa farms in Ghana averaged three acres in size. They did not lend themselves to the mechanized agriculture that Nkrumah, a believer in high-modernist ideas, envisaged. Nkrumah also entertained genuine concern about the longevity of the cocoa industry, as its expansion devastated the forest environment in which it flourished, and swollen shoot disease threatened its very survival. Nkrumah viewed industrialization as the path to Ghana's economic success and autonomy. He adopted the colonial vision of building a large dam at Akosombo on the Volta River to produce electricity to smelt Ghana's bauxite and power its industries. Nkrumah, despite his preference for socialism, viewed the United States, the wealthiest and most technologically developed nation in the world, as the potential source of the funding for the dam. But in his pursuit of positive neutralism, he hoped to combine the US-funded dam with factories built through the financial and technical support of Eastern Bloc countries. Positive neutralism would allow him to avoid becoming dependent on either Cold War power and to avoid neocolonialism.

This chapter examines the place of the United States in Nkrumah's pursuit of industrialization and the crucial role of Ghana's cocoa in this process. It argues that Nkrumah overestimated his capacity to play the superpowers against each other in his quest for industrialization. He also devalued the importance of cocoa in Ghana's economy—while eager to draw on the cocoa reserve fund for his developmental agenda, he ignored the importance of the scientific research and economic incentives that had kept the cocoa industry vibrant despite the detection of swollen shoot disease in 1936. Nkrumah's policies undercut the cocoa industry, though the results would not be evident until the late 1960s, with Ghana declining as the world's leading producer of cocoa and the Ivory Coast emerging as the premier producer in 1977. Nkrumah was outmaneuvered by Kaiser Aluminum of the United States, which negotiated to build the aluminum smelter without utilizing Ghana's bauxite, an integral part of the comprehensive Volta River Project. The major beneficiary of Ghana's new source of electricity was the Volta Aluminum Company (VALCO), 90 percent owned by Kaiser Aluminum, which secured electricity at heavily discounted rates for thirty years to smelt imported alumina. And with the overthrow of Nkrumah in February 1966, a month after the inauguration of the Akosombo Dam, the CIA ensured he would not be around to build factories with the input of the Eastern Bloc countries powered by the American-funded dam. Nkrumah left Ghana handicapped in both its agricultural and industrial sectors. In depleting the national coffers in his unsuccessful drive for industrialization, Nkrumah weakened the capacity of the state to provide robust support for the cocoa industry. He was succeeded by a military regime and then a liberal government, disinterested in continuing Nkrumah's industrial plans with the Eastern Bloc countries.

Nkrumah's relations with the United States were also ambivalent. The years he spent in the United States as a student from 1935 to 1945 were formative and highly memorable. They shaped him in important ways, as he documents in his *Autobiography*. But over the course of his political tenure, he came to see the United States as *the* bastion of neocolonialism, as industrial capital took the place of European colonial power in the maintenance of Western influence in Africa. These sentiments, given full expression in his book *Neo-colonialism*, deeply displeased the American government, which had facilitated the funding of the Akosombo Dam. But Nkrumah also valued his ties to the United States. The United States after World War II had surpassed Europe as the largest market for Ghana's cocoa. The leading producer of chocolate in the United States was the Hershey Corporation in Pennsylvania, the state where Nkrumah lived from 1935 to 1945. He obtained his college and graduate education at Lincoln University and the University of Pennsylvania respectively. Pennsylvania figured prominently in Nkrumah's plans for Ghana's development, as he tapped into networks at his alma maters to connect to people in business and government and to the lobbying power of cocoa and chocolate manufacturers in the United States. Ghana—together with Nigeria—became a beneficiary of the Teachers in West Africa Program (TWAP), funded by the Hershey Corporation and administered by Elizabethtown College in Pennsylvania. For the decade of TWAP's existence from 1962 to 1972, Ghanaian universities, polytechnics, and secondary schools, seventy-one institutions in all, received a total of 162 teachers for periods of service ranging from one to five years per teacher.[1] Other American institutions like the African-American Institute preceded TWAP in Ghana's educational space. African American professionals responded enthusiastically to Nkrumah's invitation to relocate to Ghana from the early 1950s to assist in nation-building.[2]

This chapter examines cocoa and the economic and political revolution in rural Gold Coast; Nkrumah's time in the United States and some of the formative influences in his decade in America; and the important place the United States came to play in Nkrumah's developmental agenda.

Cocoa and the Rural Revolution in the Gold Coast

In 1911, the Gold Coast emerged as the world's leading producer of cocoa, producing more than a third of the global supply of an indigenous South American crop that Gold Coasters did not eat. How did this happen? It is all the more remarkable considering that commercial structures were not even in place for the marketing of cocoa when the first Gold Coast farmers experimented with this exotic crop. We will examine shortly the two prevailing accounts of cocoa's introduction to the Gold Coast: one by the Basel missionaries; the second by an intrepid Ga carpenter and entrepreneur, Tetteh Quarshie, who encountered the crop in Fernando Po. Both accounts are acknowledged in *Ghana Farmer* (formerly *Gold Coast Farmer*), the publication of the Cocoa Research Institute.

This fact, is, however, of academic importance only since the introductions of the Basel Mission were evidently not intended for commercial purposes and did not attract attention until the efforts of Tetteh Quarshie had aroused interest of the people in Akwapim in cocoa cultivation as witnessed by him in Fernando Po. Even when the first sample of 40 lbs [pounds] of prepared cocoa was taken to the Basel Mission Factory in Mampong [Akuapem Mampong] and thence to Accra it could not be valued as the product was unknown. It had to be sent to Europe and a price of 30s [shillings] was offered after a few months with request for more supplies. Thus an industry started to grow from the few cocoa trees planted around the town of Mampong on the persuasion of Tetteh Quarshie.[3]

This initial shipment of forty pounds was made in the late 1880s, as it takes five to seven years for cocoa to mature and bear pods for harvesting. In 1891, the Gold Coast exported eighty pounds of cocoa. In 1911, the Gold Coast exported 40,356 tons, emerging as the leading exporter of cocoa in the world and beating to second and fourth place Ecuador (38,803 tons) and Brazil (34,994 tons) respectively. In third place was another West African colony, São Tomé and Principe (35,512 tons), indicating a seismic shift in the production of an indigenous South American crop, exported by countries like Ecuador, Brazil, the Dominican Republic, and Venezuela from the mid-eighteenth century, to West Africa from the turn of the twentieth century.[4]

Historical context is relevant to the story of the rise of cocoa in the Gold Coast. The nineteenth century witnessed entrepreneurial Gold Coast farmers and traders enter the palm oil, rubber, and cocoa industries successively. Always looking for market opportunities, Gold Coast farmers experimented with new crops pioneered in the botanical gardens of the Basel Mission Society in their hillside station of Aburi, north of Accra. Cocoa was introduced through two sources. Basel missionaries at the botanical garden in Aburi experimented with crops such as coffee and cocoa and dispensed seeds and seedlings to African Christians to encourage them to take up cash crops and move away from slaveholding as a form of property.[5] Chocolate was an important drink in Switzerland, home base of the Basel Mission Society—the Swiss Roderich Lindt invented "melting chocolate" in 1879, and Lindt remains a famous chocolate brand.[6] The second source of cocoa's introduction was through Tetteh Quarshie, a carpenter from Accra, who had worked on contract at Fernando Po in Spanish Equatorial Guinea. The Spaniards had introduced cocoa from their colonial possessions in Venezuela and Columbia to their West African colony. Oral traditions recount that Tetteh Quarshie saw the cocoa trees with their ripe pods, smuggled a few pods on the ship to the Gold Coast in 1879, and went north to the Akuapem

Mountains in the Eastern Region of the Gold Coast in search of forested land to experiment with the seeds. He had observed that cocoa was grown in forested regions in Fernando Po and was told that the crop thrived in forests. Accra lay on a sandy coastal plain and was hence unsuitable for growing cocoa. Tetteh Quarshie acquired land in Mampong Akuapem on the Akuapem range and started the first indigenous farm, which still exists and has become a tourist attraction. This would become a second source for the dispersion of cocoa seedlings, though it is Tetteh Quarshie's adventure and farm that has entered the nationalist narrative rather than the Basel missionary source. Clearly the Basel missionaries experimented with cocoa without immediate commercial purposes in mind, as the Basel Mission Factory in Mampong could not even put a market value on the first cocoa sample presented at the factory. Gold Coast and West African farmers, after the glut of palm oil and palm kernels on the world market and the resultant decline in prices in the mid-nineteenth century, were looking for an alternative commercial crop.[7]

Akuapem farmers embraced cocoa farming, and the crop spread quickly on the range. Soon running out of suitable land, Akuapem farmers descended to nearby Akyem Abuakwa, also in the Eastern Province of the Gold Coast (now Eastern Region of Ghana), where suitable forestland existed in abundance. At this point, they were joined by an entrepreneurial group of farmers from the Krobo region, who had dominated the export of palm oil and were eager to find a replacement. At the peak of the oil boom, Krobo farmers had organized themselves in companies called *huza* and migrated to areas in Akyem Abuakwa in search of land.[8] This system was now deployed toward cocoa, and the Krobo joined the Akuapem as leading cocoa farmers in Akyem Abuakwa. These dynamics propelled the Gold Coast to its position as the world's leading producer of cocoa in 1911. By the 1920s, cocoa had entered the Ashanti region, which emerged as the leading cocoa producer in the Gold Coast by the 1940s. Brong Ahafo was then part of Ashanti, and cocoa also spread to the Western Province.[9] The shift of the center of cocoa production from the Eastern Province to Ashanti is explained by the continuing extension of cocoa frontiers, as farmers sought new forest land, and the emergence of cocoa swollen shoot virus (CSSV), first detected in Effiduasi in the Eastern Province in 1936. As CSSV had no known cure, the only remedy was to cut out diseased and surrounding trees to prevent the virus from spreading to neighboring healthy cocoa trees. The impact of swollen shoot would be transformative in the history of the Gold Coast, economically and politically. Agricultural historian Francis Danquah describes the gloomy prognosis of Ghana's cocoa industry in the 1940s: "Of the 400,000,000 [400 million] cocoa trees in Ghana by 1947, about 46,000,000 [46 million] were infected and doomed to die within the year. Of these 45,000,000 [45 million] were situated in the Eastern Province. Due to CSSV, Ghana's cocoa output had dropped from 300,000 tons in 1936–7 to 200,000 in the mid-nineteen-forties. The rate of spread was proceeding at the rate of 15,000,000 [15 million trees] a year, and if left unchecked, the cocoa industry would disappear in 20 years."[10] The economic impact of swollen shoot on government revenues and farmers' finances was disastrous. But responding to a plant virus with no known cure—first detected in the Gold Coast—with a policy of cutting out infected trees in a prosperous cocoa industry entirely pioneered by indigenous farmers was bound to be politically explosive.

The cutting out policy reinforced rural discontent over volatile cocoa prices in the 1920s and 1930s, which had witnessed increasingly effective cocoa holdups by rural cocoa farmers against expatriate firms that dominated the marketing of cocoa in the Gold Coast. In these holdups, farmers refused to sell cocoa to the expatriate companies that controlled the marketing of cocoa at low prices. The holdups were sometimes accompanied by a boycott of European imported goods. With cocoa as the financial lifeline of the colony, the government could not stand by unconcerned, for cocoa contributed as much as 62.6 percent of the total value of Gold Coast exports between 1930 and 1936.[11] The government's intervention in the industry from the 1930s changed the infrastructure for marketing cocoa in the Gold Coast and put in place institutions for scientific research into cocoa diseases. Whereas the 1930s is typically seen as the decade of global economic depression, Susan Martin has argued that West Africa experienced a long economic depression from 1914 to 1945, with the terms of trade declining throughout this period.[12] Using West Africa's main export crops of palm oil, groundnuts, and cocoa, Martin demonstrates that the barter terms of trade for these commodities throughout the 1920s was lower than the levels for 1910–14.[13] That cocoa exports from West Africa continued to grow despite unfavorable world prices in the 1920s and 1930s underscores the dilemma of Gold Coast and western Nigerian cocoa farmers. By the late 1920s, the Gold Coast and western Nigeria controlled 72 percent of the global exports of cocoa between them.[14] Favorable cocoa prices in the early 1910s had encouraged many West African farmers to take up cocoa cultivation. Unlike groundnuts, a perennial crop usually grown as an annual, cocoa is a permanent tree crop that takes five to seven years to mature and can then bear pods for more than forty years. This makes it difficult to reallocate land assigned to cocoa, unlike groundnut. When cocoa prices declined, often a result of a glut on the world market, farmers harvested more cocoa to maintain their standard of living, further depressing world prices. Thus, the increase in cocoa exports from West Africa in the 1930s should not necessarily be taken as a sign of farmers' economic prosperity.[15]

The cocoa holdups in the 1930s reflected rural economic distress and indebtedness among farmers. Gareth Austin demonstrates how the existence of permanent cocoa farms created a stock of fixed capital against which loans could be made.[16] The value of permanent cocoa trees made it possible for chiefs, as landlords to stranger or nonsubject farmers, to impose the first agricultural rent in Asante history, adding to the financial burden of cocoa farmers. In Amansie (Bekwai District) in South Asante, the earliest evidence of the mortgaging of cocoa farms is present in 1930 with the onset of the Great Depression and unusually low cocoa prices. A government inquiry in 1933 established that about a third of farmers in Amansie had one or more farms mortgaged to rich farmers, cocoa brokers (often themselves cocoa farmers), and professional money lenders.[17] There were three major cocoa holdups in the Gold Coast in 1930–31, 1934–35, and 1937–38, the third one also involving Nigeria. These holdups were generated by the suspicion of farmers that European expatriate companies were artificially depressing cocoa prices, particularly compared to the prices of European manufactured imports. The 1930–31 and 1937–38 holdups were accompanied by the boycott of European imported goods. In Ashanti, chiefs as major landowners had also entered cocoa cultivation. Despite the British system of indirect rule that sought to rule through traditional structures of authority, chiefs in the 1930s found themselves on the side of their subjects in the economic struggle against European expatriate firms, pitting chiefs against the colonial administration for the first time in twentieth-century Gold Coast.[18] Farmers' associations and cooperatives emerged to organize the boycott with the support—both overt and tacit—of chiefs in Ashanti and the colony. In Ashanti, farmers formed the Ashanti Farmers Association Limited in 1934, and in 1937 the

Ashanti Farmers Union.[19] Across the colony, cocoa cooperative societies proliferated in the 1930s, and during the 1937–38 holdup John Ayew and Ashie Nikoi formed the Gold Coast Farmers' Association.[20] The 1937–38 cocoa holdup, Austin observes, was "industry-wide, and season-long [and] . . . by far the largest economic protest in Gold Coast history."[21] Alarmed by the imminent danger to colonial revenues and the threat of political instability to its model colony, the colonial government offered to mediate the conflict between farmers and European expatriate companies.

What had precipitated the 1937–38 holdup was the coming together in a buying agreement of the thirteen major European companies that bought cocoa in the Gold Coast. The agreement, entered in 1937, aimed at manipulating producer prices and dividing market shares among the thirteen firms. With the United Africa Company (UAC) as the lead instigator, the buying agreement was presented to the Colonial Office in London as a fait accompli, and Governor Arnold Hodson of the Gold Coast was informed after the fact.[22] Over the course of the 1910s and 1920s, as the railway and road system extended into the interior and the cocoa frontier stretched north into Ashanti and west into the Western Province, European companies had opened stores and agencies up-country for the purchase of the cocoa. Unlike in the early decades of cocoa production, when producer associations had brought their cocoa down to the European firms at the coast, a class of middlemen, salaried agents, store clerks, and brokers, came to control cocoa purchasing in the 1920s and 1930s, directing cocoa to the main branches of the European firms at the coast for a commission. As commissions rose with the increasing dependence of European firms on brokers and cut into the profits of companies, European companies came together in a buying agreement with the intent of reining in the middlemen and reducing their financial reward.[23] Using and building off the monies advanced to them by metropolitan capital for the purchase of cocoa, brokers had themselves emerged as important moneylenders to cocoa farmers, making advances toward cocoa harvest and offering loans against mortgaged cocoa farms. Brokers had acquired cocoa farms, and some successful cocoa farmers had branched out into broking. While ordinarily aligned with the interests of metropolitan capital, the buying agreement pushed brokers into the same camp as cocoa farmers and chiefs, equally invested in the cocoa industry. As lines were drawn with African interests completely on one side and European commercial capital on the other in the longest (six months) and most effective cocoa holdup in the Gold Coast, the colonial government decided it was not time to bully chiefs into submission, as it had in the 1930 holdup, but to appear impartial and arbitrate between contending sides. Not only was cocoa too important to colonial finances for the government to risk jeopardizing the industry, but the government also had on its hands a potentially destabilizing political situation. Indeed, rural political mobilization drew national attention for the first time, and some key individuals in the holdup "described the hold-up as the beginning of the nationalist movement."[24]

The colonial government, alarmed that the holdup might transform into a challenge of colonial rule, offered to arbitrate. At the end of January 1938, Governor Hodson approached the secretary of the state for the colonies and requested that a commission be formed to inquire into the causes of the 1937–38 holdup and make recommendations for the marketing of cocoa in the Gold Coast and Nigeria. The secretary of state announced the commission of inquiry in February 1938 to be chaired by William Nowell, former director of the East African Agricultural Institute. Hodson announced the formation of the commission of inquiry in the Gold Coast and called for an end to the holdup. The commission's members arrived in the Gold Coast on March 23 to conduct their inquiry, and the Nowell Commission released its report in September 1938.[25] The report referenced the intense competition among European cocoa buying firms, the critical role of cocoa brokers, and the rather weak state of the cocoa cooperative societies, which could have provided an alternative infrastructure for farmers to deliver their cocoa to the market. It recognized the legitimate grievances of both producers and shippers and recommended the termination of the buying agreement and creation of a Gold Coast Farmers' Association with a statutory monopsony for the purchase of cocoa in cocoa producing areas. "The Nowell Commission's reports were never implemented. They did not receive enthusiastic support among Europeans or among Africans. Hodson was not satisfied with the specifics of the plan, although he did not reject the idea of the state playing a more active role in structuring commercial institutions."[26] The intervention of World War II prevented the Gold Coast government from pursuing the implications of the Nowell Commission report. Aware that the Gold Coast could not return to the marketing system that had provoked the 1937–38 holdup and learning from the experience of WWI, when the shortage of shipping space due to the war effort had depressed the cocoa industry and led farmers to abandon their cocoa farms, the government introduced a government-controlled marketing system for cocoa that lasted through the war and guaranteed the purchase of the entire cocoa crop in the Gold Coast.[27]

Two important outcomes of the 1937–38 cocoa holdup shaped the future of the cocoa industry in the Gold Coast. The first was the government's creation of the Central Cocoa Research Station in Tafo in the Eastern Province to research cocoa diseases and communicate findings to cocoa farmers through extension work. Considering the importance of cocoa to the colonial government's revenues, it is remarkable that a research station for cocoa did not exist until 1937, precipitated by the detection of swollen shoot in the Gold Coast in 1936. Indeed, before this date, there was not a single agricultural station in cocoa-producing areas.[28] The Central Cocoa Research Station, renamed the West African Cocoa Research Institute (WACRI) in 1944, would become one of the leading institutes in the world in research on cocoa.[29] The cumulative work of its plant botanists, virologists, pathologists, entomologists, soil scientists, and others under the sponsorship of the state produced research that allowed the Gold Coast cocoa industry to combat various plant diseases, improve farm sanitation, and produce disease-resistant, earlier-bearing, higher-yielding cocoa hybrids to avert the collapse of the industry feared with the onset of swollen shoot disease in 1936. After a marked decline in cocoa exports from the record 304,800 tons in 1936–37, the efforts of WACRI and new plantings in the early 1950s led to a resurgence in the cocoa industry. Independent Ghana would have another record cocoa export in 1959–60.[30]

The second outcome was the government-controlled marketing system for cocoa used during World War II, intended as an ad hoc measure, that became the foundation for a permanent Cocoa Marketing Board in 1946. With the outbreak of World War II, the British government guaranteed the purchase of all cocoa produced in its West African colonies, which accounted for half the world's production. Merchants, understandably, would not buy cocoa in a war situation, when they had no guarantee of selling it. During the war, the British government, through the Ministry of Food and later the West African Cocoa Control Board, each year fixed the producer price of cocoa below the prevailing world price with the intent of guaranteeing a decent price for cocoa farmers despite price volatility. This provided some insulation for the government for cocoa stocks it was unable to sell and had to carry over to the next season. The British government committed to returning any accrued profits from its wartime control of cocoa purchasing to either the West African producers or the colonial governments to be used for purposes that benefited cocoa producers. This wartime measure worked so well for the government that a government white paper in 1944 considering the future of the cocoa industry in West Africa recommended some continuance of the wartime system. The major difference would be that separate boards in the Gold Coast and Nigeria would be responsible to their respective colonial governments. To capitalize these new Cocoa Marketing Boards, the white paper recommended that a substantial proportion of the funds generated from the controlled purchase and sale of cocoa from 1939, estimated at £3,676,253 in 1943, be placed at the disposal of the colonial governments of Nigeria and the Gold Coast.[31] Rod Alence reminds us that the Cocoa Marketing Boards were not an imposition on the colonies by Britain, but rather institutions demanded by the colonial governments in the Gold Coast and Nigeria, which held effective veto rights. The Cocoa Marketing Board in the Gold Coast committed to promoting agricultural research and ensuring interseasonal stabilization of cocoa prices.[32]

Developments peaked with another boycott of European commercial firms in January 1948. The boycott was fueled by the persistence of wartime economic conditions and soaring prices for imported goods; the grievances of ex-servicemen who had fought in World War II against low pensions and the absence of rehabilitation funds to transition those unable to continue in government service; and the cutting out of diseased cocoa trees in response to swollen shoot. The cutting out of cocoa trees infected by swollen shoot had commenced on a voluntary basis by the cocoa farmers. Noting the reluctance of farmers to cut out diseased cocoa trees still bearing pods, the colonial government in January 1947 passed legislation to make the cutting compulsory, carried out by hired gangs from the Department of Agriculture. In January 1948, serious opposition broke out against the compulsory cutting out of cocoa amid rumors that the colonial government intended the destruction of the cocoa industry.[33] A protest march organized by the ex-servicemen's union to present grievances to the governor at Christiansborg Castle on February 28, 1948, ended in a confrontation with the police, the shooting dead of two ex-servicemen, and the wounding of several others. Accra and other major urban centers broke out in riots and looting, and the newly formed United Gold Coast Convention (UGCC) positioned itself to benefit politically from this mass urban and rural expression of political discontent.[34] The Watson Commission, appointed to inquire into the 1948 disturbances, concluded that nationalism had dawned in the Gold Coast and recommended steps toward internal self-government. Kwame Nkrumah, the general secretary of the UGCC, broke away from the UGCC in June 1949 with the youth wing of the party to create the Convention People's Party, which demanded "self-government NOW." As the CPP prepared in 1951 for the first general elections based on universal adult suffrage in the Gold Coast, it promised cocoa farmers in its manifesto that "Special Attention will be given to the Swollen Shoot Disease."[35]

Southall points to the irony of the situation: the "CPP rose to power on the crest of cocoa farming support, after having promised the farmers control over the vast funds accumulated by the Cocoa Marketing Board during the war."[36] But once in power, the CPP came to appreciate the patronage these funds represented and their utility in the nationalist government's developmental agenda to industrialize Ghana. Nkrumah's relations with the cocoa farmers' movement in the Gold Coast dates to 1945–47, when he spent two years in Britain after his ten-year sojourn in the United States before returning to the Gold Coast to take up the position as secretary-general to the UGCC. It has been noted in chapter 4 that Padmore roped Nkrumah into assisting as secretary to the 1945 Pan-African Congress in Manchester. The Gold Coast Farmers' Association sent a generous contribution for the funding of the congress, as well as a delegation led by Ashie Nikoi. As mentioned above, the Gold Coast Farmers' Association was founded during the 1937–38 cocoa holdup by Ashie Nikoi and John Ayew. Nkrumah, Ashie Nikoi, Wallace-Johnson, Kojo Botsio, and others met after the 1945 Manchester Congress to work for the formation of a radical organization to spearhead the emancipation of Africa from colonial rule. This was the origin of the West African National Secretariat (WANS) in London, for which Nkrumah served as secretary. In this capacity, he corresponded with several key nationalists in the Gold Coast and West Africa, soliciting subscriptions and articles for WANS's monthly magazine, the *New African*.[37] Nkrumah rightly discerned the revolutionary moment in the Gold Coast and that the farmers' movement and cocoa would be the path to political power. Ashie Nikoi was again one of the central movers in the formation of the CPP in June 1949. In December 1949, he and John Ayew created the Farmers'

Congress as a political wing of the CPP.[38] The years abroad were instrumental in shaping Nkrumah's political philosophy and organizational skills; the ten years in the United States and Pennsylvania were among the most formative years in Nkrumah's life. We turn to these years for context of what the United States came to represent in Nkrumah's vision for Ghana.

NKRUMAH IN THE UNITED STATES: THE MAKING OF A PHILOSOPHER-POLITICIAN

Nkrumah's admiration for the United States began as a youth in Ghana through two role models he encountered. The first was Dr. James E. Kwegyir Aggrey, born in Anomabu, Gold Coast, and a graduate of Livingstone College in Salisbury, North Carolina. Aggrey obtained a doctorate in divinity and joined the faculty of Livingstone College. In 1924, he returned to the Gold Coast to become vice principal of the first government secondary school, Achimota College. Aggrey made a profound impression on the young Nkrumah at Achimota College, where Nkrumah enrolled in the teacher training section at the age of seventeen. Nkrumah reflects on the official opening of Achimota College in 1927 by Governor Gordon Guggisberg in his *Autobiography*:

> But the figure to whom all Africans looked that day was Dr. Kwegyir Aggrey, assistant vice-principal and the first African member of the staff. To me he seemed the most remarkable man that I had ever met and I had the deepest affection for him. He possessed intense vitality and enthusiasm and a most infectious laugh that seemed to bubble up from his heart, and he was a very great orator. He was extremely proud of his colour but was strongly opposed to race segregation in any form and, although he could understand Marcus Garvey's principle of "Africa for the Africans," he never hesitated to attack this principle. He believed that conditions should be such that the black and white races should work together. Co-operation between the black and white peoples was the key note of his message and the essence of his mission.[39]

On the school vacation in April or May, Aggrey undertook a trip to England and the United States, fell ill in New York, and died in the United States. Students in Achimota received the news in shock and Nkrumah wrote of how he was unable to eat for at least three days. Indeed, it was Nkrumah's admiration for Aggrey that first implanted the idea of studying in the United States in his mind.[40]

The second role model was the Nigerian Nnamdi Azikiwe, who moved to Accra in 1935 after an education and academic career in the United States to become the editor of the *African Morning Post*. Azikiwe was the first person Nkrumah met who had attended Lincoln University in Pennsylvania, and he encouraged Nkrumah to apply to Lincoln. It is noteworthy that Aggrey had made an equally profound impression on Azikiwe when in 1921 he preached at the Wesleyan High School in Lagos. Azikiwe was then sixteen years old. In his autobiography, he recalls the sermon Aggrey preached in his high school: "Soft and melodious, his voice struck my soul with the force of a supernatural wand. Symbolic and suave, his message found my heart a ready soil for the dreams of a new social order."[41] Aggrey on this occasion declared that "nothing but the best is good enough for Africa," and ended his sermon with the words "If I, one of you, could go to the new world, and make a man of myself, then you can too. May God help you."[42] Azikiwe resolved one day to find his way to America. In 1925, Azikiwe enrolled in Storer College, West Virginia, at the recommendation of D. J. Stanley, president of Howard University. After two years at Storer, Azikiwe transferred to Howard. Azikiwe recalls the privilege of studying under philosopher Alain Locke at Howard and historian William Leo Hansberry, also at Howard, and becoming friends with other foreign students like Malcolm I. Nurse, later known as George Padmore, and Bankole Wright of Sierra Leone. Even then, there was a cross-fertilization of intellectual currents between African students in the US and those in Britain. Unable to pursue his education at Howard due to a lack of funds, Azikiwe transferred to Lincoln University as a senior in the fall semester of 1929 to complete his BA. Azikiwe graduated from Lincoln in June 1930. He successfully applied for a graduate assistant position at Lincoln on graduating as an instructor in political science, also enrolling in the MA program at Lincoln Theological Seminary with a major in religion and a minor in philosophy. Azikiwe obtained his MA in 1932.[43] Azikiwe obtained a second master's degree from the University of Pennsylvania in 1934 and was appointed full-time lecturer at Lincoln.[44] Azikiwe was thus well positioned to advise Nkrumah about his alma mater, Lincoln University.

In March 1935, Lincoln University received Francis Nwia-Kofi Nkrumah's application for college admission from the Gold Coast. This was Nkrumah's legal name for his time in the United States (during his stay in London from 1945, he dropped his forenames for "Kwame"). In October

1935, Nkrumah arrived at Lincoln with only £50 in cash and a determination to succeed in education that won over the dean of the college, Professor George Johnson.[45] Professor Johnson had been Azikiwe's adviser at Lincoln.[46] Sherwood writes that "it was Azikiwe who inspired Nkrumah and other Gold Coasters such as Ako Adjei and K. A. B. Jones-Quartey to study in the US and particularly at Lincoln where African students received every possible financial assistance."[47] On that shaky start, Nkrumah began his university education in the United States, which ended a decade later with two bachelors' degrees from Lincoln and two masters' degrees from the University of Pennsylvania. He obtained bachelors' degrees from Lincoln in Economics and Sociology (1939) and Theology (1942) and masters' degrees from the University of Pennsylvania in Education (MSc 1942) and Philosophy (MA 1943). Nkrumah during his period of study was supported by charitable interests, especially the Presbyterian Church, and became a licensed preacher in the Presbyterian Church in Westchester County, Pennsylvania.

It was in the United States that Nkrumah encountered the legacies of African American slavery as well as the sharp inequities of capitalism. The Depression of the 1930s was not an auspicious time for any worker, immigrant, or foreign student in America. Nkrumah's time in America (1935–45) also overlapped with the Italian annexation of Ethiopia and World War II, an event that sharpened his understanding of empire. In his engagement with African American students at Lincoln University, social work in African American communities in Philadelphia, odd jobs during school vacations to earn money, and encounters with notable African American activists such as Du Bois, C. L. R. James, and others in New York, Nkrumah received an education in race matters and capitalism. While Lincoln offered students on-campus work during the school year—and Nkrumah received grants from philanthropic institutions with an interest in the education of Africans, such as the Phelps-Stokes Fund—Nkrumah was often pressed for cash, especially during vacations, when he needed to earn his keep.[48] Nkrumah spent quite some time in Harlem and tried his hand at several odd jobs during school vacation, including a stint selling fish one summer on Lenox Avenue. The retired curator of the Schomburg Collection, where Nkrumah often went to read, recalled how Nkrumah would come in smelling of fish.[49]

In his study of history, philosophy, and theology at Lincoln and the University of Pennsylvania, Nkrumah struggled to make sense of the changing world and his place in it. In his *Autobiography*, he recounts acquainting himself with the works of Kant, Hegel, Descartes, Schopenhauer, Nietzsche, Freud, and others to equip himself to teach as assistant lecturer in philosophy at Lincoln after graduating with his bachelor's.[50] He was a member of the philosophy club at Lincoln, and on becoming president would create a philosophy club in Ghana in the early 1960s, including philosophers like William Abraham from the Philosophy Department at the University of Ghana. As Nkrumah became more interested in political organization in the early 1940s, he followed the activities of several political organizations in the United States, including the Democrats, Republicans, Communists, and Trotskyites. It is through the activities of the last that Nkrumah met C. L. R. James, who provided Nkrumah with an introduction to Padmore when Nkrumah relocated to London. Nkrumah extended his reading to include Marx, Engels, Lenin, and Mazzini. He was deeply sensitive about race and race relations, and on becoming head of state in Ghana he keenly followed race matters in the United States. He confesses in his *Autobiography* that of all the books he read, the one that most influenced him was the *Philosophy and Opinions of Marcus Garvey* (1923).[51] America transformed the identity of the young man from rural Nzima in southwestern Ghana, and peers at Lincoln University commented that he always referred to himself as "Nkrumah of Africa," never of the Gold Coast.

That his years at Lincoln and in America occupied a special place in Nkrumah's own understanding of his formative experiences is clear in his preface to his *Autobiography*, which begins with his application to Lincoln in 1934. He reflects on his decade's sojourn in America: "Those years in America and England were years of sorrow and loneliness, poverty and hard work. But I have never regretted them because the background that they provided has helped me to formulate my philosophy of life and politics."[52] In his masterful centenary history of Lincoln University, Horace Mann Bond, president of Lincoln from 1945 to 1957, devotes some space to Lincoln's Africa connection and its two distinguished African alumni who went on to become heads of state, Azikiwe and Nkrumah. Bond's insights on what Lincoln and America meant to Azikiwe and Nkrumah are astute. Committed to providing African Americans and Africans with an academic education for leadership distinct from a vocational or technical education, Lincoln very early on attracted students from Africa, beginning with Liberians of American origin in the 1870s.[53] Horace Mann Bond writes insightfully on the impact of racial oppression and capitalist exploitation on Azikiwe and Nkrumah, who frequented African American churches and the homes of African Americans in Pennsylvania and nearby great cities. That both entered Lincoln during the Great Depression, Azikiwe in 1929 and Nkrumah in 1935, shaped their experiences and understanding of the country.

While disturbed by the inequality he saw in America, especially along racial lines, Nkrumah was impressed by America's level of economic development. Nkrumah was a believer in high modernism. That America, the proponent of modernization theory, also represented the richest country on earth after World War II, exerted a magnetic force on Africa's new rulers. Lewis was in favor of Ghana reaching out to the United States in search of foreign investment, much to the dismay of the British, for whom "development plans were intended to prolong the life of the empire and support the balance sheets of British firms, not ease the Americans into territories once controlled by the British."[54] Nkrumah would visit the United States twice in the 1950s: in 1951 to receive an honorary doctorate from his alma mater Lincoln University and in 1958 to seek foreign investment for the Akosombo Dam and associated industries. During United Nations General Assembly meetings in 1960 and 1961, he would meet with Presidents Dwight Eisenhower and John F. Kennedy respectively. Both were qualifiedly supportive of Nkrumah's Volta River Project.

The United States in Nkrumah's Development Agenda

David Birmingham notes that Nkrumah's vision of industrialization for Ghana had been shaped by his years in America and Britain. "His experience of the developed world had been gained in the old coal-fired industrial communities of Pennsylvania and Britain. The most radical model of economic growth available to date appeared to be the electrification of the Soviet Union. Nkrumah thought that industry must be his path and that electrical energy was the fuel of the future. The people of Ghana will never be happy, he said, until industrial smoke and grime make it impossible to see from one side of the Volta River to the other."[55] The history of the Volta River Project dates back to the 1910s, when A. E. Kitson, director of geological survey in the Gold Coast, established in 1914 the existence of extensive bauxite deposits at Ejuanema Mountain in Kwahu.[56] The following year, Kitson explored the Volta River and commented on the suitability of

Akosombo (near Ajena Gorge) for a hydroelectric dam. In 1924–25, Kitson submitted a report (or bulletin) to the Gold Coast government. He proposed an integrated development plan for the Volta Basin, which would involve the transformation of bauxite into alumina and the smelting of aluminum from alumina based on the waters and hydroelectric power of the propounded dam. Kitson also recommended the creation of a canal on the lower Volta and the irrigation of the Accra Plains. Already saddled with a ten-year development plan, Governor Frederick Guggisberg shelved Kitson's proposal.[57]

The project was resurrected in the late 1930s, this time as a private initiative. South African engineer Duncan Rose read Kitson's bulletin in a Johannesburg public library in November 1938. Intrigued by Kitson's proposal, Rose visited the Gold Coast in February 1939. With World War II on the horizon, Rose appreciated the value of a sterling source of aluminum. On his return to South Africa, Rose formed the Africa Aluminum Company. He returned to the Gold Coast with his partner Christopher St John Bird to negotiate for bauxite concessions from the colonial government in Mpraeso (Kwahu) and Yenahin (Asante) and to further investigate the suitability of the Ajena Gorge for a dam. Their plans had to be put on hold until 1944 because of the war. By the time Rose and Bird returned to the Gold Coast in 1944–45, the integrated Volta River Project had gained international attention, and larger concerns were interested in Rose's newly formed West African Aluminum Limited. There was a strong demand for aluminum on the world market. In June 1949, the Aluminum Company of Canada secured a 25 percent share in Rose's company. The British government, through the British Aluminum Company Limited, was exploring prospects for producing aluminum in North Borneo. It was doubted that the sterling community needed two large aluminum producers, and a joint commission comprising the British and Canadian aluminum companies was established to investigate the Gold Coast and North Borneo schemes and recommend one.[58] Even the United States by early January 1950 had become interested in the project.[59] Then came the general elections of 1951 and the advent of Nkrumah's nationalist government. It soon became clear that foreign investors were not comfortable about an "integrated industrial complex under the actual or potential control of indigenous politicians."[60]

But Nkrumah had become infatuated with the Volta River Project, and he was intent on getting a hydroelectric dam for Ghana as the basis for his industrialization plans. Lewis, who had begun to consult for Nkrumah's government from the early 1950s, even before accepting Nkrumah's appointment as economic adviser in 1957, worried about Nkrumah's obsession with the Akosombo Dam (see chap. 3). Lewis put together clear guidelines for the Gold Coast in its negotiation over the Volta River Project concerning the power contract for the smelter, the mining of local bauxite, the railway to be constructed to convey bauxite to the smelter, and the financial structure of the smelter company. Though this document is not dated, the reference to the "Aluminum Ltd.," suggests that these negotiations were with the British and Canadian interests before the formal grant of Ghana's independence. The size of the dam and the capacity of power to be generated required a major consumer of electricity to make the project financially viable, so the smelter was key to the success of the Volta River Project. Lewis suggested that the smelter should commit itself to take 340 megawatts of power, and the Aluminum Ltd. should guarantee to construct a smelter capable of producing no less than 120,000 tons of aluminum. He insisted that "the importation of alumina is not acceptable, unless the imports are limited to a defined initial period of, say, 3 years."[61] Lewis was also particular that the greater part of the funding for the Volta River Project must come from external sources and not from the CPP government. Indeed, the company to establish the smelter could take over the construction of the dam and railway to ensure that construction costs were kept to a minimum. Negotiations for the Volta River Project stalled between 1951 and 1957. After Ghana's independence, Nkrumah turned to the United States for funding. The more desperate Nkrumah became to secure his dam, the more unfavorable the financial terms for the Volta River Project became. As the project made more and more demands on the financial resources of the Ghanaian state, Nkrumah turned to cocoa and the tax on cocoa to pay for the state's investment in the dam. As Nkrumah looked to the United States for assistance, some of the most welcoming doors were opened by vested interests in Ghana's cocoa.

Pennsylvania "Home" Support: Hershey, TWAP, and Ghana's Educational Partnerships

Pennsylvanians and African Americans across the United States celebrated Ghana's formal attainment of independence on March 6, 1957. In June 1951, Lincoln University had invited its distinguished alumnus, Nkrumah, then leader of government business in the Gold Coast, to deliver the commencement address. Nkrumah was on that occasion awarded an honorary doctorate by Lincoln. Nkrumah used his commencement speech to invite African Americans to come to Ghana to assist in the novel experiment of building sub-Saharan Africa's first independent Black nation. Several African Americans responded to his call. Prominent Caribbean Africans and African Americans attended Ghana's independence celebrations in March 1957. The list included George Padmore, who relocated to live in Ghana; Norman Manley, who later became the prime minister of Jamaica; UN official and Nobel Laureate Ralph Bunche; Martin Luther King Jr. and his wife, Coretta; Lucille Armstrong representing her husband Louis Armstrong; and labor leaders and educators from historically Black universities like Howard University and Lincoln University. The vice president of the United States, Richard Nixon, led an American delegation. Ironically, it was in Accra at a reception on March 5 that Martin Luther King Jr. first met Richard Nixon. "'I'm very glad to meet you here,' King remarked, no doubt pleased by the irony of the encounter, 'but I want you to come to visit us down in Alabama where we are seeking the same kind of freedom the Gold Coast is celebrating.' Nixon promptly invited King to Washington for a meeting."[62] The deep impact King's trip to Ghana had on him is evident in the fact that the first sermon he preached on his return to his congregation in Alabama on April 7 was entitled "The Birth of a New Nation."[63] King commented on how Nkrumah had shared with him his desire to diversify and industrialize Ghana's economy and how cocoa was "too flimsy a foundation for Ghana's economy." King elaborated further in his sermon. To quote Kevin Gaines's commentary, "'Nkrumah said that one of the first things he will do is work toward industrialization.' Universal free education was needed to battle illiteracy. King hoped that Americans by the 'hundreds and thousands' would emigrate to Ghana to lend their technical assistance. Noting the rich opportunities, King told his congregation that 'American Negroes can lend their technical assistance to a growing new nation. . . . And Nkrumah made it very clear to me that he would welcome any persons coming there as immigrants to live there.'"[64] Clearly, Nkrumah saw King and other African Americans who attended Ghana's independence celebrations as ambassadors for the new nation. Pennsylvania had close ties to Nkrumah and Ghana and responded to this broader call to assist in Ghana's nation-building.

The *Pittsburg Courier* dedicated its issue of March 6, 1957, to Ghana's independence, calling it the "Ghana Salute Edition."[65] The edition provided for its readers a background history of Ghana, photos of Accra, photos of Nkrumah's cabinet ministers (African Americans locked in a civil rights struggle would have been thrilled to see an all-African cabinet), an imposing photograph of the chief justice Sir Arku Korsah, images of the University of Ghana, and more. One-page congratulatory adverts were taken out by the National Association for the Advancement of Colored People (NAACP), the African Methodist Episcopal Zion Church (which had a long history of struggle against slavery and for African liberation), and, naturally, the Association of Cocoa and Chocolate Manufacturers of the United States. In July 1958, Nkrumah paid a state visit to the United States, and he made sure that he spent quality time in Pennsylvania. He was honored at a luncheon in Harrisburg as Lincoln University's most illustrious alumnus and made a personal visit to the Hershey Chocolate Corporation. The visit was reported in *Hershey News*, which noted that the "Hershey Chocolate Corporation is the largest consumer of Ghana's cocoa bean crop, the African Gold Coast nation's major export."[66]

Hershey, the company and the town (for the two are one), has a fascinating history. A *Wall Street Journal* story from 1969 provides a history of Hershey, as well as a contemporary look at its fortunes:

> [In 1903] Mr. Hershey took the proceeds from a caramel factory that he previously had sold and put them into the then-infant chocolate business. He built the first Hershey factory and the nucleus of a town in a cornfield 13 miles east of Harrisburg, then turned around and gave the venture to a group of orphan boys.
>
> Today the Milton Hershey School is one of the most richly endowed orphanages in the country. It has a 66% interest in Hershey Foods, a holding worth $400 million even at current depressed stock prices. The school owns nearly everything else of value in the town as well—all three hotels, 38 businesses, most of the utilities and 10,000 acres of rice farmland.[67]

Hershey's growth overlapped with that of Ghana's cocoa industry, connecting intimately the history of the two. The earliest factory in the United States to manufacture chocolate was Walter Baker and Company, established in Dorchester, Boston, in 1820. Chocolate factories had emerged in Europe in the mid-eighteenth century, and by the mid-nineteenth century Germany and Switzerland had become leading producers of machinery for chocolate factories. It was at a visit to the Chicago International Exposition in 1893 that Milton Hershey encountered and was impressed by Lehmann machines for making chocolate manufactured in Germany. When he decided to move into chocolate manufacture after selling his caramel factory, Hershey opted for German and Swiss machinery.[68] In the early twentieth century, the United States became the world's largest chocolate industry.

Hershey, the town, as depicted by the *Wall Street Journal* in 1969 would not have been very different from Hershey during Nkrumah's visit a decade before. Chocolate, and by extension Ghana's cocoa, had come to define Hershey. "On the surface, all seems well at 'Chocolate Town, U.S.A.' the unofficial designation for this community of 8,000 persons. As the record 785,000 visitors who toured the company's factory last year might attest, the local product is hard to overlook. The main intersection is at Chocolate and Cocoa Avenues where the street lights are shaped like Hershey's Kisses. Company documents are printed in brown ink. Overnight guests at Hershey, the Cocoa Inn or Hershey Lodge bathe with soap made with cocoa butter."[69] Here was an image of cocoa and industrialization that should have impressed Nkrumah. But as noted above in his discussions with King, Nkrumah perceived cocoa as "too flimsy" to be the basis of Ghana's economy, despite the fact that by 1957 it had been the mainstay of the Ghanaian economy for almost half a century.[70]

Hershey executives had prepped for Nkrumah's visit in 1958, and their key talking points were outlined in a memorandum dated June 7, 1958. Ironically, the crux of their argument spoke to the very reason Nkrumah felt he had to turn Ghana's economy away from its dependence on cocoa. "Express our concern over the cocoa shortage and its high price; point out the similarity of the Ghana and Hershey position. Ghana is a one-product country and Hershey is a one-product corporation. This gives them something very much in common since the economy of both is vitally dependent upon the cocoa crop."[71] A Hershey memorandum from the end of 1958 spoke to another fear that motivated Nkrumah's turn away from cocoa: that Ghana's cocoa industry might be dying. This memo was a result of Hershey's own economic intelligence gathering, based on discussions with American and British cocoa dealers and manufacturer representatives, officials at the United States Department of State, and representatives of the Ghanaian government at the Embassy of Ghana in Washington, DC. "The English and American cocoa people are fearful of the stability of the government and also of Ghana's ability to increase or even maintain its production of its chief cash-crop—cocoa beans—which now provides about 70% of the country's revenue. They state that many of the cocoa trees are a half century old and that the soil in the cocoa growing areas is spent. Plant diseases such as swollen shoot, black pod and capsid have wreaked havoc and new plantings cannot replace the losses."[72] The American chocolate industry was understandably anxious when Nkrumah visited in July 1958.

Nkrumah sought to reassure chocolate and cocoa manufacturers that he shared their concerns and was committed to Ghana's cocoa industry. Nkrumah visited the New York Cocoa Exchange and was invited to a dinner at the Waldorf Astoria in New York on July 28, 1958. The hosts were the New York Cocoa Exchange Inc., the Cocoa Merchants' Association of America Inc., the Association of Cocoa and Chocolate Manufacturers' Association of America Inc., and the National Confectioners' Association of the United States.[73] Nkrumah's speech was rife with contradictions.

> We in Ghana are making every effort to expand our production of cocoa in the confident belief that we shall always be able to sell, at reasonable prices, all we produce, in a growing American and world market.
>
> It is, of course, the intention of my Government to diversify the national economy, especially in the agricultural sector, and to find employment for the non-farming population. We are also anxious to do everything we can to reduce the risks inherent in depending too greatly on one cash crop. Nevertheless, we wish to emphasize that we will continue to give absolute priority to our cocoa industry—the industry which above all, is the key to our prosperity and our economic and social progress.[74]

Nkrumah went on to outline how the cocoa reserve fund maintained by the Ghana Cocoa Marketing Board had funded rural schools, hospitals, and roads, and provided educational scholarships for all and sundry, including a hundred students in American universities. It would have been helpful to outline the research WACRI was doing to ensure the long-term viability of Ghana's cocoa industry. Nkrumah valued the cocoa reserve fund, but his policies did not prioritize the cocoa industry as declared in his New York Cocoa Exchange speech.

Hershey demonstrated its commitment to the cocoa-producing nations of Ghana and Nigeria through its Teachers in West Africa Program (TWAP). The brainchild of S. F. Hinkle, president of Hershey Foods Corporation, former chairman of the board, and Nkrumah's host at Hershey in July 1958, the idea was to forge an educational partnership between academic institutions in the United States and Africa "in which industry, institutions of higher education, ministries of education, and secondary schools in Africa worked together for a common goal."[75] Hinkle reached out to A. C. Baugher, former president of Elizabethtown College in Pennsylvania, to help develop the framework for this educational partnership and serve as the program's first executive director. It is not clear whether this idea had been discussed when Nkrumah visited Hershey in 1958. It has been noted above how Nkrumah mentioned to King that as a newly independent country, one of Ghana's major challenges was illiteracy, which required universal free education. President Hinkle of Hershey Foods Corporation and the president of the Milton Hershey School, Dr. John O. Hershey, certainly responded to a real need in Ghana.

As a newly independent former British colony, Ghana's educational system was oriented toward that of Britain. The university system was modeled on the Oxbridge universities and the University of London. Missionary education had left its impact on secondary schools, most boarding, after several decades. In March 1962, President Roy E. McAuley of Elizabethtown College and Dr. John Hershey of the Milton Hershey School visited Ghana and Nigeria on a feasibility trip. In Ghana they met with the chief education officer, Mr. B. A. Brown, and the principal education officer in charge of secondary education, Mr. J. W. L. Mills. Reflecting a Ghanaian condescension toward American education, McAuley and Hershey noted in their report that "we were told that in most instances first degrees from only a few American colleges were acceptable. Their advice was to present several top candidates from the ECAP program through regular African-American [Institute] channels and the Ministry would consider them with other candidates."[76] By 1960, Ghana had one of the most educated populations in tropical Africa. It is instructive that an internal memorandum at Hershey's from late 1958 notes that in terms of the Ghana Embassy staff in Washington, DC, "those responsible for the Ghana-United States relationships are well educated (Oxford and Cambridge), well spoken, friendly and able."[77] Hershey was an important player for Ghana. Elizabethtown College was an unknown institution, but the officials at Ghana's Ministry of Education had come to trust the African-American Institute, which had an educational program in Ghana. Hence the recommendation that TWAP route its candidates through the African-American Institute.[78]

Elizabethtown College followed the advice of the Ghanaian officials and approached the African-American Institute. Fortuitously, the African-American Institute was considering phasing out its program in Ghana and Nigeria and was happy to assist the establishment of TWAP, using its field staff personnel in Ghana and Nigeria to place TWAP teachers at no cost. On November 1, 1961, the Hershey Chocolate Corporation made the first payment of $250,000 to Elizabethtown College to cover the expenses of sending American teachers to Ghana and Nigeria for the years 1962 and 1963.[79] That the program lasted a decade (1962–72) underscores Hershey's financial commitment to the program. Over that decade, ninety-six teachers went to fifty-six different schools in Nigeria, and one hundred sixty-two teachers served in seventy-one academic institutions in Ghana, including the University of Ghana and the University College of Cape Coast. TWAP teachers touched most of the leading secondary schools in every region in Ghana. In all, two hundred thirty-eight teachers, sixty-three with graduate degrees, served in TWAP.[80] The impact of the program may not have been examined in the Ghanaian setting, but TWAP definitely played a major role in making American education an attractive option for Ghanaians. By the mid-1970s, to be awarded an opportunity to participate in the AFS Intercultural Program and spend a year in an American high school with an American host family had become one of the most coveted honors in Ghanaian secondary schools.

The United States, the Akosombo Dam, and Ghana's Vision of Industrialization[81]

The very year Ghana became independent (1957), Nkrumah wrote to President Eisenhower of the United States about the Volta River Project, which he had hoped would be a partnership between the governments of Ghana and Britain with the Aluminum Limited of Canada and the British Aluminum Company as private partners. Now Britain claimed "economic difficulties," and Nkrumah hoped that the United States would step in to assist with the financing of the project.[82] Nothing much happened until an incident in Delaware brought Nkrumah's need firmly before Eisenhower. In October 1957, Ghana's finance minister, Komla Gbedemah, traveled to Canada for discussions with the Aluminum Limited of Canada (Alcan) on the Volta River Project, continuing from there to the United States to meet with officials at the International Bank for Reconstruction and Development (the World Bank). Driving through Delaware on October 9 with Bill Sutherland, an African American who had settled in Ghana in 1953 in response to Nkrumah's invitation, the team stopped at a Howard Johnson restaurant to order fruit juice and snacks. Sutherland was then the private secretary to Gbedemah. About to sit down at a table, they were informed by the waitress and the manager that they would have to take their purchase out and could not sit because they were "colored." Gbedemah explained that he was the finance minister of Ghana, but the restaurant staff were not impressed, so he and his team left the restaurant without touching the order they had paid for.[83] In New York the following day, Gbedemah released a press statement about the incident that made headlines around the world.[84]

Gbedemah's incident was part of a broader context of indignities suffered by African guests in a racialized America. African diplomats posted to embassies in Washington, DC and the United Nations in New York in the late 1950s and 1960s struggled to find accommodation befitting their status, as white landlords denied them rental houses and apartments in a segregated America. This became a sore point for Senator John F. Kennedy, chair of the newly formed Senate Foreign Relations Sub-Committee for Africa (1959–60), who asked Winifred Armstrong, his African affairs consultant and speechwriter, to conduct further research on the matter. Kennedy was also campaigning for the presidency. In a report from December 1960, Armstrong noted that "at least forty cases of known discrimination have taken place in the past two to three years involving African diplomats seeking apartments or houses. Some diplomats have sought housing for upwards of six months, with responses ranging from 'No Niggers here' to returned deposit checks from brokers. Such instances often cause bitterness, hurt, resentment. They are a measure of the welcome and respect the U. S. affords African diplomats and their nations. U. S. racial practices are to other nations a measure of U. S. integrity."[85] Indeed, on the list of diplomats struggling to find accommodation in their new station was the Ghanaian ambassador to the United Nations in New York, Daniel Chapman, who was looking for a luxury apartment but had been declined "in many instances because of color."[86] Senator Kennedy wrote formally to the Department of State on August 25, 1960, about the housing situation of African diplomats and the "unfortunate reflection which is cast on the United States by the events, particularly when they occur in the nation's capitol."[87] He noted that sixteen African nations had become independent in 1960 (with more to come), making this question increasingly imperative. Under pressure, the Department of State reached out to real estate leaders in Washington, DC and New York and assured Kennedy that they would consult on a continuing basis.[88]

But something good came out of the embarrassing incident with Gbedemah in Delaware. When the incident went public, Eisenhower invited Gbedemah to the White House for a breakfast meeting that included Vice President Nixon. It was an opportunity for Gbedemah to discuss the Volta River Project. Nkrumah's insistence that Ghana not pursue and escalate Gbedemah's Delaware incident earned the respect of Eisenhower, who instructed his government to explore the possibility of assisting Ghana.[89] Nkrumah wrote to Eisenhower on November 10, 1957, formally requesting American financial assistance with the Volta River Project. "We are not asking for any gifts. At most we wish to borrow substantial sums of money at a reasonable rate of interest. The economic viability of the project is such that the loans and interest would be paid off on time. In this connection we have studied with great interest the establishment by Congress of the Development Loan Fund and we wonder whether this might be one possible source of finance which would be suitable for the scheme."[90] Nkrumah was convinced of the financial viability of an integrated Volta River Project. It was his country's path away from overdependence on cocoa. World Bank projections of a strong market for aluminum through the 1970s boosted Nkrumah's confidence: "Therefore a smelter and local bauxite could provide Ghana with a permanent and valuable manufactured export which would bolster revenue when the cocoa price fluctuated."[91] Eisenhower responded to Nkrumah's letter on January 3, 1958, extending an invitation to the Ghanaian prime minister to visit the White House. He expressed an interest in assisting with the Volta River Project once due diligence had been conducted on the financial viability of the project and the active participation of the aluminum industry had been engaged. Then the United States government would work with the government of Ghana on "the possibility of assistance in financing a part of the project, such as the portion of the hydroelectric installation."[92] US ambassador to Ghana Wilson Flake on January 13, 1958, confirmed the American government's interest in the Volta River Project and its exploration of American private interest in Ghana's aluminum project.[93]

Thus began Nkrumah's relationships with three American presidents over the Volta River Project: Eisenhower, Kennedy, and Johnson.[94] This was a saga framed by Cold War politics, on and off again, with the United States considering going ahead with financing, pulling out completely, or putting on the brakes to inject sanity into Nkrumah's politics when he pulled too close to the Eastern Bloc for American comfort. This generation of African leaders was infatuated with hydroelectric dams and the promise of modernity and industrialization, leading to what Zaki Laïdi has called "dam diplomacy" in the rivalry between the superpowers.[95] Nkrumah visited the White House in July 1958, which (as noted above) was also an occasion to visit Pennsylvania and Hershey. For Eisenhower, the visit was an opportunity to court Nkrumah and bring the influential African leader, who was being wooed assiduously by the Eastern Bloc, into the Western camp. Eisenhower introduced Nkrumah to Edgar Kaiser, who headed one of the largest aluminum corporations in the world. Kaiser offered to visit Ghana and update the 1955 engineering study of the Volta River Project. The United States offered to pay for half the cost of Kaiser's study, and the Ghana government paid for the other half. Kaiser's report was positive: he recommended moving the site of the dam from Ajena to Akosombo, and his assessment of the revised project actually reduced the estimated cost by 30 percent and made it even more economically viable. On completion of Kaiser's study, Eisenhower wrote to Nkrumah on May 9, 1959, confirming previous discussions that when Ghana received firm commitment from the aluminum industry to participate and necessary assurances for a major part of the financing from public or private sources, the US government would be pleased to explore ways to fund a portion of the hydroelectric project. Acting secretary of state C. Douglas Dillon followed up with Ghanaian Ambassador Chapman on May 11 advising the government of Ghana to approach the World Bank, since the Volta River Project might involve multiple lenders and would require the World Bank to act as a focal point. The World Bank conducted its own survey of the Volta River Project and in June 1960 declared the project "economically feasible."[96]

Assured of the financial viability of the Volta River Project by the endorsement of Kaiser Engineering and the World Bank, Eisenhower informed the government of Ghana on August 17, 1960, that the US was prepared to provide funds totaling $30 million toward the financing of the Volta River Project once Ghana reached a satisfactory agreement with the owners of the proposed aluminum smelter and found financial support to cover the rest of the project. The US issued a press release to this effect on August 18, 1960.[97] Then, Congo happened. The Belgian Congo had gained independence on June 30, 1960, under Ceremonial President Joseph Kasavubu and Prime Minister Patrice Lumumba. Lumumba was a protégé of Nkrumah, and the two first met when Lumumba attended the All-African People's Conference hosted by Nkrumah in Accra in December 1958 (see chap. 4). Nkrumah provided mentorship as Lumumba guided Congo toward independence, and it is reported that Lumumba planned for Congo to join the Ghana-Guinea Union, which Nkrumah saw as a nucleus for his United States of Africa (see chaps. 2 and 4).[98] But within days of Congo's independence, the country disintegrated into chaos, beginning with an army mutiny on July 5 at Thysville, with Congolese soldiers, still under the supervision of Belgian commanders, demanding better pay and the Africanization of the command structure of the army. The mutiny quickly spread to other military bases, and the country descended into violence. The Belgian government sent troops to protect Belgian lives and property without consulting the new African government. Lumumba in turn appealed to the UN to send in a peacekeeping force and demanded the removal of Belgian troops. The UN approved this request on July 13, and Nkrumah offered the services of Ghanaian soldiers to the UN. The situation in the Congo got messier. Kasavubu and Lumumba turned against each other. The CIA was heavily involved in the Congo because of the country's mineral wealth and Lumumba's socialist leanings. The CIA portrayed Congo as ripe for capture by the Soviets, reporting the arrival of Soviet technicians and weapons. The CIA station chief in Leopoldville (now Kinshasa), Lawrence Devlin, had instructions to move against Lumumba, whose removal the CIA considered desirable. Devlin supported the military coup staged by Colonel Joseph Mobutu on September 14, 1960, that removed Lumumba from power. Devlin subsequently informed Mobutu of a plot to assassinate him.[99] Mobutu ordered the arrest of Lumumba, who eventually was killed on January 17, 1961.

Nkrumah was distraught and accused the United States of complicity in Lumumba's murder in several statements. Nkrumah's relations with the United States worsened with the coup against Lumumba, and he berated the United Nations for its inefficiency. The United Nations General Assembly in September 1960 saw Nkrumah forcefully voice his opinions about how the West had mishandled the situation in the Congo. Nkrumah's meeting with

Eisenhower during his visit in September 1960 was a disaster. US national security interests now branded Nkrumah a communist. As Eisenhower's tenure as president drew to a close, he decided to suspend the $30 million his government had offered toward the Volta River Project.[100] It would be up to John F. Kennedy to breathe new life into the project.

In chapter 4, we saw how Kennedy moved away from Eisenhower's foreign policy in his approach to African leaders, viewing them as nationalists, not communists. Kennedy had met with many African nationalist representatives in 1959–60; he took their development concerns seriously as president and prepped for their visits. Kennedy made the effort to know African leaders and their wives, introduced them to the first family during visits to the White House, and followed developments in African countries. Kennedy believed that African leaders, "no matter how radical their rhetoric, would rather work with the U. S. than the Soviets, provided we dealt with them sympathetically and showed some understanding of their problems."[101] The first visit by a head of state under the Kennedy Administration in 1961 was Nkrumah on March 8. Barbara Ward Jackson was instrumental in facilitating this invitation from the White House to Nkrumah. She knew Kennedy from their student days at Harvard. An economist married to Sir Robert Jackson, one of the world's leading experts on multiple purpose river development schemes and closely associated with Ghana's Volta River Project from 1953, Ward Jackson was an important influence on Kennedy's thinking on Ghana and Nkrumah. Barbara Ward Jackson and Sir Robert Jackson were very close friends of Nkrumah.[102] The personal diplomacy of Kennedy worked to great effect during Nkrumah's visit to the White House. From the account of Angier Biddle Duke, who was chief of protocol for the White House and State Department (1961–65), this was a meeting of minds.

> When President Nkrumah of Ghana was here, he appeared to be surprisingly emotional and unreserved. . . . I was completely taken in by him, as I thought he caught the fire of the President's youth [Kennedy was 44]. He talked in terms of understanding the appeal of the President, not only to the youth of America but to the youth of the world. I thought he understood the symbolism of it. They talked about the future of Africa, the future of the world, civil rights. It was most fascinating—it looked like a fusion of minds. Really, to me it was an excitingly successful meeting. The President asked if he wanted to go up and meet Mrs. Kennedy and the children, and I thought Nkrumah looked terribly touched as he bounded

Fig 5.1 Nkrumah and John F. Kennedy laughing at the White House, March 8, 1961. Credit: Abby Rowe, National Park Service, John F. Kennedy Library and Museum.

out of there. The two of them went out into the Rose Garden and up into the mansion. I waited for them to come back. When they came back, the President of Ghana was leading Caroline by the hand, almost with tears in his eyes at this family confidence.[103]

This was a very special moment for Nkrumah, even though when Biddle recollected the visit in 1964, he considered Nkrumah deceptive and manipulative because of his close ties to communist leaders like Mao Zedong. Indeed, that very summer after Nkrumah's visit to the White House, he visited several Eastern Bloc countries. But that the connection with the first family was deeply meaningful for Nkrumah in his relations with Kennedy is evidenced in how he extended the same courtesy to the US ambassador to Ghana from May 1962, William P. Mahoney, a lawyer and close friend of President Kennedy. Mahoney suspected, perhaps rightly, that the first family was lonely. Nkrumah and Fathia had three children. Fathia, who was born and grew up in Egypt, did not have much of a social network in

Ghana. The Mahoney family was large, and their eighth child was born in a Ghanaian hospital, to Nkrumah's pleasure. Nkrumah suggested their children play together, which became a weekly ritual of the Mahoneys going to Flagstaff House to play with the Nkrumahs.[104] Nkrumah's link with the US was personal.

Nkrumah's relationship with Kennedy went through several hiccups. But it persevered, perhaps owing to the bond from that initial meeting in March 1961. The Kennedy administration worried about Nkrumah's flirtation with the Eastern Bloc—visits, trade agreements, sending Ghanaian students to universities in the Bloc and Ghanaian military officers for training in the Soviet Union. Kennedy questioned Nkrumah's nonalignment, and over the early 1960s Nkrumah's relations with communist countries were scrutinized closely. The CIA suspected, perhaps correctly, that Nkrumah was gaming the system, defining his own version of positive neutrality as an open-door policy to benefit Ghana. "Nkrumah and the extreme radicals among his followers are attracted by the apparent success of the Communists in promoting rapid economic development, and their avowed anticolonialism. He almost certainly believes he can use the Bloc to further his own objectives without becoming inextricably committed to the Communists. Nevertheless, Nkrumah will probably try to maintain a Western presence in Ghana to offset the Bloc, and improve his prospects for aid from both sides."[105] While the Americans resented being played, they had learned a lesson from Eisenhower canceling funding for Egypt's Aswan Dam because of Nasser's growing ties with the Soviet Union. The result was that the Soviets immediately offered Egypt funding for the Aswan Dam, and the United States lost a key ally in the Middle East and the Arab world. Kennedy did not intend to repeat this mistake. Not only would the Soviet Union seize on this project to tar the United States, but the Afro-Asian nations would also make capital of a denial of American funding. Nkrumah, perhaps, knew this.

Nkrumah's nationalist government and move toward socialism after Ghana became a republic in 1960 discomforted Western investors. In 1961, the year of the CIA report cited above, Ghana had signed sixty-three economic, technical, scientific, and cultural agreements with foreign countries, forty-four with Eastern Bloc countries and only one with the United States (see chap. 4). When Kennedy decided that the US should still support the Volta River Project, he conveyed his decision and misgivings to Nkrumah in a personal letter to be hand-delivered by the American ambassador in

Ghana. Acting Secretary of State Ball sent a telegram to the ambassador on December 14, 1961, with talking points for the meeting with Nkrumah that the ambassador and Clarence Randall were to schedule to deliver Kennedy's letter. Kennedy's sentiments were as follows: "After long and careful study and many considerations, both pro and con, relating to US participation in the Volta River Project, I have, with some reluctance and misgiving, decided to authorize US financial assistance to project. Decision in no sense endorsement of President Nkrumah or his policies, and it is of utmost importance to US Government that no one, either in Ghana, US or elsewhere in Africa, regards it as such."[106] Kennedy asked the ambassador to seek assurances from Nkrumah, in a written communiqué if possible, concerning the freedom of the press, noninterference in the internal affairs of other African nations, internal political liberty in Ghana itself, the move toward socialism precluding any attempt to nationalize the proposed smelter or other foreign-owned businesses, and Ghana arranging to receive as soon as possible a resident representative of the World Bank.[107]

On January 22, 1962, an exultant Nkrumah sent a cable to Kennedy relaying news of the signing of a master agreement with the Volta Aluminum Company Limited (VALCO), the consortium Edgar Kaiser put together to build and operate the smelter. "I want to thank you most sincerely for your unfailing support and assistance in helping to make the project a reality (STOP). I am sure it will strengthen the already cordial relations between Ghana and the United States of America and further consolidate our personal friendship (STOP). [Original in all capital letters.]"[108] The following month, the World Bank finalized the loan agreement with the Volta River Authority (VRA), the body established by an act of the government of Ghana to operate and manage the Akosombo Dam. The loan agreement lists the multiple sources of funding that made the Volta River Project possible: the US Agency for International Development (USAID)—$27 million; the Export-Import Bank of Washington (Exim Bank)—$10 million; the UK government—£5 million; and the International Bank for Reconstruction and Development (the Bank)—$47 million. The vice president for the World Bank signed, and F. J. Dobson, chief executive of VRA, signed on behalf of Ghana.[109] Nkrumah's government invested £35 million ($100 million) from Ghanaian funds.

Drama characterized Ghana–United States relations through to the inauguration of the Akosombo Dam on January 1966. The assassination of

Kennedy on November 22, 1963, and the assumption to office of Lyndon Johnson injected new uncertainty into the Volta River Project, on which construction had already begun. Nkrumah was going through his own personal hell with several assassination attempts made on his life. In 1961, Nkrumah had dismissed his old associates Gbedemah and Kojo Botsio from government, and more radical politicians on the left came to the fore of the party. The first, nearly successful attempt to assassinate Nkrumah was in Kulungugu in northern Ghana on August 1, 1961, when a grenade was lobbed at him, killing and wounding many. The president was not seriously hurt. More old associates fell foul, and foreign minister Ako Adjei, among others, was accused of involvement in the assassination plot. Assassination attempts on Nkrumah's life then became incessant. On January 1, 1964, one of the president's security detail, police constable Seth Ametewee, fired several shots at Nkrumah at close range on the grounds of Flagstaff House but missed. When President Johnson chaired a meeting at the White House that included British prime minister Alec Douglas-Home and key members of both governments on February 12, 1964, to discuss the security of their investments in Ghana's Volta River Project, it was reported that a paranoid Nkrumah had not left the impregnable Christiansborg Castle since January 2. Further US government deliberations were convened on the Ghana situation that month. What kept the Volta River Project on track was Edgar Kaiser's insistence that "he had a contract that had not been broken by Ghana despite the exasperating situation and that he intended to fulfill his contract."[110]

The Akosombo Dam was completed in January 1966 and inaugurated on January 22 with several dignitaries present. Pope Paul VI sent a papal nuncio to represent the papacy. Nkrumah had hoped that the plaque commemorating Kennedy's role in the project would be unveiled by Jacqueline Kennedy, but she was not able to attend.[111] This was a landmark moment for Ghana and the developing world, and the Akosombo Dam created the Volta Lake, then the largest man-made lake in the world. The sight of the dam was magnificent. But Nkrumah was not to have the pleasure of having brought this major undertaking to fruition. On February 24, 1966, while Nkrumah was in Beijing on his way to Hanoi to mediate in the Vietnam war, a group of senior police and military officers in Ghana overthrew him in a coup d'état.[112] The CIA was aware of the plans of the coup plotters and had facilitated their planning. Indeed, the CIA had knowledge of several assassination attempts on Nkrumah's life through 1964 as Gbedemah, who had become a key instigator of these attempts, also served as a CIA informant.[113] The American government may have decided from the time of Kennedy that to renege on funding the Volta River Project would be bad press for the US. But as they watched Nkrumah became more authoritarian and draw closer to the Soviet Bloc and China (chap. 4), the government clearly resolved that the removal of Nkrumah would be the best protection for American investments in Ghana. James Moxon notes that "with the completion of the Akosombo Dam the safe keeping of Valco's smelter became a top priority to the US government, and Edgar Kaiser himself was assured from more than one quarter that before his smelter was in operation Kwame Nkrumah would not be there to covet it."[114] Would Nkrumah's relationship with the United States have ended this way under Kennedy? One cannot know. But both the National Liberation Council that overthrew Nkrumah in February 1966 and the Progress Party government under K. A. Busia that took over in 1969 with the return to civilian government were solidly pro-American.

To insulate its investment from appropriation, Kaiser Aluminum revised the original development plan and insisted on importing alumina for refinement at the smelter rather than using the bauxite in Ghana, a desire at the center of Nkrumah's integrated Volta River Project. Why did Nkrumah jettison Arthur Lewis's sound guidelines on the Volta River Project and persist even as the vision changed to exclude local bauxite and Ghana's financial contribution exceeded the bar Lewis had set? Several explanations have pointed to Nkrumah's ego and how the Akosombo Dam had become the centerpiece of the legacy he sought to bequeath to Ghana. In chapter 4, we referenced the report of the Accra correspondent of the *Frankfurter Allgemeine Zeitung* in December 1961, which astutely perceived what Nkrumah was orchestrating with his problematic definition of positive neutrality. Nkrumah by the late 1950s had come to the realization that only the United States could make possible the Volta River Project. But Nkrumah was deeply ambivalent about capitalism, as chapter 4 demonstrated. A Pan-Africanist and anti-imperialist, he certainly did not plan to exchange the suzerainty of Britain for the hegemonic influence of either the United States or the Soviet Union. Nkrumah did not want to choose a camp; he wanted the well-heeled United States to fund his dam and the cash-strapped, industrialized Soviet Bloc countries with their credits in machinery and technicians to build the factories he hoped would diversify Ghana's economy away from cocoa. The *Frankfurter Allgemeine Zeitung* correspondent pointed out how the economic agreements with the Soviet Bloc countries would create the "industrial plant that Ghana badly needs, and some of it will consume a great deal of power. Without the Volta Project this power would simply not be available."[115] Nkrumah set up numerous state enterprises through the instrumentality of communist countries. Several never became operative, and the few that did performed miserably.[116] Nkrumah was outplayed at his own game.

The major losers were Ghana's cocoa farmers, who bore the financial burden of the Volta River Project as the state steadily took from their earnings through the Cocoa Marketing Board to fund its developmental projects. Declining world prices for cocoa meant the country could not replenish its foreign exchange reserves. As the state's finances worsened, the government's efforts to rehabilitate cocoa farms that had been ravaged by swollen shoot and other diseases lapsed. Nkrumah's priorities and his privileging of industrialization laid prostrate the cocoa industry that had borne the country's economy for half a century. Danquah describes the distressed state of the cocoa industry by the end of Nkrumah's political tenure: "The state withdrew subsidies and inputs from cocoa disease control and the importation of spraying equipment and chemicals ceased. What further worsened matters was the evolution of capsid strains resistant to the likes of *Gammalin-20*. Capsid resistance to chemical sprays was most prominent in the Eastern Region where spraying had been carried out longest. The situation led to a dangerous resurgence of capsid attacks, particularly in the 1967–68 production period and Ghana's cocoa economy began to languish."[117] Not only did economic diversification fail, but cocoa production also plunged.

CONCLUSION

Despite the remarkable success story of peasant cocoa farmers in Ghana, Nkrumah could not see farmers as the basis of modernizing Ghana's economy. The small acres of cocoa farms with irregularly planted cocoa trees interspersed with food crops that resisted mechanization jarred with Nkrumah's very image of the industrialized nation-state he sought to create. Concerns about swollen shoot, Ghana's aging cocoa trees, soil exhaustion, and deforestation worried planners—not to mention the overdependence of

Ghana's economy on cocoa. In a paper he delivered on the need to diversify Ghana's economy dated March 28, 1958, Lewis commented that "the trouble with Ghana's agriculture is not that we have too much cocoa, but that we don't have enough of other things. What we seek is not substitutes for cocoa in the cocoa belt, but ways of making the rest of the country more productive."[118] We have seen in chapter 3 that Lewis advised Ghana to privilege agriculture, not industry, to grow the economy. Lewis, whose earlier writings also critiqued small peasant farms, later came to appreciate the efficiency of peasant versus plantation agriculture.[119] But for Nkrumah, who was attracted to development economics and modernization theory, both advocates of industrialization, the dream was to build an industrialized nation-state. And despite Lewis's contestation that electricity did not necessarily translate into economic growth, Nkrumah's mind was set on having his Akosombo Dam.

The Akosombo Dam in the integrated Volta River Project had economic merit. Nkrumah's original plan counted on the mining of Ghana's bauxite, new industries linked to the mining of bauxite, and irrigation of the Accra Plains for large-scale farming as sources of revenue to help pay off the loan for the dam. K. B. Asante, then in the Ministry of Foreign Affairs, spoke to me of the day the telegram arrived from the United States with the terms of the Volta River Project loan. Nkrumah, Asante, and a few government officials were sitting around a table in Nkrumah's office. What struck Nkrumah was the thirty years and the terms of repayment. He read the telegram and sat there quietly. Suddenly he banged on the table and exclaimed, "Thirty years in a nation's life is not that long."[120] Dr. Kwesi Botchwey, finance minister from the early 1980s under the Provisional National Defense Council (PNDC) and then the National Democratic Congress (NDC), is of the opinion that Nkrumah believed that once he had the dam and the smelter, he could interest Kaiser into considering backward linkages into Ghana's local bauxite.[121] This thinking may not have been misplaced. In 1975, Dr. Kwame Donkoh Fordwor was appointed by the Acheampong government as chair of an Aluminum Industries Commission. He managed to convince Kaiser and a Japanese group to reconsider mining Ghana's bauxite. He was in Oakland, California, for the signing of the document for the feasibility study when Acheampong announced the decision to capture the commanding heights of the Ghanaian economy through acquiring shares in all mining concerns in the country. Kaiser told Donkoh Fordwor that with that announcement, the circumstances had changed substantially, and Kaiser was no longer interested in Ghana's bauxite.[122] Whether Kaiser seriously reconsidered mining Ghana's bauxite in the mid-1970s is questionable, as it seemed to have viewed the absence of an integrated aluminum industry involving Ghana's bauxite as protection against nationalist aspirations in the first place.[123] The colonial vision of an industrial Ghana based on hydroelectricity, bauxite, and the manufacture of aluminum remained powerful through Nkrumah and successive governments. With his overthrow in February 1966, a month after the Akosombo Dam was commissioned, we will never know to what use Nkrumah would have put his electricity.

CONCLUSION

THE PROMISE OF INDEPENDENCE

The relationship between political and economic independence pushed its way to the forefront of the minds of colonial officials and African nationalists in the period of decolonization. The economic reforms that marked the late colonial developmental state were meant to extend the life of empire, not end it. To transform the nature of colonial rule from a basis on the rationale of the civilizing mission to a basis on development required colonial partners other than the traditional chiefs. British colonial rule turned to educated Africans as new partners, making political concessions meant to secure acquiescence to the new direction in colonial rule. Intrusive post–World War II colonial reforms deepened rural and urban unrest, reinforcing political movements that would lead to colonial rulers being "ousted by their favorite clients—or their clients' more impatient rivals," in the case of the United Gold Coast Convention and the Convention People's Party in Ghana.[1]

The early decades of independence witnessed remarkable creativity in imagining the African nation-state, even if some efforts can, with hindsight, be seen as misguided. These misguided efforts include Sékou Touré's Demystification Program, which targeted peoples such as the Loma of the Forest Region of Guinea, and Nyerere's deeply intrusive Ujamaa, which earned a chapter in Scott's *Seeing like a State* alongside other statist projects like

249

Soviet collectivization under Stalin and the building of the high-modernist city under the influence of Swiss-born French architect Le Corbusier (also known as Charles-Edouard Jeanneret).[2] The level of social engineering in the early decades of African independence was extreme. Straker notes of Guinea under Sékou Touré that "no postcolonial regime took matters of youth cultural development and authenticity more seriously than the one led by Sékou Touré from 1958 to 1984."[3] The energy and resources invested in economic planning and development were also immense. The necessity and urgency of development explains the phenomenon of states with little capacity to plan becoming obsessed with planning. In chapter 3, I referenced Lewis's observation of how backward countries plan because their need is greater, even though their efforts are marked by error and incompetence. It is not surprising that the capacity to create and execute economic plans, together with an ideology that made rapid economic growth imperative, became criteria for defining the African developmental state (see chap. 4). For poor countries, the resources directed into industrialization, particularly import-substitution industrialization, were huge. Debt burdens became untenable over the 1970s, aggravated by the OPEC oil crisis and the rising cost of international loans. Unsustainable indebtedness would lead African countries to the doors of the World Bank and the IMF in the 1980s—and to the imposition of ill-fated structural adjustment programs. Even South Africa, which had escaped the economic vicissitudes of the 1970s and 1980s and achieved a remarkable level of economic autonomy under apartheid because of its international pariah status, was quickly brought into the international economic system in the 1990s under the ANC government through the guidance of the "technical" and "scientific" policies of the World Bank and IMF.[4] After strenuous efforts to assert the African voice in the international arena and build African economic autonomy in the early decades of independence, African countries once again slipped under the economic hegemony of the West, becoming wards of international finance institutions from the 1980s.

A key agenda of this book has been to recuperate the effort, the imagination, and the resources invested in nation-building, economic development, and worldmaking in the first two decades of African independence. These have been too easily dismissed because they failed. From today's perspective, some of these initiatives seem like pipe dreams, such as Nkrumah's huge investment in infrastructure, including the development of nuclear power.[5] By situating efforts at nation-building and economic development within the context of the 1950s through the 1970s, when the international environment and social science disciplines and theories such as development economics and modernization theory were receptive and supportive of African developmental efforts, we capture the enthusiasm and excitement of the early decades of African independence with all of its possibilities (see chaps. 2, 3 and 4). Scientific socialism was a modernist ideology that offered a cosmopolitan framework for engaging the world, but, as McGovern notes, it "insisted upon a single path to modernity" and "did not hesitate to treat non-European societies with Eurocentric disdain."[6] Socialist internationalism's dismissal of race in favor of class, and the primacy given to the Soviet model, agency, and international priorities, would spawn Black internationalism in the interwar period as an alternative to the Third International (see chap. 4).[7]

The Developmental State Loses Its Way

While the late colonial state was developmental, there is a sense in which developmentalism in the early years of independence also had local African roots. Lonsdale has examined how African nationalisms in the post–World War II period jostled for space with ethnic patriotisms and local moral economies. In West and East Africa, precolonial slaving had encouraged the rise of small autonomous communities that fought to defend the security of their communities and the rights of householders. Colonial rule brought new impositions and exactions in labor, taxes, and produce. The colonial forces that shaped nationalisms also shaped ethnic patriotisms and local moral economies. Nationalist governments on the attainment of independence were met with an interrogative stance after the recent history of colonial exploitation: what would the government provide for the public, and at what cost? "Africans were scarce and slippery subjects; kings [in the precolonial period] had to enslave strangers to get work done. History could also be cruel . . . Africans understood the paradox of power: To exist, power must be greedy, eating its subjects' substance; to work, it must be generous, sharing its fruits with allies or conditionally with clients."[8] The new political dispensation after independence, the enfranchisement of all as citizens, and universal adult suffrage meant that all had expectations of the newly independent governments. Berman notes that "nation-building tried both to create a discourse of legitimacy for the state and a doctrine of popular sovereignty and citizenship."[9]

In the optimistic and heady days of independence, social contracts were forged between governments and publics to pursue rapid economic development with an eye to social equity and inclusion. Sacrifices would have to be made; development would not be an easy process. But the benefits were attractive: universal primary education, basic health care, piped water, electricity, decent housing, jobs. External and internal factors undercut the developmental effort. Heavy social and economic investment on the part of governments intersected with declining world prices for primary commodities from the late 1950s. Import-substitution industrialization expanded the ranks of the urban working class and witnessed the ballooning of state bureaucracy to oversee the newly established state-owned enterprises. The peasantry bore the burden of the African developmental state. Not only was infrastructural development often urban based, but the peasants also paid for it. As the largest sector of the African economy, farmers were expected to provide the foreign exchange for modernization and industrialization through agricultural exports, produce cheap food for vocal urban classes, and constitute a market for products of new urban industries. Across Africa we see the paradox of the state both subsidizing and taxing agriculture.[10] Bates notes that "as part of the modernization process, the peasantry is compelled to surrender its resources to the upper classes, to the state, and to the industrial sector."[11] The results of these contradictory policies in Ghana, Guinea, Senegal, and Tanzania are evident in chapters 4 and 5. Ironically for Ghana, cocoa farmers financed Nkrumah's industrialization project, but they were not a part of his modernist vision (chap. 5). Farmers, highly intelligent economic actors, withdrew from the production of cash crops into food crops or carried their produce across borders to neighboring countries with more attractive prices. Across Africa in the 1970s, the Food and Agriculture Organization noted the decline in agricultural productivity of a continent of farmers.

With dwindling national resources, the state became more selective in its extension of patronage to powerful interests. Authoritarianism accompanied clientelism as one-party states became the phenomenon across Africa, and the state squashed all dissent. Trade unions, farmers' cooperatives, women, and youth were all brought under the umbrella of the one-party state.[12] But the ethnic patriotisms and local moral economies Lonsdale so incisively discusses for the colonial period, which had informed the nationalisms that seized political power on independence and the experiment of the developmental state, did not fade away. Communities turned inward, seeking meaning in local moral economies. Africans have not given up on their nation-states, and Lonsdale notes that Africans continue to ask how the renewal of past moral economies might infuse their states with nationhood.[13] The challenge has been holding the state to account. In the late twentieth century and the twenty-first century, advances in technology have witnessed the rise and displacement of industrial capital by financial capital on the global scene. Capital has become untethered from national moorings, and multinational companies have gone truly global, seeking strategic and often temporary nodes of operation. The global South competes against itself to attract international investment, rendering the African state weak in its capacity to withstand the demands of international capital. Extending Lonsdale's insights on ethnic patriotisms and local moral economies into the present, Pheng Cheah notes that while contending forces may account for the strain between state and nation, they also have the potential to invigorate the nation-state, making the postcolonial nation both "a specter of global capital" in its capacity to hold global capital to account and the "most apposite figure for freedom today."[14]

The Failure of Pan-Africanism and Its Implications for Africa's Economies

Having made a fetish of national sovereignty and the sanctity of national boundaries, the OAU did not take long to degenerate into a club of dictators. But the deviation from meaningful regional and continental integration, hamstrung in the late 1950s and 1960s by suspicions of Nkrumah's political ambitions (see introduction and chap. 4), deprived the quest for economic independence of a crucial enabling environment. Mkandawire comments that "the shallowness of our individual national visions has not permitted us to see that regional integration is an important ingredient in any meaningful transformation of our countries and the continent."[15] In chapter 4, we saw how the work of the ECLA and Prebisch inspired the Third World in the 1950s. Having recommended import-substitution industrialization as the path out of Latin America's peripheral position in the global economy, the ECLA advocated regional integration and expanded markets by the end of the 1950s as a result of industrializing countries' inability to export. This phenomenon was replayed in Africa in the 1960s and 1970s, and I have argued in the introduction and chapter 4 that in the latter years of his tenure, Nkrumah's arguments for continental integration took on a decidedly economic note.

Narrow national political and economic visions enabled the industrial achievements of the early years of independence, significant in retrospect, to be easily derailed by the World Bank and the IMF. Africa in the 1980s did not need to deindustrialize; it needed markets for its industries and for these industries to be made more viable. Africa needed to expand on its industrial base, not retrench. Several African countries successfully diversified their economies through manufacturing in the 1960s and 1970s, adding to their per capita income. Indeed, many African countries today have yet to reach the per capita incomes they achieved in the 1970s.[16] Their industrial or manufacturing base was lost in the 1980s and 1990s under structural adjustment, which, Mkandawire perceptively points out, "was not one aimed at redirecting these new industries towards new markets, but one that fundamentally aimed at their elimination and the direction of Africa towards its comparative advantage as 'discovered' or defined by the erstwhile colonial masters."[17] Throughout the 1970s, Nyerere remained dismissive of the IMF and its conditions for the reform of Tanzania's troubled economy. His party had to await his stepping down from power in 1985 to embrace the IMF's policies. Nyerere had the last laugh, though he would have preferred not to.

In an interview with *Business Mirror* on August 19, 2009, Benjamin Mkapa, president of Tanzania from 1995 to 2005 and chief architect of the privatization and liberalization of the Tanzanian economy under the auspices of the World Bank and the IMF, reflected on the disappointing results of the structural adjustment program: "We privatized everything the state had. Everything was bought by foreign capital because we had no national capital to compete. The foreign companies almost always closed local businesses, which were not competitive, transformed them into distributors of foreign products and driving up unemployment. The experts of the World Bank and the IMF predicted that this would happen, but they told us: Now the influx of foreign investment will lead to the creation of new, competitive and technologically current businesses that will provide the foundations for a lasting, modern development. None of this happened for us."[18] This scenario was repeated across sub-Saharan Africa with the implementation of structural adjustment programs. But these adverse economic developments under the guidance of the IMF were not limited to

Africa. Looking at Indonesia in the late 1990s, one commentator observed that "some of the IMF policies are wrong and deadly. Asking the IMF for assistance may well cause a moderately sick patient to develop a serious and life-threatening disease that will take much suffering and many years to get out of, if at all."[19]

AFRICA IN THE TWENTY-FIRST CENTURY: THE SIGNIFICANCE OF THE EARLY DECADES OF INDEPENDENCE

As we contemplate the world after COVID-19, with economists predicting a moderation of the hyperglobalization that has marked the past few decades and a return to the primacy of national (domestic) economic and social considerations, it is critical that we revisit, understand, and learn from the early decades of independence, when African countries sought to define autonomous economic and social agendas. In a recent important essay on the global economy post-COVID-19, Dani Rodrik, Ford Professor for International Development at Harvard University, opines that three trends will shape the world economy. First, we will see a rebalancing of the relationship between states and markets, with a stronger role for states and public regulation. Second, he foresees a turn toward greater national sovereignty and autonomy and a move away from the hyperglobalization that has characterized the last few decades. Third, there will be lesser economic growth, hence the need for governments and publics to moderate their growth ambitions and expectations. These three trends imply a prioritization of domestic economic and social concerns.[20]

But Africa's models of economic growth are presently all externally derived. Issa Shivji notes how current neoliberal discourse "demonizes the nationalist period."[21] Economic policies from before the onset of structural adjustment in the 1980s have been dismissed as flawed. The result has been the erasure of the experiment of the African developmental state. Since the 1960s, when the IMF and the World Bank first ventured into Africa with little context (as observed by Samir Amin in my introduction), these institutions have produced a huge body of invaluable knowledge on the continent's political economy and facilitated the training of specialists on Africa and from Africa. The result, however, is that the substance of knowledge about African political economies is framed by the received wisdom of the World Bank and the IMF, functioning as knowledge bearers, funders, program managers, and assessors of Africa's economic performance. Will the

IMF and the World Bank be the ones to determine economic priorities for Africa in the turn toward greater national sovereignty and autonomy in economic decisions anticipated by Rodrik?

Lastly, the intersection of two developments today makes the return to the early decades of independence even more urgent: first is the recent renewal of enthusiasm for import-substitution industrialization (ISI), and second is the inception of the African Continental Free Trade Area (ACFTA) in 2021.[22] Africa has been down this path before—advocates like Nkrumah, Touré, Senghor, and Nyerere sought to couple import-substitution industrialization and regional integration (see chap. 4). Did ISI in Africa fail in the 1960s and the 1970s? Two decades of industrialization, compared to the long periods over which industrialization unfolded in the West, is not sufficient time to pronounce a verdict on the prospects for industrialization in Africa. Africa's industrialization attempt did not fail; it was aborted prematurely with the Bretton Woods institutions as midwives. Is the African Union better positioned, equipped, and disposed to pursue continental integration in ways that its ill-fated predecessor, the OAU, could not? Only time will tell. In pursuit of prosperous societies, it behooves Africa to remember Adam Smith's observation that prosperous societies are by necessity well governed and that economics, politics, and morality are fused. COVID-19 has laid bare deep inequalities of gender, class, and race in the global North and South and brought into question the legitimacy of many governments and their capacity to protect and provide for their citizens. In a recent survey of public perception of COVID-19 in fourteen African countries, Afrobarometer, which sees its goal as giving the public a voice in policy making, noted the glaring inability of many governments to provide social support to vulnerable populations. Of those surveyed, 68 percent commented on the level of government corruption in COVID-19 response efforts, and 60 percent indicated that they had little or no trust in information the government disseminates on COVID-19.[23] How do we rebuild trust between governments and their publics? There are no easy answers, but no generation in Africa has given as much deep thought to the twin questions of how best to organize society and how to grow an economy and produce prosperity like the first generation of independent African leaders. Their abundant writings testify to this effort. There is no doubt that they made many mistakes. But Africa cannot venture into the twenty-first century ignorant of the lessons of the early decades of independence.

NOTES

Introduction

1. Worldmaking includes the extension of international relations to incorporate nonsovereign actors. I discuss worldmaking in detail later in this chapter and in chapter 4.

2. M. M. Goldsmith, "Regulating Anew the Moral and Political Sentiments of Mankind: Bernard Mandeville and the Scottish Enlightenment," *Journal of the History of Ideas* 49, no. 4 (1988): 587–606.

3. Jerry Evensky, *Adam Smith's Wealth of Nations: A Reader's Guide* (New York: Syracuse University Press, 2015), 16. Smith advocated a shift from mercantilist policies to a commercial society, convinced that in such a society the division of labor would lead to higher productivity and that the invisible hand of the market would provide incentives and rewards. These became fundamental principles in classical economics. Adam Smith, *The Wealth of Nations*, ed. with an introduction and notes by Edwin Cannan (New York: Ixia Press, 2019 [1776]).

4. Charles Tilly, *Coercion, Capital, and European States, AD 990–1992* (Cambridge, MA: Blackwell, 1992), 2–3.

5. John M. Lonsdale, "Anti-colonial Nationalism and Patriotism in Sub-Saharan Africa," in *The Oxford Handbook of the History of Nationalism*, ed. John Breuilly (Oxford: Oxford University Press, 2013), 334. DOI: 1093/oxfordhb/9780199209194.013.0016.

6. Bruce J. Berman and John M. Lonsdale, "Nationalism in Colonial and Post-colonial Africa," in *The Oxford Handbook of the History of Nationalism*, ed. John Breuilly (Oxford: Oxford University Press, 2013), 315–16. DOI: 1093/oxfordhb/9780199209194.013.0015.

7. Ghassan Hage, *Against Paranoid Nationalism: Searching for Hope in a Shrinking Society* (Sydney: Pluto Press, 2003), 3.

8. Thandika Mkandawire, "Thinking about Developmental States in Africa," *Cambridge Journal of Economics* 25, no. 3 (2000): 289–313.

9. Claude Ake, *A Political Economy of Africa* (Harlow, Essex: Longman, 1981), 141.

10. Joseph Ki-Zerbo, "African Intellectuals, Nationalism and Pan-Africanism: A Testimony," in *African Intellectuals: Rethinking Politics, Language, Gender and Development*, ed. Thandika Mkandawire (Dakar: CODESRIA Books, 2005), 82.

11. Berman and Lonsdale, "Nationalism in Colonial and Post-colonial Africa," 309.

12. In chapter 4, I point to how central economics was to Nkrumah's quest for a United States of Africa, which has often been ascribed to his political ambition. His preoccupation with the challenges of decolonizing Africa's economies is evident in Kwame Nkrumah, *Neocolonialism: The Last Stages of Imperialism* (New York: International, 1966 [1965]).

13. Adom Getachew, *Worldmaking after Empire: The Rise and Fall of Self-Determination* (Princeton, NJ: Princeton University Press, 2019).

14. Stephen Chan, *The Commonwealth in World Politics: A Study of International Action 1965–1985* (London: Lester Crook Academic, 1988). The centrality of the three objectives outlined above and their twined nature is affirmed by Guinea's Ahmed Sékou Touré, *Africa on the Move* (London: Panaf Books, 1979), 13: "The freedom regained by Africa and Asia, the eco-

nomic advances to be recorded in all the underdeveloped countries and their claim to equality in the international sphere should enable them to regroup themselves on the basis of true fraternity, equality of the most conscious and active kind." Touré's book was originally published as *L'Afrique en Marche* (Conakry: Imprimerie National Patrice Lumumba, 1967). This is the fourth edition; internal evidence suggests the first edition was published in 1963, before the foundation of the Organization of African Unity in May 1963.

15. Vijay Prasad, *The Darker Nations: A People's History of the Third World* (New York: New Press, 2007); and Christopher J. Lee, ed., *Making a World after Empire: The Bandung Moment and Its Political Afterlives* (Athens: Ohio University Press, 2010).

16. Nelson Goodman, *Ways of Worldmaking* (Indianapolis: Hackett, 1978), 6.

17. Pheng Cheah, *What Is a World? On Postcolonial Literature as World Literature* (Durham, NC: Duke University Press, 2016), 8.

18. Carola Lentz and David Lowe, *Remembering Independence* (London: Routledge, 2018), 47–49.

19. Ibid., 6.

20. Martin Lynn, *Commerce and Economic Change in West Africa: The Palm Oil Trade in the Nineteenth Century* (Cambridge: Cambridge University Press, 1997).

21. Though palm oil was introduced by the British government into British Malaya from Nigeria in the 1870s, it was not until the 1960s that palm oil cultivation really took off in Malaysia. The world's two largest palm oil companies are in Malaysia. Since 2006, palm oil biodiesel has been used in biodiesel sold in Malaysia. See Claire Stam, "Malaysia Relies on Sustainable Palm Oil to Keep Entry into European Market," *EURACTIV*, February 4, 2020, euractiv.com.

22. Crawford Young, *The African Colonial State in Comparative Perspective* (New Haven, CT: Yale University Press, 1994), 7.

23. Hippolyte Fofack, "Overcoming the Colonial Development Model of Resource Extraction for Sustainable Development in Africa," *Brookings*, January 31, 2019, https://www.brookings.edu/blog/africa-in-focus/2019/01/31/overcoming-the-colonial-development-model-of-resource-extraction-for-sustainable-development-in-africa/.

24. Ake, *Political Economy of Africa*, 88.

25. Achille Mbembe, *On the Postcolony* (Berkeley: University of California Press, 2001), 183.

26. Samir Amin, *Le développement du capitalisme en Côte d'Ivoire* (Paris: Editions de Minuit, 1967).

27. Lawrence Stone usefully defines prosopography as "the investigation of the common background characteristics of a group of actors in history by means of a collective study of their lives." Lawrence Stone, *The Past and the Present Revisited* (London: Routledge and Keegan Paul, 1987), 45. See chapter 2 of Stone's book, entitled "Prosopography," 45–73. Though prosopography has seldom been deployed in transnational settings, it had promise for this study. I have decided to write a journal article outlining the approach and what we learn about the post–World War II period through 1980 through the collective biographies of Nkrumah, Touré, Senghor, and Nyerere. Other works that have informed my understanding of prosopography include Michael Erben, "The Problem of Other Lives: Social Perspectives on Written Biography," *Sociology* 27, no. 1 (1993): 15–25; and Diana K. Jones, "Research Groups of Lives: A Collective Biographical Perspective on the Protestant Ethic Debate," *Qualitative Research* 1, no. 3 (2001): 325–46.

28. Young, *African Colonial State*, 4.

29. Samir Amin, *A Life Looking Forward: Memoirs of an Independent Marxist*, trans. Patrick Camiller (London: Zed Books, 2006), 118.

30. W. Arthur Lewis Papers, Call No. MC092, Box 9, Series 2: Correspondence, Folder 5. Seeley G. Mudd Manuscript Library, Princeton University Archives.

31. Tony Killick, *Development Economics in Action: A Study of Economic Policies in Ghana* (London: Heinemann, 1978).

32. W. Arthur Lewis, *Politics in West Africa* (Toronto: Oxford University Press, 1965).

33. P. T. Bauer, *West African Trade: A Study of Competition, Oligopoly and Monopoly in a Changing Economy* (Cambridge: Cambridge University Press, 1954). I have benefited from discussions with Kofi Adjepong Boateng on the works of Lewis and Bauer.

34. Janet Roitman, *Fiscal Disobedience: An Anthropology of Economic Regulation in Central Africa* (Princeton, NJ: Princeton University Press, 2005), 6.

35. Ake, *Political Economy of Africa*; Robert H. Bates, *Markets and States in Tropical Africa: The Political Basis of Agricultural Policies* (Berkeley: University of California Press, 1981). Ake's approach was based on dialectical materialism and Bates's on rational choice.

36. Thandika Mkandawire and Charles C. Soludo, *Our Continent, Our Future: African Perspectives on Structural Adjustment* (Dakar: CODESRIA, 1999).

37. Bruce J. Berman, "Nationalism in Post-colonial Africa," in *The Oxford Handbook of the History of Nationalism*, ed. John Breuilly (Oxford: Oxford University Press, 2013), 362. DOI: 1093/oxfordhb/9780199209194.013.0018.

38. Hernando de Soto, *The Mystery of Capitalism: Why Capitalism Triumphs in the West and Fails Everywhere Else* (New York: Basic Books, 2000).

39. A revealing study of this transition is Patrick Chabal and Jean-Pascal Daloz, *Africa Works: Disorder as Political Instrument* (Oxford: James Currey, 1999).

40. Mbembe, *On the Postcolony*.

41. Ibid., 5.

42. Ibid., 6.

43. Emmanuel Akyeampong, *Drink, Power and Cultural Change: A Social History of Alcohol in Ghana, c.1800 to Recent Times* (Portsmouth, NH: Heinemann, 1996); and Emmanuel Akyeampong, *Between the Sea and the Lagoon: An Eco-social History of the Anlo of Southeastern Ghana, c.1850 to Recent Times* (Oxford: James Currey, 2001).

44. Issa G. Shivji, Saida Yahya-Othman, and Ng'wanza Kamaya, *Development as Rebellion: A Biography of Julius Nyerere* (Dar es Salaam: Mkuki na Nyota, 2020), 3:135.

45. Jean M. Allman, *The Quills of the Porcupine: Asante Nationalism in an Emergent Ghana* (Madison: University of Wisconsin Press, 1993).

46. Lonsdale, "Anti-colonial Nationalism and Patriotism," 323.

47. See Baffour Agyeman-Duah, *General Acheampong: The Life and Times of Ghana's Head of State* (Tema: Digibooks, 2021).

48. Hage, *Against Paranoid Nationalism*, 10.

49. Roger Genoud, *Nationalism and Economic Development in Ghana* (New York: Frederick A. Praeger, 1969), 215–16.

50. Ama Biney, *The Political and Social Thought of Kwame Nkrumah* (New York: Palgrave Macmillan, 2011); Harcourt Fuller, *Building the Ghanaian Nation-State: Kwame Nkrumah's Symbolic Nationalism* (New York: Palgrave Macmillan, 2014); Justin Williams, *Pan-Africanism in Ghana: African Socialism, Neoliberalism, and Globalization* (Durham, NC: Carolina Academic Press, 2016); and Jeffrey Ahlman, *Living with Nkrumahism: Nation, State, and Pan-Africanism in Ghana* (Athens: Ohio University Press, 2017).

51. Meredith Terretta, *Nation of Outlaws, State of Violence: Nationalism, Grassfields Tradition, and State Building in Cameroon* (Athens: Ohio University Press, 2013). See also, Meredith

Terretta, "Cameroonian Nationalists Go Global: From Forest *Maquis* to a Pan-African Accra," *Journal of African History* 51, no. 2 (2010): 189–212.

52. Later in this introduction I provide a note on sources.

53. Fuller, *Building the Ghanaian Nation-State*, chap. 3.

54. Abou Bamba, *African Miracle, African Mirage: Transnational Politics and the Paradox of Modernization in Ivory Coast* (Athens: Ohio University Press, 2016).

55. Jon Woronoff, *West African Wager: Houphouët versus Nkrumah* (Metuchen, NJ: Scarecrow Press, 1972); Amin, *Le développement du capitalisme en Côte d'Ivoire*. See also, Samir Amin, *Neo-colonialism in West Africa*, trans. Francis McDonagh (Harmondsworth, Middlesex: Penguin Books, 1973).

56. Priya Lal, *African Socialism in Post-colonial Tanzania: Between the Village and the World* (Cambridge: Cambridge University Press, 2015).

57. Emmanuel Akyeampong, "'African Socialism'; or, the Search for an Indigenous Model of Economic Development?" *Economic History of Developing Regions* 33, no. 1 (2018): 69–87.

58. James D. Straker, *Youth, Nationalism, and the Guinean Revolution* (Bloomington: Indiana University Press, 2009); Mike McGovern, *Unmasking the State: Making Guinea Modern* (Chicago: University of Chicago Press, 2012); Kelly M. Askew, *Performing the Nation: Swahili Music and Cultural Politics in Tanzania* (Chicago: University of Chicago Press, 2002).

59. Peter van der Veer, "Nationalism and Religion," in *The Oxford Handbook of the History of Nationalism*, ed. John Breuilly (Oxford: Oxford University Press, 2013), 659. DOI: 1093/oxfordhb/9780199209194.013.0033.

60. Paul Bjerk, *Julius Nyerere* (Athens: Ohio University Press, 2017), 9.

61. John S. Mbiti, *African Religions and Philosophy* (Nairobi: Heinemann, 1969), describes Africans as "incurably religious." For continuing discussions of this assertion, see Jan Platvoet and Henk van Rinsum, "Is Africa Incurably Religious?" *Exchange* 32, no. 2 (2003): 123–53; and Frans Wijsen, "Are Africans Incurably Religious? Discursive Analysis of a Debate, Direction of a Discipline," *Exchange* 46, no. 4 (2017): 370–97.

62. McGovern, *Unmasking the State*; Straker, *Youth, Nationalism, and the Guinean Revolution*; Steven Feierman, *Peasant Intellectuals: Anthropology and History in Tanzania* (Madison: University of Wisconsin Press, 1990); and Richard Rathbone, *Nkrumah and the Chiefs: The Politics of Chieftaincy in Ghana 1961–60* (Oxford: James Currey, 2000). Religious cults and power associations were protective systems in noncentralized states during the era of slave trade. See Robert M. Baum, *Shrines of the Slave Trade: Diola Religion and Society in Precolonial Senegambia* (New York: Oxford University Press, 1999); Rosalind Shaw, *Memories of the Slave Trade: Ritual and the Historical Imagination in Sierra Leone* (Chicago: University of Chicago Press, 2002); and G. Ugo Nwokeji, *The Slave Trade and Culture in the Bight of Biafra* (New York: Cambridge University Press, 2010).

63. See Ebenezer Obiri Addo, *Kwame Nkrumah: A Case Study of Religion and Politics in Ghana* (Lanham, MD: University Press of America, 1997); and John S. Pobee, *Kwame Nkrumah and the Church in Ghana: 1949–1966* (Denver: IAcademic Books, 2000).

64. Kwame Nkrumah, *Ghana: The Autobiography of Kwame Nkrumah* (New York: International Publishers, 1976 [1957]), 12. I am working on a separate journal article that examines religion and spirituality in the life and political career of Nkrumah.

65. On Nyerere's complicated relations with the predominantly Muslim leadership of the Tanganyika African National Union (TANU) in the 1950s and 1960s, see Mohamed Said, *The Life and Times of Abdul Wahid Sykes (1924–1968): The Untold Story of the Muslim Struggle against British Colonialism in Tanganyika* (London: Minerva Press, 1998). The deep Christian

influence on Nyerere's life is evident in Shivji, Yahya-Othman, and Kamaya, *Biography of Julius Nyerere.*

66. Senghor considered himself a Christian Socialist. On the Catholic influence in his life and political thought, see Léopold Sédar Senghor, *Pierre Teilhard de Chardin et la Politique Africaine* (Paris: Editions du Seuil, 1962).

67. Ladipo Adamolekun, "The Socialist Experience in Guinea," in *Socialism in Sub-Saharan Africa: A New Assessment*, ed. Carl G. Rosberg and Thomas M. Callaghy (Berkeley: University of California Institute of International Studies, 1979), 76–80. Fula entrepreneurs in Futa Jallon moved to neighboring Sierra Leone to escape persecution by Sékou Touré. See Alusine Jalloh, *African Entrepreneurship: Muslim Fula Merchants in Sierra Leone* (Athens: Ohio University Press, 1999); and Alusine Jalloh, *Muslim Fula Business Elites and Politics in Sierra Leone* (Rochester, NY: University of Rochester Press, 2018).

68. McGovern, *Unmasking the State*; and Straker, *Youth, Nationalism, and the Guinean Revolution.*

69. Gary Wilder, *Freedom Time: Negritude, Decolonization, and the Future of the World* (Durham, NC: Duke University Press, 2015); Frederick Cooper, *Citizenship between Empire and Nation: Remaking France and French Africa, 1945–1960* (Princeton, NJ: Princeton University Press, 2014); and Getachew, *Worldmaking after Empire.*

70. Wilder, *Freedom Time*, chap. 9.

71. On the economic influence of Prebisch and the ECLA on international development, see Kathryn Sikkink, "Development Ideas in Latin America: Paradigm Shift and the Economic Commission for Latin America," in *International Development and the Social Sciences: Essays on the History and Politics of Knowledge*, ed. Frederick Cooper and Randall M. Packard (Berkeley: University of California Press, 1997), 228–56; and Luis Eugenio di Marco, ed., *International Economics and Development: Essays in Honor of Raúl Prebisch* (New York: Academic Press, 1972).

72. Mkandawire, "Thinking about Developmental States in Africa."

73. Getachew, *Worldmaking after Empire*, chap. 5.

74. Shivji, Saidya-Othman, and Kamaya, *Biography of Julius Nyerere*, 2:276–79, 3:80–93.

75. Goodman, *Ways of Worldmaking*, 102–3.

76. Vera Nünning, Ansgar Nünning, and Birgit Neumann, eds., *Cultural Ways of Worldmaking: Media and Narratives* (Berlin: De Gruyter, 2010).

77. Frantz Fanon, *The Wretched of the Earth*, trans. Constance Harrington (New York: Grove Press, 1968 [1961]); and Frantz Fanon, *Black Skin, White Masks*, trans. Richard Philcox (New York: Grove Press, 2008 [1952]).

78. Toyin Falola, *Nationalism and African Intellectuals* (Rochester, NY: University of Rochester Press, 2001), 92.

79. Ibid., 94.

80. Erez Manela, *The Wilsonian Moment: Self-Determination and the International Origins of Anticolonial Nationalism* (Oxford: Oxford University Press, 2007), 224.

81. John D. Kelly and Martha Kaplan, "Nation and Decolonization: Toward a New Anthropology of Nationalism," *Anthropological Theory* 1, no. 4 (2001): 419. For Kelly and Kaplan, American hegemony and its agenda in the post-1945 era are so distinct that we might need to disassociate "American Power" from "Western Power" (432).

82. Basil Davidson, *The Black Man's Burden: Africa and the Curse of the Nation-State* (New York: Times Books, 1992).

83. Young, *African Colonial State*, 242.

84. Ibid., 243.

85. Mahmood Mamdani, *Citizen and Subject: Contemporary African and the Legacy of Late Colonialism* (Princeton, NJ: Princeton University Press, 1996).

86. Martin Chanock, *Law, Custom and Social Order: The Colonial Experience in Malawi and Zambia* (Portsmouth, NH: Heinemann, 1998).

87. J. F. Ade Ajayi, "The Continuity of African Institutions under Colonial Rule," in *Tradition and Change in Africa: The Essays of J. F. Ade Ajayi*, ed. Toyin Falola (Trenton, NJ: Africa World Press, 2000), 159.

88. Ibid., 156.

89. Worldmaking activities on the international level after World War II included the movement toward a European Common Market, America's sponsorship of the Bretton Woods institutions, and the endeavor by Albert Einstein and other nuclear scientists to forge "One World."

90. Lentz and Lowe, *Remembering Independence*, 4.

91. Cooper, *Citizenship between Empire and Nation*.

92. Michael Collins, "Decolonization and the 'Federal Moment,'" *Diplomacy and Statecraft* 24, no. 1 (2013): 21–40.

93. Julius K. Nyerere, *Freedom and Unity: A Selection from Writings and Speeches 1952–1965* (Dar es Salaam: Oxford University Press, 1966), 89. This paper was prepared for the Second Conference of Independent African States in June 1960 and later elaborated for the PAFMECA Conference at Mbale (Uganda) in October 1960.

94. Susan Geiger, *TANU Women: Gender and Culture in the Making of Tanganyikan Nationalism, 1955–1965* (Portsmouth, NH: Heinemann, 1997), 189.

95. Emil Rado estimates that by 1985, Ghana had lost between half and two-thirds of its top professionals to other English-speaking countries and the United Nations. Emil Rado, "Notes Towards a Political Economy of Ghana Today," *African Affairs* 85, no. 841 (1986): 563–72.

96. Benedict Anderson, *Imagined Communities: Reflections on the Origin and Spread of Nationalism*, rev. ed. (London: Verso, 1991), 6.

97. Ibid., 81.

98. Ibid., 35.

99. Ibid., 133.

100. Yaw Twumasi, "Press Freedom and Nationalism under Colonial Rule in the Gold Coast (Ghana)," *Journal of the Historical Society of Nigeria* 7, no. 3 (1974): 499–520; Fred I. A. Omu, "The Dilemma of Press Freedom in Colonial Africa: The West African Example," *Journal of African History* 9, no. 2 (1968): 279–98; and Stephanie Newell, *The Power to Name: A History of Anonymity in Colonial West Africa* (Athens: Ohio University Press, 2013), chap. 3.

101. Newell, *Power to Name*, 74–75. Whereas African-owned newspapers appeared in British West Africa from the mid-nineteenth century, African-owned newspapers emerged in French West Africa only in the 1940s and 1950s.

102. Fred I. A. Omu, *Press and Politics in Nigeria, 1880–1937* (London: Longman, 1978), 247.

103. J. B. Danquah edited the *Times of West Africa*, Nkrumah the *Accra Evening News* from the 1950s, Azikiwe the *West African Pilot* in Nigeria from 1937, and Awolowo the *Nigerian Tribune*.

104. Newell, *Power to Name*, 43.

105. Obafemi Awolowo, *Path to Nigerian Freedom* (London: Faber and Faber, 1947), 47.

106. Wale Adebanwi, *Nation as Grand Narrative: The Nigerian Press and the Politics of Meaning* (Rochester, NY: University of Rochester Press, 2016).

107. Ernest Gellner, *Nations and Nationalism* (Ithaca, NY: Cornell University Press, 1983), 1.

108. Feierman, *Peasant Intellectuals*, 45.

109. On market women in Gold Coast nationalist politics, see, for example, C. L. R. James, *Nkrumah and the Ghana Revolution* (Durham, NC: Duke University Press, 2022 [1977]), 45–46.

110. Dennis Austin, *Politics in Ghana 1946–1960* (London: Oxford University Press, 1964); and Emmanuel Akyeampong, "What's in a Drink: Class Struggle, Popular Culture, and the Politics of *Akpeteshie* (Local Gin) in Ghana, 1930–1967," *Journal of African History* 37, no. 2 (1996): 215–36.

111. See Geiger, *TANU Women*; and Askew, *Performing the Nation*. On the intersection of football and the budding nationalist movement in Zanzibar, see Laura Fair, *Pastimes and Politics: Culture, Community and Identity in Post-abolition Urban Zanzibar, 1890–1945* (Oxford: James Currey, 2001), chap. 5.

112. The question of race in independent Africa is discussed later in this chapter.

113. Anthony D. Smith, *Ethnic Origins of Nations* (Oxford: Basil Blackwell, 1986).

114. Anthony D. Smith, *Theories of Nationalism* (London: Gerald Duckworth, 1971), 4.

115. Ibid., 6.

116. Irving Leonard Markovitz, *Léopold Sédar Senghor and the Politics of Negritude* (New York: Atheneum, 1969), 102.

117. Smith, *Ethnic Origins of Nations*, 97.

118. Anthony D. Smith, "The Origins of Nations," *Ethnic and Racial Studies* 12, no. 3 (1989): 342.

119. Ibid., 341.

120. Ibid., 343.

121. Lonsdale, "Anti-colonial Nationalism and Patriotism," 318–20.

122. Markovitz, *Senghor*, 112.

123. Ibid., 112ç17.

124. Smith, "Origins of Nations," 348.

125. Ibid.

126. Ibid., 352.

127. Ibid., 350.

128. Anderson, *Imagined Communities*, 139.

129. Lonsdale, "Anti-colonial Nationalism and Patriotism," 318.

130. Partha Chatterjee, *Nationalist Thought and the Colonial World: A Derivative Course* (London: Zed Books, 1993), 10.

131. Young, *African Colonial State*, 76.

132. Mbembe, *On the Postcolony*, is incisive in its examination of the European colonial mind and the rationalization of violence against the African. See especially chap. 5.

133. Young, *African Colonial State*, 191.

134. Smith, *Theories of Nationalism*, 8.

135. P. T. Bauer, *Dissent on Development*, rev. ed. (Cambridge, MA: Harvard University Press, 1976 [1971]), 105. On Bauer, see also chapter 3.

136. Chatterjee, *Nationalist Thought and the Colonial World*, 17.

137. Lonsdale, "Anti-colonial Nationalism and Patriotism," 321.

138. Joseph Appiah, *Joe Appiah: The Autobiography of an African Patriot* (Accra: Asempa, 1990), 159–60. For a discussion of Padmore's politics and internationalism, see Brent Hayes Edwards, *The Practice of Diaspora: Literature, Translation, and the Rise of Black Internationalism* (Cambridge, MA: Harvard University Press, 2003), chap. 5. See also, Robin D. G. Kelley, *Freedom Dreams: The Black Radical Imagination* (Boston: Beacon Press, 2002), especially chap. 2 on Black internationalism.

139. Nkrumah, *Autobiography*, 57. See also, Marika Sherwood, *Kwame Nkrumah: The Years Abroad 1935–1947* (Accra: Freedom, 1996), 130. The London conference Nkrumah referenced was held on August 30–September 1, 1946, with the theme "Unity and Independence for All West Africa."

140. Shivji, Yahya-Othman, and Kamaya, *Biography of Julius Nyerere*, 2:8.

141. Ibid., 2:17.

142. Biney, *Political and Social Thought of Kwame Nkrumah*, 154.

143. June Milne, *Kwame Nkrumah: The Conakry Years* (London: Panaf Books, 2001 [1991]), 6, describes the moving circumstances of this announcement in Conakry.

144. Shivji, Yahya-Othman, and Kamaya, *Biography of Julius Nyerere*, 1:142. In my interview with Mrs. Andrée Sékou Touré, she took pains to correct me when I described Nkrumah as "living in exile in Conakry"; Nkrumah was not in exile, he was copresident of Guinea. Interview with Mrs. Andrée Sékou Touré, Conakry, August 22, 2018.

145. Shivji, Yahya-Othman, and Kamaya, *Biography of Julius Nyerere*, 3:268.

146. Ibid., 1:142.

147. On the growth of an international infrastructure for the production of knowledge about Africa in the social sciences, see Fredrick Cooper and Randall M. Packard, "Introduction," in *International Development and the Social Sciences: Essays on the History and Politics of Knowledge*, ed. Frederick Cooper and Randall M. Packard (Berkeley: University of California Press, 1997), 1–41.

148. The relevant writings of these leaders include Kwame Nkrumah, *Autobiography*; Nkrumah, *Africa Must Unite* (London: Heinemann, 1963); Nkrumah, *Consciencism* (New York: Modern Reader Paperbacks, 1970 [1964]); and Nkrumah, *Neo-colonialism: The Last Stage of Imperialism* (New York: International, 1966 [1965]). Compilations of some of Nyerere's writings can be found in Julius K. Nyerere, *Freedom and Unity: A Selection from Writings and Speeches 1952–65* (Dar es Salaam: Oxford University Press, 1966); Nyerere, *Freedom and Socialism: A Selection of Writings and Speeches 1965–1967* (Dar es Salaam: Oxford University Press, 1968); and Nyerere, *Freedom and Development: A Selection from Writing and Speeches 1968–1973* (London: Oxford University Press, 1973). Touré's writings consulted include Ahmed Sékou Touré, *L'action politique du Parti démocratique du Guinée* (Paris: Présence Africaine, 1959); Touré, *La Révolution Culturelle*, 3rd ed. (Geneva: Kundig, 1972); and Touré, *Africa on the Move* (London: Panaf Books, 1979). Of Senghor's vast body of writings, those I found particularly useful to this book dealt with his push for federation under the auspices of the Fourth and Fifth Republics; his thoughts on language, culture, and race; and his approach to African socialism. These are cited in subsequent chapters, but key works include Léopold Sédar Senghor, "Balkanization ou fédération," *Afrique nouvelle* (December 1956); Senghor, "Union française et fédéralisme," *Université des Annales* (November 1956); Senghor, "Le Français, Langue de Culture," *Esprit* (November 1962); Senghor, *On African Socialism*, trans. with an introduction by Mercer Cook (New York: Frederick A Praeger, 1964 [1961]); and Senghor, *The Foundations of "Africanité" or "Négritude" and "Arabité,"* trans. Mercer Cook (Paris: Présence Africaine, 1971).

149. June Milne was Nkrumah's research assistant for fifteen years and worked closely with him on his publications in Conakry. See Milne, *Kwame Nkrumah: The Conakry Years*.

1. Africa in the Twentieth Century

1. Safia Aidid, "Pan-Somali Dreams: Ethiopia, Greater Somalia, and the Somali Nationalist Imagination" (PhD diss., Department of History, Harvard University, 2020).

2. Adom Getachew, *Worldmaking after Empire: The Rise and Fall of Self-Determination* (Princeton, NJ: Princeton University Press, 2019).

3. Myron J. Echenberg, *Plague Ports: The Global Urban Impact of Bubonic Plague, 1894–1901* (New York: New York University Press, 2007).

4. J. D. Hargreaves, "The European Partition of West Africa," in *History of West Africa*, ed. J. F. Ade Ajayi and Michael Crowder (London: Longman, 1987), 2:402–23.

5. William Tordoff, *Ashanti under the Prempehs, 1888–1935* (London: Oxford University Press, 1965), 66–67; Thomas Lewin, *Asante before the British: The Prempean Years, 1875–1900* (Lawrence: Regents Press of Kansas, 1978), 47–48.

6. Daniel R. Headrick, *The Tools of Empire: Technology and European Imperialism in the Nineteenth Century* (New York: Oxford University Press, 1981), 9.

7. J. F. Ade Ajayi, "Colonialism: An Episode in African History," in *Tradition and Change in Africa: The Essays of J. F. Ade Ajayi*, ed. Toyin Falola (Trenton, NJ: Africa World Press, 2000), 170–71. Originally published in L. H. Gann and Peter Duignan, eds., *Colonialism in Africa, 1870–1960*, vol. 1, *History and Politics of Colonialism, 1870–1914* (Cambridge: Cambridge University Press, 1969), 497–509.

8. Peter P. Ekeh, "Colonialism and the Two Publics in Africa: A Theoretical Statement," *Comparative Studies in Society and History* 17, no. 1 (1975): 111.

9. Crawford Young, *The African Colonial State in Comparative Perspective* (New Haven, CT: Yale University Press, 1994), 283.

10. Ibid., 217. Frederick Cooper, *Colonialism in Question: Theory, Knowledge, History* (Berkeley: University of California Press, 2005), 230, notes that "the process of decolonization, not just the heritage of colonialism, shaped the patterns of post-colonial politics."

11. Young, *African Colonial State*, 45.

12. Ibid., 76.

13. Gregory Mann, "What Was the Indigénat? The 'Empire of Law' in French West Africa," *Journal of African History* 50, no. 3 (2009): 331–53.

14. Mahmood Mamdani, *Define and Rule: Native as Political Identity* (Cambridge, MA: Harvard University Press, 2012), 2–3.

15. For examples of artisanal gold mining, see Moses Ochonu, *Colonial Meltdown: Northern Nigeria in the Great Depression* (Athens: Ohio University Press, 2009); and Robyn d'Avignon, "'Customary' Mining and Colonialism in French West Africa" (Paper delivered at the African Studies Workshop, Harvard University, September 17, 2018).

16. On Indians in East African commerce, see, for example, Dana April Seidenberg, *Mercantile Adventurers: The World of East African Asians, 1750–1985* (New Delhi: New Age International, 1996); and Abdul Sheriff, *Dhow Cultures of the Indian Ocean: Cosmopolitanism, Commerce and Islam* (London: C. Hurst, 2010). On the Lebanese in West Africa, see H. L. van der Laan, *The Lebanese Traders in Sierra Leone* (The Hague: Mouton, 1975); Chris Bierwrith, "The Lebanese Communities of Côte d'Ivoire," *African Affairs* 39, no. 390 (1999): 79–99; and Emmanuel Akyeampong, "Race, Identity and Citizenship in Black Africa: The Case of the Lebanese in Ghana," *Africa* 76, no. 3 (2006): 297–323.

17. Emmanuel Akyeampong, "Commerce, Credit, and Mobility in Late Nineteenth-Century Gold Coast: Changing Dynamics in Euro-African Trade," in *Africa's Development in Historical Perspective*, ed. Emmanuel Akyeampong et al. (New York: Cambridge University Press, 2014), 231–63; Raymond E. Dumett, "John Sarbah, the Elder, and African Mercantile Entrepreneurship in the Gold Coast in the Late Nineteenth Century," *Journal of African History* 14, no. 4 (1973): 653–79.

18. Bruce Fetter, ed., *Colonial Rule in Africa: Readings from Primary Sources* (Madison: University of Wisconsin Press, 1979), 109.

19. BBC, "Africa & Europe (1800–1914)," The Story of Africa, accessed September 18, 2013, https://www.bbc.co.uk/worldservice/africa/features/storyofafrica/index_section11.shtml.

20. Nilanjin Banik and C. A. Yoonus, "Trade as an Answer to Sustainable Economic Growth—The ECOWAS Story," *Global Business Review* 13, no. 2 (2012): 320.

21. Richard Bullock, "Off Track: Sub-Saharan African Railways." African Infrastructure Country Diagnostic Background Paper 17 (Washington, DC: World Bank, 2009).

22. Banik and Yoonus, "The ECOWAS Story," 320.

23. Masami Kojima and Chris Trimble, *Making Power Affordable for Africa and Viable for Utilities* (Washington, DC: World Bank, 2016).

24. A. G. Hopkins, *Economic History of West Africa* (New York: Columbia University Press, 1973).

25. Ibid., 266.

26. S. M. Martin, "The Long Depression: West African Export Producers and the World Economy, 1914–1945," in *The Economies of Africa and Asia in the Inter-War Depression*, ed. Ian Brown (New York: Routledge, 1989), 74–94.

27. David Anderson and David Throup, "The Agrarian Economy of Central Province, Kenya, 1918 to 1939," in Brown, *The Economies of Africa and Asia in the Inter-War Depression*, 8.

28. Ochonu, *Colonial Meltdown*, chap. 3.

29. Jean Marie Allman, "Rounding Up Spinsters: Gender Chaos and Unmarried Women in Colonial Asante," *Journal of African History* 37, no. 2 (1996): 195–214. On gender tensions on the Copperbelt during the depression, see Jane Parpart, "'Where Is your Mother?': Gender, Urban Marriage, and Colonial Discourse on the Zambian Copperbelt, 1925–1945," *International Journal of African Historical Studies* 27, no. 2 (1994): 241–71.

30. Basil Davidson, *Modern Africa: A Social and Political History*, 2nd ed. (London: Longman, 1989), 78–79.

31. On African American responses to Italy's invasion of Ethiopia, see Brice Harris, *The United States and the Italo-Ethiopian Crisis* (Stanford: Stanford University Press, 1964); William Randolph Scott, *The Sons of Sheba's Race: African-Americans and the Italo-Ethiopian War, 1935–1941* (Bloomington: Indiana University Press, 1993); and Joseph Harris, *African-American Reactions to War in Ethiopia, 1936–1941* (Baton Rouge: Louisiana State University Press, 1994).

32. Hopkins, *Economic History of West Africa*, 267.

33. See Erez Manela, *The Wilsonian Moment: Self-Determination and the International Origins of Anticolonial Nationalism* (Oxford: Oxford University Press, 2007).

34. Anthony Clayton, *France, Soldiers and Africa* (London: Brassey's Defense, 1988); Myron J. Echenberg, *Colonial Conscripts: The Tirailleurs Senegalais in French West Africa, 1857–1960* (Portsmouth, NH: Heinemann, 1991); and Gregory Mann, *Native Sons: West African Veterans and France in the Twentieth Century* (Durham, NC: Duke University Press, 2006).

35. Richard Rathbone, "World War I and Africa: Introduction," *Journal of African History* 19, no. 1 (1978): 1–9.

36. Timothy H. Parsons, "Mobilizing Britain's African Empire for War: Pragmatism vs Trusteeship," *Journal of Modern European Studies* 13, no. 2 (2015): 183–202; and Anthony Clayton and David Killingray, *Khaki and Blue: Military and Police in British Colonial Africa* (Athens: Ohio University Center for International Studies, 1989).

37. Andrew D. Roberts, "Introduction," in *The Colonial Moment in Africa: Essays on the Movement of Minds and Materials, 1890–1940*, ed. Andrew D. Roberts (Cambridge: Cambridge University Press, 1990).

38. Labour leaders turned out to be as committed to empire once Labour won the elections of 1945. For Africans who had campaigned actively for Labour in 1945, this was a major disappointment. See Joseph Appiah, *Joe Appiah: The Autobiography of an African Patriot* (Accra: Asempa, 1990), 162–63.

39. On Africa and World War II, see Judith A. Byfield et al., eds., *Africa and World War II* (New York: Cambridge University Press, 2015).

40. Davidson, *Modern Africa*, 66.

41. Appiah, *Joe Appiah*, 167.

42. Jean Filipovich, "Destined to Fail: Forced Settlement at the Office du Niger, 1926–1945," *Journal of African History* 42, no. 2 (2001): 239–60; and Monica M. van Beusekom, *Negotiating Development: African Farmers and Colonial Experts at the Office du Niger, 1920–1960* (Westport, CT: Heinemann, 2002).

43. Steven Feierman, *Peasant Intellectuals: Anthropology and History in Tanzania* (Madison: University of Wisconsin Press, 1990), chap. 7.

44. John Gallagher, *The Revival, Decline and Fall of the British Empire* (Cambridge: Cambridge University Press, 1982).

45. "Recommendations Adopted by the Brazzaville Conference," in Fetter, *Colonial Rule in Africa*, 169.

46. Frederick Cooper, *Citizenship between Empire and Nation: Remaking France and French Africa, 1945–1960* (Princeton, NJ: Princeton University Press, 2014). See also, Jeffrey Herbst, *States and Power in Africa: Comparative Lessons in Authority and Control* (Princeton, NJ: Princeton University Press, 2000), 100–101.

47. William Roger Louis and Ronald Robinson, "Empire Preserv'd: How the Americans Put Anti-communism before Anti-imperialism," in *Decolonization: Perspectives from Now and Then*, ed. Prasenjit Duara (London: Routledge, 2004), 159.

48. Benno J. Ndulu and Stephen A. O'Connell, "Policy Plus: African Growth Performance, 1960–2000," in *The Political Economy of Economic Growth in Africa 1960–2000*, ed. Benno J. Ndulu et al. (Cambridge: Cambridge University Press, 2008), 1:4.

49. Interview with former president of Tanzania Jakaya Kikwete, Cambridge, MA, March 29, 2017.

50. Douglas Rimmer, *Staying Poor: Ghana's Political Economy, 1950–1990* (New York: Pergamon Press, 1992), 10.

51. Appiah, *Joe Appiah*, 207.

52. Ibid.

53. W. Arthur Lewis, *Politics in West Africa* (Toronto: Oxford University Press, 1965).

54. Robin Luckham, *Politicians and Soldiers in Ghana, 1966–1972* (London: Cass, 1975); Robin Luckham, *The Nigerian Military: A Sociological Analysis of Authority and Revolt 1960–1967* (Cambridge: Cambridge University Press, 1971); and A. B. Assensoh and Yvette M. Alex-Assensoh, *African Military History and Politics: Coups and Ideological Incursions, 1900–Present* (New York: Palgrave, 2001).

55. Examples of such agreements between African commodity producers and consumers in developed countries include the Lome Conventions from 1975 through 1999 between African, Caribbean, and Pacific countries and the European Economic Community. The Lome Conventions originated in the arrangement between France and its former African colonies

as the European Economic Community (EEC) emerged. Through Yaounde I (1963–69) and Yaounde II (1969–75), France arranged for its former colonies to have preferential access to the EEC's market. When Britain joined the EEC in 1973, this arrangement was expanded to include Britain's former colonies in Africa, the Caribbean, and the Pacific, and the Lome Conventions were born.

56. This section draws on African Export-Import Bank, *Coming of Age: 25 Years of the African Export-Import Bank* (Cairo: African Export-Import Bank, 2018), 23–24. I was privileged to lead a small team in putting together a twenty-fifth anniversary book for the bank.

57. John Iliffe, *The African Aids Epidemic: A History* (Athens: Ohio University Press, 2006).

58. World Bank, *Adjustment Landing: An Evaluation of Ten Years of Experience* (Washington, DC: World Bank, 1988), 20.

59. I. G. Patel, ed., *Policies for African Development: From the 1980s to the 1990s* (Washington, DC: International Monetary Fund, 1992).

60. I. G. Patel, "A View from Africa," IMF eLibrary, IMF, published December 1992, www .elibrary.imf.org.

61. A trained economist, Adebayo Adedeji had served as Nigeria's Federal Commissioner for Economic Development and Reconstruction from 1971 to 1975, tasked with the economic development and reconstruction of post–civil war Nigeria. He moved from this position to head the UNECA.

62. Adebayo Adedeji, "From the Lagos Plan of Action to the New Partnership for African Development and from the Final Act of Lagos to the Constitutive Act: Whither Africa?" (Keynote address, African Forum for Envisioning Africa, Nairobi, April 26–29, 2002).

63. Ibid., 4.

64. See especially Frederick Cooper, "Development and Disappointment: Economic and Social Change in an Unequal World, 1945–2018," chap. 5 in *Africa Since 1940: The Past of the Present*, 2nd ed. (Cambridge: Cambridge University Press, 2019).

65. Adedeji, "From the Lagos Plan of Action to the New Partnership for African Development," 10.

66. World Bank, *Sub-Saharan Africa: From Crisis to Sustainable Growth* (Washington, DC: World Bank, 1989); and World Bank, *Adjustment in Africa: Reforms, Results, and the Road Ahead* (Oxford: Oxford University Press, 1994).

67. Adedeji, "From the Lagos Plan of Action to the New Partnership for African Development," 13.

68. See, for example, Kwame Boafo-Arthur, "Ghana: Structural Adjustment, Democratization, and the Politics of Continuity," *African Studies Review* 42, no. 2 (1999): 41–72.

69. Memorable titles include Jean-François Bayart, *The State in Africa: The Politics of the Belly* (New York: Longman, 1993); Robert Fatton Jr., *Predatory Rule: State and Civil Society in Africa* (Boulder, CO: Lynne Rienner, 1992); Jean-François Bayart, Stephen Ellis, and Béatrice Hibou, *The Criminalization of the State in Africa* (Oxford: James Currey, 1999); and Patrick Chabal and Jean-Pascal Daloz, *Africa Works: Disorder as Political Instrument* (Oxford: James Currey, 1999).

70. Patrick Manning, *Francophone Sub-Saharan Africa 1880–1995* (Cambridge: Cambridge University Press, 1998), chap. 8 provides an excellent discussion.

71. Ibid.

72. Ibid.

73. A landmark publication was Thandika Mkandawire and Charles C. Soludo, *Our Continent, Our Future: African Perspectives on Structural Adjustment* (Dakar: CODESRIA, 1999);

followed by Thandika Mkandawire and Charles Soludo, eds., *African Voices on Structural Adjustment* (Dakar: CODESRIA, 2003). Important country studies also began to emerge, such as Eboe Hutchful, *Ghana's Adjustment Experience: The Paradox of Reform* (Oxford: James Currey and UNRISD, 2002).

74. Adedeji, "From the Lagos Plan of Action to the New Partnership for African Development," 6.

75. Austin Strange, "Seven Decades of Chinese State Financing in Africa: Tempering Current Debates," *Economic History of Developing Regions* 34, no. 3 (2019): 259–79.

76. Jamie Monson, *Africa's Freedom Railway: How a Chinese Development Project Changed Lives and Livelihoods in Tanzania* (Bloomington: Indiana University Press, 2009).

77. Anna Lindley, "African Remittances and Progress: Opportunities and Challenges," *Real Instituto Elcano*, May 27, 2008, www.realinstitutoelcano.org.

78. Benu Modi and Seema Shekhawat, "China and India in Africa," *Pambazuka News*, Issue 456, November 5, 2009, http://pambazuka.org/en/category/africa_china/60030.

79. Shanta Devarjan and Sudhir Shetty, "Africa: Leveraging the Crisis into a Development Takeoff," *Economic Premise* 30 (2010): 1–4.

80. For the case of West Africa, see Nilanjin Banik and C. A. Yoonus, "Trade as an Answer to Sustainable Economic Growth—The ECOWAS Story," *Global Business Review* 13, no. 2 (2012): 312.

81. An excellent study is presented in Deborah Brautigam, *The Dragon's Gift: The Real Story of China in Africa* (Oxford: Oxford University Press, 2009).

82. Hippolyte Fofack, "Retrospective Analysis of Africa's Post-HIPC Growth Resurgence" (conference paper, Harvard University, 2015).

83. Ibid.

84. Strange, "Seven Decades of Chinese State Financing in Africa," 271.

85. Ibid., 274.

86. Hippolyte Fofack, "Overcoming the Colonial Development Model of Resource Extraction for Sustainable Development in Africa," *Brookings*, January 31, 2019, https://www.brookings .edu/blog/africa-in-focus/2019/01/31/overcoming-the-colonial-development-model-of-resource -extraction-for-sustainable-development-in-africa/.

2. Religion, Culture, and the Arts in the Making of the African Nation-State

1. Richard Rathbone, "From Kingdom to Nation: Challenging African Constructions of Identity," in *Chieftaincy in Ghana: Culture, Governance and Development*, ed. Irene K. Odotei and Albert K. Awedoba (Accra: Sub-Saharan, 2006), 43–54.

2. Steven Feierman, *Peasant Intellectuals: Anthropology and History in Tanzania* (Madison: University of Wisconsin Press, 1990), 23–24.

3. Ibid., 6. In the Gold Coast, the influence of priest-chiefs (*asofo*) in Guan towns like Late and Abiriw extended into the mid-nineteenth century. Kwame Amoah Labi, "Cross-Cultural Appropriation of Regalia and Royal Art, and Contemporary Adaptations in Ghana," in Odotei and Awedoba, *Chieftaincy in Ghana*, 275–94. The same applied to the Dangme in the Gold Coast. Nii O. Quarcoopome, "Rituals and Regalia of Power: Arts and Politics among the Dangme and Ewe, 1800 to Present" (PhD diss., University of California at Los Angeles, 1993).

4. Kwame Nkrumah, *Consciencism* (New York: Modern Reader Paperbacks, 1970 [1964]), 13.

5. Ibid., 68.

6. John S. Pobee, *Nkrumah and the Church in Ghana: 1949–1966* (Denver: IAcademic Books, 2000), chap. 3.

7. See, for example, David Amponsah, "(Un)Desirable Customs: A History of Religion in the Making of Modern Ghana, c.1806–1966" (PhD diss., Harvard University, 2015); and Jean Allman and John Parker, *Tongnaab: The History of a West African God* (Bloomington: Indiana University Press, 2005).

8. Feierman, *Peasant Intellectuals*, 22.

9. Modibo Keita, Mali's first head of state, also reportedly was a direct descendant of an ancient Mali chief, which added to his pedigree as nationalist leader and as independent Mali's first ruler from 1960 to 1968. Robert H. Jackson and Carl G. Rosberg, *Personal Rule in Black Africa: Prince, Autocrat, Prophet, Tyrant* (Berkeley: University of California Press, 1982), 188.

10. Joseph Boakye Danquah, *The Ghanaian Establishment: Its Constitution, Its Detentions, Its Traditions, Its Justice and Statecraft, and Its Heritage of Ghanaism*, ed. Albert Adu Boahen (Accra: Ghana Universities Press, 1997).

11. Kelly M. Askew, *Performing the Nation: Swahili Music and Cultural Politics in Tanzania* (Chicago: University of Chicago Press, 2002).

12. Nate Plageman, *Highlife Saturday Night: Popular Music and Social Change in Urban Ghana* (Bloomington: Indiana University Press, 2013).

13. James D. Straker, *Youth, Nationalism, and the Guinean Revolution* (Bloomington: Indiana University Press, 2009).

14. Askew, *Performing the Nation*, 26.

15. Ibid., 288.

16. Senghor spoke of de Chardin in several of his publications. They met while Senghor was a student in Paris. On a visit to New York in 1963, Senghor arranged to go to the cemetery at St. Andrews on Hudson to de Chardin's grave. Thomas Patrick Melady and Margaret Badum Melady, *Ten African Heroes: The Sweep of Independence in Black Africa* (Maryknoll, NY: Orbis Books, 2011), 26–27.

17. Jackson and Rosberg, *Personal Rule in Black Africa*, 182.

18. Léopold Sédar Senghor, *Liberté 1: négritude et humanisme* (Paris: Editions du Seuil, 1964), 284.

19. Issa G. Shivji, Saida Yahya-Othman, and Ng'wanza Kamaya, *Development as Rebellion: A Biography of Julius Nyerere* (Dar es Salaam: Mkuki na Nyota, 2020), 1:52.

20. John Iliffe, *A Modern History of Tanganyika* (Cambridge: Cambridge University Press, 1994 [1979]), 543.

21. Mohamed Said, *The Life and Times of Abdul Wahid Sykes: The Untold Story of the Muslim Struggle against British Colonialism in Tanganyika* (London: Minerva Press, 1998). See also, Salma Maoulidi, "Racial and Religious Tolerance in Nyerere's Political Thought and Practice," in *Africa's Liberation: The Legacy of Nyerere*, ed. Chambi Chachage and Annar Cassam (Cape Town: Pambazuka Press, 2010), 134–48.

22. Shivji, Yahya-Othman, and Kamaya, *Biography of Julius Nyerere*, 2:117. The fact that Muslims had associations separate from TANU, such as the East African Muslim Welfare Society (EAMWS) with the wealthy Aga Khan as patron, made Nyerere uncomfortable. He viewed the Aga Khan as opposed to his socialist agenda and the EAMWS as an alternative base of power. The government banned the EAMWS in 1968. Shivji, Yahya-Othman, and Kamaya, *Biography of Julius Nyerere*, 3:57–63.

23. Geoffrey Ross Owens, "The Secret History of TANU: Rumor, Historiography and Muslim Unrest in Contemporary Dar es Salaam," *History and Anthropology* 16, no. 4 (2005): 455.

24. Feierman, *Peasant Intellectuals*, 229.

25. Shivji, Yahya-Othman, and Kamaya, *Biography of Julius Nyerere*, 1:18.

26. Feierman, *Peasant Intellectuals*, 257.

27. Ibid.

28. Julius Nyerere, "Poverty, Christianity and Revolution," *New Blackfriars* 52, no. 618 (1971): 484–95, quote on 485. The address is also reproduced in Julius K. Nyerere, *Freedom and Development: A Selection of Writings and Speeches 1968–1973* (London: Oxford University Press, 1973), 213–28.

29. Simeon Mesaki and Mrisho Malipula, "Julius Nyerere's Influence and Legacy: From a Proponent of Familyhood to a Candidate for Sainthood," *International Journal of Sociology and Anthropology* 3, no. 3 (2011): 93–100.

30. Shivji, Yahya-Othman, and Kamaya, *Biography of Julius Nyerere*, 3:54.

31. Iliffe, *Modern History of Tanganyika*, 551.

32. Shivji, Yahya-Othman, and Kamaya, *Biography of Julius Nyerere*, 3:65–69.

33. Trevor Huddleston, "The Person Nyerere," in *Mwalimu: The Influence of Nyerere*, ed. Colin Legum and Geoffrey Mmari (London: James Currey, 1995), 6–7.

34. Shivji, Yahya-Othman, and Kamaya, *Biography of Julius Nyerere*, 3:69.

35. Donal B. Cruise O'Brien, *Saints and Politicians: Essays in the Organization of a Senegalese Peasant Society* (Cambridge: Cambridge University Press, 1975). On Kajoor in the nineteenth century, see Mamadou Diouf, *La Kajoor au XIXe siècle: Pouvoir ceddo et Conquête Coloniale* (Paris: Karthala, 1990).

36. Cruise O'Brien, *Saints and Politicians*, 188.

37. Ibid.

38. Ibid., 10.

39. See more generally David Robinson, *Muslim Societies in African History* (Cambridge: Cambridge University Press, 2004), chap. 13 in particular on Muslim brotherhoods under French colonial rule in Senegal.

40. Cruise O'Brien, *Saints and Politicians*, 11.

41. Lucy Behrman, *Muslim Brotherhoods and Politics in Senegal* (Cambridge, MA: Harvard University Press, 1970), 10. I am grateful to my colleague Ousmane Kane, grandson to Ibrahima Niasse, for shedding light on Nkrumah's relationship with Niasse. During Nkrumah's administration, a few members of the Niasse family lived in Ghana and served as advisers to Nkrumah in various capacities. Personal communication from Ousmane Kane, May 1, 2022.

42. Ibid., 120.

43. Jackson and Rosberg, *Personal Rule in Black Africa*, 84.

44. Behrman, *Muslim Brotherhoods*, 178.

45. Senghor, *Liberté 1: Négritude et Humanisme*, 267.

46. Mike McGovern, *Unmasking the State: Making Guinea Modern* (Chicago: University of Chicago Press, 2012), 123–24. McGovern argues that a mixture of Marxist and Islamist reform idioms underpinned Touré's politics throughout his political tenure (131).

47. Straker, *Youth, Nationalism, and the Guinean Revolution*, 22. Touré wanted Guinean youth connected directly to the state and ruling party, not to "different associations according to their creed [religion]." Ahmed Sékou Touré, *Africa on the Move* (London: Panaf Books, 1979), 475.

48. Straker, *Youth, Nationalism, and the Guinean Revolution*. See also, Claude Rivière, *Mutations Sociales en Guinée* (Paris: Marcel Rivière, 1971).

49. McGovern, *Unmasking the State*, 22.

50. Ahmed Sékou Touré, *La Révolution Culturelle* (Geneva: Kundig, 1972).

51. McGovern, *Unmasking the State*.

52. Straker, *Youth, Nationalism, and the Guinea Revolution*, 102.

53. McGovern, *Unmasking the State*, 13, speaks to how Demystification "bridged the distance between Marxism and Pan-Africanism by simultaneously outlawing and foklorizing the same objects," then exporting the product through ballet as an authentic but sanitized aspect of Guinea's past.

54. Straker, *Youth, Nationalism, and the Guinean Revolution*, 12.

55. Ibid., 114. McGovern, *Unmasking the State*, 182, places this murder in 1962.

56. Straker, *Youth, Nationalism, and the Guinean Revolution*, 190. McGovern, *Unmasking the State*, 77, notes that during his research among the Loma in Macenta Prefecture in the 1990s and early 2000s, the Loma brushed off monotheism and continued their sacrifices.

57. On the religious and ritual dimensions of the Liberian civil war, see Stephen Ellis, *The Mask of Anarchy: The Destruction of Liberia and the Religious Dimension of an African Civil War*, 2nd rev. ed. (New York: New York University Press, 2006 [1999]).

58. Religious pluralism was a key feature of Nkrumah's private life during his political tenure as head of state, as he forged close relations with Muslim and indigenous religious leaders. I explore this in a forthcoming journal article. Whereas the state remained secular, Nkrumah's spirituality privately informed important state matters like when to declare Ghana a republic, as is evident in Nkrumah's correspondence with Sheikh A. A. Hussein of Cairo, father-in-law of Alhaji Sinar. See Nkrumah's correspondence in 1958 with Sheikh A. A. Hussein, Kwame Nkrumah Private and Personal Letters, Public Records and Archives Administration Department (PRAAD), Accra, SC/BAA/513, Set 4. The Ghanaian Alhaji Sinar had studied in Cairo and married into a Muslim Egyptian family. He was instrumental in the matchmaking of Nkrumah and his Egyptian wife, Fathia Halim Rizk. Personal communication from Sangu Delle, grandson of Alhaji Sinar, April 14, 2020.

59. Pobee, *Nkrumah and the Church in Ghana*, chap. 3.

60. Kwesi Dickson, "Religion and Society," in *The Life and Work of Kwame Nkrumah*, ed. Kwame Arhin (Accra: Sedco, 1991), 144.

61. Ibid., 140.

62. On the Young Pioneer Movement, see Jeffrey Ahlman, *Living with Nkrumahism: Nation, State, and Pan-Africanism in Ghana* (Athens: Ohio University Press, 2017), chap. 3.

63. Interview with Dr. Elizabeth Amoah, Accra, August 1, 2012.

64. Pobee, *Nkrumah and the Church in Ghana*, 131.

65. Ibid.

66. Ebenezer Obiri Addo, *Kwame Nkrumah: A Case Study of Religion and Politics in Ghana* (Lanham, MD: University Press of America, 1997), 145–46.

67. Pobee, *Nkrumah and the Church in Ghana*, 171.

68. Ibid., 172.

69. Interview with George Hagan, Accra, July 31, 2012.

70. Pew Forum on Religion and Public Life, "Tolerance and Tension: Islam and Christianity in Sub-Saharan Africa," April 2010, https://www.pewforum.org/2010/04/15/executive-summary-islam-and-christianity-in-sub-saharan-africa/.

71. Alexander Keese, "Understanding Colonial Chieftaincy from Its Final Phase: Responses to the Crisis of an Institution in French-Ruled West Africa and Beyond, 1944–1960," *Africana Studia* 15 (2010): 11–28.

72. Leonardo Villalón, *Islamic Society and State Power in Senegal: Disciples and Citizens in Fatick* (Cambridge: Cambridge University Press, 1995), 12.

73. Ibid., chap. 7.

74. Jackson and Rosberg, *Personal Rule in Black Africa*, 93–94.

75. Mahmood Mamdani, *Citizen and Subject: Contemporary African and the Legacy of Late Colonialism* (Princeton, NJ: Princeton University Press, 1996).

76. Elizabeth Schmidt, *Cold War and Decolonization in Guinea, 1946–1958* (Athens: Ohio University Press, 2007), 53.

77. Ibid., 107.

78. Mahmood Mamdani, *Define and Rule: Native as Political Identity* (Cambridge, MA: Harvard University Press, 2012), 109.

79. Andreas Eckert, "Useful Instruments of Participation? Local Government and Cooperatives in Tanzania, 1940s to 1970s," *International Journal of African Historical Studies* 40, no. 1 (2007): 108–9.

80. Feierman, *Peasant Intellectuals*, 222.

81. Irving Leonard Markovitz, *Léopold Sédar Senghor and the Politics of Negritude* (New York: Atheneum, 1969), 112–13.

82. Villalón, *Islamic Society and State Power in Senegal*, 264.

83. Jean M. Allman, *The Quills of the Porcupine: Asante Nationalism in an Emergent Ghana* (Madison: University of Wisconsin Press, 1993); and Dennis Austin, *Politics in Ghana 1946–1960* (London: Oxford University Press, 1964).

84. Richard Rathbone, *Nkrumah and the Chiefs: The Politics of Chieftaincy in Ghana 1951–60* (Oxford: James Currey, 2000), 4.

85. Ibid., viii.

86. Ibid., 17.

87. Ibid., 31.

88. Ibid., 96–97.

89. Ibid., 149.

90. Sara Berry, "Chieftaincy, Land, and the State in Ghana and South Africa," in *The Politics of Custom: Chiefship, Capital, and the State in Contemporary Africa*, ed. John L. Comaroff and Jean Comaroff (Chicago: University of Chicago Press, 2018), 79–109.

91. See, for example, Piet Konings, "Capitalist Rice Farming and Land Allocation in Northern Ghana," *Journal of Legal Pluralism and Unofficial Law* 16, no. 22 (1984): 89–119.

92. Berry, "Chieftaincy, Land, and the State," 86–87.

93. Rathbone, *Nkrumah and the Chiefs*, 110–11.

94. Interview with Professor George P. Hagan, Accra, July 31, 2012.

95. Ibid.

96. See, for example, Karin Barber, *I Could Speak Until Tomorrow: Oriki Women and the Past in a Yoruba Town* (Edinburgh: International African Institute, 1991).

97. Kristen Neuschel, *Word of Honor: Interpreting Noble Gesture in Sixteenth-Century France* (Ithaca, NY: Cornell University Press, 1989).

98. See, for example, J. H. Kwabena Nketia, *Ayan*, vol. 1, *The Poetry of the Atumpan Drums of the Asantehene* (Accra: Institute of African Studies, University of Ghana, 1966); and more

generally, J. H. Kwabena Nketia, *Reinstating Traditional Music in Contemporary Contexts* (Akropong-Akuapem: Regnum Africa, 2016).

99. Suzanne Preston Blier, *The Royal Arts of Africa: The Majesty of Form* (New York: Harry Abrams, 1998).

100. Labi, "Cross-Cultural Appropriation of Regalia and Royal Art," 275.

101. Interview with Agya Ko Nimo, Ayeduase, July 27, 2012.

102. Brittany Sheldon, "Becoming Ghana: The Role of Artwork in Forming Ghanaian National Identity," *Montage* 5 (2011): 46.

103. Book's cover photo.

104. On Akan linguist staffs, see Doran H. Ross, "The Verbal Arts of Akan Linguist Staffs," *African Arts* 16, no. 1 (1982): 56–67, 95–96.

105. On the history, place, and meanings of kente cloth, see Doran H. Ross, *Wrapped in Pride: Ghanaian Kente and African American Identity* (Los Angeles: UCLA Fowler Museum of Cultural History, 1999).

106. Doran H. Ross, "The Iconography of Asante State Swords," *African Arts* 11, no. 1 (1977): 16–25, 90–91. See also, A. A. Y. Kyerematen, *Kingship and Ceremony in Ashanti* (Kumasi: UST Press, 1969).

107. Harcourt Fuller, *Building the Ghanaian Nation-State: Kwame Nkrumah's Symbolic Nationalism* (New York: Palgrave Macmillan, 2014), 7.

108. Nketia, *Reinstating Traditional Music in Contemporary Contexts*, 78–79.

109. Isaac D. Riverson, *Songs of the Akan Peoples* (Accra: Methodist Book Depot, 1939). See also, T. E. Andoh, "The Nationalistic Music of I. D. Riverson," *Legon Journal of the Humanities* 18 (2007): 159–77.

110. Kofi Antubam, *Ghana's Heritage of Culture* (Leipzig: Koehler and Amelang, 1963), 18. I am yet to explore how the early demand for restitution of African art from European museums in the 1970s by African intellectuals like Amadou Mahtar M'Bow, the Senegalese director general for UNESCO from 1974 to 1988, fits into the larger state endeavor to represent the arts in Africa. Bénédicte Savoy, "Amnesia: Forty Years' Debate on African Cultural Heritage in European Museums" (paper presented at conference "The Restitution Debate: African Art in a Global Society," Columbia University, October 18, 2019).

111. Interview with Professor J. H. Kwabena Nketia, Accra, August 4, 2012. Other state designated artists included Oku Ampofu and Vincent Kofi. Nii O. Quarcoopome points out that a larger pool of community craftsmen made the numerous works of art presented as gifts to foreign dignitaries, not just state-designated artists. Janet Hess and Nii O. Quarcoopome, "Spectacular Nation: Nkrumahist Art and Resistance Iconography in the Ghanaian Independence Era," *African Arts* 39, no. 1 (2006): 16–25, 91–92.

112. George P. Hagan, "Nkrumah's Cultural Policies," in *The Life and Work of Kwame Nkrumah*, ed. Kwame Arhin (Accra: Sedco, 1991), 10–11.

113. Ibid., 11. Some contemporaries like Nancy Tsiboe, an NLM activist, would allege in 1956 that Nkrumah came from "a genealogical line with potentially non-Gold Coast roots." Jeffrey S. Ahlman, *Kwame Nkrumah: Visions of Liberation* (Athens: Ohio University Press, 2021).

114. Samuel Obeng, *Selected Speeches: Kwame Nkrumah* (Accra: Afram, 1979), 1:244.

115. Ndiouga Benga, "Mise en scène de la culture et espace public au Sénégal," *Africa Development* 35, no. 4 (2010): 237–60.

116. Elizabeth Harney, *In Senghor's Shadow: Art, Politics and the Avant-Garde in Senegal, 1960–1995* (Durham, NC: Duke University Press, 2004), 49.

117. Benga, "Culture et espace au Sénégal," 240. Kenneth Kaunda, independent Zambia's first president, agreed that the worth of an individual or country did not come to the material. For Kaunda, who forged an ideology he called "humanism," "Africa's gift to world culture must be in the realm of Human Relationships." Colin M. Morris, *A Humanist in Africa: Letters to Colin M. Morris from Kenneth D. Kaunda President of Zambia* (London: Longmans, 1966), 22.

118. Touré, *La Révolution culturelle*, 117.

119. Léopold Sédar Senghor, "La Décolonisation, Condition de la Communauté Franco-Africaine," *Le Monde*, September 4, 1957.

120. Touré, *Africa on the Move*, 440.

121. Straker, *Youth, Nationalism, and the Guinean Revolution*.

122. Fuller, *Building the Ghanaian Nation-State*, 6.

123. On the agenda to create a new African, see, for example, Ahlman, *Living with Nkrumahism*; Straker, *Youth, Nationalism, and the Guinean Revolution*; and McGovern, *Unmasking the State*. The overlap with modernization theory is instructive, as the latter sought to birth a new person positioned for the transition of undeveloped societies from tradition to modernity (see chap. 3).

124. Frantz Fanon, *The Wretched of the Earth*, trans. Constance Harrington (New York: Grove Press, 1968 [1961]), 245–46.

125. Touré, *Africa on the Move*, 40–41.

126. Paul Bjerk, *Julius Nyerere* (Athens: Ohio University Press, 2017), 60.

127. Straker, *Youth, Nationalism, and the Guinean Revolution*, 80.

128. Askew, *Performing the Nation*, especially chaps. 3 and 5.

129. Plageman, *Highlife Saturday Night*, 156. Highlife music evolved from the late nineteenth century through a mix of local and foreign influences, with the two world wars and the presence of foreign troops being key stimulants to its development. See the many publications by John Collins, particularly "Ghanaian Highlife," *African Arts* 10, no. 1 (1976): 62–68; and *West African Pop Roots* (Philadelphia: Temple University Press, 1992).

130. Plageman, *Highlife Saturday Night*, 147.

131. Ibid., 149.

132. See an article in retrospect, Jack Royston, "How Queen Elizabeth II Danced with Ghana's President Months after Civil Rights Bus Burns," *Newsweek*, May 21, 2022.

133. Plageman, *Highlife Saturday Night*, 175.

134. Obeng, *Selected Speeches: Kwame Nkrumah*, 2:279.

135. Ibid., 280.

136. Ibid., 430–31.

137. See, for example, Terence O. Ranger, *Dance and Society in East Africa: The Beni Ngoma* (London: Heinemann, 1975).

138. Susan Geiger, *TANU Women: Gender and Culture in the Making of Tanganyikan Nationalism, 1955–1965* (Portsmouth, NH: Heinemann, 1997), 50.

139. Ibid., 58.

140. Vicensia Shule, "Mwalimu Nyerere: The Artist," in *Africa's Liberation: The Legacy of Nyerere*, ed. Chambi Chachage and Annar Cassam (Cape Town: Pambazuka Press, 2010), 164.

141. Penina Mlama, "Emergence: The Indelible Face of Artistic Creativity in the Struggle for Self-Determination in Africa," *Africa Development* 42, no. 4 (2017): 17–36.

142. As cited in Askew, *Performing the Nation*, 171.

143. Ibid., 186.

144. Mlama, "Emergence," 25. In the early 1960s, liberation movements based in Dar es Salaam—first under the umbrella of the PAFMECA and after 1964 under the OAU's African Liberation Committee—often arranged planned processions of freedom fighters. This was an important way of bringing the causes of freedom movements before the ordinary people of Tanzania. ANC Archives, National Heritage and Cultural Studies (NAHECS), University of Fort Hare. ANC Morogoro Office (1960–1990), Box 8, Folder 71, FRELIMO 1962–1965.

145. Shule, "Mwalimu Nyerere," 164.

146. The ANC in exile had a Department of Arts and Culture. See Oliver Tambo Papers (1960–92), Office of the President Records, Box 38, ANC Archives, National Heritage and Cultural Studies (NAHECS), University of Fort Hare.

147. Sindiso Mfenyana, *Walking with Giants: Life and Times of an ANC Veteran* (Cape Town: South African History Online, 2017), 255–56.

148. Joshua Cohen describes the group as the first globally touring African performance company. The group's first visit to the United States in 1959 had a major impact on African American dance and on artists like Miles Davis. Joshua Cohen, "Stages in Transition: Les Ballets Africains and Independence, 1959 to 1960," *Journal of Black Studies* 43, no. 1 (2012): 11–48.

149. Lansiné Kaba, "The Cultural Revolution, Artistic Creativity, and Freedom of Expression in Guinea," *Journal of Modern African Studies* 14, no. 2 (1976): 202.

150. Kaba, "Cultural Revolution," 202.

151. Ibid., 203.

152. Ibid.

153. Ibid., 205.

154. This cultural renaissance was not without its contradictions. A good example is the Demystification Program pursued in the Forest Region to rid Loma- and Manya-speaking peoples of "superstitious" practices while appropriating their confiscated masks and other ritual objects into the new national culture the state was fabricating.

155. Cohen, "Stages in Transition"; and Straker, *Youth, Nationalism, and the Guinean Revolution*.

156. Cohen, "Stages in Transition," 16. It was in Guinea in 1967 that African American activist Stokely Carmichael would meet Makeba, who he later married. Carmichael changed his name to Kwame Ture after his two mentors Kwame Nkrumah and Sékou Touré. Makeba lived in Guinea from 1968 to 1986, produced music under the Guinean national label Syliphone, and represented Guinea at international festivals. Yair Hashachar, "Playing the Backbeat in Conakry: Miriam Makeba and the Cultural Politics of Sékou Touré's Guinea, 1968–1986," *Social Dynamics* 43, no. 2 (2017): 259–73.

157. See Straker, *Youth, Nationalism, and the Guinean Revolution*, chap. 3.

158. Hashachar, "Makeba and the Cultural Politics of Touré's Guinea," 213.

159. Laura L. Cochrane, "The Growth of Artistic Nationalism in Senegal," *Nations and Nationalism* 17, no. 2 (2011): 378.

160. Ibid., 392.

161. Benga, "Culture et espace au Sénégal."

162. Alioune Diop, "From the Festival of Negro Arts at Dakar to the Lagos Festival: Itinerary," *Présence Africaine*, n.s., 92 (1974): 9–14.

163. Penny M. von Eschen, "Soul Call: The First World Festival of Negro Arts as a Pivot of Black Modernities," *Nka: Journal of Contemporary African Arts* 42–43 (November 2018): 124–35; and Tracy D. Snipe, *Arts and Politics in Senegal: 1960–1996* (Trenton, NJ: Africa World Press, 1998), 48. William Greaves directed a forty-minute documentary on the First World

Festival of Negro Arts (Dakar 1966). On the relationship between African nationalists and African American nationalists, see Daryl Michael Scott, "How Black Nationalism Became Sui Generis," *Fire!!!* 1, no. 2 (2012): 6–63.

164. Anthony J. Ratcliff, "When Négritude Was in Vogue: Critical Reflections of the First World Festival of Negro Arts and Culture in 1966," *Journal of Pan African Studies* 6, no. 7 (February 2014): 167–86.

165. The Dakar Festival of 1966 and the Algiers Festival of 1969 underscore the tension between cultural nationalism underpinned by racial solidarity and revolutionary nationalism with its vision of radical political reform. Scott, "How Black Nationalism Became Sui Generis."

166. Andrew Apter, "Beyond Négritude: Black Cultural Citizenship and the Arab Question in FESTAC 77," *Journal of African Cultural Studies* 28, no. 3 (2016): 313–26.

167. Obeng, *Selected Speeches: Kwame Nkrumah*, 2:277.

168. Apter, "Beyond Négritude." The Guinean delegation to the Algiers Festival distinguished itself in the artistic contests and won the grand prize, seen by Touré as affirmation of his cultural revolution. Yair Hashachar, "Guinea Unbound: Performing Pan-African Cultural Citizenship between Algiers 1969 and the Guinean National Affairs," *Interventions* (2018). DOI: 10.1080/1369801X.2018.1508932.

169. Léopold Sédar Senghor, *The Foundations of "Africanité" or "Négritude" and "Arabité,"* trans. Mercer Cook (Paris: Présence Africaine, 1971).

170. Apter, "Beyond Négritude," 318.

171. Andrew Apter, *The Pan-African Nation: Oil and the Spectacle of Culture in Nigeria* (Chicago: University of Chicago Press, 2005). See also, J. Southern, "FESTAC '77," *Black Perspective in Music* 5, no. 1 (1977): 104–17.

172. Fritz Schatten, *Communism in Africa* (London: George Allen and Unwin, 1966), 71–72, discusses the "Two-Camp" Slogan as outlined in *Pravda*, October 22, 1947; and Philip E. Muehlenbeck, *Betting on the Africans: John F. Kennedy's Courting of African Nationalist Leaders* (Oxford: Oxford University Press, 2012), chap. 1, provides a discussion of Eisenhower's Africa policy in the 1950s.

173. Samir Amin, *The Long Revolution of the Global South: Toward a New Anti-imperialist International*, trans. James Membrez (New York: Monthly Review Press, 2019), 16–18. See also, Demba Moussa Dembélé, *Samir Amin: Intellectuel organique au service de l'émancipation du Sud* (Dakar: CODESRIA, 2011).

174. Christopher J. Lee, "Introduction: Between a Moment and an Era: The Origins and Afterlives of Bandung," in *Making a World after Empire: The Bandung Moment and Its Political Afterlives*, ed. Christopher J. Lee (Athens: Ohio University Press, 2010), 25–26.

175. Romi Crawford, "The Event of the Photograph: Black Consciousness from the *Wall of Respect '67* to FESTAC 77," *Nka: Journal of Contemporary African Art* 42–43 (November 2018): 154–63.

176. Arthur Monroe, "FESTAC 77—The Second World Black and African Festival of Arts and Culture: Lagos, Nigeria," *Black Scholar* 9, no. 1 (1977): 37.

177. Askew, *Performing the Nation*, 190.

178. Ibid., 54.

179. McGovern, *Unmasking the State*, 232.

180. The privileging of national and territorial sovereignty in a weakly structured OAU undercut any serious attempt at continental integration and undermined uncoordinated efforts at national economic development. The formation of the African Union (AU) in 2002 to replace the OAU and rekindle the vision of continental integration—now crystallized in the

form of the African Continental Free Trade Agreement—made a new outreach to the African diaspora, which the AU declared in 2008 as Africa's Sixth Region. There are important connections between worldmaking at the national, continental, and international levels.

3. Economic Imaginaries

1. Colonial economics was birthed in the latter years of World War II, as the Colonial Office in Britain explored ways to accelerate economic growth in its tropical colonies to assist the reconstruction of war-torn Britain. This was the preface to the second colonial occupation in Africa after World War II (see chap. 1). As early as 1943–44, William Arthur Lewis offered a course on colonial economics at the London School of Economics. See Robert L. Tignor, *W. Arthur Lewis and the Birth of Development Economics* (Princeton, NJ: Princeton University Press, 2006), chap. 2.

2. Robert Skidelsky, *Keynes: The Return of the Master* (New York: Public Affairs, 2009).

3. W. W. Rostow, *The Process of Economic Growth* (Oxford: Clarendon, 1953); and W. W. Rostow, *The Stages of Economic Growth: A Non-communist Manifesto* (Cambridge: Cambridge University Press, 1961 [1960]).

4. Since America was the first country to achieve high mass-consumption in the 1920s, with Western Europe and Japan only probing this phase in the 1950s, America was clearly positioned to guide the Third World in these stages of growth that climaxed with the high mass-consumption society. Rostow, *Stages of Economic Growth*, 10.

5. Frederick Cooper, "Modernizing Bureaucrats, Backward Africans, and the Development Concept," in *International Development and the Social Sciences: Essays on the History and Politics of Knowledge*, ed. Frederick Cooper and Randall M. Packard (Berkeley: University of California Press, 1997), 64–92.

6. Dean C. Tipps, "Modernization Theory and the Comparative Study of Societies: A Critical Perspective," *Comparative Studies in Society and History* 15, no. 2 (1973): 204.

7. Abou B. Bamba, *African Miracle, African Mirage: Transnational Politics and the Paradox of Modernization in Ivory Coast* (Athens: Ohio University Press, 2016), 26–28.

8. Jon Woronoff, *West African Wager: Houphouët versus Nkrumah* (Metuchen, NJ: Scarecrow Press, 1972), 11–12.

9. Ralph Austen, *African Economic History* (Oxford: James Currey, 1987), 238. In chapter 4, I argue that the developmental state offers a better framework for understanding the economic agenda in Ghana, Guinea, and other radical countries than socialism, or "African socialism" in the rhetoric of the time.

10. Ahmed Sékou Touré, *Africa on the Move* (London: Panaf Books, 1979), 593–94.

11. Tony Killick, *Development Economics in Action: A Study of Economic Policies in Ghana* (London: Heinemann, 1978).

12. The economic success of the Asian Tigers—South Korea, Taiwan, Malaysia, Indonesia, and Singapore—in the 1970s and 1980s in state-led economic growth might seem to qualify my argument on the deficiency of top-down approaches to economic development in Africa. A statist approach to economic development requires a fine balance between economics and governance. Improved living standards for the majority may earn public endorsement of statist approaches, but people also value personal liberties, even in the context of material improvement. In the African context, the decline in world prices for Africa's primary commodities from the late 1950s undercut developmental efforts and reinforced the shift to authoritarianism. While the Asian Tigers were developmental but initially undemocratic, "the most successful

of these states eventually developed more open political systems, with citizens renegotiating and constitutionalizing the power of the state." Laura Mann and Marie Berry, "Understanding the Political Motivations That Shape Rwanda's Emergent Developmental State," *New Political Economy* 21, no. 1 (2016): 119–44 (quote on 139). Rwanda from 2000 has assumed the mantle of the developmental state, or more accurately of a postdevelopmental state, in its efforts to merge developmental and neoliberal approaches with Singapore as its conscious model. The Rwandan state's embrace of neoliberalism has been motivated by the desire of an authoritarian government to maintain its grip on power and society through economic growth, improved living standards, and security. In spite the Rwandan government's remarkable achievements in these areas postgenocide, the issues of civil liberty, the plight of poorer groups, and rising inequalities have now surfaced, raising questions about the durability of the Rwandan experiment going forward. See Ibid; David Booth and Frederick Golooba-Mutebi, "Developmental Patrimonialism? The Case of Rwanda," *African Affairs* 111, no. 444 (2012): 379–403; and Catherine A. Honeyman, *The Orderly Entrepreneur: Youth, Education, and Governance in Rwanda* (Stanford: University of Stanford Press, 2016).

13. This distinction is not just semantics, as Deepak Lal underscores in *The Poverty of 'Development Economics'* (London: Institute of Economic Affairs, 2002 [1983]). I access Lewis's works through Patrick A. M. Emmanuel, ed., *Sir William Arthur Lewis Collected Papers 1941–1988*, 3 vols. (Barbados: Institute of Social and Economic Research, University of the West Indies, 1994); and Bauer's through P. T. Bauer, *Dissent on Development*, rev. ed. (Cambridge, MA: Harvard University Press, 1976), first published 1971; and P. T. Bauer, *Reality and Rhetoric: Studies in the Economics of Development* (Cambridge, MA: Harvard University Press, 1984).

14. Killick, *Development Economics in Action*, 2.

15. Ibid., 12.

16. Ragnar Nurkse, *Problems of Capital Formation in Underdeveloped Countries* (New York: Oxford University Press, 1953). See also, Ragnar Nurkse, "Some International Aspects of the Problems of Economic Development," *American Economic Review* 40, no. 2 (1952): 571–83.

17. Harvey Leibenstein, *A Theory of Economic-Demographic Development* (Princeton, NJ: Princeton University Press, 1954); and Harvey Leibenstein, *Economic Backwardness and Economic Growth: Studies in the Theory of Economic Development* (New York: Wiley, 1957).

18. Gunnar Myrdal, *Economic Theory and Underdeveloped Regions* (London: G. Duckworth, 1957).

19. Raúl Prebisch, "Commercial Policy in Underdeveloped Countries," *American Economic Review* 49, no. 2 (1959): 251–73.

20. Rostow, *Process of Economic Growth*; and Rostow, *Stages of Economic Growth*.

21. Paul Rosenstein-Rodan, "Problems of Industrialization of Eastern and South-Eastern Europe," *Economic Journal* 53 (1943): 202–11; Nurkse, *Problems of Capital Formation in Underdeveloped Countries*; Leibenstein, *Economic Backwardness and Economic Growth*; and Albert O. Hirschman, *The Strategy of Economic Development* (New Haven, CT: Yale University Press, 1958). Rosenstein-Rodan's 1943 article laid the foundation for the "big push" model.

22. Hans Wolfgang Singer, "Gains and Losses from Trade and Investment in Underdeveloped Countries," *American Economic Review* 40 (1950): 473–85. Singer was best known for the Singer-Prebisch thesis, which states that the terms of trade tend to move adversely against producers of primary products. Singer became an advocate of foreign aid to underdeveloped countries to offset the disproportionate gains developed countries earned from international trade. See also, Hans Wolfgang Singer, *International Development: Growth and Change* (New York: McGraw-Hill, 1962).

23. Myrdal, *Economic Theory and Underdeveloped Regions*; Dudley Seers, "International Aid: The Next Steps," *Journal of Modern African Studies* 2, no. 4 (1964): 471–89; and Prebisch, "Commercial Policy in Underdeveloped Countries."

24. Killick, *Development Economics in Action*, 15.

25. Tibor Scitovsky, "Two Concepts of External Economies," *Journal of Political Economy* 62, no. 2 (1954): 143–51.

26. Killick, *Development Economics in Action*, 15, 19.

27. Ibid., 24.

28. William Arthur Lewis, *The Principles of Economic Planning* (London: Unwin University Books, 1949), 2nd ed. 1952. Tignor notes how the period from the late 1930s through 1953, when Lewis served as a consultant for the British Colonial Office and had frequent contacts with colonial officials, was formative in Lewis's development of ideas on economic development in tropical colonies. Tignor, *W. Arthur Lewis*, 43.

29. Lewis, *Principles of Economic Planning*, 3.

30. Ibid., 20.

31. Ibid., 120.

32. Ibid., 123.

33. Ibid., 126.

34. Ibid., 127. I develop this line further in chapter 4. By the late 1950s, regional economic integration had come to the fore of Prebisch's thinking as the most coherent response to Latin America's underdevelopment. Aldo Antonio Dadone and Luis Eugenio di Marco, "The Impact of Prebisch's Ideas on Modern Economic Analysis," in *International Economics and Development: Essays in Honor of Rául Prebisch*, ed. Luis Eugenio di Marco (New York: Academic Press, 1972), 20.

35. Benno J. Ndulu, "The Evolution of Global Development Paradigms and Their Influence on African Economic Growth," in *The Political Economy of Economic Growth in Africa 1960–2000*, ed. B. J. Ndulu et al. (Cambridge: Cambridge University Press, 2008), 2:325.

36. Jeff Grischow and Holger Weiss, "Pan-Africanism, Socialism and the Future: Development Planning in Ghana, 1951–1966," in *The Struggle for the Long-Term in Transnational Science and Politics: Forging the Future*, ed. Jenny Andersson and Egle Rindzeviciute (London: Routledge, 2015), 236.

37. Lewis, *Principles of Economic Planning*, 127. For the World Bank, which sponsored Tanzania's initial villagization project, this was in line with modernization theory (see chap. 4).

38. Ibid.

39. William Arthur Lewis, "Colonial Development," in Emmanuel, *Sir William Arthur Lewis Collected Papers 1941–1988*, 761.

40. Ibid., 765.

41. Ibid., 769.

42. Ibid., 775.

43. Ibid., 777–78.

44. William Arthur Lewis, *Report on Industrialization and the Gold Coast* (Accra: Government Printing Department, 1963 [1953]).

45. Ibid., 1.

46. Ibid., 2.

47. Ibid.

48. Ibid., 22.

49. William Arthur Lewis, "Economic Development with Unlimited Supplies of Labour," *Manchester School* 22, no. 2 (May 1954): 131–91, reproduced in Emmanuel, *Sir William Arthur Lewis Collected Papers 1941–1988*, 2:900–60.

50. Ibid., 904.

51. Walter Rodney, *How Europe Underdeveloped Africa* (London: Bogle-L'Ouverture, 1972).

52. Bauer, *Dissent on Development*, 17.

53. Frederick Cooper and Randall M. Packard, "Introduction," in Cooper and Packard, *International Development and the Social Sciences*, 21, points to how the Rockefeller Foundation's global financial support for centers of demographic research in the 1950s produced a cohort of demographers in the 1960s who endorsed population control measures.

54. Bauer, *Dissent on Development*, 37.

55. Ibid., 95. This would be the subject of Dambisa Moyo's much-debated book forty years later, *Dead Aid: Why Aid Is Not Working and How There Is a Better Way for Africa* (London: Allen Lane, 2009). Bauer was not wrong in observing that foreign aid was not designed to facilitate economic growth. In the opening sentence of a draft paper in 1956 entitled "The Objectives of Foreign Aid," Rostow declared that "economic aid is simply a tool of foreign and military policy." Max F. Millikan Papers (AC-0188), Box 10, Folder 343, MIT Archives. But as noted above, others like Singer viewed foreign aid as a moral obligation. Two years after publishing *Dissent on Development*, Nicholas Stern questioned whether Bauer's work was a worthy addition to the field of development arguments. Unlike Bauer, he believed that foreign aid is a moral obligation simply because rich countries have extremely more wealth than poor ones. See Nicholas H. Stern, "Professor Bauer on Development," *Journal of Development Economics* 1 (1974): 191–211.

56. Bauer, *Dissent on Development*, 96, 98.

57. Ibid., 109–10.

58. Ibid., 84.

59. Ibid., 92.

60. Ibid., 111.

61. Bauer, *Reality and Rhetoric*, 18.

62. Ibid., 40.

63. Bauer, *Dissent on Development*, 41.

64. Ibid., 24.

65. P. T. Bauer, *West African Trade: A Study of Competition, Oligarchy, and Monopoly in a Changing Economy* (Cambridge: Cambridge University Press, 1954).

66. Tignor, *W. Arthur Lewis*, 176. On marketing boards in Africa, see Robert H. Bates, *Markets and States in Tropical Africa: The Political Basis of Agricultural Policies* (Berkeley: University of California Press, 2014). Lal, *Poverty of 'Development Economics,'* 172–73, notes the paternalistic attitude of development economists, shared with African and Asian elites, when it came to the ordinary, poor, uneducated masses. It was as if they doubted that ordinary people in the Third World would conform to the expectations of neoclassical economics that people act economically when presented with the opportunity of an advantage.

67. Bauer, *Reality and Rhetoric*, 58.

68. Ibid.

69. See, for example, Allen B. Richard, *European Slave Trading in the Indian Ocean, 1500–1850* (Athens: Ohio University Press, 2014).

70. Bauer, *Dissent on Development*, 78.

71. Killick, *Development Economics in Action*, ix.

72. J. H. Mensah earned a bachelor in economics from the University of London and a master of science in economic theory and development from Stanford University. E. N. Omaboe received his training in economics from the University of Ghana and in statistics from the London School of Economics, where he graduated with first class honors. Both played instrumental roles in Nkrumah's National Planning Commission that worked on Ghana's Seven-Year Development Plan, launched in 1964.

73. With a military government that professed allegiance to the West after the overthrow of Nkrumah, Ghana and the Harvard University Development Advisory Services engaged in a five-year economic consultancy project (1967–72) funded by the Ford Foundation. It was as a member of this Harvard advisory group that Killick visited Ghana in 1969 after his departure from the University of Ghana in 1965. Ford Foundation Records, Ford Grant 07000350, Rockefeller Archives Center.

74. Killick, *Development Economics in Action*, 54–56.

75. Ibid., 58.

76. Tignor, *W. Arthur Lewis*, 190.

77. Bauer, *Dissent on Development*, 158.

78. Killick, *Development Economics in Action*, 26.

79. Zoltán Ginelli, "Hungarian Experts in Nkrumah's Ghana," *Mezosfera*, May 2018, mezosfera.org, especially 47n.

80. Nils Gilman, *Mandarins of the Future: Modernization Theory in Cold War America* (Baltimore: Johns Hopkins University Press, 2003), 72.

81. Ibid., 158.

82. Max F. Millikan Papers (AC-0188), Box 10, Folders 275, 309, 310 & 343, MIT Archives.

83. Kevin T. Baker, "Virtually Nigeria: USAID, Simulated Futures, and the Politics of Postcolonial Expertise, 1964–1980," in Andersson and Rindzeviciute, *The Struggle for the Long-Term in Transnational Science and Politics*, 196.

84. Geoffrey Traugh, "Becoming a 'Central African Denmark': Capitalism and the Agrarian Imagination in Late Colonial Malawi" (Paper presented at the African Studies Association Annual Meeting, Boston, November 21–23, 2019).

85. Ibid.

86. Baker, "Virtually Nigeria," 198.

87. Thandika Mkandawire recounts how he covered this important conference as a young journalist in Malawi. Eager to prepare, he asked Chisiza for a good book to read and was referred to Rostow's *Stages of Economic Growth*. Thandika Mkandawire, *Fifty Years of Independence: Personal Reflections* (Dar es Salaam: Mkuki na Nyota, 2013), 13. On the appeal of Rostow in Africa in the early 1960s, see also, W. T. Newlyn, "'Take-off' Considered in an African Setting," *Yorkshire Bulletin of Economic and Social Research* 13, no. 1 (1961): 19–32.

88. E. F. Jackson, ed., *Economic Development in Africa: Papers Presented to the Nyasaland Economic Symposium Held in Blantyre 18 to 28 July 1962* (Oxford: Basil Blackwell, 1965), 360–68: "Closing Address by Dr. H. K. Banda, Prime Minister of Nyasaland," quote on 360. I am grateful to Geoffrey Traugh for bringing this symposium and publication to my attention.

89. D. K. Chisiza, "The Temper, Aspirations, and Problems of Contemporary Africa," in Jackson, *Economic Development in Africa*, 7.

90. Bauer, *Dissent on Development*, 164–65.

91. Killick, *Development Economics in Action*, 26.

92. Africa Confidential, "J. H. Mensah, 1928–2018," *Africa Confidential* 60, no. 1 (January 11, 2019). Obituary.

93. Killick, *Development Economics in Action*, 40.

94. Lewis's correspondence with Nkrumah on the Volta River Project dates at least to 1953. By 1956, there were signs that Nkrumah was determined to press on with the project even as the British government became lukewarm and the terms offered by the aluminum companies changed, much to the concern of Lewis. Lewis had provided guidelines for Ghana's negotiations on the Volta Project and when to step back if the project became uneconomical. See W. Arthur Lewis Papers, MC 092, Box 10, Folder 3. Seely G. Mudd Manuscript Library, Princeton University.

95. Douglas Rimmer, *Staying Poor: Ghana's Political Economy, 1950–1990* (New York: Pergamon Press, 1992), 63. See also, Killick, *Development Economics in Action*, 36.

96. Tignor, *W. Arthur Lewis*, 136–38. In a letter dated November 4, 1957, Nkrumah outlined to Lewis the scope of his work as economic adviser. This included framing a five-year development plan, the Volta River Project, the development of industries (particularly smaller industries), and the construction of the new port at Tema and the new township of Tema. W. Arthur Lewis Papers, MC 092, Box 10, Folder 3.

97. Lewis to Nkrumah, May 29, 1957. W. Arthur Lewis Papers, MC092, Box 10, Folder 3.

98. It is odd that Nkrumah's offer to Lewis of a chair in economics position at the University of Ghana was made in the postscript of a letter that discussed the state of negotiations over the Volta River Project (Nkrumah to Lewis, April 2, 1957). Lewis politely declined in his reply of April 16, 1957. W. Arthur Lewis Papers, MC 092, Box 10, Folder 3.

99. Tignor, *W. Arthur Lewis*, 152. The perception of Lewis as procapitalist and pro-Western was in evidence in February and March 1965, when Britain and the United States pressured Lewis to put together a development plan for British Guiana on short notice after its Marxist prime minister, Dr. C. B. Jagan, was defeated in elections. William Arthur Lewis to Dr. Amos Manor, March 19, 1965, W. Arthur Lewis Papers, MC 092, Box 9, Folder 4.

100. Stephan F. Miescher, "'Nkrumah's Baby': The Akosombo Dam and the Dream of Development in Ghana, 1952–1966," *Water History* 6 (2014): 341–66.

101. Tignor, *W. Arthur Lewis*, 154.

102. W. Arthur Lewis to Kwame Nkrumah, October 31, 1958. W. Arthur Lewis Papers, MC 092, Box 10, Folder 3.

103. Kwame Nkrumah to W. Arthur Lewis, November 1, 1958. W. Arthur Lewis Papers, MC 092, Box 10, Folder 3.

104. Rimmer, *Staying Poor*, 10.

105. W. Arthur Lewis Papers, MC 092, Box 21, Folder 7: "Second Development Plan, Analysis by Lewis, 1958."

106. Ibid.

107. Lewis to Nkrumah, December 18, 1958. W. Lewis Papers, MC092, Box 10, Folder 3. See also, Tignor, *W. Arthur Lewis*, 169–73, on the deteriorating relations between Lewis and Nkrumah.

108. Nkrumah to Lewis, December 19, 1958. W. Arthur Lewis Papers, MC092, Box 10, Folder 3.

109. Government of Ghana, *Seven-Year Development Plan 1963/64 to 1969/70* (Accra: Office of the Planning Commission, 1964), vi.

110. Ginelli, "Hungarian Experts in Nkrumah's Ghana."

111. Ibid.

112. Tignor, *W. Arthur Lewis*, 185–86.

113. Ibid., 187. It is interesting to set this list side-by-side with those who attended the Nyasaland Symposium on Economic Development in Africa. Kaldor and Raj attended both meetings. Present in Nyasaland but not invited to Ghana was Bauer. Jackson, *Economic Development in Africa.*

114. Killick, *Development Economics in Action*, 53.

115. Tignor, *W. Arthur Lewis*, 190.

116. Ibid., 189.

117. Ghana, *Seven-Year Development Plan*, 53, notes that "of the total of £G700 million [Ghana pounds] earned from the export of cocoa in the period 1951 to 1961 the cocoa farmers have received £G420 million while the remaining £G280 million has gone to man the public services, to finance development and to build up the external reserves of Ghana."

118. Tignor, *W. Arthur Lewis*, 192. For Lal, *Poverty of 'Development Economics,'* the ideas of the field were theoretical fads, and he believes that neoclassical economics, especially its branch of welfare economics, would have been capacious enough to guide the aspirations of development economists.

119. Killick, *Development Economics in Action*, 53.

120. Rimmer, *Staying Poor*, 69.

121. Peter Marden, *The Ivory Coast: Economic Miracle or Blocked Development? Implications for the Geography of Development* (Melbourne: Monash University, 1990), 1.

122. Bamba, *African Miracle, African Mirage.*

123. Woronoff, *West African Wager.*

124. Samir Amin, *Le développement du capitalisme en Côte d'Ivoire* (Paris: Editions de Minuit, 1967); and Samir Amin, *Neo-colonialism in West Africa*, trans. Francis McDonagh (Harmondsworth, Middlesex: Penguin Books, 1973), 45.

125. Bamba, *African Miracle, African Mirage*, 63. Bamba comments that on Houphouët-Boigny's visit to the United States in 1959 as part of a French UN delegation, he reportedly told the American President Dwight D. Eisenhower to decline aid to African countries that had sought assistance from communist countries.

126. Bamba, *African Miracle, African Mirage*, 23. Frederick Cooper, "Modernizing Bureaucrats, Backward Africans, and the Development Concept," 73, notes that by the early 1950s the Ivory Coast accounted for 40 percent of exports from French West Africa, representing 64 percent of foreign exchange earnings from the region.

127. Bamba, *African Miracle, African Mirage.*

128. Ibid., 71.

129. The influence of Rostow's model of the stages of economic growth and the TVA are examined by Bamba, *Ivorian Miracle, Ivorian Mirage*, chap. 4. Ivorian politicians visited the TVA's headquarters in Knoxville in 1963, and by the Rostovian model, the Ivory Coast envisaged that it would reach self-sustaining economic growth in 1975.

130. In short, embodying the liabilities examined in James C. Scott, *Seeing like a State: How Certain Schemes to Improve the Human Condition Have Failed* (New Haven, CT: Yale University Press, 1998). It is instructive that in their typology of African rulers of the early independence era, Jackson and Rosberg label Houphouët-Boigny as an "autocrat." Robert H. Jackson and Carl G. Rosberg, *Personal Rule in Black Africa: Prince, Autocrat, Prophet, Tyrant* (Berkeley: University of California Press, 1982).

131. Samir Amin, "Capitalism and Development in the Ivory Coast," in *African Politics and Society: Basic Issues and Problems of Government and Development*, ed. Irving L. Markovitz (New York: Free Press, 1970), 288.

132. Amin, "Capitalism and Development in the Ivory Coast," 283.

133. Bamba, *African Miracle, African Mirage*, 129.

134. Ibid., 180–81.

135. Robert M. Hecht, "The Ivory Coast Economic 'Miracle': What Benefits for Peasant Farmers?" *Journal of Modern African Studies* 21, no. 1 (1983): 25–53.

136. See Andre Gunder Frank, *Latin America: Underdevelopment or Revolution* (New York: Monthly Review Press, 1969); and Andre Gunder Frank, *Crisis in the Third World* (New York: Holmes and Meier, 1981).

137. William Arthur Lewis, *The Evolution of Foreign Aid* (Inaugural David Owen Memorial Lecture, University College, Cardiff, November 9, 1971), 18.

138. Bamba, *African Miracle, African Mirage*, 180.

139. Killick, *Development Economics in Action*, 27.

140. W. W. Rostow, "The Historian and the Analysis of Economic Growth" (n.d.), 13, Millikan Papers, Box 10, Folder 314, MIT Archives.

141. Killick, *Development Economics in Action*, 127. See also, Bauer, *Dissent on Development*.

142. See, for example, Keri Lambert, "'It's All Work and Happiness on the Farms': Agricultural Development between the Blocs in Nkrumah's Ghana," *Journal of African History* 60, no. 1 (2019): 25–44; Jeffrey S. Ahlman, "A New Type of Citizen: Youth, Gender, and Generation in the Ghanaian Builders Brigade," *Journal of African History* 53, no. 1 (2012): 87–105; Piet Konings, "Capitalist Rice Farming and Land Allocation in Northern Ghana," *Journal of Legal Pluralism and Unofficial Law* 16, no. 22 (1984): 89–119; and P. Hodge, "The Ghana Workers Brigade: A Project for Unemployed Youth," *British Journal of Sociology* 15, no. 2 (1964): 113–28.

143. Albert O. Hirschman, "The Rise and Decline of Development Economics," in *The Essential Hirschman*, ed. Jeremy Adelman (Princeton, NJ: Princeton University Press, 2013), 61.

144. Tignor, *W. Arthur Lewis*, 58–59.

145. William Arthur Lewis to David Owen, Executive Chairman, UN Technical Assistance Board (New York), February 3, 1958. W. Arthur Lewis Papers, MC 092, Box 10, Series 2, Folder 5.

146. Douglas Rimmer, "Learning about Economic Development from Africa," *African Affairs* 102, no. 408 (2003): 469–91.

147. Baker, "Virtually Nigeria," 199.

148. Ibid. Wolfgang Frederick Stolper, *Planning without Facts: Lessons in Resource Allocation from Nigeria's Development: With an Input-Output Analysis of the Nigerian Economy, 1959–60* (Cambridge, MA: Harvard University Press, 1966). On the persistence of poor statistics into the present, see Morten Jerven, *Poor Numbers: How We Are Misled by African Development Statistics and What to Do about It* (Ithaca, NY: Cornell University Press, 2013).

149. Polly Hill, *Development Economics on Trial: The Anthropological Case for a Prosecution* (Cambridge: Cambridge University Press, 1986), xii–xiii.

150. Ibid., 145.

151. Ibid., xii–xiii.

152. Hirschman, "Rise and Decline of Development Economics," 66.

153. William Arthur Lewis, *Politics in West Africa* (Toronto: Oxford University Press, 1965), 12.

154. Ibid., 86.

155. African Export-Import Bank, *Coming of Age: 25 Years of the African Export-Import Bank* (Cairo: African Export-Import Bank, 2018), 23.

156. Patrick Manning, *Francophone Sub-Saharan Africa 1880–1995* (Cambridge: Cambridge University Press, 1998), chap. 5. See also, John Waterbury, "Dimensions of State Intervention

in the Groundnut Basin," in *The Political Economy of Risk and Choice in Senegal*, ed. John Waterbury and Mark Gersovitz (London: Frank Cass, 1987), 188–222.

157. Manning, *Francophone Sub-Saharan Africa*, 126.

158. African Export-Import Bank, *25 Years of the African Export-Import Bank*, 24.

159. Tony Killick, *A Reaction Too Far: Economic Theory and the Role of the State in Developing Countries* (London: Overseas Development Institute, 1989), 7–11.

160. Samir Amin, *Only People Make Their Own History: Writings on Capitalism, Imperialism, and Revolution* (New York: Monthly Review Press, 2019), 45.

161. Marion Fourcade, *Economists and Societies: Discipline and Profession in the United States, Britain, and France, 1890s to 1990s* (Princeton, NJ: Princeton University Press, 2009), xii. Fourcade is here citing the American economist Wassily Leontief.

162. Ibid., xi–xii.

163. Paul Krugman, "The Fall and Rise of Development Economics," Massachusetts Institute of Technology, 2012, https://web.mit.edu/krugman/www/dishpan.html.

164. Ibid., 6.

165. Ibid.

166. Hirschman, "Rise and Decline of Development Economics," 50–51.

167. Krugman, "Fall and Rise of Development Economics," 6.

168. Moses Abramovitz to W. Arthur Lewis, October 17, 1979. W. Arthur Lewis Papers, MC 092, Box 2 Folder 3.

169. Fourcade, *Economists and Societies*, xii.

170. Ibid., xiii.

171. Ibid., 5.

172. Ibid., 8.

173. Ibid., 10.

174. Ibid., 11.

175. Killick, *A Reaction Too Far*, 7.

176. Killick, Development Economics in Action, 11.

4. Pan-African Socialism

1. Kwame Nkrumah, *Ghana: The Autobiography of Kwame Nkrumah* (New York: International, 1976 [1957]), 12.

2. Léopold Sédar Senghor, *On African Socialism*, trans. with introduction by Mercer Cook (New York: Praeger, 1964 [1961]), 26. This was written after 1956, when Senghor shifted from endeavoring to package Marx for the African context to being a critic of Marxism. Gary Wilder, *Freedom Time: Negritude, Decolonization, and the Future of the World* (Durham, NC: Duke University, 2015), 218.

3. Issa G. Shivji, Saida Yahya-Othman, and Ng'wanza Kamaya, *Development as Rebellion: A Biography of Julius Nyerere* (Dar es Salaam: Mkuki na Nyota, 2020), 1:274.

4. Sékou Touré in conversation with US ambassador William Attwood, Conakry, May 3, 1961. Incoming telegram from Conakry to Department of State; dispatched May 4, 1961, received May 5, 1961. John F. Kennedy Presidential Library and Museum, Papers of President Kennedy, National Security Files, Countries, Box 102, 1961.

5. Roger Genoud, *Nationalism and Economic Development in Ghana* (New York: Frederick A. Praeger, 1969), 4.

6. Ladipo Adamolekun, "The Socialist Experience in Guinea," in *Socialism in Sub-Saharan Africa: A New Assessment,* ed. Carl G. Rosberg and Thomas M. Callaghy (Berkeley: University of California Press, 1979), 61–82.

7. Wilder, *Freedom Time,* 236, notes that the imprisonment of Dia in 1962 "marked the collapse of Senghor's postwar vision of African socialism."

8. Mamadou Diouf, "Senegalese Development: From Mass Mobilization to Technocratic Elitism," in *International Development and the Social Sciences: Essays on the History and Politics of Knowledge,* ed. Frederick Cooper and Randall M. Packard (Berkeley: University of California Press, 1997), 314.

9. Samir Amin, *The Long Revolution of the Global South: Toward a New Anti-imperialist International,* trans. James Membrez (New York: Monthly Review Press, 2019), 124.

10. Frantz Fanon, *Toward the African Revolution,* trans. Haakon Chevalier (New York: Grove Press, 1967 [1964]), 186.

11. See, for example, Andrew Apter, "Socialism, Africa," *International Encyclopedia of the Social Sciences,* vol. 7, 2nd ed. (Detroit: Macmillan Reference, 2008), 638–42. Samir Amin in 1971 distinguished between "an apparently radical socialism" and the "more moderate approach of African socialism." Samir Amin, *Neo-colonialism in West Africa,* trans. Francis McDonagh (Harmondsworth, Middlesex: Penguin Books, 1973), 48–49.

12. This paper was presented as the LEAP Lecture at the University of Stellenbosch on October 25, 2017, and was subsequently published as "African Socialism; or, the Search for an Indigenous Model of Economic Development?" *Economic History of Developing Regions* 33, no. 1 (2018): 69–87.

13. Thandika Mkandawire notes how for the first generation of independent African leaders, "development" was a theoretical legitimization and central preoccupation. Thandika Mkandawire, "Thinking about Developmental States in Africa," *Cambridge Journal of Economics* 25, no. 3 (2001): 295.

14. American Embassy Conakry to Secretary of State, Washington, DC, December 28, 1961. John F. Kennedy Library and Museum, Papers of President Kennedy. National Security Files, Countries, Box 102.

15. Frederick Cooper, "Modernizing Bureaucrats, Backward Africans, and the Development Concept," in Cooper and Packard, *International Development and the Social Sciences,* 64.

16. Genoud, *Nationalism and Economic Development in Ghana,* 12, 85; and Andrew Coulson, *Tanzania: A Political Economy,* 2nd ed. (Oxford: Oxford University Press, 2013), 179.

17. Fanon was disappointed by Senghor's support of France in the Algerian war of independence and described Houphouët-Boigny as "objectively the most conscious curb on the evolution and the liberation of Africa." See, respectively, Frantz Fanon, *The Wretched of the* Earth, trans. Constance Harrington (New York: Grove Press, 1968 [1961]), 235; and Fanon, *Toward the African Revolution,* 183.

18. Erez Manela, *The Wilsonian Moment: Self-Determination and the International Origins of Anticolonial Nationalism* (Oxford: Oxford University Press, 2007).

19. Ibid., 40–42.

20. Ibid., 43.

21. American wartime propaganda was unprecedented, spread through burgeoning international news agencies such as Reuters, Havas, and Associated Press, and cable telegraph and wireless radio technology. See Daniel R. Headrick, *The Tentacles of Progress: Technology Transfer in the Age of Imperialism, 1850–1940* (New York: Oxford University Press, 1988). Manela

notes that "millions of pamphlets extolling American ideals and life in dozens of languages, were printed and circulated at home and abroad." Manela, *Wilsonian Moment*, 48–49.

22. Though written in 1916, the ninety-page pamphlet was not published until the middle of 1917. For a recent reprint with an introduction by Doug Lorimer, see V. I. Lenin, *Imperialism, The Highest Stage of Capitalism* (Chippendale, Australia: Resistance Books, 1999).

23. Adom Getachew, *Worldmaking after Empire: The Rise and Fall of Self-Determination* (Princeton, NJ: Princeton University Press, 2019), 37–38; and Manela, *Wilsonian Moment*, 37.

24. Manela, *Wilsonian Moment*, 62.

25. Ibid., 60. The first Pan-African Congress was convened in 1900 in London by the West Indian lawyer Henry Sylvester-Williams. On the Pan-African movement, see George Padmore, *Pan-Africanism or Communism? The Coming Struggle for Africa* (New York: Roy, 1956); and J. Ayodele Langley, *Pan-Africanism and Nationalism in West Africa, 1900–1945* (Oxford: Clarendon Press, 1973).

26. Manela, *Wilsonian Moment*, 60.

27. Ibid., 138–39.

28. Ibid., 26–29.

29. Getachew, *Worldmaking after Empire*, 10.

30. Manela, *Wilsonian Moment*, 7.

31. Robin D. G. Kelley, *Freedom Dreams: The Black Radical Imagination* (Boston: Beacon Press, 2002), 44.

32. V. I. Lenin, *Two Tactics of Social Democracy in the Democratic Revolution* (Peking: Foreign Language Press, 1965). Reprinted from V. I. Lenin, *Selected Works*, English ed. (Moscow: Foreign Language Press, 1952).

33. Fritz Schatten, *Communism in Africa* (London: George Allen and Unwin, 1966), 54.

34. V. I. Lenin, *"Left-Wing" Communism, an Infantile Disorder* (New York: International, 1940 [1920]).

35. Manela, *Wilsonian Moment*, 225.

36. Emmanuel Asiedu-Acquah, "Youth Culture and Popular Politics in Ghana, c.1900 to Recent Times" (PhD diss., Department of History, Harvard University, 2015).

37. Leo Spitzer and LaRay Denzer, "I. T. A. Wallace-Johnson and the West African Youth League," *International Journal of African Historical Studies* 6, no. 3 (1973): 413–52.

38. Getachew, *Worldmaking after Empire*, 7, 51.

39. In the scramble and partition of Africa at the end of the nineteenth century, Italy had been soundly defeated by Ethiopia at the Battle of Adwa in 1896. Its national pride blemished, Italy had long waited to avenge itself of the ignominy of defeat at the hands of an African state. See George Webster Baer, *Test Case: Italy, Ethiopia, and the League of Nations* (Stanford: Hoover Institution Press, 1976).

40. Getachew, *Worldmaking after Empire*, especially chap. 2.

41. See, for examples, Roger Thomas, "Forced Labour in British West Africa: The Case of the Northern Territories of the Gold Coast, 1906–1927," *Journal of African History* 14, no. 1 (1973): 79–103; Alexander Keese, "Slow Abolition within the Colonial Mind: British and French Debates about 'Vagrancy,' 'African Laziness,' and Forced Labor in West Central and South Central Africa, 1945–1965," *International Review of Social History* 59, no. 3 (2014): 377–407.

42. "Memorandum by the Italian Government on the Situation in Ethiopia," September 11, 1935, in League of Nations, Official Journal, 88th and 89th Council Sessions. As cited in Getachew, *Worldmaking after Empire*, 64–65.

43. Basil Davidson, *Modern Africa: A Political and Social History*, 2nd ed. (London: Longman, 1989), 60–61.

44. J. Calvitt Clarke III, "Soviet Appeasement, Collective Security, and the Italo-Ethiopian War of 1935 and 1936," in *Collision of Empires: Italy's Invasion of Ethiopia and Its International Impact*, ed. G. Bruce Strang (Surrey, UK: Ashgate, 2013), 261–86.

45. Ibid., 283–84.

46. Ibid., 280. See also, Sergius Yakobson, "The Soviet Union and Ethiopia: A Case of Traditional Behavior," *Review of Politics* 25, no. 3 (1963): 329–42.

47. Schatten, *Communism in Africa*, chap. 5. Communist China's activities in Africa under Mao Zedong privileged the training and arming of liberation movements and the spread of communist propaganda through radio and print. See Donovan C. Chau, *Exploiting Africa: The Influence of Maoist China in Algeria, Ghana, and Tanzania* (Annapolis, MD: Naval Institute Press, 2014).

48. Brent Hayes Edwards, *The Practice of Diaspora: Literature, Translation, and the Rise of Black Internationalism* (Cambridge, MA: Harvard University Press, 2003), 241–305.

49. Kelley, *Freedom Dreams*, chap. 2, points to the political trajectories of other African Americans and West Indians in the United States, such as Otto Huiswood and Claude McKay, who were drawn into international communist networks in the early 1920s.

50. On Soviet appeasement of Italy, see Clarke III, "Soviet Appeasement, Collective Security, and the Italo-Ethiopian War."

51. On Padmore's life and political thought, see Edwards, *Practice of Diaspora*, chap. 5; Leslie James, *George Padmore and Decolonization from Below: Pan-Africanism, the Cold War, and the End of Empire* (New York: Palgrave Macmillan, 2015); Fitzroy Baptiste and Rupert Lewis, eds., *George Padmore: Pan-African Revolutionary* (Kingston: Ian Randle, 2009); and Getachew, *Worldmaking after Empire*. The similar itinerant trajectories of Wallace-Johnson and Padmore point to the mobile circuits of the Third International.

52. Davidson, *Modern Africa*, 78–79. See also, Fred I. A. Omu, *Press and Politics in Nigeria, 1880–1937* (London: Longman, 1978), 239.

53. Nkrumah, *Autobiography*, 27.

54. Marika Sherwood, *Kwame Nkrumah: The Years Abroad 1935–1947* (Accra: Freedom, 1996), chap. 8. This was the first Pan-African congress that had significant African participation. Indeed, the most generous contribution to the congress's expenses came from the Gold Coast Farmers' Delegation. Hakim Adi and Marika Sherwood, *The 1945 Manchester Pan-African Congress Revisited* (London: New Beacon Books, 1995).

55. Adi and Sherwood, *1945 Manchester Pan-African Congress Revisited*. On Manchester's attractiveness for multiracial gatherings, see Marika Sherwood, *Manchester and the 1945 Pan-African Congress* (London: Savannah Press, 1995).

56. Sherwood, *Kwame Nkrumah*, 116.

57. Getachew, *Worldmaking after Empire*, 72.

58. Joseph Appiah, *Joe Appiah: The Autobiography of an African Patriot* (Accra: Asempa, 1990), 166–67; and Nkrumah, *Autobiography*, 52–53.

59. Edwards, *Practice of Diaspora*, 282–83.

60. Cyril K. Daddieh, "Ethnicity, Conflict and the State in Contemporary West Africa," in *Themes in West Africa's History*, ed. Emmanuel Akyeampong (Athens: Ohio University Press, 2006), 265–85.

61. Sindiso Mfenyana, *Walking with Giants: Life and Times of an ANC Veteran* (Cape Town: South African History Online, 2017), 120–21.

62. Interview with Advocate Nathaniel Mashilo Masemola, Somerset West, Western Cape Province, South Africa, February 2, 2021.

63. Sékou F. Doumbouya and Fodé Camara, "Explaining Economic Growth in Africa: The Case of Guinea," in *The Political Economy of Economic Growth in Africa 1960–2000*, ed. Benno J. Ndulu et al. (Cambridge: Cambridge University Press, 2008), 2:600, 608–9.

64. Mansour Ndiaye, "State Control and Poor Economic Growth Performance in Senegal," in Ndulu et al., *Political Economy of Economic Growth in Africa*, 401–25.

65. Genoud, *Nationalism and Economic Development in Ghana*, 46.

66. Ibid., 22.

67. A reality noted by Douglas Rimmer, *Staying Poor: Ghana's Political Economy, 1950–1990* (New York: Pergamon Press, 1992), 4.

68. Genoud, *Nationalism and Economic Development in Ghana*, 23.

69. Coulson, *Tanzania*, 33.

70. Ibid., 179–81. The thirty-six independent nation-states in the OAU had passed a resolution that, short of Britain showing concrete evidence that it was working to reverse the UDI and put Southern Rhodesia firmly on the road to majority rule by December 15, 1965, they would sever diplomatic relations with Britain. Britain did nothing to convince the African countries of this commitment, so Nyerere explained in an address to Tanzania's National Assembly on December 14, 1965, that it was a matter of honor for Tanzania to sever diplomatic relations with Britain. If Africa ignored its own resolutions, how could it be taken seriously in the international context, Nyerere queried. "The President Mwalimu Julius K. Nyerere's Address to the National Assembly" (Dar es Salaam, National, 1965). CCM Library, Dodoma, Tanzania.

71. Thandika Mkandawire, *Fifty Years of Independence: Personal Reflections* (Dar es Salaam: Mkuki na Nyota, 2013), 35–36. See also, Kathryn Sikkink, "Development Ideas in Latin America: Paradigm Shift and the Economic Commission for Latin America," in Cooper and Packard, *International Development and the Social Sciences*, 228–56.

72. "Unification Is Master Key to Africa's Future," *Ghana Today*, vol. 6, no. 2, March 28, 1962. Nkrumah at the opening of a conference of African farmers' organizations at the University of Ghana, Legon.

73. Ibid.

74. Mkandawire, "Thinking about Developmental States in Africa," 290–91.

75. Ibid.

76. Chambi Seithy Chachage and Chachage Seithy L. Chachage, "Nyerere: Nationalism and Post-colonial Developmentalism," *African Sociological Review* 8, no. 2 (2004): 163.

77. Kathryn Sikkink, "Development Ideas in Latin America: Paradigm Shift and the Economic Commission for Latin America," in Cooper and Packard, *International Development and the Social Sciences*; and Aldo Antonio Dadone and Luis Eugenio di Marco, "The Impact of Prebisch's Ideas on Modern Economic Analysis," in *International Economics and Development: Essays in Honor of Raúl Prebisch*, ed. Luis Eugenio di Marco (New York: Academic Press, 1972).

78. Martha Finnemore, "Redefining Development at the World Bank," in Cooper and Packard, *International Development and the Social Sciences*, 203–27.

79. Sikkink, "Development Ideas in Latin America," 231. See Raúl Prebisch, *The Economic Development of Latin America and Its Principal Problems* (Santiago: Economic Commission for Latin America and the Caribbean, 1950).

80. Sikkink, "Development Ideas in Latin America," 229.

81. Mkandawire, *Fifty Years of Independence*, 22.

82. Diouf, "Senegalese Development," 294.

83. For Prebisch, regional integration represented the most coherent response to the underdevelopment of Latin America. Dadone and de Marco, "Impact of Prebisch's Ideas on Modern Economic Analysis," 20.

84. Genoud, *Nationalism and Economic Development in Ghana*, 4.

85. Ibid., 74.

86. This observation is based on the CPP's *Program of the Convention People's Party for Work and Happiness* (Accra: Government Printer, 1962) and the Seven-Year Development Plan proposed in 1963–64 for the period 1964–70. Genoud asserts that "neither the CPP Program of 1962 nor the Seven-Year Development Plan of 1963 represent a fundamental departure from previous strategical options. Although more systemically presented, if not always implemented, the strategy remained essentially the same after 1961 as before 1961." Ibid., 83–84.

87. Kwesi Jonah, "Imperialism, the State and the Indigenization of the Ghanaian Economy 1957–84," *African Development* 10, no. 3 (1985): 66.

88. Genoud, *Nationalism and Economic Development in Ghana*, 132–33.

89. William F. Steel, "Import Substitution and Excess Capacity in Ghana," *Oxford Economic Papers* 24, no. 2 (1972): 212–40.

90. Kwame Akyeampong, *Educational Expansion in Ghana: A Review of 50 Years of Challenge and Progress* (University of Sussex Centre for International Education, Monograph No. 33, 2020), 1–2. On education in Ghana under Nkrumah, see also, H. O. A. McWilliam and M. A. Kwamena-Poh, *The Development of Education in Ghana* (London: Longman, 1975).

91. Genoud, *Nationalism and Economic Development in Ghana*, 219.

92. Albert O. Hirschman, "The Political Economy of Import-Substituting Industrialization in Latin America," *Quarterly Journal of Economics* 62 (1968): 1–32.

93. Steel, "Import Substitution," 213. See also, Charles Ackah, Charles Adjosi, and Festus Turkson, "Industrial Policy in Ghana: Its Evolution and Impact," in *Manufacturing Transformation: Comparative Studies of Industrial Development in Africa and Emerging Asia*, ed. Carol Newman et al. (Oxford: Oxford University Press, 2016), 50–70.

94. Schatten, *Communism in Africa*, 159.

95. Cited in Obed Yao Asamoah, *The Political History of Ghana (1950–2013): The Experience of a Non-conformist* (Bloomington: AuthorHouse, 2014), 77.

96. Cited in Schatten, *Communism in Africa*, 161.

97. Nana Osei-Opare, "Uneasy Comrades: Postcolonial Statecraft, Race, and Citizenship, Ghana-Soviet Relations, 1957–1966," *Journal of West African History* 5, no. 2 (2019): 87.

98. Zoltán Ginelli, "Hungarian Experts in Nkrumah's Ghana," *Mezosfera*, May 2018, mezosfera.org.

99. Steel, "Import Substitution," 217–18.

100. E. N. Omaboe, "An Introductory Survey," in *A Study of Contemporary Ghana*, ed. Walter Birmingham, I. Neustadt, and E. N. Omaboe, vol. 1, *The Economy of Ghana* (London: George Allen and Unwin, 1966), 29–31.

101. Steel, "Import Substitution," 214.

102. Genoud, *Nationalism and Economic Development in Ghana*, 143.

103. Jonah, "Indigenization of the Ghanaian Economy," 67.

104. Ibid., 76.

105. PRAAD, Accra, ADM 5/3/114. Local Purchasing of Cocoa.

106. PRAAD, Accra, ADM 5/3/154. Republic of Ghana, "Report of the Commission of Enquiry into the circumstances surrounding the establishment of the Ghana Cargo Handling Company."

107. Jonah, "Indigenization of the Ghanaian Economy."

108. Steel, "Import Substitution," 232.

109. Booth and Golooba-Mutebi point to how the government of Rwanda, or more accurately, the present Rwandan Patriotic Front (RPF) regime, has used party-funded businesses such as Tri-Star Investments, Crystal Ventures Ltd., the military investment company Horizon, and the public-private consortium Rwanda Investment Group to pioneer investments in critical areas of social need after the 1994 genocide destroyed Rwanda's economy and made it unattractive to external investors. The operations of these outfits have built entrepreneurial and business management capacity, and the spillover effect has been seen in a "crowding in" rather than a "crowding out" of local firms. David Booth and Frederick Golooba-Mutebi, "Developmental Patrimonialism? The Case of Rwanda," *African Affairs* 111, no. 444 (2012): 379–403.

110. Genoud, *Nationalism and Economic Development in Ghana*, 215.

111. Ibid., 215–16.

112. Steel, "Import Substitution," 236.

113. Hirschman, "Political Economy of Import-Substituting Industrialization," 29.

114. Chachage and Chachage, "Nationalism and Post-colonial Developmentalism."

115. Nkunde Mwase and Benno J. Ndulu, "Tanzania: Explaining Four Decades of Episodic Growth," in Ndulu et al., *Political Economy of Economic Growth in Africa*, 2:427.

116. Coulson, *Tanzania*, 34. Coulson's *Tanzania* provides the spine for the following discussion of Tanzania's political economy.

117. Shivji, Yahya-Othman, and Kamaya, *Biography of Julius Nyerere*, 3:233.

118. Coulson, *Tanzania*, 179.

119. Ibid., 180.

120. Issa G. Shivji, "The Village in Mwalimu's Thought and Political Practice," in *Africa's Liberation: The Legacy of Julius Nyerere*, ed. Chambi Chachage and Annar Cassam (Cape Town: Pambazuka Press, 2010), 121.

121. Finnemore, "Redefining Development at the World Bank."

122. Shivji, "The Village in Mwalimu's Thought and Political Practice," 123.

123. Ibid., 132. Ironically, the bureaucratic bourgeoisie that emerged through the Africanization of the state, the nationalization of foreign businesses, and the proliferation of state-owned enterprises would be the same bureaucratic bourgeoisie to oversee the dismantling of the socialist state and the liberalization of the economy after 1985. Chambi Chachage, "A Capitalizing City: Dar es Salaam and the Emergence of an African Entrepreneurial Elite (c.1862–2015)" (PhD diss., Department of African and African American Studies, Harvard University, 2018).

124. Coulson, *Tanzania*, 206–10.

125. Ibid., 183.

126. Mwase and Ndulu, "Tanzania," 431.

127. Julius K. Nyerere, "The Arusha Declaration," chap. 2 in *Ujamaa: Essays on Socialism* (London: Oxford University Press, 1968). See also, Samuel Wangwe et al., "The Performance of the Manufacturing Sector in Tanzania: Challenges and the Way Forward" (WIDER Working Paper 2014/085, 2014, www.wider.unu.edu).

128. Nyerere, *Ujamaa*, 12.

129. Coulson, *Tanzania*, 217.

130. Shivji, "The Village in Mwalimu's Thought and Political Practice," 122–23; Julius K. Nyerere, *The Arusha Declaration Ten Years Later* (Dar es Salaam: United Republic of Tanzania, 1977), 41–42.

131. Dean E. McHenry Jr., "The Struggle for Rural Socialism in Tanzania," in Rosberg and Callaghy, *Socialism in Sub-Saharan Africa*, 37–60.

132. Coulson, *Tanzania*, 219.

133. Nyerere, *The Arusha Declaration*, 19.

134. Ibid., 33.

135. Coulson, *Tanzania*, 234.

136. Ibid., 328.

137. Ibid., 228–30.

138. Mwase and Ndulu, "Tanzania," 427.

139. McHenry Jr., "Struggle for Rural Socialism in Tanzania," 60.

140. Coulson, *Tanzania*, 364.

141. Ibid., 365. See also, Finnemore, "Redefining Development at the World Bank."

142. Coulson, *Tanzania*, 3; and Shivji, Yahya-Othman, and Kamaya, *Biography of Julius Nyerere*, 3:283. Shivji, Yahya-Othman, and Kamaya, *Biography of Julius Nyerere*, 1:209, notes how Nyerere "would launch caustic attacks on the IMF from the early 1960s."

143. Shivji, Yahya-Othman, and Kamaya, *Biography of Julius Nyerere*, 3:275–76.

144. Mwase and Ndulu, "Tanzania," 432.

145. Alex Akurgo, *Kwame Nkrumah: A Story from the CIA Files* (Accra: Staricom, 2018).

146. Genoud, *Nationalism and Economic Development in Ghana*, 139–140.

147. Lansiné Kaba, *Kwame Nkrumah and the Dream of African Unity* (New York: Diasporic Africa Press, 2017), 93. On the Declaration of the Ghana-Guinea Union on May 1, 1959, see Colin Legum, *Pan-Africanism: A Short Political Guide* (New York: Frederick A. Praeger, 1962), 160–61.

148. Mohamed Saliou Camara, *Political History of Guinea since World War Two* (New York: Peter Lang, 2014), 105.

149. Ibid., 122.

150. Ahmed Sékou Touré, *Africa on the Move* (London: Panaf Books, 1979), 82.

151. Camara, *Political History of Guinea*, 118.

152. Lansiné Kaba, "Guinean Politics: A Critical Review History," *Journal of Modern African Studies* 15, no. 1 (1977): 36.

153. Ibid., 37.

154. Department of State, Memorandum of Conversation with Guinean delegation including Moussa Diakité, Governor of the Central Bank, and Mamadou Bah, Director of the National Credit Bank, May 1, 1962. Papers of President John F. Kennedy, National Security Files, Countries, Box 102, Guinea. John F. Kennedy Presidential Library and Museum.

155. On the "Teachers' strike," see James D. Straker, *Youth, Nationalism, and the Guinean Revolution* (Bloomington: Indiana University Press, 2009), chap. 3.

156. Schatten, *Communism in Africa*, chap. 8.

157. Philip E. Muehlenbeck, *Betting on the Africans: John F. Kennedy's Courting of African Nationalist Leaders* (Oxford: Oxford University Press, 2012).

158. Twenty-eight African heads of state visited the White House during Kennedy's presidency. Ibid., xv.

159. See profile of William Attwood in Spartacus Educational, which profiles international personalities and historical figures (www.spartacus-educational.com/JFKattwood.htm).

160. Papers of President Kennedy. National Security Files, Countries, Box 102 (1961). Incoming Telegram from Conakry (Attwood) to Department of State, Dispatch May 4, Received May 5, 1961. Kennedy Presidential Library and Museum.

161. Ibid.

162. Muehlenbeck, *Betting on the Africans*, 63.

163. Incoming Telegram from Conakry to Secretary of State, received June 2, 1961. Papers of President Kennedy, National Security Files, Countries, Box 102, Guinea. Kennedy Presidential Library and Museum.

164. Department of State, Memorandum of Conversation with Guinean delegation including Moussa Diakité, Governor of the Central Bank, and Mamadou Bah, Director of the National Credit Bank, May 1, 1962. Papers of President Kennedy, National Security Files, Countries, Box 102, Guinea. Kennedy Presidential Library and Museum.

165. William Attwood to George Ball, "The Current Situation in Guinea and Its Implications for U.S. Policy," May 12, 1961. Papers of President Kennedy, National Security Files, Countries, Box 102, Guinea. Kennedy Presidential Library and Museum.

166. Muehlenbeck, *Betting on the Africans*, 69.

167. Doumbouya and Camara, "The Case of Guinea," 591.

168. Muehlenbeck, *Betting on the Africans*, 227.

169. Adamolekun, "Socialist Experience in Guinea," 75.

170. Kaba, "Guinean Politics," 38.

171. Ibid., 40.

172. Doumbouya and Camara, "The Case of Guinea," 591–97.

173. Wilder, *Freedom Time*.

174. Senghor, "The Facts of the Problem," as cited in Diouf, "Senegalese Development," 296.

175. Diouf, "Senegalese Development."

176. Ibid. See also, Irving Leonard Markovitz, *Léopold Sédar Senghor and the Politics of Negritude* (New York: Atheneum, 1969), chap. 6.

177. Laura Tuck, "Financial Markets in Rural Senegal," in *The Political Economy of Risk and Choice in Senegal*, ed. John Waterbury and Mark Gersovitz (London: Frank Cass, 1987), 160–87.

178. Ibid., 163.

179. Ibid., 165–66. John Waterbury examines how the groundnut farmer's "amoralism" in Senegal is matched by the state's exactions on the industry, which largely supported the huge expansion in government bureaucracy. John Waterbury, "Dimensions of State Intervention in the Groundnut Basin," in Waterbury and Gersovitz, *Political Economy of Risk and Choice in Senegal*, 188–222.

180. Diouf, "Senegalese Development," 307.

181. Ibid., 310–14.

182. Ndiaye, "State Control and Poor Economic Growth Performance," 403.

183. Ibid., 420.

184. For Senghor, nationalization was only a disincentive to capital formation in poor countries. Markovitz, *Senghor*, 144.

185. "Africa in Too Much of a Hurry," *Daily Nation*, April 21, 1967. CCM Library, Dodoma.

186. Wilder, *Freedom Time*, 243.

187. Ibid., 152. Wilder points out that Senghor's promotion of federalism between 1946 and 1958 was in tune with the spirit of the times and not just a response to the need for metropolitan investment or aid. Senghor envisaged a plural French republic that included African territories in a united Europe.

188. Coulson, *Tanzania*, 241–43.

189. Ruben Um Nyobé is memorialized in Mongo Beti's *Remember Ruben* (London: Heinemann, 1974). Before the independence of Ghana, Guinea, and Tanganyika, African independence movements had mostly operated from Cairo.

190. Chau, *Exploiting Africa*, 76.

191. CIA Files, OCI No. 1359/63. Current Intelligence Memorandum. Subject: Orientation of Nkrumah Regime, April 17, 1963. Approved for release March 7, 2007.

192. CIA Files, OCI No. 1359/63. Current Intelligence Memorandum. Subject: Orientation of Nkrumah Regime, April 17, 1963.

193. Mfenyana, *Walking with Giants*, 186.

194. Numerous correspondence from 1959 in BAA/RLAA/455 address these issues. Bureau of African Affairs records, George Padmore Research Library (GPRL), Accra. On relations with ZANU, see BAA/RLAA/358. On correspondence with South African liberation movements and political organizations between 1960 and 1964, see BAA/RLAA/752. On Nkrumah's relations with southern Africa liberation movements, see also, Jeffrey S. Ahlman, "Road to Ghana: Nkrumah, Southern Africa and the Eclipse of a Decolonizing Africa," *Kronos* 37, no. 1 (2011): 23–40.

195. Joe Matlou to J. J. Hadebe, Accra, August 13, 1965. ANC Archives, University of Fort Hare, Morogoro Office (1960–90), Box 1, Folder 1, Accra (1965–66).

196. Jeffrey S. Ahlman, *Living with Nkrumahism: Nation, State, and Pan-Africanism in Ghana* (Athens: Ohio University Press, 2017), 131. J. B. Danquah and the executive of the opposition United Party, in a press conference following the September 1961 strike by Ghanian trade union workers against the rising cost of living and the introduction of a compulsory savings scheme, complained about the millions of pounds "poured into the coffers of Guinea, Mali, and Upper Volta" over the course of regional integration with no financial returns. This was a clear swipe at the Ghana-Guinea-Mali Union. "Statement Issued at a Press Conference by the Executive of the United Party," September 15, 1961. Reproduced in Joseph Boakye Danquah, *The Ghanaian Establishment: Its Constitution, Its Detentions, Its Traditions, Its Justice and Statecraft, and Its Heritage of Ghanaism*, ed. Albert Adu Boahen (Accra: Ghana Universities Press, 1997), chap. 4. The Ghana-Guinea-Mali Union saw itself as the nucleus of the Union of African States. For its charter, see Legum, *Pan-Africanism*, 183–86.

197. Interview with Dr. Albie Sachs, Clifton, Cape Town, February 19, 2021.

198. Alfred Hutchinson, *Road to Ghana* (London: Victor Gollancz, 1960).

199. Abdoulaye Diallo, Secretary General AAPC, Accra, to Office of the High Commissioner for the Republic of Ghana in Dar es Salaam, June 17, 1963, extending an invitation to steering committee members of the liberation movements based in Tanganyika to an emergency meeting of the AAPC in Accra. TNA, Accession No. 589, File No. BMC 25/03. AAPC—Accra—Ghana 1961–63.

200. Shivji, Yahya-Othman, and Kamaya, *Biography of Julius Nyerere*, 3:151–52.

201. Azaria Mbughuni, "Tanzania and the Pan African Quest for Unity, Freedom, and Independence in East, Central, and Southern Africa: The Case of the Pan African Freedom Movement for East, Central, and Southern Africa," *Journal of Pan African Studies* 7, no. 4 (2014): 211–38; and Shivji, Yahya-Othman, and Kamaya, *Biography of Julius Nyerere*, 2:176.

202. Mbughuni, "Tanzania and the Pan African Quest for Unity," 212. The organization was renamed the Pan-African Freedom Movement for East, Central and Southern Africa (PAFMECSA) in 1962 to include southern African countries. The organization was dissolved with the establishment of the OAU's African Liberation Committee.

203. W. Scott Thompson, *Ghana's Foreign Policy, 1957–1966: Diplomacy, Ideology and the New State* (Princeton, NJ: Princeton University Press, 1969), 331–32. Indeed, Thompson notes that at the PAFMECSA Conference in Addis Ababa in 1962, a group of Ghana militants disrupted the conference, claiming the primacy of the AAPC.

204. Shivji, Yahya-Othman, and Kamaya, *Biography of Julius Nyerere*, 2:186.

205. Nkrumah to Nyerere, July 4, 1963, Amir Jamal Papers, MISR. Cited in Shivji, Yahya-Othman, and Kamaya, *Biography of Julius Nyerere*, 2:160. The British had pushed unsuccessfully for an East African Federation in the 1920s and 1930s and again in 1953. Uganda had been the main stumbling block. Wary of settler influence from Kenya, Buganda used its protectorate status based on the Buganda Agreement of 1900 to oppose federation. M. S. M. Kiwanuka, "Uganda under the British," in *Zamani: A Survey of East African History*, ed. B. A. Ogot and J. A. Kieran (New York: Humanities Press, 1971), 312–33.

206. Nkrumah, through Ghana's diplomatic representatives in Uganda, worked hard to dissuade Ugandan politicians on the East African Federation, exploiting the personal friendship between Ghana's high commissioner in Kampala, David Bosumtwi-Sam, and Ugandan head of state Milton Obote. Scott Thompson, *Ghana's Foreign Policy*, 331.

207. Kiwanuka, "Uganda under the British," 314. Interview with Edward Kirumira, Stellenbosch, Western Cape Province, June 10, 2021.

208. Mbughuni, "Tanzania and the Pan African Quest for Unity," 227–29.

209. Shivji, Yahya-Othman, and Kamaya, *Biography of Julius Nyerere*, 1:228.

210. President Julius K. Nyerere, "Stability and Change in Africa" (Address at the University of Toronto, Canada, October 2, 1969). CCM Library, Dodoma.

211. *Nationalist*, January 19, 1967. Cited in Shivji, Yahya-Othman, and Kamaya, *Biography of Julius Nyerere*, 3:117.

212. Shivji, Yahya-Othman, and Kamaya, *Biography of Julius Nyerere*, 1:142.

213. Schatten, *Communism in Africa*, 74–79.

214. Ibid., 98.

215. Letter from D. Nokwe, Secretary General of ANC to Secretary General of AAPSO (Cairo), February 3, 1967. ANC Morogoro Office, Box 2, Folder 7, Afro-Asian People's Solidarity Organization, 1966–70. ANC Archives, University of Fort Hare.

216. Youssef Al-Sebni, Secretary General of AAPSO to Oliver Tambo, President of ANC, Dar es Salaam, May 4, 1974. Oliver Tambo Papers, Personal Documents, Box 11, Folder 82. ANC Archives, University of Fort Hare.

217. Statement of Oliver Tambo to the United Nations Special Committee on the Policies of Apartheid of the Government of the Republic of South Africa, Stockholm, June 17, 1968. Oliver Tambo Papers, Personal Documents, Box 17, Folder 0133.

218. Stephen Ellis, *External Mission: The ANC in Exile, 1960–1990* (Oxford: Oxford University Press, 2013), 103.

219. Ibid., 63–64.

220. Ibid., 287.

221. Dar-es-Salaam Office (1973–91), Box 20, Folder 56, OAU Liberation Committee (1972–91). ANC Archives, University of Fort Hare.

222. Schatten, *Communism in Africa*, 139.

223. William Attwood to George Ball, Under Secretary of State, May 12, 1961. Papers of President Kennedy, National Security Files, Countries, Box 102 (1961). John F. Kennedy Library and Museum.

224. Thandika Mkandawire, "The New International Economic Order, Basic Needs Strategies and the Future of Africa," *Africa Development* 5, no. 3 (1980): 68–90.

225. Mkandawire, *Fifty Years of Independence*, 24.

226. Luis Eugenio di Marco, "Biographical Notes on Dr. Prebisch," in di Marco, *International Economics and Development*, xiii.

227. Ibid.

228. Getachew, *Worldmaking after Empire*, 145.

229. Ibid., 158.

230. Finnemore, "Redefining Development at the World Bank."

231. Mkandawire, "New International Economic Order."

232. Getachew, *Worldmaking after Empire*, 157.

233. Mkandawire, "New International Economic Order."

234. Getachew, *Worldmaking after Empire*, 173–74.

235. Shivji, Yahya-Othman, and Kamaya, *Biography of Julius Nyerere*, 3:286.

236. Mkandawire, "New International Economic Order," 84.

237. Ahlman, *Living with Nkrumahism*, 3.

5. Nkrumah, Cocoa, and the United States

1. James M. Berkebile, "The Teachers for West Africa Program: A Decade of Service" (Program Report in 1972). TWAP Papers, Elizabethtown College Library Archive.

2. Kevin K. Gaines, *American Africans in Ghana: Black Expatriates and the Civil Rights Era* (Chapel Hill: University of North Carolina Press, 2006).

3. J. O. Torto, "History of Cocoa in Ghana," *Ghana Farmer* 3, no. 3 (1959): 88.

4. William Gervase Clarence-Smith, *Cocoa and Chocolate, 1765–1915* (New York: Routledge, 2000), 239. The Portuguese introduced cocoa seeds from Brazil to São Tomé in 1822 and the Spanish brought the crop to Fernando Po in 1840. Olisa Godson Muojama, "The First World War and the Cocoa Industry in Ghana: A Study of the Hazards of Economic Dependency," *Global Journal of Human-Social Science* 16, no. 6 (2016): 35. William Gervase Clarence-Smith, ed., *Cocoa Pioneer Fronts since 1800: The Role of Smallholders, Planters and Merchants* (London: Macmillan Press, 1996), provides five case studies that examine the relocation of cocoa to different West African countries from the nineteenth century.

5. Peter Haenger, *Slaves and Slaveholders on the Gold Coast: Towards an Understanding of Social Bondage in West Africa* (Basel: P. Schlettwein, 2000).

6. Clarence-Smith, *Cocoa and Chocolate*, 77.

7. On the palm oil and palm kernel trade in nineteenth-century West Africa, see Martin Lynn, *Commerce and Economic Change in West Africa: The Palm Oil Trade in the Nineteenth Century* (Cambridge: Cambridge University Press, 1997). R. H. Green and S. H. Hymer, "Cocoa in the Gold Coast: A Study of the Relations between African Farmers and Agricultural Experts," *Journal of Economic History* 26, no. 3 (1966): 299–319, comments on the swiftness with which West African farmers in the Gold Coast, Nigeria, and French West Africa embraced new crops and techniques of production in the early decades of the twentieth century.

8. Louis E. Wilson, "The 'Bloodless Conquest' in Southeastern Ghana: The *Huza* and Territorial Expansion of the Krobo in the 19th Century," *International Journal of African Historical Studies* 23, no. 2 (1990): 269–97.

9. On the cocoa industry in Ghana, the two major works are Polly Hill, *The Migrant Cocoa Farmers of Southern Ghana: A Study in Rural Capitalism* (Cambridge: Cambridge University Press, 1961); and Gareth Austin, *Labour, Land and Capital in Ghana: From Slavery to Free Labour in Asante, 1807–1956* (Rochester, NY: University of Rochester Press, 2005). The first focuses on the Eastern Province and the second on Ashanti.

10. Francis K. Danquah, "Sustaining a West African Cocoa Economy: Agricultural Science and the Swollen Shoot Contagion in Ghana, 1936–1965," *African Economic History* 31 (2003): 46.

11. Rod Alence, "The 1937–1938 Gold Coast Cocoa Crisis: The Political Economy of Commercial Stalemate," *African Economic History* 19 (1991): 87.

12. S. M. Martin, "The Long Depression: West African Export Producers and the World Economy, 1914–1945," in *The Economies of Africa and Asia in the Inter-war Depression*, ed. Ian Brown (New York: Routledge, 1989).

13. Ibid., 77.

14. Ibid., 78.

15. A. G. Hopkins, *An Economic History of West Africa* (New York: Columbia University Press, 1973), 254–55.

16. Austin, *Labour, Land and Capital*, chap. 15.

17. Gareth Austin, "Capitalists and Chiefs in the Cocoa Hold-Ups in South Asante, 1927–1938," *International Journal of African Historical Studies* 21, no.1 (1988): 63–95.

18. The paramount chiefs of the Eastern Province passed a resolution in December 1930 deprecating any attempt by chiefs to use the Native Administrative Ordinance to pass bylaws to penalize farmers participating in the 1930 holdup. In short, the chiefs refused to be the punitive arm of the government in a holdup that had witnessed district commissioners fining and imprisoning native authority figures. See *Gold Coast Spectator*, December 13, 1930. The paramount chief of New Juaben was explicit in forbidding under oath all his subjects and strangers residing and farming on New Juaben land from selling "any cocoa beans till such time that the state will notify the sale of same." See *Independent*, November 1, 1930.

19. Austin, "Capitalists and Chiefs in the Cocoa Hold-Ups in South Asante," 81.

20. Francis K. Danquah, "Rural Discontent and Decolonization in Ghana, 1945–1951," *Agricultural History* 68, no. 1 (1994): 7.

21. Austin, "Capitalists and Chiefs in the Cocoa Hold-Ups in South Asante," 91.

22. Alence, "The 1937–1938 Gold Coast Cocoa Crisis," 77–104.

23. Roger J. Southall, "Farmers, Traders and Brokers in the Gold Coast Cocoa Economy," *Canadian Journal of African Studies* 12, no. 2 (1978): 185–211.

24. Austin, "Capitalists and Chiefs in the Cocoa Hold-ups in South Asante," 89.

25. *Report of the Commission on the Marketing of West African Cocoa*, Cmd 5485 (London, 1938).

26. Alence, "The 1937–1938 Gold Coast Cocoa Crisis," 103.

27. On the Gold Coast cocoa industry in World War I, see Muojama, "The First World War and the Cocoa Industry in Ghana." During World War I, Britain classified cocoa as a luxury crop, giving shipping preference to crops that contributed directly to the war effort, like palm oil and rubber. Farmers neglected the sanitation of their cocoa farms, allowing ripened cocoa pods to go unpicked, which encouraged pests and diseases that proved disastrous. Francis Danquah, "Capsid Pests as 'Cocoa Mosquitoes': A Study in Cash Crop Infestation and Control in Ghana, 1910–1965," *Journal of Third World Studies* 21, no. 2 (2004): 147–66.

28. G. B. Kay, *The Political Economy of Colonialism in Ghana: A Collection of Documents and Statistics 1900–1960* (Cambridge: Cambridge University Press, 1972), 231.

29. J. D. Boateng, "Problems of Cocoa Growing in the Gold Coast I," *New Gold Coast Farmer* 1, no. 1 (1956–57): 2–3. Boateng was the Gold Coast's director of agriculture.

30. Gareth Austin, "Vent for Surplus or Productivity Breakthrough? The Ghanaian Cocoa Take-off, c.1890–1936" (African Economic History Working Paper Series, No. 81, 2012), 7. The scientists at WACRI came up with a new cocoa hybrid, *Tafo Hybrid*, that was a cross between the *Amelonado* and the *Amazonia* cocoa trees. More resistant to disease and earlier bearing, the *Tafo Hybrid* was provided to Ghanaian farmers in 1963–64 for the rehabilitation of farms devastated by swollen shoot. The government declared swollen shoot to be under control in 1960. The only remedy to the disease remained the cutting out of infected trees. Danquah, "Sustaining a West African Cocoa Economy," 59–62. See also, Alex Attafuah, "A Brief Introduction to the Virus Diseases of Cacao," *Ghana Farmer* 3, no. 2 (1959): 63–65; and S. T. Quansah, "The Future of Cocoa," *Ghana Farmer* 8, no. 3 (1964): 98–100.

31. *Report on Cocoa Control in West Africa and Statements on Future Policy*, Cmd. 6554 (London, 1944).

32. Rod Alence, "Colonial Government, Social Conflict and State Involvement in Africa's Open Economies: The Origins of the Ghana Cocoa Marketing Board, 1939–1946," *Journal of African History* 42, no. 3 (2001): 397–416.

33. See the *Report of the Commission of Enquiry into Disturbances in the Gold Coast* (London: Colonial Office, 1948), also referred to as the Watson Commission Report.

34. On the 1948 riots, see Emmanuel Akyeampong, *Drink, Power, and Cultural Change: A Social History of Alcohol in Ghana, c.1800 to Recent Times* (Portsmouth, NH: Heinemann, 1996), 120–24.

35. Danquah, "Rural Discontent and Decolonization in Ghana," 16.

36. Southall, "Farmers, Traders and Brokers in the Gold Coast Economy," 210.

37. Marika Sherwood, *Kwame Nkrumah: The Years Abroad 1935–1947* (Accra: Freedom, 1996), chap. 9.

38. Danquah, "Rural Discontent and Decolonization in Ghana," 16.

39. Kwame Nkrumah, *Ghana: The Autobiography of Kwame Nkrumah* (New York: International, 1976 [1957]), 14.

40. Ibid., 15.

41. Nnamdi Azikiwe, *My Odyssey: An Autobiography* (London: C. Hurst, 1970), 37.

42. Ibid.

43. Ibid.

44. Sherwood, *Kwame Nkrumah*, 29.

45. A. B. Assensoh, *Kwame Nkrumah: Six Years in Exile 1966–1972* (Devon, UK: Arthur H. Stockwell, 1978), 65.

46. Azikiwe, *My Odyssey*, 155.

47. Sherwood, *Kwame Nkrumah*, 30.

48. Nkrumah's correspondence at Lincoln University Library Archives includes several exchanges with the Phelps-Stokes Fund. In 1940, Nkrumah received a grant of $55 toward his tuition from the National Missions of the Presbyterian Church in the USA (New York office). In a letter to his mentor, Dr. Johnson, Nkrumah mentions how "almost every one of my Sundays has been devoted to preaching either in Philadelphia, New York or Washington." Nkrumah to Dr. George Johnson, August 6, 1942, Lincoln University Library Archives.

49. Sherwood, *Kwame Nkrumah*, 42–43. A branch of the New York Public Library, the Schomburg Collection was then located at 103 West 135th Street. The *New York Times* in 1958 recalled Nkrumah's fish-selling days when Harlem turned out to welcome its old friend, now prime minister of Ghana. Ten thousand Harlemites lined up along Seventh Avenue to welcome the visiting head of state, "who fifteen summers ago vainly tried to peddle fish on a Harlem street corner." *New York Times*, July 28, 1958.

50. Nkrumah, *Autobiography*, 32.

51. Ibid., 44–45.

52. Ibid., vii.

53. Horace Mann Bond, *Education for Freedom: A History of Lincoln University, Pennsylvania* (Princeton, NJ: Princeton University Press, 1976).

54. Robert L. Tignor, *W. Arthur Lewis and the Birth of Development Economics* (Princeton, NJ: Princeton University Press, 2006), 64. The same uneasiness is seen in the tense French relations with the Americans in Ivory Coast, which Bamba describes as a parallel, lowercase "cold war." Abou B. Bamba, *African Miracle, African Mirage: Transnational Politics and the Paradox of Modernization in Ivory Coast* (Athens: Ohio University Press, 2016).

55. David Birmingham, *Kwame Nkrumah: The Father of African Nationalism* (Athens: Ohio University Press, 1998), 63.

56. Kwamina Barnes, *Economics of the Volta River Project* (Tema: State, 1966), 1.

57. Gold Coast, *Development of the Volta River Basin: A Statement by the Government of the Gold Coast on the Volta River Project and Related Matters* (Accra: Government Printer, 1952); James Moxon, *Volta, Man's Greatest Lake: The Story of Ghana's Akosombo Dam* (London: Andre Deutsch, 1984), 49–50.

58. National Archives of Britain (NAB), CO 96/825/5, Development of the Volta River Basin.

59. Ibid. Memorandum by Sir Hilton Poynton of a conversation with Ervin Anderson (US Economic Corporation Administration), London, January 18, 1950.

60. Birmingham, *Kwame Nkrumah*, 66.

61. "Statement by the Gold Coast Delegation" (n.d.). Box 20, Folder 4. W. Arthur Lewis Papers, Call No. MC 092. Seeley G. Mudd Manuscript Library, Princeton University Archives.

62. Gaines, *American Africans in Ghana*, 81.

63. Ibid., 83.

64. Ibid., 84.

65. *Pittsburgh Courier*, Wednesday, March 6, 1957. Hershey Foods Corporation Archives, Hershey, PA. Hereafter Hershey Archives.

66. *Hershey News*, July 31, 1958. Hershey Archives.

67. *Wall Street Journal*, Vol. CLXXV, No. 34, 1969. Hershey Archives.

68. Clarence-Smith, *Cocoa and Chocolate*, 78.

69. *Wall Street Journal*, Vol. CLXXV, No. 34, 1969.

70. Nkrumah invited Dr. Noel Drevici in 1963 to build a cocoa processing plant in Tema. Known today as the Tema Cocoa Processing Company, it began production in 1965 and processes raw cocoa into semifinished products. But cocoa was not at the center of Nkrumah's vision of industrialization.

71. "Memorandum re visit of Prime Minister Kwame Nkrumah of Ghana, Africa," June 7, 1958. Hershey Archives, Accession No. 87006.

72. Memorandum dated December 31, 1958. Hershey Archives, Accession No. 87006.

73. Dinner program. Hershey Archives, Accession No. 85006.

74. Speech to be delivered by Dr. Kwame Nkrumah, Prime Minister of Ghana, at a dinner given by the New York Cocoa Exchange, July 28, 1958. Nkrumah Papers, Moorland Spingarn Library, Howard University.

75. James M. Berkebile, "The Teachers for West Africa Program: A Decade of Service" (August 1972). Elizabethtown College Library Archives.

76. "Report of Investigations in Behalf of the Elizabethtown College African Program Made by Dr. John O. Hershey and Dr. Roy E. McAuley in the Instance of Their Visits to Ghana and Nigeria, March 6–16, 1962" (March 1962). Elizabethtown College Library Archives. TWAP Collection. The program was initially called the Elizabethtown College African Program (ECAP).

77. Memorandum dated December 31, 1958. Hershey Archives, Accession Number 87006.

78. The African-American Institute, a private, nonpolitical American organization, was founded in 1953 with the explicit purpose of fostering closer relations between the peoples of Africa and America. Its educational programs included the placement of American teachers in African secondary schools and colleges in cooperation with African authorities. The institute had its West African office in Accra. It also administered scholarships to African students in the United States and operated the Africa House in Washington, DC, which hosted events and served as the headquarters of the All African Students Union of the Americas. Information contained in a publication by the African-American Institute in file on "African-American Institute," Winifred Armstrong Papers (No. 356), Box 2, General Correspondence, December 1960–March 1961. John F. Kennedy Presidential Library and Museum, Boston, Massachusetts.

79. Berkebile, "The Teachers for West Africa Program: A Decade of Service."

80. Ibid.

81. Several books and articles have been written about the Volta River Project, and this section does not attempt an exhaustive discussion of the project—its financing, the framing of Cold War politics that determined its outcome, environmental and health studies, the planned townships of Tema and Akosombo that were part of the larger project, and so on. The focus is on how the United States became the final option for funding the dam, the abandoning of the integrated project, and the impact of Nkrumah's policy choices on the cocoa industry and Ghana's economy. Works on the Volta River Project include Keith Jopp, *Volta: The Story of Ghana's Volta River Project* (Accra: Volta River Authority, 1965); Moxon, *Volta*; Barnes, *Economics of the Volta River Project*; Thomas J. Noer, "The New Frontier and African Neutralism: Kennedy, Nkrumah, and the Volta River Project," *Diplomatic History* 8, no. 1 (1984): 61–79; Dzodzi Tsikata, *Living in the Shadow of the Large Dams: Long Term Responses of Downstream and Lakeside Communities of Ghana's Volta River Project* (Leiden: Brill, 2006); Stephanie Decker, "Corporate Political Activity in Less Developed Countries: The Volta River Project in Ghana, 1958–66," *Business History* 53, no. 7 (2011): 993–1017; and Stefan M. Miescher's forthcoming monograph on the dam and Akosombo township.

82. Alex Akurgo, *Kwame Nkrumah: A Story from the CIA Files* (Accra: Staricom, 2018), 35–36.

83. Ibid., 37.

84. Philip E. Muehlenbeck, *Betting on the Africans: John F. Kennedy's Courting of African Nationalist Leaders* (Oxford: Oxford University Press, 2012), 19.

85. "Housing for African Diplomats," report prepared by Winifred Armstrong for African Task Force for Kennedy Campaign, December 1960. Winifred Armstrong Papers, Box 1: Africa

and the United Nations. Discrimination against African diplomats in Washington, DC, 1959–62. John F. Kennedy Presidential Library and Museum.

86. "Brief Memo on Housing Discrimination and Its Effects on U. N. Staff and Missions" (n.d.). Winifred Armstrong Papers, Box 1. John F. Kennedy Presidential Library and Museum.

87. Letter from John F. Kennedy to Honorable Christian A. Herter, Secretary of State, Washington, DC, August 25, 1960. Winifred Armstrong Papers, Box 1. John F. Kennedy Presidential Library and Museum.

88. Letter from William B. Macomber Jr., Assistant Secretary, Department of State, Washington, DC, to John F, Kennedy, US Senate, September 7, 1960. Winifred Armstrong Papers, Box 1. John F. Kennedy Presidential Library and Museum.

89. Akurgo, *Kwame Nkrumah*, 39–41.

90. Nkrumah's letter is reproduced in Akurgo, *Kwame Nkrumah*, 41–42.

91. David Rooney, *Kwame Nkrumah: The Political Kingdom in the Third World* (New York: St. Martin's Press, 1988), 154.

92. "Chronology of United States Interest in the Volta Project," Appendix to "The Volta Project," Report submitted by the Department of State for consideration by the National Security Council on December 5, 1961. Papers of President Kennedy. National Security Files, Countries, Box 99a (Ghana). John F. Kennedy Presidential Library and Museum. Hereafter "Chronology."

93. Ibid.

94. Two excellent accounts on the twists and turns of America's engagement with the Volta River Project are Muehlenbeck, *Betting on the Africans*, and Akurgo, *Kwame Nkrumah*.

95. Zaki Laïdi, *The Superpowers and Africa: The Constraints of a Rivalry, 1960–1990* (Chicago: University of Chicago Press, 1990). Allen Isaacman and Barbara Isaacman, *Dams, Displacement and the Delusion of Development: Cahora Bassa and Its Legacies in Mozambique, 1965–2007* (Athens: Ohio University Press, 2013), 8–9, observes that in the second half of the twentieth century, African governments constructed more than one thousand dams. On Nkrumah's obsession with the Akosombo Dam, see Stephan F. Miescher, "'Nkrumah's Baby': The Akosombo Dam and the Dream of Development in Ghana, 1952–1966," *Water History* 6 (2014): 341–66; and Stephan F. Miescher and Dzodzi Tsikata, "Hydro-power and the Promise of Modernity and Development in Ghana: Comparing the Akosombo and Bui Projects," *Ghana Studies* 12/13 (2009/2010): 15–33.

96. "Chronology." Papers of President Kennedy – National Security Files. Box 99a, John F. Kennedy Presidential Library and Museum. See also, International Bank for Reconstruction and Development, "Preliminary Appraisal of the Volta River Hydroelectric Project Ghana," June 30, 1960. Department of Technical Operations. Report No. TO – 2499. World Bank Archives.

97. "Chronology."

98. On the secret agreement between Nkrumah and Lumumba, see Richard D. Mahoney, *JFK: Ordeal in Africa* (New York: Oxford University Press, 1983), 164.

99. Lawrence Devlin, *Chief of Station, Congo* (New York: Public Affairs, 2007). On how Africa became a battleground for Cold War conflicts, see also, John Stockwell, *In Search of Enemies* (New York: W. W. Norton, 1978).

100. Muehlenbeck, *Betting on the Africans*, 24.

101. Philip E. Muehlenberg, "Kennedy and Touré: A Success in Personal Diplomacy," *Diplomacy and Statecraft* 19, no. 1 (2008): 78.

102. William P. Mahoney, Oral History Interview, John F. Kennedy Presidential Library and Museum, May 14, 1975, comments on the close relationship between the Jacksons and Nkrumah. Mahoney was the US ambassador to Ghana from June 22, 1962, to May 26, 1965.

103. Interview with Angier Biddle Duke, April 7, 1964. Conducted by Frank Sieverts. Oral History Series, John F. Kennedy Presidential Library and Museum.

104. Interview with William P. Mahoney, May 14, 1975. Oral History Series, John F. Kennedy Presidential Library and Museum.

105. Central Intelligence Agency, "Subject: Prospects for Ghana," dated November 16, 1961. Papers of President Kennedy – National Security Files, countries. Box 99a (Ghana).

106. Outgoing Telegram from Department of State (Acting Secretary of State Ball) to American Embassy Accra – Eyes only Ambassador. No distribution. Dated December 14, 1961. Papers of President Kennedy – National Security Files, Countries, Box 99a (Ghana).

107. Ibid.

108. Cable from President Nkrumah to President Kennedy, January 22, 1962. Papers of President Kennedy – National Security Files, Countries. Box 99A (Ghana).

109. Loan Agreement (Volta Project) between IBRD and VRA, dated February 8, 1962. Loan No. 310 GH. World Bank Archives.

110. Memorandum for the Record, drafted by McCone, Department of State, Washington, DC, February 26, 1964. Cited in Akurgo, *Kwame Nkrumah*, 237.

111. Akurgo, *Kwame Nkrumah*, 284.

112. For an account of the coup by one of its key architects, see Colonel A. A. Afrifa, *The Ghana Coup: 24th January 1966* (London: Frank Cass, 1966). Intriguingly, the preface to the book was written by K. A. Busia, the leader of the opposition party under Nkrumah, before he went into exile in the United Kingdom. He returned with the 1966 coup and his Progress Party won the elections of 1969 that returned Ghana to civilian rule.

113. The CIA's role in Nkrumah's downfall is documented exhaustively in CIA and other American government records in Akurgo, *Kwame Nkrumah*. On Gbedemah and the CIA, see especially CIA Document Number (FOIA)/RSDN (CREST): CIA-RPD75-00001R000300210022-8, "The Truth about Komla Gbedemah" (Department of State, December 1, 1964).

114. Moxon, *Volta*, 270.

115. Cited in Fritz Schatten, *Communism in Africa* (London: George Allen and Unwin, 1966), 161.

116. See chapter 4. See also, Obed Yao Asamoah, *The Political History of Ghana (1950–2013): The Experience of a Non-conformist* (Bloomington: AuthorHouse, 2014), 73–79.

117. Danquah, "Capsid Pests as 'Cocoa Mosquitoes'," 158.

118. W. Arthur Lewis, "Diversifying Ghana's Economy" (March 26, 1958). Box 20, Folder 7, W. Arthur Lewis Papers.

119. Ibid. Lewis now called for government assistance for peasant farming: "The idea that plantations are more efficient than peasant farms is derived from comparing progressive plantations with unassisted peasants."

120. Interview with K. B. Asante, La, July 31, 2017.

121. Interview with Dr. Kwesi Botchwey, August 10, 2017.

122. Interview with Kantinka Dr. Kwame Donkoh Fordwor, Kumasi (by phone), July 13, 2017.

123. Personal communication from Nana Dr. S. K. B. Asante, March 19, 2018. See, as well, his "Presidential Lecture" as president of the Ghana Academy of Arts and Sciences, Accra, December 1, 2006.

Conclusion

1. John M. Lonsdale, "Anti-colonial Nationalism and Patriotism in Sub-Saharan Africa," in *The Oxford Handbook of the History of Nationalism*, ed. John Breuilly (Oxford: Oxford University Press, 2013), 321. DOI: 1093/oxfordhb/9780199209194.013.0016.

2. James C. Scott, *Seeing like a State: How Certain Schemes to Improve the Human Condition Have Failed* (New Haven, CT: Yale University Press, 1998).

3. James D. Straker, *Youth, Nationalism, and the Guinean Revolution* (Bloomington: Indiana University Press, 2009), 2.

4. Bruce J. Berman, "Nationalism in Post-colonial Africa," in *The Oxford Handbook of the History of Nationalism*, ed. John Breuilly (Oxford: Oxford University Press, 2013), 362. DOI: 1093/oxfordhb/9780199209194.013.0018.

5. Abena Osseo-Asare, *Atomic Junction: Nuclear Power in Africa after Independence* (New York: Cambridge University Press, 2019).

6. Mike McGovern, *Unmasking the State: Making Guinea Modern* (Chicago: University of Chicago Press, 2012), 19.

7. See John Schwarzmantel, "Nationalism and Socialist Internationalism," in *The Oxford Handbook of the History of Nationalism*, ed. John Breuilly (Oxford: Oxford University Press, 2013). DOI: 1093/oxfordhb/9780199209194.013.0032.

8. Lonsdale, "Anti-colonial Nationalism and Patriotism," 324.

9. Berman, "Nationalism in Post-colonial Africa," 359.

10. Robert H. Bates, *Markets and States in Tropical Africa: The Political Basis of Agricultural Policies* (Berkeley: University of California Press, 2014), 5.

11. Ibid., 7.

12. Jeffrey S. Ahlman, *Kwame Nkrumah: Visions of Liberation* (Athens: Ohio University Press, 2021), is a good portrait of this process.

13. Lonsdale, "Anti-colonial Nationalism and Patriotism," 321.

14. Pheng Cheah, *Spectral Nationality: Passages of Freedom from Kant to Postcolonial Literatures of Liberation* (New York: Columbia University Press, 2003), 395. Instructively, Achille Mbembe, in a wide-ranging essay on "Afropolitanism" in his more recently published *Out of the Dark Night: Essays on Decolonization* (Johannesburg: Witwatersrand University Press, 2021), 173–222, translated from the 2010 French original publication *Sortir de la grande nuit*, has a more optimistic perspective on the future of Africa not dissimilar to Lonsdale and Cheah. Unlike *On the Postcolony*, where state power had become brutal, grotesque, and carnal, in "Afropolitanism" Mbembe sees new agency in Africans, in their literature, music, art, and relationship with technology. Whereas Hegel had been at the center of Mbembe's understanding of the European mind that colonized and denigrated Africa, Mbembe now discards Hegel as he contemplates Africa in the twenty-first century, asserting that "the Hegelian mythology—along with its multiple actualizations—manifestly no longer holds" (222). Indeed, Mbembe's conclusion in this essay is even more remarkable: "As a matter of fact, the destiny of our planet will be played out, to a large extent, in Africa" (222).

15. Thandika Mkandawire, *Fifty Years of Independence: Personal Reflections* (Dar es Salaam: Mkuki na Nyota, 2013), 24–25.

16. Ibid., 50.

17. Ibid., 36.

18. Issa G. Shivji, Saida Yahya-Othman, and Ng'wanza Kamaya, *Development as Rebellion: A Biography of Julius Nyerere* (Dar es Salaam: Mkuki na Nyota, 2020), 3:399.

19. Martin Khor, "IMF 'Cure' Pushes Indonesia to Crisis," *Star*, May 11, 1998, as cited in Cheah, *Spectral Nationality*, 395.

20. Dani Rodrik, "Africa after COVID-19: De-globalization and Recalibrating Nations' Growth Prospects," *Contemporary Issues in African Trade and Trade Finance* 6, no. 1 (December 2020): 14–17.

21. Foreword to Mkandawire, *Fifty Years of Independence*, vii.

22. Liam Taylor, "Import Substitution Makes a Comeback in Africa," *African Business Magazine*, November 6, 2020, Africa.business/2020/11/trade-investment/import-substitution-makes-a-comeback-in-africa/.

23. Joseph Asunka, "Covid-19, Integration, and Development Cooperation: Selected Afrobarometer Findings" (Paper delivered at the African Philanthropy Conference 2021, "Surviving Covid-19—The Role of African Philanthropy" Virtual Conference, August 3–5, 2021). On Afrobarometer, see https://afrobarometer.org.

BIBLIOGRAPHY

1. Archival Collections

African National Congress (ANC) Archives, University of Fort Hare, Alice, Eastern Cape, South Africa.

Center for International Studies Records, Department of Distinctive Collections, Massachusetts Institute of Technology, Cambridge, Massachusetts.

Chama Cha Mapinduzi (CCM) Library, Dodoma, United Republic of Tanzania.

Committee for the Comparative Study of New Nations Records 1958–75, Special Collections Research Center, University of Chicago, Chicago, Illinois.

Dabu Gizenga Collection on Kwame Nkrumah, Moorland Spingarn Research Center, Manuscripts Division, Howard University, Washington, DC.

Ford Foundation Records, International Division, Office of the Vice President, Rockefeller Archive Center, Sleepy Hollow, New York.

George Padmore Research Library, Accra, Ghana.

Hershey Community Archives, Hershey, Pennsylvania.

International Association for Cultural Freedom Records 1941–78, Special Collections Research Center, University of Chicago, Chicago, Illinois.

John F. Kennedy Oral History Collection, John F. Kennedy Presidential Library and Museum, Boston, Massachusetts.

Kwame Nkrumah Papers, Moorland-Spingarn Research Center, Manuscripts Division, Howard University, Washington, DC.

Lincoln University Library Archives, Lincoln, Pennsylvania.

Max F. Millikan Papers, Department of Distinctive Collections, Massachusetts Institute of Technology, Cambridge, Massachusetts.

National Archives of Britain, Kew Gardens, London, United Kingdom.

Papers of John F. Kennedy, Presidential Papers, President's Office Files, John F. Kennedy Presidential Library and Museum, Boston, Massachusetts.

Public Records and Archives Administration Department (PRAAD), Accra, Ghana.

Shirley Graham Du Bois Papers, 1865–1998, Schlesinger Library, Harvard University, Cambridge, Massachusetts.

Tanzania National Archives, Dar es Salaam.

The Teachers for West Africa Program, Hess Archives and Special Collections, Elizabethtown College, Elizabethtown, Pennsylvania.

United States Central Intelligence Agency Archives.

W. Arthur Lewis Papers, Seeley G. Mudd Manuscript Library, Princeton University, Princeton, New Jersey.

World Bank Group Archives Holding, Washington, DC.

2. Published Sources

Ackah, Charles, Charles Adjosi, and Festus Turkson. "Industrial Policy in Ghana: Its Evolution and Impact." In *Manufacturing Transformation: Comparative Studies of Industrial Development in Africa and Emerging Asia*, edited by Carol Newman, John Page, John Rand, Abebe Shimeles, Mans Söderbom, and Finn Tarp. Oxford: Oxford University Press, 2016.

Adamolekun, Ladipo. "The Socialist Experience in Guinea." In *Socialism in Sub-Saharan Africa: A New Assessment*, edited by Carl G. Rosberg and Thomas M. Callaghy. Berkeley: University of California Institute of International Studies, 1979.

Addo, Ebenezer Obiri. *Kwame Nkrumah: A Case Study of Religion and Politics in Ghana*. Lanham, MD: University Press of America, 1997.

Adebanwi, Wale. *Nation as Grand Narrative: The Nigerian Press and the Politics of Meaning*. Rochester, NY: University of Rochester Press, 2016.

Adedeji, Adebayo. "From the Lagos Plan of Action to the New Partnership for African Development and from the Final Act of Lagos to the Constitutive Act: Whither Africa?" Keynote address, African Forum for Envisioning Africa, Nairobi, April 26–29, 2002.

Adi, Hakim, and Marika Sherwood. *The 1945 Manchester Pan-African Congress Revisited*. London: New Beacon Books, 1995.

African Export-Import Bank. *Coming of Age: 25 Years of the African Export-Import Bank*. Cairo: African Export-Import Bank, 2018.

Afrifa, A. A. *The Ghana Coup: 24th February 1966*. London: Frank Cass, 1966.

Agyeman Duah, Baffour. *General Acheampong: The Life and Times of Ghana's Head of State*. Tema: Digibooks, 2021.

Ahlman, Jeffrey S. *Kwame Nkrumah: Visions of Liberation*. Athens: Ohio University Press, 2021.

———. *Living with Nkrumahism: Nation, State, and Pan-Africanism in Ghana*. Athens: Ohio University Press, 2017.

———. "A New Type of Citizen: Youth, Gender and Generation in the Ghanaian Builders Brigade." *Journal of African History* 53, no. 1 (2012): 87–105.

———. "Road to Ghana: Nkrumah, Southern Africa and the Eclipse of a Decolonizing Africa." *Kronos* 37, no. 1 (2011): 23–40.

Ajayi, J. F. Ade. "Colonialism: An Episode in African History." In *Tradition and Change in Africa: The Essays of J. F. Ade Ajayi*, edited by Toyin Falola. Trenton, NJ: Africa World Press, 2000.

———. "The Continuity of African Institutions under Colonial Rule." In *Tradition and Change in Africa: The Essays of J. F. Ade Ajayi*, edited by Toyin Falola. Trenton, NJ: Africa World Press, 2000.

Ajayi, J. F. Ade, and Michael Crowder, eds. *History of West Africa*. Vol. 2. London: Longman, 1987.

Ake, Claude. *A Political Economy of Africa*. Harlow, Essex: Longman, 1981.

Akurgo, Alex. *Kwame Nkrumah: A Story from the CIA Files*. Accra: Staricom, 2018.

Akyeampong, Emmanuel. "African Socialism; or, The Search for an Indigenous Model of Economic Development?" *Economic History of Developing Regions* 33, no. 1 (2018): 69–87.

———. *Between the Sea and the Lagoon: An Eco-social History of the Anlo of Southeast-ern Ghana, c.1850 to Recent Times*. Oxford: James Currey, 2001.

———. "Commerce, Credit, and Mobility in Late Nineteenth-Century Gold Coast: Changing Dynamics in Euro-African Trade." In *Africa's Development in His-torical Perspective*, edited by Emmanuel Akyeampong, Robert H. Bates, Nathan Nunn, and James A. Robinson. New York: Cambridge University Press, 2014.

———. *Drink, Power, and Cultural Change: A Social History of Alcohol in Ghana, c.1800 to Recent Times*. Portsmouth, NH: Heinemann, 1996.

———. "Race, Identity and Citizenship in Black Africa: The Case of the Lebanese in Ghana." *Africa* 76, no. 3 (2006): 297–323.

———. "What's in a Drink: Class Struggle, Popular Culture, and the Politics of *Akpeteshie* (Local Gin) in Ghana, 1930–1967." *Journal of African History* 37, no. 2 (1996): 215–36.

Akyeampong, Kwame. *Educational Expansion in Ghana: A Review of 50 Years of Chal-lenge and Progress*. University of Sussex Centre for International Education, Monograph No. 33, 2020.

Alence, Rod. "Colonial Government, Social Conflict and State Involvement in Africa's Open Economies: The Origins of the Ghana Cocoa Marketing Board, 1939–1946." *Journal of African History* 42, no. 3 (2001): 397–416.

———. "The 1937–1938 Gold Coast Cocoa Crisis: The Political Economy of Commercial Stalemate." *African Economic History* 19 (1991): 77–104.

Allen, Danielle. *Our Declaration*. New York: W. W. Norton, 2014.

Allman, Jean Marie. *The Quills of the Porcupine: Asante Nationalism in an Emergent Ghana*. Madison: University of Wisconsin Press, 1993.

———. "Rounding Up Spinsters: Gender Chaos and Unmarried Women in Colonial Asante." *Journal of African History* 37, no. 2 (1996): 195–214.

Allman, Jean Marie, and John Parker. *Tongnaab: The History of a West African God*. Bloomington: Indiana University Press, 2005.

Amin, Samir. "Capitalism and Development in the Ivory Coast." In *African Politics and Society: Basic Issues and Problems of Government and Development*, edited by Irving L. Markovitz. New York: Free Press, 1970.

———. *Le développement du capitalisme en Côte d'Ivoire*. Paris: Editions de Minuit, 1967.

———. *A Life Looking Forward: Memoirs of an Independent Marxist*. Translated by Pat-rick Camiller. London: Zed Books, 2006.

———. *The Long Revolution of the Global South: Toward a New Anti-imperialist Interna-tional*. Translated by James Membrez. New York: Monthly Review Press, 2019.

———. *Neo-colonialism in West Africa*. Translated by Francis McDonagh. Harmond-sworth, Middlesex: Penguin Books, 1973.

———. *Only People Make Their Own History: Writings on Capitalism, Imperialism, and Revolution*. New York: Monthly Review Press, 2019.

Anderson, Benedict. *Imagined Communities: Reflections on the Origin and Spread of Nationalism*. Rev. ed. London: Verso, 1991.

Anderson, David, and David Throup. "The Agrarian Economy of Central Province, Ke-nya, 1918 to 1939." In *The Economies of Africa and Asia in the Inter-War Depression*, edited by Ian Brown. New York: Routledge, 1989.

Andoh, T. E. "The Nationalistic Music of I. D. Riverson." *Legon Journal of the Humani-ties* 18 (2007): 159–77.

Antubam, Kofi. *Ghana's Heritage of Culture*. Leipzig: Koehler and Amelang, 1963.

Appiah, Joseph. *Joe Appiah: The Autobiography of an African Patriot*. Accra: Asempa, 1990.

Apter, Andrew. "Beyond Négritude: Black Cultural Citizenship and the Arab Question in FESTAC 77." *Journal of African Cultural Studies* 28, no. 3 (2016): 313–26.

———. *The Pan-African Nation: Oil and the Spectacle of Culture in Nigeria*. Chicago: University of Chicago Press, 2005.

———. "Socialism, Africa." *International Encyclopedia of the Social Sciences*. Vol. 7. 2nd ed. Detroit: Macmillan Reference, 2008.

Aryeetey, Ernest, and Augustin Kwasi Fosu. "Economic Growth in Ghana, 1960–2000." In *Country Case Studies*, edited by Benno J. Ndulu, Stephen A. O'Connell, Jean-Paul Azam, Robert H. Bates, Augustin K. Fosu, Jan Willem Gunning, and Dominique Njinkeu. Vol. 2 of *Political Economy of Economic Growth in Africa 1960–2000*. Cambridge: Cambridge University Press, 2008.

Asamoah, Obed Yao. *The Political History of Ghana (1950–2013): The Experience of a Non-conformist*. Bloomington: AuthorHouse, 2014.

Asante, S. K. B. "Presidential Lecture." Accra, Ghana Academy of Arts and Sciences, Accra, December 1, 2006.

———. "The 'Yentua' Saga: A Chapter in Ghana's External Debt History." Paper delivered at the Friedman Conference on the Regulation of Transnational Corporations, Columbia University Law School, February 26, 1976.

Askew, Kelly M. *Performing the Nation: Swahili Music and Cultural Politics in Tanzania*. Chicago: University of Chicago Press, 2002.

Assensoh, A. B. *Kwame Nkrumah: Six Years in Exile 1966–1972*. Devon, UK: Arthur H. Stockwell, 1978.

Assensoh, A. B., and Yvette M. Alex-Assensoh. *African Military History and Politics: Coups and Ideological Incursions, 1900–Present*. New York: Palgrave, 2001.

Attafuah, Alex. "A Brief Introduction to the Virus Diseases of Cacao." *Ghana Farmer* 3, no. 2 (1959): 63–65.

Austen, Ralph A. *African Economic History*. London: James Currey, 1987.

Austin, Dennis. *Politics in Ghana 1946–1960*. London: Oxford University Press, 1964.

Austin, Gareth. "Capitalists and Chiefs in the Cocoa Hold-Ups in South Asante, 1927–1938." *International Journal of African Historical Studies* 21, no. 1 (1988): 63–95.

———. *Labour, Land and Capital in Ghana: From Slavery to Free Labour in Asante, 1807–1956*. Rochester, NY: University of Rochester Press, 2005.

———. "Vent for Surplus or Productivity Breakthrough? The Ghanaian Cocoa Take-off, c.1890–1936." African Economic History Working Paper Series, No. 81, 2012.

Awolowo, Obafemi. *Path to Nigerian Freedom*. London: Faber and Faber, 1947.

Azikiwe, Nnamdi. *My Odyssey: An Autobiography*. London: C. Hurst, 1970.

Babu, Abdul R. M. *African Socialism or Socialist Africa?* London: Zed Press, 1981.

Baer, George Webster. *Test Case: Italy, Ethiopia, and the League of Nations*. Stanford: Hoover Institution Press, 1976.

Baker, Kevin T. "Virtually Nigeria: USAID, Simulated Futures, and the Politics of Postcolonial Expertise, 1964–1980." In *The Struggle for the Long-Term in Transnational*

Science and Politics: Forging the Future, edited by Jenny Andersson and Egle Rindzeviciute. London: Routledge, 2015.

Bamba, Abou B. *African Miracle, African Mirage: Transnational Politics and the Paradox of Modernization in Ivory Coast*. Athens: Ohio University Press, 2016.

Banik, Nilanjin, and C. A. Yoonus. "Trade as an Answer to Sustainable Economic Growth—The ECOWAS Story." *Global Business Review* 13, no. 2 (2012): 311–26.

Baptiste, Fitzroy, and Rupert Lewis, eds. *George Padmore: Pan-African Revolutionary*. Kingston: Ian Randle, 2009.

Barber, Karin. *I Could Speak Until Tomorrow: Oriki Women and the Past in a Yoruba Town*. Edinburgh: International African Institute, 1991.

Barnes, Kwamina. *Economics of the Volta River Project*. Tema: State, 1966.

Basch, Linda G., Nina Glick Schiller, and Cristina Szanton Blanc. *Nations Unbound: Transnational Projects, Postcolonial Predicaments, and Deterritorialized Nation-States*. Langhorne, PA: Gordon and Breach, 1994.

Bates, Robert H. *Markets and States in Tropical Africa: The Political Basis of Agricultural Policies*. Berkeley: University of California Press, 2014.

Bauer, P. T. *Dissent on Development*. Rev. ed. Cambridge, MA: Harvard University Press, 1976 [1971].

———. *Reality and Rhetoric: Studies in the Economics of Development*. Cambridge, MA: Harvard University Press, 1984.

———. *West African Trade: A Study of Competition, Oligarchy, and Monopoly in a Changing Economy*. Cambridge: Cambridge University Press, 1954.

Baum, Robert M. *Shrines of the Slave Trade: Diola Religion and Society in Precolonial Senegambia*. New York: Oxford University Press, 1999.

Bayart, Jean-François. *The State in Africa: The Politics of the Belly*. New York: Longman, 1993.

Bayart, Jean-François, Stephen Ellis, and Béatrice Hibou. *The Criminalization of the State in Africa*. Oxford: James Currey, 1999.

Behrman, Lucy. *Muslim Brotherhoods and Politics in Senegal*. Cambridge, MA: Harvard University Press, 1970.

Benga, Ndiouga. "Mise en scène de la culture et espace public au Sénégal." *Africa Development* 35, no. 4 (2010): 237–60.

Berman, Bruce J. "Nationalism in Post-colonial Africa." In *The Oxford Handbook of the History of Nationalism*, edited by John Breuilly. Oxford: Oxford University Press, 2013. DOI: 1093/oxfordhb/9780199209194.013.0018.

Berman, Bruce J., and John M. Lonsdale. "Nationalism in Colonial and Post-colonial Africa." In *The Oxford Handbook of the History of Nationalism*, edited by John Breuilly. Oxford: Oxford University Press, 2013. DOI: 1093/oxfordhb/9780199209194.013.0015.

Berry, Sara. "Chieftaincy, Land, and the State in Ghana and South Africa." In *The Politics of Custom: Chiefship, Capital, and the State in Contemporary Africa*, edited by John L. Comaroff and Jean Comaroff. Chicago: University of Chicago Press, 2018.

Beti, Mongo. *Remember Ruben*. London: Heinemann, 1974.

Bierwirth, Chris. "The Lebanese Communities of Côte D'Ivoire." *African Affairs* 98, no. 390 (1999): 79–99.

Biney, Ama. *The Political and Social Thought of Kwame Nkrumah*. New York: Palgrave Macmillan, 2011.

Birmingham, David. *Kwame Nkrumah: The Father of African Nationalism*. Athens: Ohio University Press, 1998.

Bjerk, Paul. *Julius Nyerere*. Athens: Ohio University Press, 2017.

Blier, Suzanne Preston. *The Royal Arts of Africa: The Majesty of Form*. New York: Harry Abrams, 1998.

Boafo-Arthur, Kwame. "Ghana: Structural Adjustment, Democratization, and the Politics of Continuity." *African Studies Review* 42, no. 2 (1999): 41–72.

Boateng, J. D. "Problems of Cocoa Growing in the Gold Coast I." *New Gold Coast Farmer* 1, no. 1 (1956–57): 2–3.

Bond, Horace Mann. *Education for Freedom: A History of Lincoln University, Pennsylvania*. Princeton, NJ: Princeton University Press, 1976.

Booth, David, and Frederick Golooba-Mutebi. "Developmental Patrimonialism? The Case of Rwanda." *African Affairs* 111, no. 444 (2012): 379–403.

Bozzoli, Belinda, with the assistance of Mmantho Nkotsoe. *Women of Phokeng: Consciousness, Life Strategy, and Migrancy in South Africa, 1900–1983*. Portsmouth, NH: Heinemann, 1991.

Brautigam, Deborah. *The Dragon's Gift: The Real Story of China in Africa*. Oxford: Oxford University Press, 2009.

Bravmann, René. *African Islam*. Washington, DC: Smithsonian Institute, 1983.

Bretton, Henry L. *The Rise and Fall of Kwame Nkrumah: A Study of Personal Rule in Africa*. New York: Praeger, 1966.

Brockway, Fenner. *African Socialism*. London: Bodley Head, 1963.

Brokensha, David. *Social Change in Larteh, Ghana*. Oxford: Clarendon Press, 1966.

Bullock, Richard. "Off Track: Sub-Saharan African Railways." African Infrastructure Country Diagnostic Background Paper 17. Washington, DC: World Bank, 2009.

Byfield, Judith A., Carolyn A. Brown, Timothy Parsons, and Ahmad Alawad Sikainga, eds. *Africa and World War II*. New York: Cambridge University Press, 2015.

Camara, Mohamed Saliou. *Political History of Guinea since World War Two*. New York: Peter Lang, 2014.

Chabal, Patrick, and Jean-Pascal Daloz. *Africa Works: Disorder as Political Instrument*. Oxford: James Currey, 1999.

Chachage, Chambi Seithy, and Chachage Seithy L. Chachage. "Nyerere: Nationalism and Post-colonial Developmentalism." *African Sociological Review* 8, no. 2 (2004): 158–79.

Chan, Stephen. *The Commonwealth in World Politics: A Study of International Action 1965–1985*. London: Lester Crook Academic, 1988.

Chanock, Martin. *Law, Custom and Social Order: The Colonial Experience in Malawi and Zambia*. Portsmouth, NH: Heinemann, 1998.

Chatterjee, Partha. *Nationalist Thought and the Colonial World: A Derivative Course*. London: Zed Books, 1993.

Chau, Donovan C. *Exploiting Africa: The Influence of Maoist China in Algeria, Ghana, and Tanzania*. Annapolis, MD: Naval Institute Press, 2014.

Cheah, Pheng. *Spectral Nationality: Passages of Freedom from Kant to Postcolonial Literatures of Liberation*. New York: Columbia University Press, 2003.

———. *What Is in a World? On Postcolonial Literature as World Literature*. Durham, NC: Duke University Press, 2016.

Chisiza, D. K. "The Temper, Aspirations, and Problems of Contemporary Africa." In *Economic Development in Africa: Papers Presented to the Nyasaland Economic Symposium Held in Blantyre 18 to 28 July 1962*, edited by E. F. Jackson. Oxford: Blackwell, 1966.

Clarence-Smith, William Gervase. *Cocoa and Chocolate, 1765–1915*. New York: Routledge, 2000.

———, ed. *Cocoa Pioneer Fronts since 1800: The Role of Smallholders, Planters and Merchants*. London: Macmillan Press, 1996.

Clarke III, J. Calvitt. "Soviet Appeasement, Collective Security, and the Italo-Ethiopian War of 1935 and 1936." In *Collision of Empires: Italy's Invasion of Ethiopia and Its International Impact*, edited by G. Bruce Strang. Surrey, UK: Ashgate, 2013.

Clayton, Anthony. *France, Soldiers and Africa*. London: Brassey's Defense, 1988.

Clayton, Anthony, and David Killingray. *Khaki and Blue: Military and Police in British Colonial Africa*. Athens: Ohio University Center for International Studies, 1989.

Cochrane, Laura L. "The Growth of Artistic Nationalism in Senegal." *Nations and Nationalism* 17, no. 2 (2011): 377–95.

Cohen, Joshua. "Stages in Transition: Les Ballets Africains and Independence, 1959 to 1960." *Journal of Black Studies* 43, no. 1 (2012): 11–48.

Collins, John. "Ghanaian Highlife." *African Arts* 10, no. 1 (1976): 62–68.

———. *West African Pop Roots*. Philadelphia: Temple University Press, 1992.

Collins, Michael. "Decolonization and the 'Federal Moment.'" *Diplomacy and Statecraft* 24, no. 1 (2013): 21–40.

Cooper, Frederick. *Africa Since 1940: The Past of the Present*. 2nd ed. Cambridge: Cambridge University Press, 2019.

———. *Citizenship between Empire and Nation: Remaking France and French Africa, 1945–1960*. Princeton, NJ: Princeton University Press, 2014.

———. *Colonialism in Question: Theory, Knowledge, History*. Berkeley: University of California Press, 2005.

———. "Modernizing Bureaucrats, Backward Africans, and the Development Concept." In *International Development and the Social Sciences: Essays on the History and Politics of Knowledge*, edited by Frederick Cooper and Randall M. Packard. Berkeley: University of California Press, 1997.

Cooper, Frederick, and Randall M. Packard. "Introduction." In *International Development and the Social Sciences: Essays on the History and Politics of Knowledge*, edited by Frederick Cooper and Randall M. Packard. Berkeley: University of California Press, 1997.

Coulson, Andrew. *Tanzania: A Political Economy*. 2nd ed. Oxford: Oxford University Press, 2013.

Crawford, Romi. "The Event of the Photograph: Black Consciousness from the *Wall of Respect* '67 to FESTAC 77." *Nka: Journal of Contemporary African Art* 42–43 (November 2018): 154–63.

Cruise O'Brien, Donal B. *Saints and Politicians: Essays in the Organization of a Senegalese Peasant Society*. Cambridge: Cambridge University Press, 1975.

Daddieh, Cyril K. "Ethnicity, Conflict and the State in Contemporary West Africa." In *Themes in West Africa's History*, edited by Emmanuel Akyeampong. Oxford: James Currey, 2006.

Dadone, Aldo Antonio, and Luis Eugenio di Marco. "The Impact of Prebisch's Ideas on Modern Economic Analysis." In *International Economics and Development: Essays in Honor of Rául Prebisch*, edited by Luis Eugenio di Marco. New York: Academic Press, 1972.

Danquah, Francis K. "Capsid Pests as 'Cocoa Mosquitoes': A Study in Cash Crop Infestation and Control in Ghana, 1910–1965." *Journal of Third World Studies* 21, no. 2 (2004): 147–66.

———. "Rural Discontent and Decolonization in Ghana, 1945–1951." *Agricultural History* 68, no. 1 (1994): 1–19.

———. "Sustaining a West African Cocoa Economy: Agricultural Science and the Swollen Shoot Contagion in Ghana, 1936–1965." *African Economic History* 31 (2003): 43–74.

Danquah, Joseph Boakye. *The Ghanaian Establishment: Its Constitution, Its Detentions, Its Traditions, Its Justice and Statecraft, and Its Heritage of Ghanaism*. Edited by Albert Adu Boahen. Accra: Ghana Universities Press, 1997.

Davidson, Basil. *The Black Man's Burden: Africa and the Curse of the Nation-State*. New York: Times Books, 1992.

———. *Black Star: A View of the Life and Times of Kwame Nkrumah*. Oxford: James Currey, 2007 [1973].

———. *Modern Africa: A Social and Political History*. 2nd ed. London: Longman, 1989.

D'Avignon, Robyn. *A Ritual Geology: Gold and Subterranean Knowledge in Savanna West Africa*. Durham, NC: Duke University Press, 2022.

Decker, Stephanie. "Corporate Political Activity in Less Developed Countries: The Volta River Project in Ghana, 1958–66." *Business History* 53, no. 7 (2011): 993–1017.

Dekutsey, Woeli. *Kwegyir Aggrey of Africa: His Life and Achievements*. Accra: Woeli, 2012.

Dembélé, Demba Moussa. *Samir Amin: Intellectuel organique au service de l'émancipation du Sud*. Dakar: CODESRIA, 2011.

De Soto, Hernando. *The Mystery of Capitalism: Why Capitalism Triumphs in the West and Fails Everywhere Else*. New York: Basic Books, 2000.

Devarjan, Shanta, and Sudhir Shetty. "Africa: Leveraging the Crisis into a Development Takeoff." *Economic Premise* 30 (2010): 1–4.

Devlin, Lawrence. *Chief of Station, Congo*. New York: Public Affairs, 2007.

Dickson, Kwesi. "Religion and Society." In *The Life and Work of Kwame Nkrumah*, edited by Kwame Arhin. Accra: Sedco, 1991.

Di Marco, Luis Eugenio. "The Evolution of Prebisch's Economic Thought." In *International Economics and Development: Essays in Honor of Rául Prebisch*, edited by Luis Eugenio di Marco. New York: Academic Press, 1972.

Diop, Alioune. "From the Festival of Negro Arts at Dakar to the Lagos Festival: Itinerary." *Présence Africaine*, n.s., 92 (1974): 9–14.

Diouf, Mamadou. *La Kajoor au XIXe siècle: Pouvoir ceddo et Conquête Coloniale*. Paris: Karthala, 1990.

———. "Senegalese Development: From Mass Mobilization to Technocratic Elitism." In *International Development and the Social Sciences: Essays on the History and Politics of Knowledge*, edited by Frederick Cooper and Randall M. Packard. Berkeley: University of California Press, 1997.

Doumbouya, Sékou F., and Fodé Camara. "Explaining Economic Growth in Africa: The Case of Guinea." In *Country Case Studies*, edited by Benno J. Ndulu, Stephen A. O'Connell, Jean-Paul Azam, Robert H. Bates, Augustin K. Fosu, Jan Willem Gunning, and Dominique Njinkeu, 588–620. Vol. 2 of *The Political Economy of Economic Growth in Africa 1960–2000*. Cambridge: Cambridge University Press, 2008.

Dumett, Raymond E. "John Sarbah, the Elder, and African Mercantile Entrepreneurship in the Gold Coast in the Late Nineteenth Century." *Journal of African History* 14, no. 4 (1973): 653–79.

Echenberg, Myron J. *Colonial Conscripts: The Tirailleurs Senegalais in French West Africa, 1857–1960*. Portsmouth, NH: Heinemann, 1991.

———. *Plague Ports: The Global Urban Impact of Bubonic Plague, 1894–1901*. New York: New York University Press, 2007.

Eckert, Andreas. "Useful Instruments of Participation? Local Government and Cooperatives in Tanzania, 1940s to 1970s." *International Journal of African Historical Studies* 40, no. 1 (2007): 97–118.

Edwards, Brent Hayes. *The Practice of Diaspora: Literature, Translation, and the Rise of Black Internationalism*. Cambridge, MA: Harvard University Press, 2003.

Ekeh, Peter P. "Colonialism and the Two Publics in Africa: A Theoretical Statement." *Comparative Studies in Society and History* 17, no. 1 (1975): 91–112.

Ellis, Stephen. *External Mission: The ANC in Exile 1960–1990*. Oxford: Oxford University Press, 2013.

———. *The Mask of Anarchy: The Destruction of Liberia and the Religious Dimension of an African Civil War*. 2nd rev. ed. New York: New York University Press, 2006.

Ellis, Stephen, and Gerrie Ter Haar. *World of Power: Religious Thought and Political Practice in Africa*. New York: Oxford University Press, 2004.

Emmanuel, Patrick A. M., ed. *Sir William Arthur Lewis Collected Papers 1941–1988*. 3 vols. Barbados: Institute of Social and Economic Research, University of the West Indies, 1994.

Erben, Michael. "The Problem of Other Lives: Social Perspectives on Written Biography." *Sociology* 27, no. 1 (1993): 15–25.

Evensky, Jerry. *Adam Smith's Wealth of Nations: A Reader's Guide*. New York: Syracuse University Press, 2015.

Fair, Laura. *Pastimes and Politics: Culture, Community and Identity in Post-abolition Urban Zanzibar, 1890–1945*. Oxford: James Currey, 2001.

Falola, Toyin. *Nationalism and African Intellectuals*. Rochester, NY: University of Rochester Press, 2001.

Fanon, Frantz. *Black Skin, White Masks*. Translated by Richard Philcox. New York: Grove Press, 2008 [1952].

———. *Toward the African Revolution*. Translated by Haakon Chevalier. New York: Grove Press, 1967 [1964].

———. *The Wretched of the Earth*. Translated by Constance Harrington. New York: Grove Press, 1968 [1961].

Fatton Jr., Robert. *Predatory Rule: State and Civil Society in Africa*. Boulder, CO: Lynne Rienner, 1992.

Feierman, Steven. *Peasant Intellectuals: Anthropology and History in Tanzania*. Madison: University of Wisconsin Press, 1990.

Fetter, Bruce, ed. *Colonial Rule in Africa: Readings from Primary Sources*. Madison: University of Wisconsin Press, 1979.

Fields, Barbara Jeanne. "Slavery, Race and Ideology in the United States of America." *New Left Review* I, no. 181 (1990): 95–118.

Filipovich, Jean. "Destined to Fail: Forced Settlement at the Office du Niger, 1926–1945." *Journal of African History* 42, no. 2 (2001): 239–60.

Finnemore, Martha. "Redefining Development in the World Bank." In *International Development and the Social Sciences: Essays on the History and Politics of Knowledge*, edited by Frederick Cooper and Randall M. Packard. Berkeley: University of California Press, 1997.

Fourcade, Marion. *Economists and Societies: Discipline and Profession in the United States, Britain, and France, 1890s to 1990s*. Princeton, NJ: Princeton University Press, 2009.

Frank, Andre Gunder. *Crisis in the Third World*. New York: Holmes and Meier, 1981.

———. *Latin America: Underdevelopment or Revolution*. New York: Monthly Review Press, 1969.

Fuller, Harcourt. *Building the Ghanaian Nation-State: Kwame Nkrumah's Symbolic Nationalism*. New York: Palgrave Macmillan, 2014.

Gaines, Kevin K. *American Africans in Ghana: Black Expatriates and the Civil Rights Era*. Chapel Hill: University of North Carolina Press, 2006.

Gallagher, John. *The Revival, Decline and Fall of the British Empire*. Cambridge: Cambridge University Press, 1982.

Geggus, David P. "The Haitian Revolution." In *The Modern Caribbean*, edited by Franklin Knight and Colin Palmer. Chapel Hill: University of North Carolina Press, 1989.

Geiger, Susan. *TANU Women: Gender and Culture in the Making of Tanganyikan Nationalism, 1955–1965*. Portsmouth, NH: Heinemann, 1997.

Gellner, Ernest. *Nations and Nationalism*. Ithaca, NY: Cornell University Press, 1983.

Genoud, Roger. *Nationalism and Economic Development in Ghana*. New York: Frederick A. Praeger, 1969.

Getachew, Adom. *Worldmaking after Empire: The Rise and Fall of Self-Determination*. Princeton, NJ: Princeton University Press, 2019.

Gilman, Gils. *Mandarins of the Future: Modernization Theory in Cold War America*. Baltimore: Johns Hopkins University Press, 2003.

Goldsmith, M. M. "Regulating Anew the Moral and Political Sentiments of Mankind: Bernard Mandeville and the Scottish Enlightenment." *Journal of the History of Ideas* 49, no. 4 (1988): 587–606.

Gomez, Michael A. *Pragmatism in the Age of Jihad: The Precolonial State of Bundu*. Cambridge: Cambridge University Press, 1992.

Goodman, Nelson. *Ways of Worldmaking*. Indianapolis: Hackett, 1978.

Government of Ghana. *Seven-Year Development Plan 1963/64 to 1969/70*. Accra: Office of the Planning Commission, 1964.

Green, R. H., and S. H. Hymer. "Cocoa in the Gold Coast: A Study of the Relations between African Farmers and Agricultural Experts." *Journal of Economic History* 26, no. 3 (1966): 299–319.

Grischow, Jeff, and Holger Weiss. "Pan-Africanism, Socialism and the Future: Development Planning in Ghana, 1951–1966." In *The Struggle for the Long-Term in Transnational Science and Politics: Forging the Future*, edited by Jenny Andersson and Egle Rindzeviciute. London: Routledge, 2015.

Grottanelli, Vinigi L. *The Python Killer: Stories of Nzema Life*. Chicago: University of Chicago Press, 1988.

Hadjor, Kofi Buenor. *Nkrumah and Ghana: The Dilemma of Post-colonial Power*. London: Keegan Paul International, 1989.

Haenger, Peter. *Slaves and Slaveholders on the Gold Coast: Towards an Understanding of Social Bondage in West Africa*. Basel: P. Schlettwein, 2000.

Hagan, George P. "Nkrumah's Cultural Policies." In *The Life and Work of Kwame Nkrumah*, edited by Kwame Arhin. Accra: Sedco, 1991.

Hage, Ghassan. *Against Paranoid Nationalism: Searching for Hope in a Shrinking Society*. Sydney: Pluto Press, 2003.

Harney, Elizabeth. *In Senghor's Shadow: Art, Politics and the Avant-Garde in Senegal, 1960–1995*. Durham, NC: Duke University Press, 2004.

Harris, Brice. *The United States and the Italo-Ethiopian Crisis*. Stanford: Stanford University Press, 1964.

Harris, Joseph. *African-American Reactions to War in Ethiopia, 1936–1941*. Baton Rouge: Louisiana State University Press, 1994.

Hashachar, Yair. "Guinea Unbound: Performing Pan-African Cultural Citizenship between Algiers 1969 and the Guinean National Affairs." *Interventions* 20, no. 7 (2018): 1003–21. DOI: 10.1080/1369801X.2018.1508932.

———. "Playing the Backbeat in Conakry: Miriam Makeba and the Cultural Politics of Sékou Touré's Guinea, 1968–1986." *Social Dynamics* 43, no. 2 (2017): 259–73.

Headrick, Daniel R. *The Tentacles of Progress: Technology Transfer in the Age of Imperialism, 1850–1940*. New York: Oxford University Press, 1988.

———. *The Tools of Empire: Technology and European Imperialism in the Nineteenth Century*. New York: Oxford University Press, 1981.

Hecht, Robert M. "The Ivory Coast Economic 'Miracle': What Benefits for Peasant Farmers?" *Journal of Modern African Studies* 21, no. 1 (1983): 25–53.

Herbst, Jeffrey. *States and Power in Africa: Comparative Lessons in Authority and Control*. Princeton, NJ: Princeton University Press, 2000.

Hess, Janet, and Nii O. Quarcoopome. "Spectacular Nation: Nkrumahist Art and Resistance Iconography in the Ghanaian Independence Era." *African Arts* 39, no. 1 (2006): 16–25, 91–92.

Hill, Polly. *Development Economics on Trial: The Anthropological Case for a Prosecution*. Cambridge: Cambridge University Press, 1986.

———. *The Migrant Cocoa Farmers of Southern Ghana: A Study in Rural Capitalism*. Cambridge: Cambridge University Press, 1961.

Hirschman, Albert O. "The Political Economy of Import-Substituting Industrialization in Latin America." *Quarterly Journal of Economics* 62 (1968): 1–32.

———. "The Rise and Decline of Development Economics." In *The Essential Hirschman*, edited by Jeremy Adelman. Princeton, NJ: Princeton University Press, 2013.

———. *The Strategy of Economic Development*. New Haven, CT: Yale University Press, 1958.

Hodge, P. "The Ghana Workers Brigade: A Project for Unemployed Youth." *British Journal of Sociology* 15, no. 2 (1964): 113–28.

Honeyman, Catherine A. *The Orderly Entrepreneur: Youth, Education, and Governance in Rwanda*. Stanford: University of Stanford Press, 2016.

Hopkins, A. G. *An Economic History of West Africa*. New York: Columbia University Press, 1973.

Huddleston, Trevor. "The Person Nyerere." In *Mwalimu: The Influence of Nyerere*, edited by Colin Legum and Geoffrey Mmari. London: James Currey, 1995.

Hutchful, Eboe. *Ghana's Adjustment Experience: The Paradox of Reform*. Oxford: James Currey and UNRISD, 2002.

Hutchinson, Alfred. *Road to Ghana*. London: Victor Gollancz, 1960.

Iliffe, John. *The African Aids Epidemic: A History*. Athens: Ohio University Press, 2006.

———. *A Modern History of Tanganyika*. Cambridge: Cambridge University Press, 1994 [1979].

Irele, F. Abiola. *The Negritude Moment: Explorations in Francophone African and Caribbean Literature and Thought*. Trenton, NJ: Africa World Press, 2011.

Isaacman, Allen, and Barbara Isaacman. *Dams, Displacement and the Delusion of Development: Cahora Bassa and Its Legacies in Mozambique, 1965–2007*. Athens: Ohio University Press, 2013.

Jackson, E. F., ed. *Economic Development in Africa: Papers Presented to the Nyasaland Economic Symposium Held in Blantyre 18 to 28 July 1962*. Oxford: Basil Blackwell, 1965.

Jackson, Robert H., and Carl G. Rosberg. *Personal Rule in Black Africa: Prince, Autocrat, Prophet, Tyrant*. Berkeley: University of California Press, 1982.

Jalloh, Alusine. *African Entrepreneurship: Muslim Fula Merchants in Sierra Leone*. Athens: Ohio University Press, 1999.

———. *Muslim Fula Business Elites and Politics in Sierra Leone*. Rochester, NY: University of Rochester Press, 2018.

James, C. L. R. *The Black Jacobins: Toussaint L'Ouverture and the San Domingo Revolution*. London: Secker & Warburg, 2001 [1938].

———. *Nkrumah and the Ghana Revolution*. Durham, NC: Duke University Press, 2022[1977].

James, Leslie. *George Padmore and Decolonization from Below: Pan-Africanism, the Cold War, and the End of Empire*. New York: Palgrave Macmillan, 2015.

Jerven, Morten. *Poor Numbers: How We Are Misled by African Development Statistics and What to Do about It*. Ithaca, NY: Cornell University Press, 2013.

Jonah, Kwesi. "Imperialism, the State and the Indigenization of the Ghanaian Economy, 1957–84." *Africa Development* 10, no. 3 (1985): 63–99.

Jones, Diana K. "Research Groups of Lives: A Collective Biographical Perspective on the Protestant Ethnic Debate." *Qualitative Research* 1, no. 3 (2001): 325–46.

Jopp, Keith. *Volta: The Story of Ghana's Volta River Project.* Accra: Volta River Authority, 1965.

Kaba, Lansiné. "The Cultural Revolution, Artistic Creativity, and Freedom of Expression in Guinea." *Journal of Modern African Studies* 14, no. 2 (1976): 201–18.

———. "Guinean Politics: A Critical Review History." *Journal of Modern African Studies* 15, no. 1 (1977): 25–45.

———. *Kwame Nkrumah and the Dream of African Unity.* New York: Diasporic Africa Press, 2017.

Kay, G. B. *The Political Economy of Colonialism in Ghana: A Collection of Documents and Statistics 1900–1960.* Cambridge: Cambridge University Press, 1972.

Keese, Alexander. "Slow Abolition within the Colonial Mind: British and French Debates about 'Vagrancy,' 'African Laziness,' and Forced Labor in West Central and South Central Africa, 1945–1965." *International Review of Social History* 59, no. 3 (2014): 377–407.

———. "Understanding Colonial Chieftaincy from Its Final Phase: Responses to the Crisis of an Institution in French-ruled West Africa and beyond, 1944–1960." *Africana Studia* 15 (2010): 11–28.

Kelley, Robin D. G. *Freedom Dreams: The Black Radical Imagination.* Boston: Beacon Press, 2002.

Kelly, John D., and Martha Kaplan. "Nation and Decolonization: Toward a New Anthropology of Nationalism." *Anthropological Theory* 1, no. 4 (2001): 419–37.

Killick, Tony. *Development Economics in Action: A Study of Economic Policies in Ghana.* London: Heinemann, 1978.

———. *A Reaction Too Far: Economic Theory and the Role of the State in Developing Countries.* London: Overseas Development Institute, 1989.

Kiwanuka, M. S. M. "Uganda under the British." In *Zamani: A Survey of East African History*, edited by B. A. Ogot and J. A. Kieran. New York: Humanities Press, 1971.

Ki-Zerbo, Joseph. "African Intellectuals, Nationalism and Pan-Africanism: A Testimony." In *African Intellectuals: Rethinking Politics, Language, Gender and Development*, edited by Thandika Mkandawire. Dakar: CODESRIA Books, 2005.

Kojima, Masami, and Chris Trimble. *Making Power Affordable for Africa and Viable for Utilities.* Washington, DC: World Bank, 2016.

Konings, Piet. "Capitalist Rice Farming and Land Allocation in Northern Ghana." *Journal of Legal Pluralism and Unofficial Law* 16, no. 22 (1984): 89–119.

Kyerematen, A. A. Y. *Kingship and Ceremony in Ashanti.* Kumasi: UST Press, 1969.

Labi, Kwame Amoah. "Cross-Cultural Appropriation of Regalia and Royal Art, and Contemporary Adaptations in Ghana." In *Chieftaincy in Ghana: Culture, Governance and Development*, edited by Irene K. Odotei and Albert K. Awedoba. Accra: Sub-Saharan, 2006.

Laïdi, Zaki. *The Superpowers and Africa: The Constraints of a Rivalry, 1960–1990.* Chicago: University of Chicago Press, 1990.

Lal, Deepak. *The Poverty of 'Development Economics.'* London: Institute of Economic Affairs, 2002 [1983].

Lal, Priya. *African Socialism in Post-colonial Tanzania: Between the Village and the World.* New York: Cambridge University Press, 2015.

Lambert, Keri. "'It's All Work and Happiness on the Farms': Agricultural Development between the Blocs in Nkrumah's Ghana." *Journal of African History* 60, no. 1 (2019): 25–44.

Langley, J. Ayodele. *Pan-Africanism and Nationalism in West Africa, 1900–1945*. Oxford: Clarendon Press, 1973.

Lee, Christopher J. "Introduction: Between a Moment and an Era: The Origins and Afterlives of Bandung." In *Making a World after Empire: The Bandung Moment and Its Political Afterlives*, edited by Christopher J. Lee. Athens: Ohio University Press, 2010.

Legum, Colin. *Pan-Africanism: A Short Political Guide*. New York: Frederick A. Praeger, 1962.

Leibenstein, Harvey. *Economic Backwardness and Economic Growth: Studies in the Theory of Economic Development*. New York: Wiley, 1957.

———. *A Theory of Economic-Demographic Development*. Princeton, NJ: Princeton University Press, 1954.

Lenin, V. I. *Imperialism, The Highest Stage of Capitalism*. Chippendale, Australia: Resistance Books, 1999.

———. *"Left-Wing" Communism, an Infantile Disorder*. New York: International, 1940 [1920].

———. *Two Tactics of Social Democracy in the Democratic Revolution*. Peking: Foreign Language Press, 1965.

Lentz, Carola, and David Lowe. *Remembering Independence*. London: Routledge, 2018.

Lewin, Thomas. *Asante Before the British: The Prempean Years, 1875–1900*. Lawrence: Regents Press of Kansas, 1978.

Lewis, William Arthur. "Colonial Development." In *Sir William Arthur Lewis Collected Papers 1941–1988*. Vol. 2, edited by Patrick A. M. Emmanuel. Cave Hill, Barbados: Institute of Social and Economic Research, University of the West Indies, 1994 [1949].

———. "Economic Development with Unlimited Supplies of Labour." *Manchester School* 22, no. 2 (May 1954): 131–91.

———. *The Evolution of Foreign Aid*. Cardiff: University of Wales, 1971.

———. *Politics in West Africa*. Toronto: Oxford University Press, 1965.

———. *The Principles of Economic Planning*. 2nd ed. London: Unwin University Books, 1952.

———. *Report on Industrialization and the Gold Coast*. Accra: Government Printing Department, 1963 [1953].

Lonsdale, John M. "Anti-colonial Nationalism and Patriotism in Sub-Saharan Africa." In *The Oxford Handbook of the History of Nationalism*, edited by John Breuilly. Oxford: Oxford University Press, 2013. DOI: 1093/oxfordhb/9780199209194.013.0016.

Louis, William Roger. "The Dissolution of the British Empire." In *The Oxford History of the British Empire: The Twentieth Century*, edited by Judith M. Brown and William Roger Louis. Oxford: Oxford University Press, 1999.

Louis, William Roger, and Ronald Robinson. "Empire Preserv'd: How the Americans Put Anti-communism before Anti-imperialism." In *Decolonization: Perspectives from Now and Then*, edited by Prasenjit Duara. London: Routledge, 2004.

Luckham, Robin. *The Nigerian Military: A Sociological Analysis of Authority and Revolt 1960–1967*. Cambridge: Cambridge University Press, 1971.

———. *Politicians and Soldiers in Ghana, 1966–1972*. London: Cass, 1975.

Lynn, Martin. *Commerce and Economic Change in West Africa: The Palm Oil Trade in the Nineteenth Century*. Cambridge: Cambridge University Press, 1997.

Mahoney, Richard D. *JFK: Ordeal in Africa*. New York: Oxford University Press, 1983.

Mamdani, Mahmood. *Citizen and Subject: Contemporary Africa and the Legacy of Late Colonialism*. Princeton, NJ: Princeton University Press, 1996.

———. *Define and Rule: Native as Political Identity*. Cambridge, MA: Harvard University Press, 2012.

Manela, Erez. *The Wilsonian Moment: Self-Determination and the International Origins of Anticolonial Nationalism*. Oxford: Oxford University Press, 2007.

Mann, Gregory. *Native Sons: West African Veterans and France in the Twentieth Century*. Durham, NC: Duke University Press, 2006.

———. "What Was the Indigénat? The 'Empire of Law' in French West Africa." *Journal of African History* 50, no. 3 (2009): 331–53.

Mann, Laura, and Marie Berry. "Understanding the Political Motivations That Shape Rwanda's Emergent Developmental State." *New Political Economy* 21, no. 1 (2016): 119–44.

Manning, Patrick. *Francophone Sub-Saharan Africa 1880–1995*. Cambridge: Cambridge University Press, 1998.

Maoulidi, Salma. "Racial and Religious Tolerance in Nyerere's Political Thought and Practice." In *Africa's Liberation: The Legacy of Nyerere*, edited by Chambi Chachage and Annar Cassam. Cape Town: Pambazuka Press, 2010.

Marden, Peter. *The Ivory Coast: Economic Miracle or Blocked Development? Implications for the Geography of Development*. Melbourne: Monash University, 1990.

Markovitz, Irving Leonard. *Léopold Sédar Senghor and the Politics of Negritude*. New York: Atheneum, 1969.

Martin, S. M. "The Long Depression: West African Export Producers and the World Economy, 1914–1945." In *The Economies of Africa and Asia in the Inter-war Depression*, edited by Ian Brown. New York: Routledge, 1989.

Mbembe, Achille. "African Modes of Self-Writing." *Public Culture* 14, no. 1 (2002): 239–73.

———. *On the Postcolony*. Berkeley: University of California Press, 2001.

———. *Out of the Dark Night: Essays on Decolonization*. Johannesburg: Witwatersrand University Press, 2021.

Mbiti, John S. *African Religions and Philosophy*. Nairobi: Heinemann, 1969.

Mbughuni, Azaria. "Tanzania and the Pan African Quest for Unity, Freedom, and Independence in East, Central, and Southern Africa: The Case of the Pan African Freedom Movement for East, Central, and Southern Africa." *Journal of Pan African Studies* 7, no. 4 (2014): 211–38.

McCain, James A. "Ideology and Leadership in Post-Nkrumah Ghana." In *Socialism in Sub-Saharan Africa: A New Assessment*, edited by Carl G. Rosberg and Thomas M. Callaghy. Berkeley: University of California Institute of International Studies, 1979.

McGovern, Mike. *Unmasking the State: Making Guinea Modern*. Chicago: University of Chicago Press, 2012.

McHenry Jr., Dean E. "The Struggle for Rural Socialism in Tanzania." In *Socialism in Sub-Saharan Africa: A New Assessment*, edited by Carl G. Rosberg and Thomas M. Callaghy. Berkeley: Institute of International Studies, University of California, 1979.

McWilliam, H. O. A., and M. A. Kwamena-Poh. *The Development of Education in Ghana*. London: Longman, 1975.

Melady, Thomas Patrick. *Profiles of African Leaders*. New York: Macmillan, 1961.

Melady, Thomas Patrick, and Margaret Badum Melady. *Ten African Heroes: The Sweep of Independence in Black Africa*. Maryknoll, NY: Orbis Books, 2011.

Mcsaki, Simeon, and Mrisho Malipula. "Julius Nyerere's Influence and Legacy: From a Proponent of Familyhood to a Candidate for Sainthood." *International Journal of Sociology and Anthropology* 3, no. 3 (2011): 93–100.

Mfenyana, Sindiso. *Walking with Giants: Life and Times of an ANC Veteran*. Cape Town: South African History Online, 2017.

Miescher, Stephan F. "'Nkrumah's Baby': The Akosombo Dam and the Dream of Development in Ghana, 1952–1966." *Water History* 6 (2014): 341–66.

Miescher, Stephan F., and Dzodzi Tsikata. "Hydro-power and the Promise of Modernity and Development in Ghana: Comparing the Akosombo and Bui Projects." *Ghana Studies* 12/13 (2009/2010): 15–33.

Milne, June. *Kwame Nkrumah: The Conakry Years*. London: Panaf Books, 2000 [1991].

Mkandawire, Thandika. *Fifty Years of Independence: Personal Reflections*. Dar es Salaam: Mkuki na Nyota, 2013.

———. "The New International Economic Order, Basic Needs Strategies and the Future of Africa." *Africa Development* 5, no. 3 (1980): 68–89.

———. "Thinking about Developmental States in Africa." *Cambridge Journal of Economics* 25, no. 3 (2001): 289–313.

Mkandawire, Thandika, and Charles C. Soludo, eds. *African Voices on Structural Adjustment*. Dakar: CODESRIA, 2003.

Mkandawire, Thandika, and Charles C. Soludo. *Our Continent, Our Future: African Perspectives on Structural Adjustment*. Dakar: CODESRIA, 1999.

Mlama, Penina. "Emergence: The Indelible Face of Artistic Creativity in the Struggle for Self-Determination in Africa." *Africa Development* 42, no. 4 (2017): 17–36.

Molony, Thomas. *Nyerere: The Early Years*. Woodbridge, Suffolk: Boydell and Brewer, 2014.

Monroe, Arthur. "FESTAC 77—The Second World Black and African Festival of Arts and Culture: Lagos, Nigeria." *Black Scholar* 9, no. 1 (1977): 34–37.

Monson, Jamie. *Africa's Freedom Railway: How a Chinese Development Project Changed Lives and Livelihoods in Tanzania*. Bloomington: Indiana University Press, 2009.

Morgenthau, Ruth Schachter. *Political Parties in French-Speaking West Africa*. Oxford: Clarendon Press, 1964.

Morris, Colin M. *A Humanist in Africa: Letters to Colin M. Morris from Kenneth D. Kaunda President of Zambia*. London: Longmans, 1966.

Moxon, James. *Volta, Man's Greatest Lake: The Story of Ghana's Akosombo Dam*. London: Andre Deutsch, 1984.

Moyo, Dambisa. *Dead Aid: Why Aid Is Not Working and How There Is a Better Way for Africa*. London: Allen Lane, 2009.

Muehlenbeck, Philip E. *Betting on the Africans: John F. Kennedy's Courting of African Nationalist Leaders*. Oxford: Oxford University Press, 2012.

———. "Kennedy and Touré: A Success in Personal Diplomacy." *Diplomacy and Statecraft* 19, no. 1 (2008): 69–95.

Muojama, Olisa Godson. "The First World War and the Cocoa Industry in Ghana: A Study of the Hazards of Economic Dependency." *Global Journal of Human-Social Science* 16, no. 6 (2016): 33–41.

Mwase, Nkunde, and Benno J. Ndulu. "Tanzania: Explaining Four Decades of Episodic Growth." In *Country Case Studies*, edited by Benno J. Ndulu, Stephen A. O'Connell, Jean-Paul Azam, Robert H. Bates, Augustin K. Fosu, Jan Willem Gunning, and Dominique Njinkeu. Vol. 2 of *The Political Economy of Economic Growth in Africa 1960–2000*. Cambridge: Cambridge University Press, 2008.

Myrdal, Gunnar. *Economic Theory and Underdeveloped Regions*. London: G. Duckworth, 1957.

Ndiaye, Mansour. "State Control and Poor Economic Growth Performance in Senegal." In *Country Case Studies*, edited by Benno J. Ndulu, Stephen A. O'Connell, Jean-Paul Azam, Robert H. Bates, Augustin K. Fosu, Jan Willem Gunning, and Dominique Njinkeu. Vol. 2 of *The Political Economy of Economic Growth in Africa, 1960–2000*. Cambridge: Cambridge University Press, 2008.

Ndulu, Benno J. "The Evolution of Global Development Paradigms and Their Influence on African Economic Growth." In *The Political Economy of Economic Growth in Africa 1960–2000*. Vol. 1, edited by Benno J. Ndulu, Stephen A. O'Connell, Robert H. Bates, Paul Collier, and Chukwuma C. Soludo. Cambridge: Cambridge University Press, 2008.

Ndulu, Benno J., and Stephen A. O'Connell. "Policy Plus: African Growth Performance, 1960–2000." In *The Political Economy of Economic Growth in Africa 1960–2000*. Vol. 1, edited by Benno J. Ndulu, Stephen A. O'Connell, Robert H. Bates, Paul Collier, and Chukwuma C. Soludo. Cambridge: Cambridge University Press, 2008.

Neuschel, Kristen. *Word of Honor: Interpreting Noble Gesture in Sixteenth-Century France*. Ithaca, NY: Cornell University Press, 1989.

Newell, Stephanie. *The Power to Name: A History of Anonymity in Colonial West Africa*. Athens: Ohio University Press, 2013.

Newlyn, W. T. "'Take-off' Considered in an African Setting." *Yorkshire Bulletin of Economic and Social Research* 13, no. 1 (1961): 19–32.

Nketia, J. H. Kwabena. *Ayan*. Vol. 1, *The Poetry of the Atumpan Drums of the Asantehene*. Accra: Institute of African Studies, University of Ghana, 1966.

———. *Reinstating Traditional Music in Contemporary Contexts*. Akropong-Akuapem: Regnum Africa, 2016.

Nkrumah, Kwame. "African Socialism Revisited." In *The African Reader: Independent Africa*, edited by W. Cartey and M. Kilson. New York: Random House, 1970.

———. *Class Struggle in Africa*. New York: International, 1970.

———. *Consciencism*. New York: Modern Reader Paperbacks, 1970 [1964].

———. *Dark Days in Ghana*. London: Panaf Books, 1968.

———. *Ghana: The Autobiography of Kwame Nkrumah*. New York: International, 1976 [1957].

———. *Handbook of Revolutionary Warfare: A Guide to the Armed Phase of the African Revolution*. London: Panaf Books, 1968.

———. *Neo-colonialism: The Last Stage of Imperialism*. New York: International, 1966 [1965].

Noer, Thomas J. "The New Frontier and African Neutralism: Kennedy, Nkrumah, and the Volta River Project." *Diplomatic History* 8, no. 1 (1984): 61–79.

Nugent, Paul. *Africa since Independence: A Comparative History*. New York: Palgrave Macmillan, 2004.

Nünning, Vera, Ansgar Nünning, and Birgit Neumann, eds. *Cultural Ways of World-making: Media and Narratives*. Berlin: De Gruyter, 2010.

Nurkse, Ragnar. *Problems of Capital Formation in Underdeveloped Countries*. New York: Oxford University Press, 1953.

———. "Some International Aspects of the Problems of Economic Development." *American Economic Review* 40, no. 2 (1952): 571–83.

Nwokeji, Ugo G. *The Slave Trade and Culture in the Bight of Biafra*. New York: Cambridge University Press, 2010.

Nyerere, Julius K. *The Arusha Declaration Ten Years Later*. Dar es Salaam: United Republic of Tanzania, 1977.

———. *Freedom and Development: A Selection from Writings and Speeches 1968–1973*. London: Oxford University Press, 1973.

———. *Freedom and Socialism: A Selection of Writings and Speeches 1965–1967*. Dar es Salaam: Oxford University Press, 1968.

———. *Freedom and Unity: A Selection from Writings and Speeches 1952–65*. Dar es Salaam: Oxford University Press, 1966.

———. "Poverty, Christianity and Revolution." *New Blackfriars* 52, no. 618 (1971): 484–95.

———. *Ujamaa: Essays on Socialism*. Dar es Salaam: Oxford University Press, 1968.

Obeng, Samuel. *Selected Speeches: Kwame Nkrumah*. 2 vols. Accra: Afram, 1979.

Ochonu, Moses. *Colonial Meltdown: Northern Nigeria in the Great Depression*. Athens: Ohio University Press, 2009.

Omaboe, E. N. "An Introductory Survey." In *The Economy of Ghana*, edited by Walter Birmingham, I. Neustadt, and E. N. Omaboe. Vol. 1 of *A Study of Contemporary Ghana*. London: George Allen and Unwin, 1966.

Omu, Fred I. A. "The Dilemma of Press Freedom in Colonial Africa: The West African Example." *Journal of African History* 9, no. 2 (1968): 279–98.

———. *Press and Politics in Nigeria, 1880–1937*. London: Longman, 1978.

Onuoha, Bede. *The Elements of African Socialism*. London: A Deutsch, 1965.

Osei-Opare, Nana. "Uneasy Comrades: Postcolonial Statecraft, Race, and Citizenship, Ghana-Soviet Relations, 1957–1966." *Journal of West African History* 5, no. 2 (2019): 85–111.

Osseo-Asare, Abena. *Atomic Junction: Nuclear Power in Africa after Independence*. New York: Cambridge University Press, 2019.

Owens, Geoffrey Ross. "The Secret History of TANU: Rumor, Historiography and Muslim Unrest in Contemporary Dar es Salaam." *History and Anthropology* 16, no. 4 (2005): 441–63.

Padmore, George. *Pan-Africanism or Communism? The Coming Struggle for Africa*. New York: Roy, 1956.

Parpart, Jane. "'Where Is your Mother?': Gender, Urban Marriage, and Colonial Discourse on the Zambian Copperbelt, 1925–1945." *International Journal of African Historical Studies* 27, no. 2 (1994): 241–71.

Parsons, Timothy H. "Mobilizing Britain's African Empire for War: Pragmatism vs Trusteeship." *Journal of Modern European Studies* 13, no. 2 (2015): 183–202.

Patel, I. G., ed. *Policies for African Development: From the 1980s to the 1990s*. Washington, DC: International Monetary Fund, 1992.

Pitcher, Anne M., and Kelly M. Askew. "African Socialisms and Post-Socialisms." *Africa* 76, no. 1 (2006): 1–14.

Plageman, Nate. *Highlife Saturday Night: Popular Music and Social Change in Urban Ghana*. Bloomington: Indiana University Press, 2013.

Platvoet, Jan, and Henk van Rinsum. "Is Africa Incurably Religious?" *Exchange* 32, no. 2 (2003): 123–53.

Pobee, John S. *Kwame Nkrumah and the Church in Ghana: 1949–1966*. Denver: IAcademic Books, 2000.

Prasad, Vijay. *The Darker Nations: A People's History of the Third World*. New York: New Press, 2007.

Prebisch, Raúl. "Commercial Policy in Underdeveloped Countries." *American Economic Review* 49, no. 2 (1959): 251–73.

———. *The Economic Development of Latin America and Its Principal Problems*. Santiago: Economic Commission for Latin America and the Caribbean, 1950.

Quansah, S. T. "The Future of Cocoa." *Ghana Farmer* 8, no. 3 (1964): 98–100.

Rado, Emil. "Notes Towards a Political Economy of Ghana Today." *African Affairs* 85, no. 841 (1986): 563–72.

Ranger, Terence O. *Dance and Society in East Africa: The Beni Ngoma*. London: Heinemann, 1975.

Ratcliff, Anthony J. "When Négritude Was in Vogue: Critical Reflections of the First World Festival of Negro Arts and Culture in 1966." *Journal of Pan African Studies* 6, no. 7 (2014): 162–86.

Rathbone, Richard. "From Kingdom to Nation: Challenging African Constructions of Identity." In *Chieftaincy in Ghana: Culture, Governance and Development*, edited by Irene K. Odotei and Albert K. Awedoba. Accra: Sub-Saharan, 2006.

———. *Nkrumah and the Chiefs: The Politics of Chieftaincy in Ghana 1951–60*. Oxford: James Currey, 2000.

———. "World War I and Africa: Introduction." *Journal of African History* 19, no. 1 (1978): 1–9.

Richard, Allen B. *European Slave Trading in the Indian Ocean, 1500–1850*. Athens: Ohio University Press, 2014.

Rimmer, Douglas. "Learning about Economic Development from Africa." *African Affairs* 102, no. 408 (2003): 469–91.

———. *Staying Poor: Ghana's Political Economy, 1950–1990*. New York: Pergamon Press, 1992.

Riverson, Isaac D. *Songs of the Akan Peoples*. Accra: Methodist Book Depot, 1939.

Rivière, Claude. *Mutations Sociales en Guinée*. Paris: Marcel Rivière, 1971.

Roberts, Andrew D. "Introduction." In *The Colonial Moment in Africa: Essays on the Movement of Minds and Materials, 1890–1940*, edited by Andrew D. Roberts. Cambridge: Cambridge University Press, 1990.

Robinson, David. *The Holy War of Umar Tal: The Western Sudan in the Mid-nineteenth Century*. Oxford: Clarendon Press, 1985.

———. *Muslim Societies in African History*. Cambridge: Cambridge University Press, 2004.

Robinson, Ronald, Alice Denny, and John Gallagher. *Africa and the Victorians: The Official Mind of Imperialism*. London: Macmillan, 1961.

Rodney, Walter. *How Europe Underdeveloped Africa*. London: Bogle-L'Ouverture, 1972.

Rodrik, Dani. "Africa after Covid-19: De-globalization and Recalibrating Nations' Growth Prospects." *Contemporary Issues in African Trade and Trade Finance* 6, no. 1 (2020): 14–17.

Roitman, Janet. *Fiscal Disobedience: An Anthropology of Economic Regulation in Central Africa*. Princeton, NJ: Princeton University Press, 2005.

Rooney, David. *Kwame Nkrumah: The Political Kingdom in the Third World*. New York: St. Martin's Press, 1988.

Rosenstein-Rodan, Paul. "Problems of Industrialization of Eastern and South-Eastern Europe." *Economic Journal* 53 (1943): 202–11.

Ross, Corey. "The Plantation Paradigm: Colonial Agronomy, African Farmers, and the Global Cocoa Boom, 1870s–1940s." *Journal of Global History* 9, no. 1 (2014): 49–71.

Ross, Doran H. "The Iconography of Asante Sword Ornaments." *African Arts* 11, no. 1 (1977): 16–25.

———. "The Verbal Arts of Akan Linguist Staffs." *African Arts* 16, no. 1 (1982): 56–96.

———. *Wrapped in Pride: Ghanaian Kente and African American Identity*. Los Angeles: UCLA Fowler Museum of Cultural History, 1999.

Rostow, W. W. *The Process of Economic Growth*. Oxford: Clarendon Press, 1953.

———. *The Stages of Economic Growth: A Non-communist Manifesto*. Cambridge: Cambridge University Press, 1961.

Said, Mohamed. *The Life and Times of Abdul Wahid Sykes (1924–1968): The Untold Story of the Muslim Struggle against British Colonialism in Tanganyika*. London: Minerva Press, 1998.

Schatten, Fritz. *Communism in Africa*. London: George Allen and Unwin, 1966.

Schmidt, Elizabeth. *Cold War and Decolonization in Guinea, 1946–1958*. Athens: Ohio University Press, 2007.

———. *Foreign Intervention in Africa: From the Cold War to the War on Terror*. Cambridge: Cambridge University Press, 2013.

Schwarzmantel, John. "Nationalism and Socialist Internationalism." In *The Oxford Handbook of the History of Nationalism*, edited by John Breuilly. Oxford: Oxford University Press, 2013. DOI: 1093/oxfordhb/9780199209194.013.0032.

Scitovsky, Tibor. "Two Concepts of External Economies." *Journal of Political Economy* 62, no. 2 (1954): 143–51.

Scott, Daryl Michael. "How Black Nationalism became Sui Generis." *Fire!!!* 1, no. 2 (2012): 6–63.

Scott, James C. *Seeing like a State: How Certain Schemes to Improve the Human Condition Have Failed*. New Haven, CT: Yale University Press, 1998.

Scott, William Randolph. *The Sons of Sheba's Race: African-Americans and the Italo-Ethiopian War, 1935–1941*. Bloomington: Indiana University Press, 1993.

Seers, Dudley. "International Aid: The Next Steps." *Journal of Modern African Studies* 2, no. 4 (1964): 471–89.

Seidenberg, Dana April. *Mercantile Adventurers: The World of East African Asians, 1750–1985*. New Delhi: New Age International, 1996.

Senghor, Léopold Sédar. *The Foundations of "Africanité" or "Négritude" and "Arabité."* Translated by Mercer Cook. Paris: Présence Africaine, 1971.

———. *Liberté 1: négritude et humanisme*. Paris: Editions du Seuil, 1964.

———. *On African Socialism*. Translated with an introduction by Mercer Cook. New York: Praeger, 1964 [1961].

———. *Pierre Teilhard de Chardin et la Politique Africaine*. Paris: Editions du Seuil, 1962.

———. *Socialisme et Planification*. Paris: Seuil, 1983.

Shaw, Rosalind. *Memories of the Slave Trade: Ritual and Historical Imagination in Sierra Leone*. Chicago: University of Chicago Press, 2002.

Sheldon, Brittany. "Becoming Ghana: The Role of Artwork in Forming Ghanaian National Identity." *Montage* 5 (2011): 46–57.

Sheriff, Abdul. *Dhow Cultures of the Indian Ocean: Cosmopolitanism, Commerce and Islam*. London: C. Hurst, 2010.

Sherwood, Marika. *Kwame Nkrumah: The Years Abroad 1935–1947*. Accra: Freedom, 1996.

———. *Manchester and the 1945 Pan-African Congress*. London: Savannah Press, 1995.

Shivji, Issa G. "The Village in Mwalimu's Thought and Political Practice." In *Africa's Liberation: The Legacy of Julius Nyerere*, edited by Chambi Chachage and Annar Cassam. Cape Town: Pambazuka Press, 2010.

Shivji, Issa G., Saida Yahya-Othman, and Ng'wanza Kamata. *Development as Rebellion: A Biography of Julius Nyerere*. 3 vols. Dar es Salaam: Mkuki Na Nyota, 2020.

Shule, Vicensia. "Mwalimu Nyerere: The Artist." In *Africa's Liberation: The Legacy of Nyerere*, edited by Chambi Chachage and Annar Cassam. Cape Town: Pambazuka Press, 2010.

Sikkink, Kathryn. "Development Ideas in Latin America: Paradigm Shift and the Economic Commission for Latin America." In *International Development and the Social Sciences: Essays on the History and Politics of Knowledge*, edited by Frederick Cooper and Randall M. Packard. Berkeley: University of California Press, 1997.

Singer, Hans Wolfgang. "Gains and Losses from Trade and Investment in Underdeveloped Countries." *American Economic Review* 40 (1950): 473–85.

———. *International Development: Growth and Change*. New York: McGraw-Hill, 1962.

Skidelsky, Robert. *Keynes: The Return of the Master*. New York: Public Affairs, 2009.

Smith, Adam. *The Wealth of Nations*. Edited with an introduction and notes by Edwin Cannan. New York: Ixia Press, 2019 [1776].

Smith, Anthony D. *Ethnic Origins of Nations*. Oxford: Basil Blackwell, 1986.

———. "The Origins of Nations." *Ethnic and Racial Studies* 12, no. 3 (1989): 340–67.

———. *Theories of Nationalism*. London: Gerald Duckworth, 1971.

Smith, William Edgett. *Nyerere of Tanzania*. London: Victor Gollanz, 1973.

Snipe, Tracy D. *Arts and Politics in Senegal: 1960–1996*. Trenton, NJ: Africa World Press, 1998.

Southall, Roger J. "Farmers, Traders and Brokers in the Gold Coast Cocoa Economy." *Canadian Journal of African Studies* 12, no. 2 (1978): 185–211.

Southern, J. "FESTAC '77." *Black Perspective in Music* 5, no. 1 (1977): 104–17.

Spitzer, Leo, and LaRay Denzer. "I. T. A. Wallace-Johnson and the West African Youth League." *International Journal of African Historical Studies* 6, no. 3 (1973): 413–52.

Steel, William F. "Import Substitution and Excess Capacity in Ghana." *Oxford Economic Papers* 24, no. 2 (1972): 212–40.

Stern, Nicholas H. "Professor Bauer on Development." *Journal of Development Economics* 1 (1974): 191–211.

Stockwell, John. *In Search of Enemies*. New York: W. W. Norton, 1978.

Stolper, Wolfgang Frederick. *Planning without Facts: Lessons in Resource Allocation from Nigeria's Development: With an Input-Output Analysis of the Nigerian Economy, 1959–60*. Cambridge, MA: Harvard University Press, 1966.

Stone, Lawrence. *The Past and the Present Revisited*. London: Routledge and Kegan Paul, 1987.

Straker, James D. *Youth, Nationalism, and the Guinean Revolution*. Bloomington: Indiana University Press, 2009.

Strange, Austin. "Seven Decades of Chinese State Financing in Africa: Tempering Current Debates." *Economic History of Developing Regions* 34, no. 3 (2019): 259–79.

Terretta, Meredith. "Cameroonian Nationalists Go Global: From Forest *Maquis* to a Pan-African Accra." *Journal of African History* 51, no. 2 (2010): 189–212.

———. *Nation of Outlaws, State of Violence: Nationalism, Grassfields Tradition, and State Building in Cameroon*. Athens: Ohio University Press, 2013.

Thomas, Roger. "Forced Labour in British West Africa: The Case of the Northern Territories of the Gold Coast, 1906–1927." *Journal of African History* 14, no. 1 (1973): 79–103.

Thompson, Scott W. *Ghana's Foreign Policy, 1957–1966: Diplomacy, Ideology, and the Nation State*. Princeton, NJ: Princeton University Press, 1969.

Tignor, Robert L. *W. Arthur Lewis and the Birth of Development Economics*. Princeton, NJ: Princeton University Press, 2006.

Tilly, Charles. *Coercion, Capital, and European States, AD 990–1992*. Cambridge, MA: Blackwell, 1992.

Tipps, Dean C. "Modernization Theory and the Comparative Study of Societies: A Critical Perspective." *Comparative Studies in Society and History* 15, no. 2 (1973): 199–226.

Tordoff, William. *Ashanti under the Prempehs, 1888–1935*. London: Oxford University Press, 1965.

Torto, J. O. "History of Cocoa in Ghana." *Ghana Farmer* 3, no. 3 (1959): 88–90, 105–8.

Touré, Ahmed Sékou. *Africa on the Move*. London: Panaf Books, 1979.

———. *L'action politique du Parti démocratique du Guinée*. Paris: Présence Africaine, 1959.

———. *La Révolution Culturelle*. 3rd ed. Geneva: Kundig, 1972.

———. *Seminaire des Cadre du P.D.G. Seminaire de Formation Ideologique de L'Anneé Universitaire 1971–1972*. Conakry: Patrice Lumumba Press, 1972.

Tsikata, Dzodzi. *Living in the Shadow of the Large Dams: Long Term Responses of Downstream and Lakeside Communities of Ghana's Volta River Project*. Leiden: Brill, 2006.

Tuck, Laura. "Financial Markets in Rural Senegal." In *The Political Economy of Risk and Choice in Senegal*, edited by John Waterbury and Mark Gersovitz. London: Frank Cass, 1987.

Twaddle, Michael. "Decolonization in Africa: A New British Historiographical Debate." In *African Historiographies: What History for Which Africa*, edited by Bogumil Jewsiewicki and David Newbury. Beverley Hills: Sage, 1986.

Twumasi, Yaw. "Press Freedom and Nationalism under Colonial Rule in the Gold Coast (Ghana)." *Journal of the Historical Society of Nigeria* 7, no. 3 (1974): 499–520.

Van Beusekom, Monica M. *Negotiating Development: African Farmers and Colonial Experts at the Office du Niger, 1920–1960*. Westport, CT: Heinemann, 2002.

Van der Laan, H. L. *The Lebanese Traders in Sierra Leone*. The Hague: Mouton, 1975.

Van der Veer, Peter. "Nationalism and Religion." In *The Oxford Handbook of the History of Nationalism*, edited by John Breuilly. Oxford: Oxford University Press, 2013. DOI: 1093/oxfordhb/9780199209194.013.0033.

Villalón, Leonardo. *Islamic Society and State Power in Senegal: Disciples and Citizens in Fatick*. Cambridge: Cambridge University Press, 1995.

Von Eschen, Penny M. "Soul Call: The First World Festival of Negro Arts as a Pivot of Black Modernities." *Nka: Journal of Contemporary African Arts* 42–43 (November 2018): 124–35.

Wangwe, Samuel, Donald Mmari, Jehovanes Aikaeli, Neema Rutatina, Thaddeus Mboghoina, and Abel Kinyondo. "The Performance of the Manufacturing Sector in Tanzania: Challenges and the Way Forward." WIDER Working Paper 2014/085, 2014. www.wider.unu.edu.

Waterbury, John. "Dimensions of State Intervention in the Groundnut Basin." In *The Political Economy of Risk and Choice in Senegal*, edited by John Waterbury and Mark Gersovitz. London: Frank Cass, 1987.

Wijsen, Frans. "Are Africans Incurably Religious? Discursive Analysis of a Debate, Direction of a Discipline." *Exchange* 46, no. 4 (2017): 370–97.

Wilder, Gary. *Freedom Time: Negritude, Decolonization, and the Future of the World*. Durham, NC: Duke University, 2015.

Williams, Justin. *Pan-Africanism in Ghana: African Socialism, Neoliberalism, and Globalization*. Durham, NC: Carolina Academic Press, 2016.

Wilson, Louis E. "The 'Bloodless Conquest' in Southeastern Ghana: The *Huza* and Territorial Expansion of the Krobo in the 19th Century." *International Journal of African Historical Studies* 23, no. 2 (1990): 269–97.

World Bank. *Adjustment in Africa: Reforms, Results, and the Road Ahead*. Oxford: Oxford University Press, 1994.

———. *Adjustment Landing: An Evaluation of Ten Years of Experience*. Washington, DC: World Bank, 1988.

———. *Sub-Saharan Africa: From Crisis to Sustainable Growth*. Washington, DC: World Bank, 1989.

Woronoff, Jon. *West African Wager: Houphouët versus Nkrumah.* Metuchen, NJ: Scarecrow Press, 1972.

Yakobson, Sergius. "The Soviet Union and Ethiopia: A Case of Traditional Behavior." *Review of Politics* 25, no. 3 (1963): 329–42.

Young, Crawford. *The African Colonial State in Comparative Perspective.* New Haven, CT: Yale University Press, 1994.

3. Unpublished Dissertations, Conference and Workshop Papers

Aidid, Safia. "Pan-Somali Dreams: Ethiopia, Greater Somalia, and the Somali Nationalist Imagination." PhD diss., Harvard University, 2020.

Amponsah, David. "(Un)Desirable Customs: A History of Religion in the Making of Modern Ghana, c.1800–1966." PhD diss., Harvard University, 2015.

Asiedu-Acquah, Emmanuel. "Youth Culture and Popular Politics in Ghana, c.1900 to Recent Times." PhD diss., Harvard University, 2015.

Asunka, Joseph. "Covid-19, Integration, and Development Cooperation: Selected Afrobarometer Findings." Paper presented at the African Philanthropy Conference 2021, "Surviving Covid-19—The Role of African Philanthropy" Virtual Conference, August 3–5, 2021.

Chachage, Chambi. "A Capitalizing City: Dar es Salaam and the Emergence of an African Entrepreneurial Elite (c.1862–2015)." PhD diss., Department of African and African American Studies, Harvard University, 2018.

D'Avignon, Robyn. "'Customary' Mining and Colonialism in French West Africa." Paper presented at the African Studies Workshop, Harvard University, September 17, 2018.

Fofack, Hippolyte. "Retrospective Analysis of Africa's Post-HIPC Growth Resurgence." Conference paper, Harvard University, 2015.

Quarcoopome, Nii O. "Rituals and Regalia of Power: Arts and Politics among the Dangme and Ewe, 1800 to Present." PhD diss., University of California at Los Angeles, 1993.

Savoy, Bénédicte. "Amnesia: Forty Years' Debate on African Cultural Heritage in European Museums." Paper presented at conference "The Restitution Debate: African Art in a Global Society." Columbia University, New York, October 18, 2019.

Traugh, Geoffrey. "Becoming a 'Central African Denmark': Capitalism and the Agrarian Imagination in Late Colonial Malawi." Paper presented at the African Studies Association Annual Meeting, Boston, November 21–23, 2019.

4. Newspaper Articles, Videos, Reviews, and Online Material

BBC. "Africa & Europe (1800–1914)." The Story of Africa. Accessed September 18, 2013. https://www.bbc.co.uk/worldservice/africa/features/storyofafrica/index_section11.shtml.

Davidson, Basil. *Africa*. Episode 7, "The Rise of Nationalism." An MBT/RM Arts/Channel Four Co-production, 1984.

Fofack, Hippolyte. "Overcoming the Colonial Development Model of Resource Extraction for Sustainable Development in Africa." *Brookings*. January 31, 2019. https://www.brookings.edu/blog/africa-in-focus/2019/01/31/overcoming-the-colonial-development-model-of-resource-extraction-for-sustainable-development-in-africa/.

Ginelli, Zoltán. "Hungarian Experts in Nkrumah's Ghana." *Mezosfera*. May 2018. mezosfera.org.

Greaves, William. "First World Festival of Negro Arts." Documentary Film. Dakar, 1966.

Krugman, Paul. "The Fall and Rise of Development Economics." Massachusetts Institute of Technology. 2012. https://web.mit.edu/krugman/www/dishpan.html.

Lindley, Anna. "African Remittances and Progress: Opportunities and Challenges." *Real Instituto Elcano*. May 27, 2008. www.realinstitutoelcano.org.

Modi, Benu, and Seema Shekhawat. "China and India in Africa." *Pambazuka News*. Issue 456, November 5, 2009. http://pambazuka.org/en/category/africa_china/60030.

Patel, I. G. "A View from Africa." IMF eLibrary. IMF. December 1992. www.elibrary.imf.org.

Pew Forum on Religion and Public Life. "Tolerance and Tension: Islam and Christianity in Sub-Saharan Africa." April 2020. https://www.pewforum.org/2010/04/15/executive-summary-islam-and-christianity-in-sub-saharan-africa/.

Senghor, Léopold Sédar. "La Décolonisation, Condition de la Communauté Franco-Africaine." *Le Monde*. September 4, 1957.

Stam, Claire. "Malaysia Relies on Sustainable Palm Oil to Keep Entry into European Market." *EURACTIV*. February 4, 2020. euractiv.com.

Taylor, Liam. "Import Substitution Makes a Comeback in Africa." *African Business Magazine*. November 16, 2020. African.business/2020/11/trade-investment/import-substitution-makes-a-comeback-in-africa/.

INDEX

Page numbers in italics indicate figures.

Emmanuel Kwaku Akyeampong is Ellen Gurney Professor of History and of African and African American Studies at Harvard University. He also serves as Oppenheimer Faculty Director of the Center for African Studies. He is author of *Drink, Power and Cultural Change: A Social History of Alcohol in Ghana, c. 1800 to Recent Times* (1996) and *Between the Sea and the Lagoon: An Eco-social History of the Anlo of Southeast Ghana, c. 1850 to Recent Times* (2001).

For Indiana University Press

Emily Baugh, Editorial Assistant
Brian Carroll, Rights Manager
Gary Dunham, Acquisitions Editor and Director
Anna Francis, Assistant Acquisitions Editor
Brenna Hosman, Production Coordinator
Katie Huggins, Production Manager
Darja Malcolm-Clarke, Project Manager and Editor
Dan Pyle, Online Publishing Manager
Leyla Salamova, Book Designer
Stephen Williams, Marketing and Publicity Manager